HOW EVERYTHING
IN THE HOME WORKS

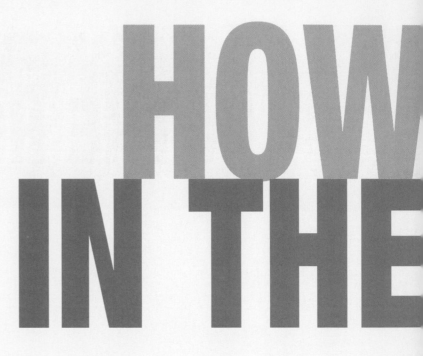

EVERYTHING HOME WORKS

and how to take the sting out of repair bills

Published by The Reader's Digest Association Limited
LONDON • NEW YORK • SYDNEY • MONTREAL

Contents

Around the house

Appliances

Audio-visual

Computer equipment

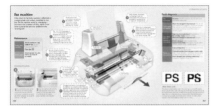

Communications

Power tools

Garden equipment

On wheels

HOW EVERYTHING IN THE HOME WORKS

From how a kettle boils water to the way a video records a film, this book explains how the technology in our homes works, and how to look after it. The book is divided into eight sections that take you around the house and into the garden.

Around the house

Learn the basics of plumbing and electrical wiring with clearly laid out introductory guides. This section also includes easy to follow, step-by-step instructions for a variety of basic repair tasks. Tackle these yourself and save time and money. ▶

Audio-visual

What really happens when you turn on the TV or put a CD on your stereo? Here we explain devices from loudspeakers to MiniDisc players, with helpful troubleshooting guides to ensure your system always gives its best possible performance.

Appliances

This section covers everything electrical you are likely to find in the kitchen, laundry or bedroom: from small items, such as electric toothbrushes, to large appliances like washing machines.
▼

Computer equipment

Don't worry if you don't know your RAM from your ROM. This section introduces all the elements of the home computer so you will understand exactly what's going on, and presents clear instructions on how to keep your PC running smoothly.

Communications

A comprehensive guide to modern communications starts here. Learn what happens when you pick up your telephone to make a call, how a mobile phone works and the ins and outs of sending and receiving a fax.
▶

Garden equipment

With just a little time and some simple maintenance procedures, your garden equipment will give you many years of trouble-free service. This section covers the popular types of electrical and petrol-driven garden tools.

Power tools

Electric tools are invaluable for saving time, but can be dangerous if not properly used or maintained. Our unique 3D illustrations explain power drills, nail guns and jigsaws in the clearest detail: what to watch out for and what to do if things go wrong.
▼

◀ On wheels

This section covers diverse items around the home that run on wheels. Find out how bicycle gears work, how inline skates glide and how radio controlled cars steer.

3D illustrations

The centrepiece of each featured item is a unique 'see through' 3D illustration. This shows how the device is constructed, and illustrates its operation with arrows and colour-coded sections, while clear labels indicate all the major components. Explanatory steps arranged around the illustration take you through the sequence of how everything works.

Conceptual diagrams

These annotated diagrams are designed to provide simple illustrations of systems or processes that operate out of sight in the mysterious 'black boxes' within your appliance. Numbers point the way to essential components or operations.

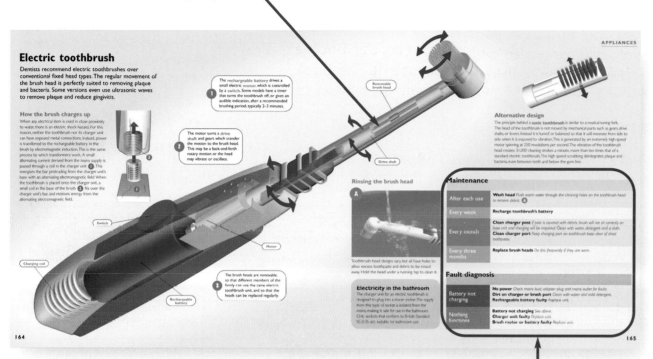

Maintenance and Fault diagnosis

Alongside every entry is a table of recommended maintenance tasks (in green), with complicated procedures explained step-by-step with photographs. However, no matter how well you look after appliances, there will still be times when things go wrong. The fault diagnosis table (in blue) indicates the most common reasons for failure, giving clear repair instructions where you can tackle the job yourself, and objective advice about what should be referred to a qualified repairer.

House diagrams

Systems such as telephone wiring, plumbing, waste water and electrical circuits are shown in the context of a complete 3D house. These illustrations explain how the whole system works and how individual components fit into the big picture.

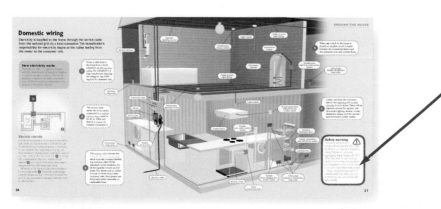

Safety warning ⚠

The red safety panels indicate areas where special care must be taken, or contain warnings of potential danger when handling or undertaking repairs on particular items.

When something goes wrong

For every item featured in *How Everything in the Home Works*, there is a fault diagnosis chart listing things that can go wrong and how to put them right – or when getting expert help is the most practical, or the only option. A good overall starting point when something goes wrong is to take a logical approach to faultfinding and problem solving.

Analysing the problem

When something goes wrong, you need to work out what has happened, what the consequences of the problem are, and what to do next. Some faults require immediate emergency action to eliminate personal danger or to limit any consequential damage. Others require simple common sense. Most faults are either a result of a system failure or an equipment failure. These pages show you how to deal with system failures; for equipment failures turn to pages 10–11.

The electrical system

Your electrical system can fail at several different levels. Follow the flow chart below to help you to diagnose the problem.

Is there any electrical power to the house? No / Yes

Is more than one item affected? Yes / No

Tripped miniature circuit breaker (MCB) or blown fuse in fuse box. Check consumer unit or fuse box, (see Domestic wiring, page 26). Reset MCB or replace or rewire fuse and check all appliances on the circuit using the electrical faultfinder flowchart on page 11.

Blown plug fuse or faulty appliance See appliance faultfinder flowchart on page 11.

Does your electrical supply have a main on/off switch? Is it in the 'off' position? No / Yes

Supply switched off Check that the on/off switch is in the 'on' position. If you have a whole-house RCD (residual current device) that has tripped off, press the reset button to restore the power supply. If you cannot reset it there is a serious electrical safety fault. Contact a qualified electrician. If your RCD keeps tripping for no apparent reason, report this to your electricity company.

Are all neighbours' homes affected? No / Yes

Phase fault Occasionally a fault will affect only one of the three phases delivered from local substations, so power continues to be supplied to some neighbouring houses. Call the emergency number of your electricity supplier (under Electricity in the telephone directory) and report the fault immediately.

Blackout Look under Electricity in your telephone directory to find the 24 hour emergency number for your electricity supplier (it should also be on your electricity bills). Call the number and report the fault as soon as possible.

Electrical emergency action

- If anyone receives a minor shock from an appliance, stop using it and have it checked by an expert.
- If someone receives a major shock, turn off the current immediately at the consumer unit. Try to avoid touching the victim, as this also puts you at risk of a major electrical shock. Refer to the guidelines on page 20.

The heating system

A central heating system consists of five main components, each of which can malfunction or fail. For more detail, see Central heating, page 66.

The boiler heats the system (and may also provide domestic hot water). It contains a number of parts that will need regular maintenance and eventual replacement and this is a job for a professional (see gas safety, page 21). Annual servicing will keep the boiler in good order.

The pump circulates heated water round the system. It may become jammed or noisy in operation, or may simply fail altogether. Regular operation and cleaning help to prevent problems, but replacement is usually straightforward.

The radiators transmit heat to individual rooms. They sometimes develop pinhole leaks due to corrosion, and may trap air, gas or sludge (by-products of corrosion), all of which can cause uneven heating or banging noises when in use. The use of a corrosion inhibitor or leak sealer will help to prevent or cure these problems. Leaks require prompt action – see plumbing system, below.

The feed-and-expansion tank tops up any water lost from the heating system through leaks or evaporation. The tank itself may also develop a leak and need replacing. The float valve that refills it may jam through lack of use, causing an overflow or allowing air to be drawn into the radiators and pump. A float valve can be repaired or replaced (see Water system, page 44).

Controls operating the heating system include a programmer, thermostats and motorised valves. Faulty wiring may lead to malfunction, and mechanical failure may be remedied through servicing or replacement of the faulty control.

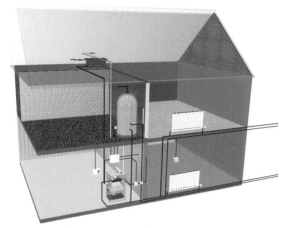

Heating emergency action ⚠
● If the system overheats or the pump fails, turn off the boiler.
● Turn off the gas at the meter if you smell a gas leak and call Transco's emergency number (look under Gas in the telephone directory).
● Until you can make a repair, drain leaking pipes, radiators and hot water cylinders via the relevant drain cock (see page 66).

The plumbing system

Your plumbing system can suffer from a wide range of faults, but they fall into four main categories. Water system (page 40) tells you more.

Taps and valves control the flow of water into and through the home. They may drip, causing stains and overflows, or may jam open or closed, or be hard to operate. Taps are mechanical devices, and might need maintenance or replacement, depending on the severity of the problem.

Supply pipes distribute water to wherever it is needed. They may leak, due to perforations developing in the pipe or faulty seals at pipe connectors. They may also gradually become blocked by scale, caused by hard water. Both faults are easily remedied, although leaks demand swift damage limitation – see Plumbing emergency action (right).

Storage tanks hold cold and hot water. They may develop leaks or, in the case of the hot tank, may become inefficient due to a build-up of limescale. Replacement is the only long-term solution.

Plumbing emergency action ⚠
● If a fault causes water to escape, aim to stop the flow as quickly as possible.
● Make sure you know in advance where the system's main on/off and flow controls are located (see Water system, page 40).
● Empty leaking water storage tanks and supply pipes by turning off the main stoptap and opening cold taps, or by attaching a garden hose to a drain valve and opening the valve with pliers or a spanner. Lead the hose outside the house.
● Clear blocked waste pipes and traps by dismantling, plunging or rodding (see Waste water, page 60).

Waste pipes convey used water from appliances and WCs to the household drains, via U-shaped traps designed to keep drain smells out of the house. They can become blocked, causing overflows, but most blockages can be cleared mechanically.

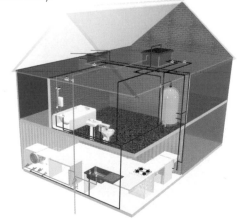

Appliance faults

It is worth working out why an appliance has stopped working, even if you don't want to do the repair yourself. Your deductions will equip you to brief a professional and anticipate his recommendations, saving time and money. Remember that DIY repairs may invalidate an appliance's warranty.

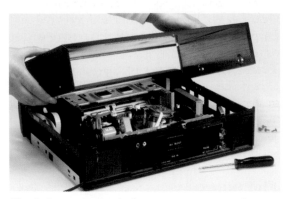

Check the guarantee before you attempt repairs – you may invalidate it simply by opening the casing.

Mechanical failure

Often items stop working for very simple reasons: moving parts may have become jammed by a foreign body; drive belts may have slipped off their pulleys; a door or lid may not have been closed properly.

On some electrical equipment, a cut-out may have operated to protect the machine from overheating or overloading and this may need resetting. Whatever the cause, spending a few minutes checking the obvious in a logical way can often save hours of frustration and expense on needless call-outs.

Operator failure

Always read the instructions. Don't assume that a new appliance will work in the same way as the old one it's replacing. Sometimes, failure is a result of not following a particular sequence of instructions, or not

taking certain safety precautions before use. Keep instruction manuals in a safe place so that they are available for future reference.

Decide what to do next

Once you have a broad understanding of where the problem lies, you have to decide what action to take next. Your choice will depend on the following related considerations: how complicated the task is; whether you think you can fix it yourself; your need for a quick solution; how much you are prepared to pay for someone else to tackle the problem; and whether repair is a feasible or economic option.

Is the appliance under warranty?

Don't attempt DIY repairs on recently purchased items as most new equipment in the home is guaranteed against parts failure for at least a year. While the warranty is in force, it pays to have problems put right by the manufacturer or a recommended service agent. Trying to effect your own repairs may invalidate the guarantee, leaving you with an expensive repair bill if you fail to put things right yourself.

Carry out repairs on a suitable work surface – use a tray or container to stop parts, screws and tools falling on the floor.

Can you fix it yourself?

Carrying out your own repairs requires knowledge, aptitude, a degree of common sense and access to the relevant tools, materials and spare parts. It also needs time and a suitable workspace.

This book will give you the knowledge to diagnose and tackle faults with individual systems or pieces of equipment. By explaining what is involved in the tasks, it will also enable you to decide whether your skills are up to the job, and to check whether you have the necessary tools and equipment to tackle it.

The time factor is likely to be the strongest in guiding you towards DIY repairs. Time is money to the professional, but free to you. Many repair jobs are very labour-intensive; stripping down and reassembling something may take a couple of hours, while curing the fault or fitting the replacement part may take only a few minutes.

Do you need a professional?

Complex tasks may call for professional repair. Repairs on major appliances can seem daunting, and you may simply be unwilling to embark on a course of action that looks potentially very complicated. If tackling a particular job requires the purchase of several expensive tools you may never use again, the case for calling in a professional becomes stronger.

The final reason for choosing professional repair is convenience. If you can't afford to have something out of action for more than a day or so, then professional repair is the only logical option (see Getting things repaired professionally, page 18).

Replacement or renewal

For many appliances, there comes a time when repairs are not economical. Small appliances can be inexpensive to buy, and all but the simplest repair could cost more than a replacement.

Larger appliances often cost even more to service or repair because of their complexity and, as with smaller appliances, you need to weigh the cost against that of a new machine, which will come with a guarantee and the likelihood of several years of trouble-free operation.

Safe disposal

If you decide to replace an appliance, make it safe for disposal first. A small appliance is likely to end up in the dustbin with other domestic rubbish and could cause harm to anyone who finds it and tries to use it. Cut off the flex close to the appliance first, to render it harmless. Deform the plug pins with a hammer so that the severed flex cannot be plugged into a socket outlet. Alternatively, you could contact an organisation such as Waste Watch (see Useful contacts, page 308) for details of schemes in your area that accept basic electrical equipment for repair and re-use by low-income households.

Larger appliances need to be safely disposed of – especially if, like fridges and freezers, they contain dangerous chemicals. This is the job of your local waste authority, which is obliged to accept unwanted appliances free of charge, if you can take them to an approved waste site, or for a small fee if it has to collect them.

New directives are on the way, aimed at reducing the amount of waste and encouraging recycling or recovery. Before you throw away any item, check that it is safe to dispose of, and that there are no recycling or recovery schemes in operation in your area.

Electrical appliance faultfinder flowchart

Follow the flow chart below to work out why an electrical appliance has stopped working – it may be something as simple as a blown fuse.

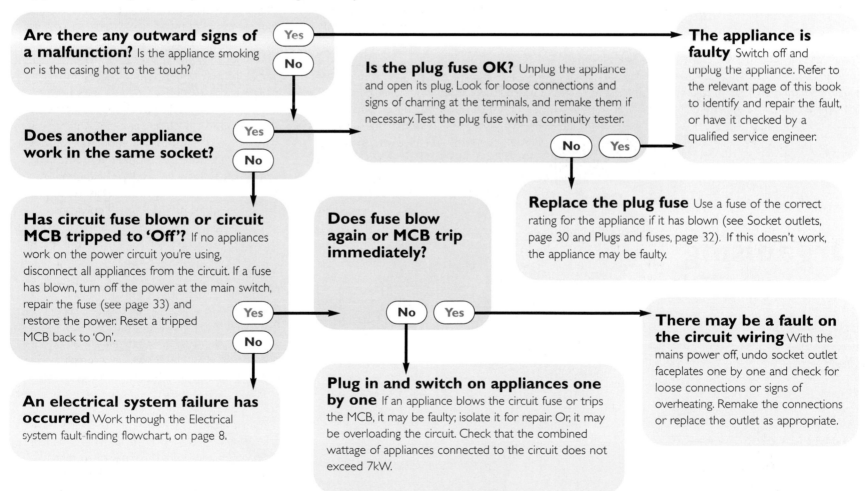

Are there any outward signs of a malfunction? Is the appliance smoking or is the casing hot to the touch? — **Yes** / **No**

Does another appliance work in the same socket? — **Yes** / **No**

Has circuit fuse blown or circuit MCB tripped to 'Off'? If no appliances work on the power circuit you're using, disconnect all appliances from the circuit. If a fuse has blown, turn off the power at the main switch, repair the fuse (see page 33) and restore the power. Reset a tripped MCB back to 'On'. — **Yes** / **No**

An electrical system failure has occurred Work through the Electrical system fault-finding flowchart, on page 8.

Is the plug fuse OK? Unplug the appliance and open its plug. Look for loose connections and signs of charring at the terminals, and remake them if necessary. Test the plug fuse with a continuity tester. — **No** / **Yes**

Does fuse blow again or MCB trip immediately? — **No** / **Yes**

Plug in and switch on appliances one by one If an appliance blows the circuit fuse or trips the MCB, it may be faulty; isolate it for repair. Or, it may be overloading the circuit. Check that the combined wattage of appliances connected to the circuit does not exceed 7kW.

The appliance is faulty Switch off and unplug the appliance. Refer to the relevant page of this book to identify and repair the fault, or have it checked by a qualified service engineer.

Replace the plug fuse Use a fuse of the correct rating for the appliance if it has blown (see Socket outlets, page 30 and Plugs and fuses, page 32). If this doesn't work, the appliance may be faulty.

There may be a fault on the circuit wiring With the mains power off, undo socket outlet faceplates one by one and check for loose connections or signs of overheating. Remake the connections or replace the outlet as appropriate.

Basic toolkit

Many of the step-by-step repair procedures listed in this book require the use of tools. There will be occasions when you may need to hire or purchase a specialist tool, but the following basic items should be in every well-equipped toolbox.

Organising your toolkit

Most modern toolboxes have multiple stacking layers. Put tools to which you need quick access in the top layer **1**. It is sensible to put cutting tools, such as junior hacksaws and retractable blade knives, in the second layer **2** where they are safely out of the way but not loose in the base of the toolbox. Oils and liquids should be stored in the bottom layer **3**, in case they leak.

Screwing, unscrewing and holding tools

These are probably the tools that you'll use most often, so they should be made easily accessible. Ensure that screwdrivers are kept in their sets so that you can readily select the correct size and tip for the type of screw.

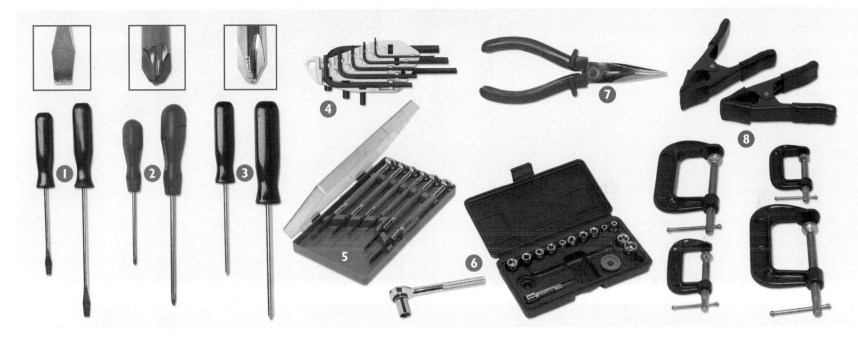

Flat tip screwdrivers ❶ fit into screws with a single slot head. **Phillips** ❷ and **Pozidriv** **screwdrivers** ❸ have a cross tip. They are regarded as safer than flat tip ones as they are less likely to slip under pressure. You will need to have at least one small and one medium-sized driver of each.

A selection of **hexagon keys** ❹ is useful for undoing nuts in cases and changing blades. **Watchmaker's screwdrivers'** ❺, are tiny screwdrivers that come in sets, providing a variety of Phillips and flat tips. These are useful when working on small devices. A **socket set** ❻ is useful for undoing

and tightening small nuts and bolts. **Long-nosed pliers** ❼ can be used for gripping small items and for bending wire objects. A set of differently-sized **clamps** ❽ can be useful for securing items to a work surface, or holding glued things together while the adhesive sets.

Cutting tools

Take care when reaching into this part of the toolbox.
Keep blades retracted and hinged cutters closed.

A **retractable blade knife** ❶, with replaceable blades, is a highly versatile tool. Whenever possible, use it with an A4 or larger **cutting mat** ❷ for safety. For small jobs, such as cutting through wood or metal, a cheap **junior hacksaw** ❸ with replaceable blades is excellent value. A pair of general purpose **scissors** ❹ will also be useful to have at hand.

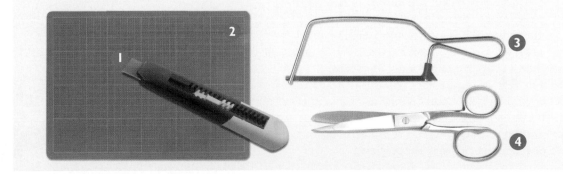

Measuring tools

If you want professional DIY results, you'll need tools to help you to measure accurately. It is always wise to keep a pencil and paper in your toolbox, where it will be at hand when you need it.

A small **steel ruler** ❶ acts as a sturdy guide for cutting and drawing and is useful for measuring too. Retractable steel **tape measures** ❷ come in a variety of lengths, with a lock button that keeps the tape extended when measuring. A **spirit level** ❸ is invaluable when installing items such as dishwashers that must be level – the longer the better, for accurate levelling. When attempting any repair project it is a good idea to have a **notepad** and **pencil** ❹ for jotting down measurements or drawing diagrams of components and connections to aid with reassembly of an item you are taking apart. Plain **white labels** ❺ are useful when dismantling appliances, for labelling parts and wires so that you know how to refit them.

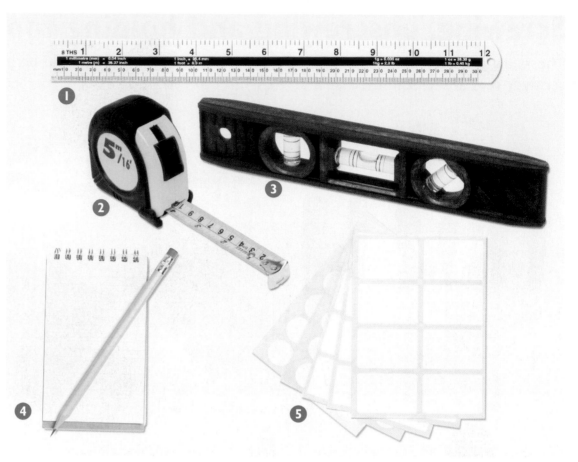

Plumbing tools

These often get wet during use, so always dry them before replacing in the toolbox.

PTFE tape ❶ is a thin, plastic tape used for sealing threaded joints in plumbing such as compression fittings and radiator connections. A **radiator key** ❷ lets you release a build-up of air in radiators so that they heat more efficiently: some have built-in drip catchers. An **adjustable spanner** ❸ is a versatile tool, allowing you to turn nuts of various different sizes. Use the spanner with a **Stilson wrench** ❹ to prevent pipes, valves or taps from twisting when undoing nuts. A **plunger** ❺ can help clear blockages in pipes and plugholes.

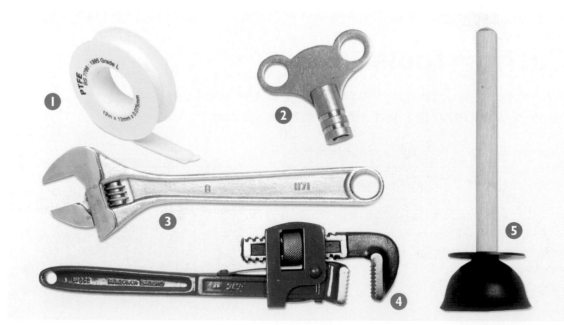

Electrical tools

The contents of this section of the toolbox range from small, plug top fuses to large torches and rolls of tape. Make sure you are fully familiar with where everything is: you'll want to be able to find the torch easily, should the lights fail.

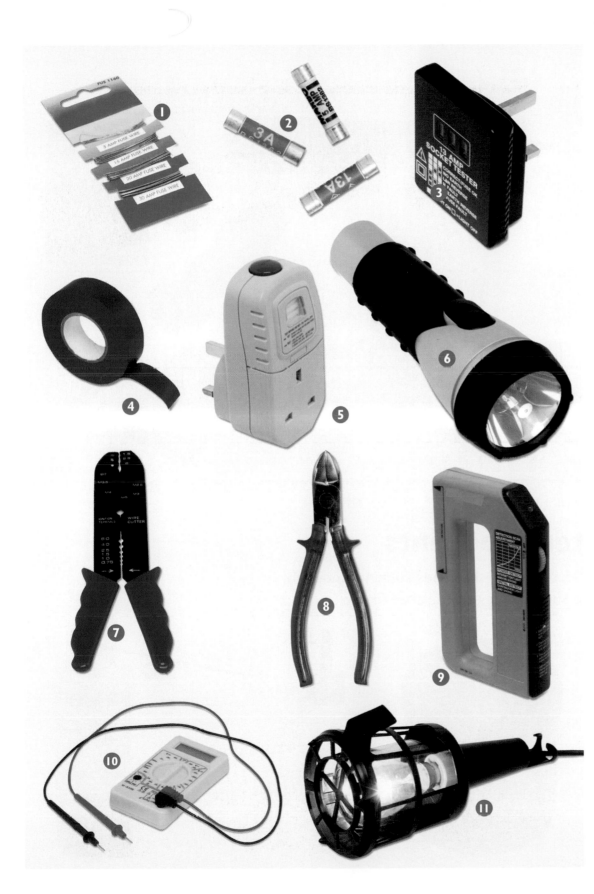

Fuse wire ① is necessary only if your house has an old-style fuse box. Make sure you have spare wire for all the common ratings. **Plug top fuses ②** should blow before the fuse in the fuse box or the miniature circuit breaker (MCB) in the consumer unit. Most household appliances need a 3A, 5A or 13A fuse: keep spares of each and always replace a blown fuse with one of the same rating. A **socket tester ③** plugs into socket outlets to test if they are wired correctly and safe to use. **Red PVC insulating tape ④** is useful for temporary repairs to damaged flex, and for identifying live cores in household wiring. An **RCD adaptor ⑤** cuts the supply of electricity to an appliance if you touch a live part, offering extra protection against electrocution. Always use one when working with electricity outdoors. A battery-powered **torch ⑥** is invaluable in a power cut – remember to check the batteries regularly and to keep a spare set in the toolbox. A **wire stripper ⑦** does several jobs. Use the larger hole to cut through flex sheaths; the smaller hole to remove the plastic insulation from around the cores; and the sharp blades to cut through the core. **Wire cutters ⑧** will also be useful to have at hand. Before drilling into walls, use a **cable detector ⑨** to check for concealed cables and water pipes. A **multimeter ⑩** lets you check the current and voltage flowing through electrical devices, simply by placing its probes on any two exposed contact points. It can also be used to check continuity, that is whether there is an electrical connection between two points. Most multimeters emit an audible sound if a circuit is made between the two probes. A mains-powered **inspection lamp ⑪** is very useful when working on lighting circuits, or when doing repair work in any awkward-to-reach or unlit spots, such as the loft.

Additional tools

The following items are not essential parts of a basic toolkit, but they can come in handy and may be necessary for some of the procedures described in this book.

An **electric screwdriver** ❶ is faster and more convenient than conventional screwdrivers. A **security screwdriver set** ❷ combines a screwdriver handle with several interchangeable tips, useful for electrical devices, mobile phones and computer equipment, which use casing screws that are not of the Phillips or slot head type. Some deeply recessed screws may require a fixed security screwdriver of the appropriate type. A **battery tester** ❸ enables you to tell whether it is the device or the batteries that are at fault when something stops working.

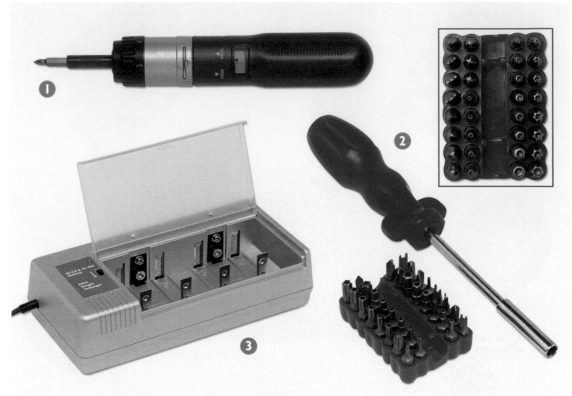

Lubrication and water repellents

Use the right lubricant to keep appliances, tools and machines running smoothly. To avoid spillages in your tool box, make sure all lids are replaced firmly.

Lithium grease ❶ is sold in pots. It is a thick grease, used to pack gear boxes and lubricate bearings. Take care when handling it as it will stain clothing. Also, be careful not to push down the disc inside the pot too quickly, as you could cause a 'volcano effect' – a gush of black gunk through the hole in its centre. **Light machine oil** ❷ – often referred to as 'three in one' or 'multipurpose' oil – is usually supplied in plastic or metal canisters, about the same size and shape as lighter fluid containers. **Aerosol water repellent** ❸ (WD40) is sold in spray cans. This light oil can be used for lubrication and for repelling water from electrical contacts.

Cleaning materials

Appliances that are kept free from dirt and dust with the correct products will last longer. Flammable solvents should ideally be stored outdoors.

Clean, **lint-free cloths** ❶ are useful for applying cleaning agents such as isopropyl alcohol, and can be purchased at hardware stores. Disposable household cloths ❷ can be used when cleaning with water and mild detergent. Sometimes sold as 'lens cleaners' in photographic shops, **air blowers** ❸ are small bellows, with brush tips, for simultaneously dusting and blowing away small particles. For more powerful dust removal, an **aerosol air duster** ❹ is recommended. These are ideal for cleaning camera lenses because they avoid physical contact, which can cause scratches. A jet of air can also remove dust particles from areas that a cloth or cotton bud cannot reach. **Isopropyl alcohol** ❺ is an effective cleaning agent and disinfectant that dries quickly without leaving a residue: it is particularly useful for cleaning electrical contacts. It is also highly flammable and you should avoid contact with the skin. Only use it in well ventilated areas. **Wet and dry abrasive paper** ❻ can be used dry or wet for cleaning, smoothing and preparing surfaces. It comes in different grades for different finishes. Used with water, a fine grade wet and dry abrasive paper can produce a very smooth finish for painting or sticking. **Switch cleaner** ❼ is used to clean inaccessible switches, such as the volume controls in audio systems. This pressurised flammable solvent can be directly applied through a fine straw. **Washing-up liquid** ❽ can be put to a variety of cleaning uses outside the kitchen. When diluted it makes a gentle but effective cleaning agent but, undiluted, it will restore tarnished silverware. **Cotton buds** ❾ are perfect for cleaning small and delicate items, and components in hard-to-reach places: look out for lint-free ones. **White spirit** ❿ is a highly flammable liquid and should be stored safely. It can be used to thin and remove wet oil-based paint, and as a general-purpose cleaner for removing grease.

Getting things repaired professionally

Whether you need to find an electrician, a plumber, a heating engineer, a locksmith or a qualified appliance repairer, the chances of your getting a quick call-out and a speedy repair at a reasonable price depend on factors that are mostly beyond your control. It is always best if a friend, neighbour or relative can recommend someone reliable. Otherwise you will have to find contractors from telephone directories.

Household repairs

Choosing someone who is a member of a recognised trade body is a good starting point in finding a reliable tradesperson for a professional repair. Members of the following bodies should be professionally competent and trustworthy. Some unscrupulous contractors claim membership of trade bodies, often using their logos in telephone directory and newspaper advertisements. It is a wise precaution to check with the relevant body that such claims are valid before employing them. Many trade bodies have a facility to check a contractor's registration on their web site or over the phone.

Electricians It is possible to get names of qualified electricians by calling the National Inspection Council for Electrical Installation Contracting (NICEIC), the Electrical Contractors Association (ECA) and the Electrical Contractors Association of Scotland. See Useful contacts, page 308, for their details.

Plumbers For registered plumbers, contact the Institute of Plumbing. Many plumbers may also be members of the National Association of Plumbing, Heating and Mechanical Services Contractors (NAPH&MSC), or of the Heating and Ventilating Contractors Association (HVCA).

Gas fitters If the plumbing or heating work involves gas pipework, it is a legal requirement that the fitter is registered with the Council for Registered Gas Installers (CORGI).

Locksmiths If you are accidentally locked out of your home or are having trouble with your locks, call a locksmith who is member of the Master Locksmiths Association (MLA).

Certain components must be repaired or replaced by a qualified washing machine repairer.

Faulty timer circuit

Door interlock failed

Faulty heater element

Pump failed

When you buy a new appliance

Store the receipt, instruction manual, warranty and any other useful documentation somewhere safe. If a fault occurs, check the warranty before approaching a repairer or attempting repairs yourself – the guarantee may be invalidated unless the appliance is repaired by the manufacturer or their agent.

Any goods that develop a fault within 28 days of purchase should be taken back to the place where they were bought, where you are entitled to a replacement or refund. Even outside the 28 day period many retailers will agree to replace or refund faulty goods.

Appliance repairs

If you cannot get a faulty appliance replaced by the retailer, you have three repair options.

Manufacturers and appointed agents
If your appliance is still under guarantee, or if you have an extended warranty on it, this should be your first point of call, after contacting the retailer from whom the appliance was purchased. These agents only tackle repairs to their own products or to specified brands. Check the instruction manual that came with the appliance for contact details, or call the manufacturer direct.

Most major appliance manufacturers are members of the Association of Manufacturers of Domestic Appliances (AMDEA), whose code of practice says that a call-out should be answered within three working days of a customer's call, that repairs should be completed on the first visit in four out of five instances, and that if a second visit is needed it should take place within seven working days.

Independent repairers These will tackle general repairs to most makes of appliance, subject to their being able to obtain spare parts. You will find them listed in your telephone directory under Electrical Appliance Repairs. They are often the fastest and most reliable option.

Electrical appliance retailers
Some electrical retailers run their own service departments, and may be prepared to repair appliances that were bought elsewhere. You will find them listed under Electrical Appliance Retailers in your telephone directory

A strict code of practice regarding customer service and workmanship, and the competence of member repair companies is maintained by the Domestic Appliance Service Association (DASA) and the Radio, Electrical and Television Retailers' Association (RETRA).

Pinch roller faulty

Heads out of alignment

Precision electronic parts need specialist attention from a qualified repairer.

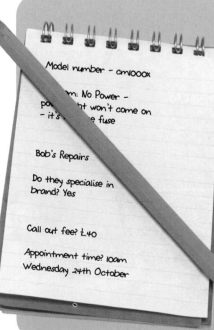

Call-out checklist

When you call a professional there are certain questions you should ask them and that they are likely to ask you. Knowing what these are can save you time and money.

✔ **What is the make and model number of the faulty appliance?** Ask if the repairer specialises in this brand.

✔ **Briefly summarise the problem** so the repairer can bring any spare parts that are obviously required, such as a motor or pump.

✔ **Is there a call-out fee and does it include labour time?** Ask what the hourly rate is, and whether the bill includes VAT.

✔ **Confirm the appointment time**, or at least whether it will be morning or afternoon. Ask whether the repairer makes evening or weekend visits, if weekdays are not convenient for you.

✔ **Give the repairer your telephone number** and ask them to call if they cannot keep the appointment.

✔ **Write down the time that the repairer arrives** and, once the fault has been diagnosed, ask for a written quotation for the repair before work starts.

✔ **Take an interest in the repair work and don't be afraid to ask questions** – the information may be useful should the appliance break down again.

✔ **Make sure you get a fully itemised receipt**, and pay by cheque rather than cash so you have proof of payment in case of any subsequent dispute. If you pay by credit or debit card, ask for a receipt.

Safety in the home

Each year, several thousand people in the UK die as a result of accidents in the home, and around three million need medical attention. Yet many of these accidents are caused by carelessness or a lack of common sense, and could be easily avoided. The advice in the following pages will help you to escape the most common safety hazards, whether you are operating a day-to-day appliance or carrying out maintenance or a repair.

Electrical safety

Electricity can kill. Follow these ten safety precautions to keep yourself safe when using electrical appliances or working with or near electric circuits.

⚠️ **Always unplug appliances from the mains** before attempting any repair work on them.

⚠️ **Isolate mains circuits at the consumer unit** (see page 28) by switching off miniature circuit breakers (MCBs) or removing circuit fuses before carrying out any work on the house wiring.

▼

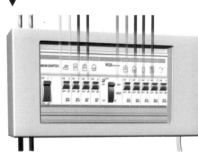

⚠️ **Uncoil extension leads fully before using them** If the lead is powering any appliance with a heating element, check that the flex rating is suitable for the wattage.

⚠️ **Do not overload socket outlets** — either mechanically, with adaptors, or electrically, by plugging in too many high-wattage appliances. If using a four or six-way adaptor, refer to its back label for the maximum load.

⚠️ **Use a cable detector** to ▲ locate hidden cables and pipes before making holes for wall fixings.

⚠️ **Check appliance plugs and flexes** regularly for damage, cuts or other signs of wear. Replace damaged parts at the earliest possible opportunity.

⚠️ **Out of doors** plug any power tool being used into a residual current device (RCD) adaptor. ▶

⚠️ **Replace blown circuit fuses** using fuse wire or cartridge fuses of the correct rating. Never use any other metallic object to repair a fuse.

⚠️ **Check that there are earth connections** for all appliances and wiring accessories, and earth all metal pipework and plumbing fittings. The only situation where an earth connection is not needed is in

the flex to a non-metallic lampholder or to power tools and portable appliances that are double-insulated.

⚠️ **Keep water and electricity apart** Never plug in appliances or operate electrical switches with wet hands. Never take an electrical appliance into the bathroom, even if the flex is long enough. Never use electrical equipment outside the house in wet conditions.

Electric shock

If somebody receives an electric shock, immediate action is vital.

1 Do not touch the victim. Turn off the source of the current as quickly as possible. If you cannot do this, grab clothing (not bare flesh, or you will get a shock too) and drag the victim away from the source of the current. Use a wooden broom handle to move them if this is not possible.

2 If the victim is conscious but visibly shocked, lay him flat on his back with his

legs raised and cover him with a blanket. Turn the head to one side to keep the airway clear and call an ambulance. Soak burns with cold water and cover them with a clean sterile dressing.

3 If the victim is breathing, but unconscious, place him in the recovery position (shown below) and keep the airway clear by tilting the head back and opening the mouth. Cover him with a blanket and call an ambulance immediately.

Gas safety

Mains gas will not poison you, but it can explode if it leaks and is ignited. It can also kill indirectly if it is not burned safely and under controlled conditions in a gas fire, boiler or water heater. Follow these guidelines to ensure that you always use gas safely.

⚠️ **Never attempt DIY work** on your gas pipes, fittings or appliances: this is illegal. Always call in a CORGI-registered fitter to do the work. See page 308 for contact details.

⚠️ **If you smell a leak** turn off the supply at the main on/off lever ❶ (you'll find it next to the gas meter) by moving it so it is at right angles to the pipe. Open all doors and windows. Put out all naked lights and extinguish cigarettes with water. Do not turn any electrical switches either on or off as this can create a spark.

Contact the Transco gas emergency number immediately (0800 111 999) if the smell of gas persists, and call a qualified gas fitter to trace the fault if it disperses.

⚠️ **Buy only gas appliances** that comply with British or European standards.

⚠️ **Have gas appliances serviced** at least annually by a qualified CORGI-registered fitter. Look out for danger signs.

If there is sooting round an appliance, if it burns with an orange or lazy flame, or if there is excessive condensation nearby, it may be faulty. Call the Transco gas emergency number and stop using it until it has been checked.

⚠️ **Ensure that rooms** containing gas-burning appliances are properly ventilated. If you get headaches or nausea when they are operating, they may be burning fuel unsafely and creating potentially lethal carbon monoxide (CO) gas. Ask your gas supplier for advice if you are concerned.

⚠️ **For complete safety**, have a gas detector installed – ideally a mains-powered one made to British Standard BS EN 50194:2000 – look for the British Standards Kitemark (right). Also fit a carbon monoxide detector made to BS 7860. This is particularly important if you have gas heaters in bedrooms and use gas or wood burning appliances when you or your family are asleep.

Water safety

Although water itself is not dangerous, a major leak inside the house can do a great deal of damage. It can also cause an electrical short circuit if it penetrates any wiring. Leaking water may be coming from one of four main sources: follow these guidelines to minimise the damage fast.

⚠️ **The rising main stoptap** controls the flow of water into the house. It supplies the cold water storage tank, any feed-and-expansion tank, the kitchen cold tap and some appliances, such as a washing machine. Turning it off prevents tanks from refilling, and stems leaks from kitchen supply pipes. The rising main can be drained (right) via the drain valve ❶, which is usually near the stoptap ❷. Attach a length of garden hose to direct the water out of doors.

⚠️ **The cold water storage tank** supplies all other cold taps in the house, and also the WC cisterns. There may be an on/off valve on the

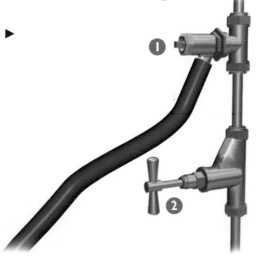

supply pipe leading from the tank. Turning it off and opening all cold taps will stop leaks from these pipes. If there is no valve, turn off the rising main stoptap and open all cold taps to drain the storage tank and stop the leak.

⚠️ **The hot water storage cylinder** is supplied from the storage tank. If the cylinder or its supply pipe develops a leak, the cylinder must be drained using the drain valve close to its base. Attach a length of garden hose to direct the contents out of doors. Turn off the supply to the cylinder or empty the storage tank as described above. Opening hot taps will not drain the cylinder.

⚠️ **The feed-and-expansion tank** tops up water losses from the heating system. If the heating system develops a leak, turn off the boiler and drain the system using the drain valve at the lowest point.

Potential hazards

Never underestimate the potential for danger in the home, particularly when performing DIY repairs. Fortunately, most dangerous situations can be easily avoided.

Fire

Be alert to the dangers of fire. A fire can be caused by an electrical fault, by careless use of tools that generate heat, such as a blowlamp or heat gun, or by careless use or storage of flammable materials. For general household protection, fit a smoke detector (see page 96) made to British Standard BS 5446-1:2000 on each floor of the house, and change the batteries every year to ensure that the detectors are always in full working order. Keep a fire blanket in the kitchen, and an all-purpose fire extinguisher in the workshop.

Heavy loads

Be aware of your strength limitations when lifting or moving heavy loads or large domestic appliances. Check the manufacturer's instructions for advice on moving large appliances, and get help if necessary to avoid back strain. In general, it is always better to move a large heavy appliance by sliding rather than lifting it, but if you must pick it up, try to keep your back as straight as possible and bend your knees so that your legs provide the lifting force. Bear in mind that some objects, such as washing machines, have very heavy built-in stability weights.

Electricity

Remember that electricity can kill if misused or not treated with respect. Always double-check that the electrical appliance or electric circuit you are about to work on is disconnected or isolated from the mains supply and warn others not to reconnect it. Follow the safety guidelines on page 20.

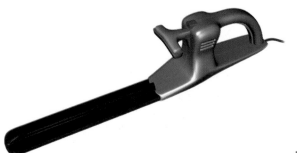

High internal voltages

Some electronic appliances such as microwaves, televisions, amplifiers and video equipment may retain high internal voltages. Pay attention to any safety warnings on the casing. If in any doubt, do not open the case; contact a qualified repairer. Wear an anti-static wrist guard when working inside a computer to prevent static electricity within your body from damaging sensitive electronic components.

Power tools

Make sure you know how to operate bladed power tools correctly and always keep your hands behind the cutting direction. Keep the blades sharp: a blunt tool is more likely to slip and injure you. Store bladed tools carefully, ideally with their blade guards in place. Never attempt to bypass or deactivate any safety guard fitted to a power tool.

Harmful chemicals

Always read the instructions supplied with any liquid or powder product before you use it, and observe any recommended safety precautions. Keep separate instruction leaflets in a file for future reference. Always store DIY products safely, out of the reach of children. Contact your local authority waste disposal department for advice on disposing of chemicals safely.

Ladders and steps

Falls from access equipment cause more deaths and injuries in the home than any other DIY activity. To avoid them, always set ladders up at the correct angle, with the base of the ladder 1m away from the wall for every 4m of ladder height. If possible, tie the top of the ladder to the building, and ensure that its foot is resting on solid ground or on a level and secure board. Make sure that stepladders are standing square and level.

Don't climb a ladder with your hands full; haul up what you need afterwards using a rope or bucket, or get someone to pass things to you through a nearby window. Don't lean out too far; you or the ladder may slip and fall. Keep your hips within the line of the ladder sides (the stiles), with both feet on the rungs at all times, and hold on to the ladder with one hand whenever possible.

Glass

If window glass, a glass shelf, a table top or a glazed door is broken, put on a pair of thick gloves and pick up, wrap and dispose of all the broken pieces as soon as possible. Consider fitting safety glass in vulnerable locations, such as low-level door and window glazing. Remove blown light bulbs using a cloth to protect your hand if the glass breaks.

Asbestos

Be aware of the danger of building materials containing asbestos fibres. If in any doubt about asbestos in your home, seek advice from your local council's Environmental Health Department. Do not attempt DIY on sprayed coatings, pipe lagging, or insulating boards – these materials should be handled only by a licensed asbestos removal contractor. If you do DIY work involving contact with asbestos fibres, wear a facemask, soak the material with water first, and avoid using power tools. Do not use a domestic vacuum cleaner to remove dust – hire a commercial one if necessary. Bag up the damp dust and offcuts in heavy-duty refuse sacks and mark them 'ASBESTOS', then contact your local authority waste disposal department for advice on its safe removal.

Safety equipment

Many DIY activities generate dust, debris, fumes, noise and heat. Buy a personal protective equipment (PPE) kit. These are available from DIY outlets and include safety goggles, a dust mask, ear defenders and gloves.

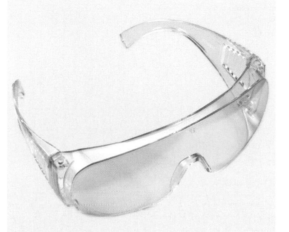

Safety goggles or spectacles made to British Standard BS EN 166:2002 will protect you from eye injuries when drilling, sawing, sanding, driving masonry nails or using chemicals, especially above head height.

A disposable face mask will stop you from inhaling the coarse, airborne, non-toxic dust and particles caused by many drilling, sawing and sanding jobs. If you are spraying paint or creating toxic dust, you should wear a specialist mask made to British Standard BS EN 140:1999.

Ear defenders or ear plugs made to British Standard BS EN 352-4:2001 will protect your hearing during noisy jobs such as sanding a floor, using a chainsaw or drilling masonry.

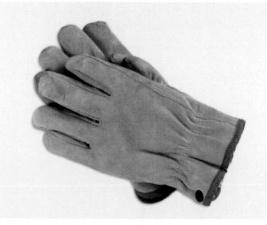

Gloves protect your hands when handling coarse building materials or working with chemicals that could harm your skin. Use leather gloves for building and gardening work; PVC ones when handling chemicals. Disposable latex gloves can provide useful light-weight protection for many dirty but not potentially harmful jobs.

Around the house

Domestic wiring

Electricity is supplied to the home through the service cable from the national grid via a local substation. The householder's responsibility for electricity begins at the cables leading from the meter to the consumer unit.

How electricity works

Electricity is a stream of negatively charged particles, called electrons, flowing from negative to positive through a conductor. The flow of electricity is called current, and is measured in amps (A). The driving force, or pressure, of the current is measured in volts (V).

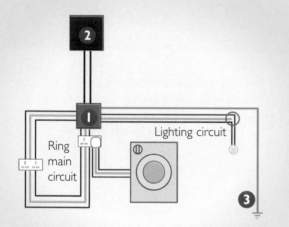

Electric circuits

In order for any appliance to function or any bulb to light, electric current must flow in a circuit through the device. Circuits connect all devices in the home to the consumer unit using cable comprising live (red) and neutral (black) copper conductors, covered in plastic insulation. The consumer unit **1** (see page 28) is connected to the power station, via substations **2**, by a circuit, which carries much higher voltages than the 230V used in the home.

All circuits in the home include a third conductor, known as the earth **3**, to provide a safe escape route for electric current in the event of a fault. The earth is also connected to exposed metalwork, such as as sinks and taps.

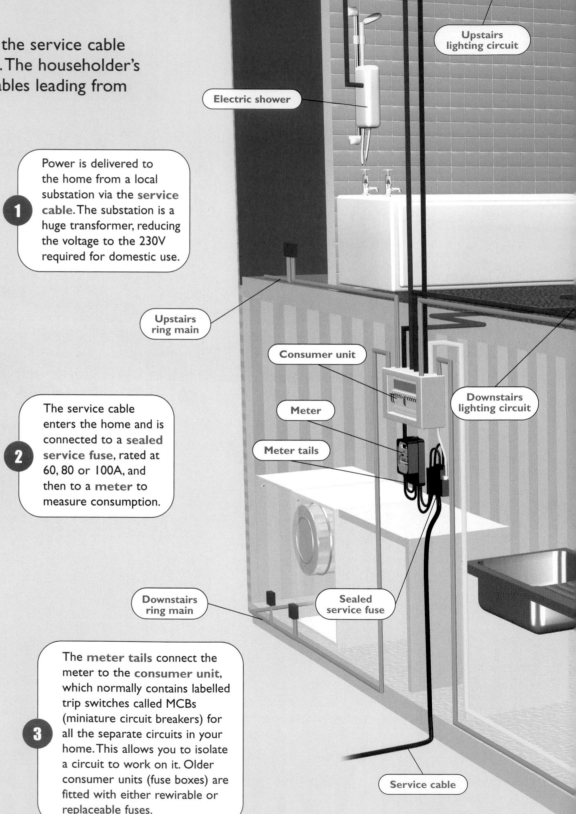

1 Power is delivered to the home from a local substation via the **service cable**. The substation is a huge transformer, reducing the voltage to the 230V required for domestic use.

2 The service cable enters the home and is connected to a **sealed service fuse**, rated at 60, 80 or 100A, and then to a **meter** to measure consumption.

3 The **meter tails** connect the meter to the **consumer unit**, which normally contains labelled trip switches called MCBs (miniature circuit breakers) for all the separate circuits in your home. This allows you to isolate a circuit to work on it. Older consumer units (fuse boxes) are fitted with either rewirable or replaceable fuses.

Upstairs lighting circuit

Electric shower

Upstairs ring main

Consumer unit

Meter

Meter tails

Downstairs lighting circuit

Downstairs ring main

Sealed service fuse

Service cable

Lighting circuit

Ring main circuit

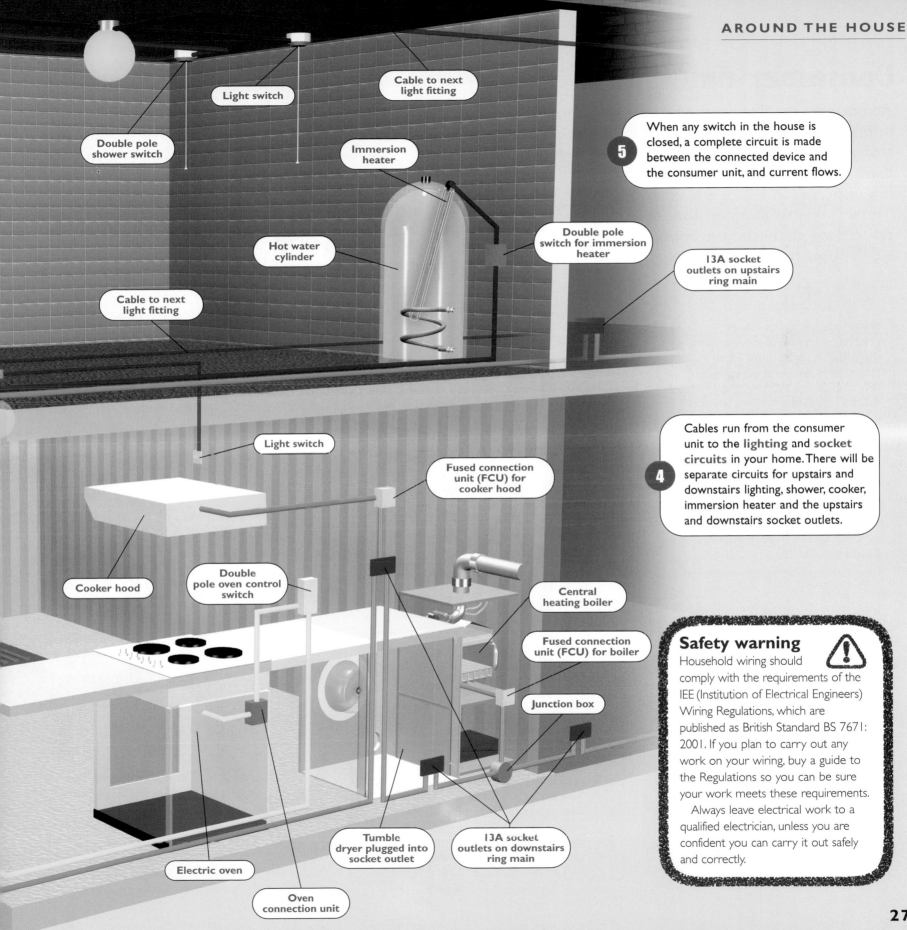

Light switch

Cable to next light fitting

Double pole shower switch

Immersion heater

Hot water cylinder

Double pole switch for immersion heater

Cable to next light fitting

5 When any switch in the house is closed, a complete circuit is made between the connected device and the consumer unit, and current flows.

13A socket outlets on upstairs ring main

Light switch

Fused connection unit (FCU) for cooker hood

4 Cables run from the consumer unit to the lighting and socket circuits in your home. There will be separate circuits for upstairs and downstairs lighting, shower, cooker, immersion heater and the upstairs and downstairs socket outlets.

Double pole oven control switch

Central heating boiler

Cooker hood

Fused connection unit (FCU) for boiler

Junction box

Safety warning ⚠

Household wiring should comply with the requirements of the IEE (Institution of Electrical Engineers) Wiring Regulations, which are published as British Standard BS 7671: 2001. If you plan to carry out any work on your wiring, buy a guide to the Regulations so you can be sure your work meets these requirements.

Always leave electrical work to a qualified electrician, unless you are confident you can carry it out safely and correctly.

Tumble dryer plugged into socket outlet

13A socket outlets on downstairs ring main

Electric oven

Oven connection unit

Consumer unit

All new houses have consumer units instead of the older-style fuse box. However, despite the differences, the basic features remain the same: there is a mains on/off switch and circuit breakers/trip switches or fuses to protect the circuits in the house against overload.

Miniature circuit breakers (MCBs) protect against overloading the circuit. A switch turns off or a button pops out when the current flow through the MCB is higher than its rated value.

Each miniature circuit breaker (MCB) should be labelled to indicate which circuit it controls. To identify yours, turn off one MCB at a time and check which circuit has stopped working. Repeat for all MCBs.

Understanding your electricity supply

Power is supplied from the power station through the national grid at an extremely high voltage but very low current. This is because energy loss through heat is lower at low currents and high voltages. The electricity is supplied as alternating current (AC) rather than direct current (DC). This means that the flow of electrons moves backwards and forwards with less energy loss than DC. It is also safer. The speed at which the current alternates is measured in Hertz (Hz). Domestic supplies alternate at 50 times a second, or 50Hz.

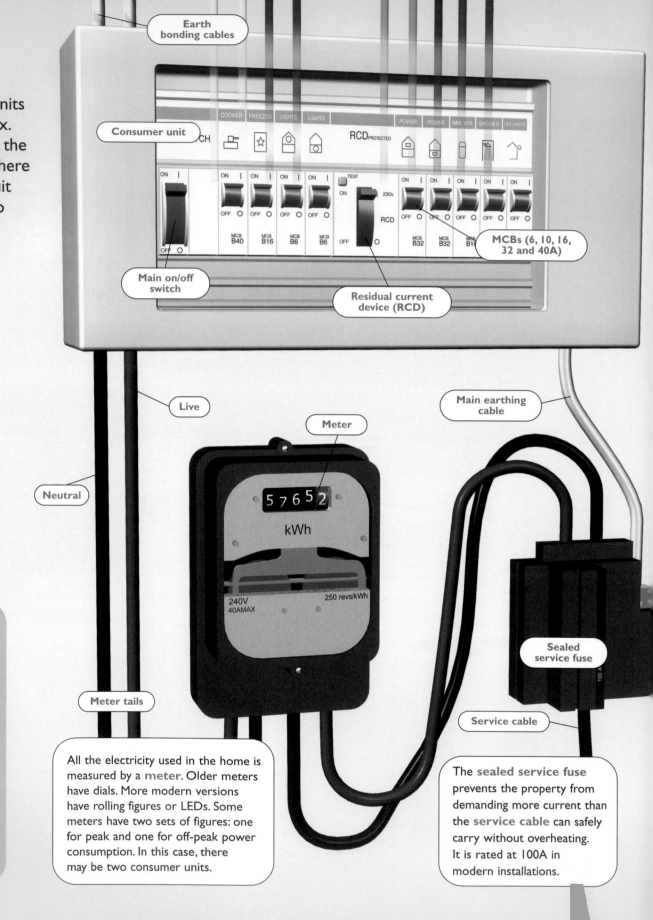

Earth bonding cables

Consumer unit

Main on/off switch

Residual current device (RCD)

MCBs (6, 10, 16, 32 and 40A)

Live

Meter

Main earthing cable

Neutral

57652 kWh

240V 40AMAX

250 revs/kWh

Sealed service fuse

Meter tails

Service cable

All the electricity used in the home is measured by a **meter**. Older meters have dials. More modern versions have rolling figures or LEDs. Some meters have two sets of figures: one for peak and one for off-peak power consumption. In this case, there may be two consumer units.

The **sealed service fuse** prevents the property from demanding more current than the **service cable** can safely carry without overheating. It is rated at 100A in modern installations.

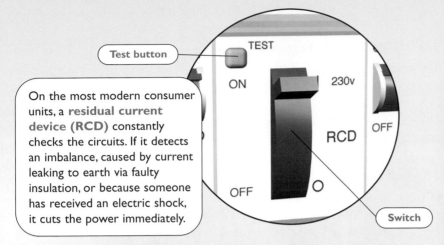

Test button

TEST

ON   230v

OFF

RCD

OFF   O

Switch

On the most modern consumer units, a **residual current device (RCD)** constantly checks the circuits. If it detects an imbalance, caused by current leaking to earth via faulty insulation, or because someone has received an electric shock, it cuts the power immediately.

Fuse box

The oldest fuse boxes have slot-in rewirable fuse carriers or cartridges **1**. Within each of these is a small length of fuse wire **2** that melts and breaks if it is overloaded. Always keep a supply of replacement wires or cartridges in a range of amp ratings: 5A for lighting, 15A for the immersion heater circuit, and 30A for socket outlet and cooker circuits. Cooker fuses rated at 45A are available only as cartridge fuses.

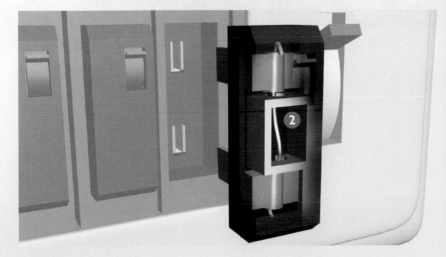

Maintenance

Before doing any electrical work	**Turn power off** *Remove fuse for the circuit you are working on, or turn off the MCB. Make sure everyone else in your home knows you are working on an electric circuit.*
Once every three months	**Test RCD in consumer unit (and/or any separate versions you might have)** *Make sure all major appliances are turned off and that everyone else in the house knows the power is to be cut temporarily. Push RCD test button (see left). Switch should flip to the off position. If nothing happens, contact electrician immediately. If switch trips correctly, reset switch to the on position to reconnect power.*

Fault diagnosis

Mild shock from metal-cased device	**Earth fault within item** *Contact a qualified repairer. This fault should have tripped an RCD, so test yours, or have one fitted if none is present.*
No power	**MCB tripped** *Turn off appliances, reset switch and identify faulty device by a process of elimination. Unplug all appliances, then reconnect them one by one to trace cause of problem.* **Whole house RCD tripped** *Reset RCD. If fault occurs again, call qualified electrician.* **Local power failure** *Check neighbouring buildings to verify, and report power failure to your electricity company.* **Service fuse blown** *Call electricity company immediately to replace.*
MCB in consumer unit trips regularly	**Circuit overload** *Caused by plugging in too many high-wattage appliances at once. Make sure that you don't overload a circuit – maximum wattage is 7kW.* **Faulty device on circuit** *If an MCB trips when a specific appliance is used, immediately stop using appliance, unplug it and have it checked. If an MCB trips periodically, plug in one appliance at a time to see which one causes the problem. Once you have identified the faulty appliance, have it repaired.*

Socket outlets

Most electrical appliances can be plugged in at any socket outlet, which may be sunk in the wall or surface mounted. Permanently fixed appliances, such as cooker hoods, are connected directly to the power circuit using fused connection units (FCUs), which are protected by a dedicated fuse.

1 As a plug is inserted, the **earth pin** enters first because it is longest. As the earth pin pushes in, the **live** and **neutral pins** push open the protective **shutters** from in front of the live and neutral pin holes.

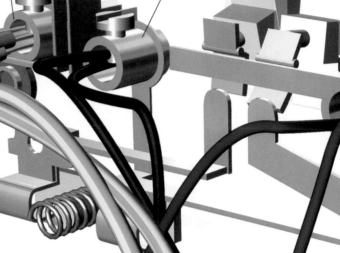

Earth terminal in mounting box

Flying earth link

Earth terminal

Switches

Neutral terminal

Live terminal

Earth pin

Shutters

Sprung connectors

Live pin

Plug flex

Understanding the ring main circuits

All the socket outlets in the home are connected in ring circuits running to and from the consumer unit **1**. There is normally one ring for downstairs **2** and one for upstairs **3**. Unlike lighting circuits, there is no limit on the number of socket outlets **4** or FCUs on a ring circuit. However, the total load on the circuit should not exceed 6900watts.

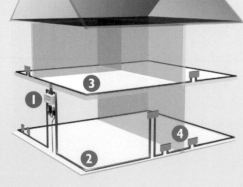

3 When the **switch** is moved to the on position, the contacts complete a circuit by linking the live terminal to the live sprung connector. Power flows from the ring main via the live pin through the flex to the appliance. The circuit is completed via the neutral pin. A **flying earth link** ensures the metal box is earthed.

Testing the socket outlets

Use a mains tester unit to check each socket outlet in turn. Up to three lights will come on in different combinations to indicate that the socket is correctly wired or that it has a fault. Check the chart on the back of the tester (or the tester manufacturer's instructions) to identify specific faults.

Neutral pin

Sprung connectors

2 When the plug has been fully inserted, all three pins make contact with their corresponding **sprung connectors** inside the socket outlet. These are connected to the wiring terminals.

Ring main

Maintenance

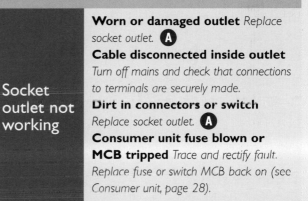

Once a year

Test socket outlets using a socket tester *This is an inexpensive device that plugs into each socket outlet and warns of wiring problems.* **A**

Fault diagnosis

Socket outlet not working

Worn or damaged outlet *Replace socket outlet.* **A**
Cable disconnected inside outlet *Turn off mains and check that connections to terminals are securely made.*
Dirt in connectors or switch *Replace socket outlet.* **A**
Consumer unit fuse blown or MCB tripped *Trace and rectify fault. Replace fuse or switch MCB back on (see Consumer unit, page 28).*

Replacing a socket outlet

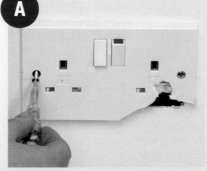  

1 Turn off the main power switch and also remove the fuse or turn off the miniature circuit breaker (MCB) (see Consumer unit, page 28) for the circuit on which you are working. Then switch the power back on to the other circuits. Test the socket outlet with a lamp to make sure the power is off. Undo the screws holding the faceplate in place and pull it away from the mounting box.

2 A socket outlet on a ring main has two wires in each terminal. If there is one wire in each terminal, the outlet is a spur (ie it is wired to a socket that is itself on the ring main). If there are three, it supplies a spur. Connect the new outlet in exactly the same way as the old one – red to live, black to neutral and green/yellow to earth. Reconnect the earth link between the faceplate and mounting box, as shown.

3 Make sure that none of the wires will be twisted or caught as you fold them back into the box. If the earth link is missing, use the earth wire from a cable offcut to create an earth link. If earth wires are bare, cover them with a green/yellow sleeving. Screw the faceplate back on and then replace the fuse or reset the MCB and switch the power on. Test the socket with a mains tester before use.

31

Plugs and fuses

Correctly fitting the appropriate plug, flex and fuse to an electrical appliance is crucial to avoid the risks of fire and electric shocks. The key factor in deciding what rating of fuse to use is the wattage of the appliance. Modern appliances are supplied with factory-fitted moulded plugs – all that is required is to fit the correct fuse if the original blows.

Maintenance

<table>
<tr><td>Once every six months</td><td>**Check flexes and plugs** *This is particularly important with appliances which are portable or which are moved during use, such as a hairdryer, iron, vacuum cleaner or power tools.* **A**</td></tr>
</table>

Checking flexes

A

Look for signs of wear and tear on the flex, especially near the plug and where the flex enters the appliance. Unplug and open the plug, and make sure the flex grip is tight and is gripping the flex sheath, not the conductors. Check that each conductor is firmly attached to the correct terminal, that there are no loose strands of wire, and that there is no blackening on the inside of the plug.

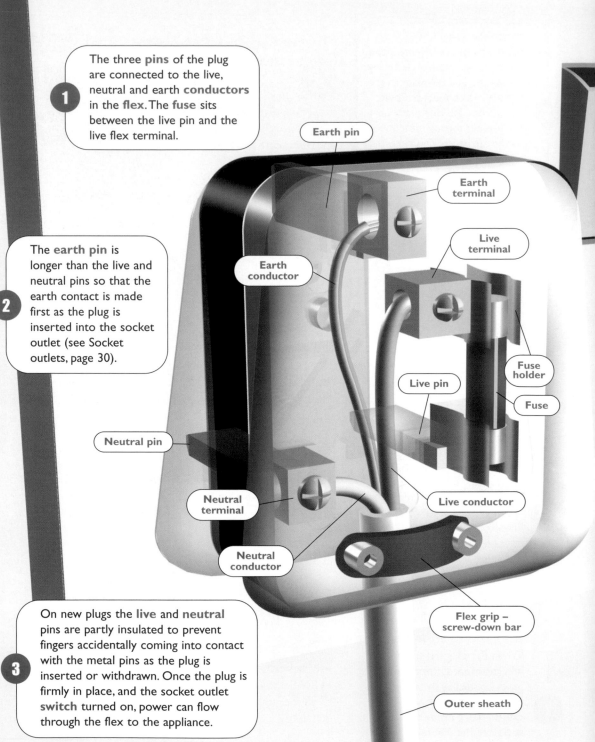

1 The three **pins** of the plug are connected to the live, neutral and earth **conductors** in the **flex**. The **fuse** sits between the live pin and the live flex terminal.

2 The **earth pin** is longer than the live and neutral pins so that the earth contact is made first as the plug is inserted into the socket outlet (see Socket outlets, page 30).

3 On new plugs the **live** and **neutral** pins are partly insulated to prevent fingers accidentally coming into contact with the metal pins as the plug is inserted or withdrawn. Once the plug is firmly in place, and the socket outlet **switch** turned on, power can flow through the flex to the appliance.

4 To get power to the appliance the current must pass through the **fuse**. The fuse contains a fine strip of metal. If the current drawn from the mains is too large the fuse wire will overheat and melt, stopping the excessive current from damaging the appliance.

Earth pin

Earth terminal

Live terminal

Earth conductor

Fuse holder

Fuse

Live pin

Neutral pin

Neutral terminal

Live conductor

Neutral conductor

Flex grip – screw-down bar

Outer sheath

Flex

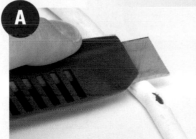

Safety standards

Buy plugs marked 'Made to British Standard BS1363', and fuses made to BS1362. Fit tough rubber plugs to power tools and to garden equipment, to prevent them being damaged if dropped.

If discarding a moulded-on plug, cut through the flex close to the plug body. Then deform the pins with hammer blows so the plug, if found, cannot be inserted in a socket outlet and cause the user to receive a shock.

Switches

Fault diagnosis

No power to appliance

Cracked plug/live parts exposed *Replace plug.* **A**
Fuse blown *Unplug appliance and check plug and flex for evidence of short circuit causing charring. Replace flex if necessary. Fit replacement fuse of correct rating and test appliance.*
MCB tripped or circuit fuse blown *Reset MCB or replace blown fuse. If fault recurs, consult an electrician (see Consumer unit, page 28).*
Flex discontinuity *Check each conductor with continuity tester (see Basic toolkit, page 12) and replace flex if faulty.*

Fitting a new plug

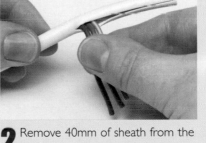

5 The earth wire forms a safety route for the electricity to flow to earth in case of electrical faults. All flex cores are individually insulated by a coating of coloured plastic, and are contained within a flexible insulating **outer sheath**.

1 Disconnect the appliance from the mains and remove the plug from the flex. Use a sharp knife to cut the end off the flex near where it entered the flex grip or at the point where the flex is damaged.

2 Remove 40mm of sheath from the flex. Take care not to cut the insulation on the conductors. Thread the flex through the plug cover, if necessary, and under the loosened flex grip. Trim each conductor with side cutters so it reaches its terminal easily.

3 Use wire strippers to expose a section of metal on each conductor. Twist the wires tightly. Remove the fuse to gain access to the live terminal and connect the conductors to their respective terminals: brown to live, blue to neutral and green-and-yellow to earth.

Plug fuse ratings

3A (red)	Use in plugs for appliances up to 690 watts, such as electric blankets, hi-fi systems and table lamps.
13A (brown)	Use in plugs for appliances between 690 and 2990 watts. This includes anything with a heating element.

4 Leave a little slack on the earth conductor. For pillar terminals (above), undo the screw, push the bare wire through the hole and tighten the screw. With screw-on stud terminals, remove the stud and wind the bare wires clockwise round the pin.

5 Make sure the conductors lie in their channels within the plug and don't obstruct the retaining screw hole, then tighten the flex grip to hold the sheath firmly.

6 Make sure that no unsheathed cores are visible outside the plug, and check the fuse is the correct rating for the appliance (see table). Remove and replace if necessary. Then fit the plug cover firmly in place and tighten the retaining screw.

Lighting

All the light fittings in a circuit are connected in a chain, with switch cables connected into each lighting point. There are usually separate circuits for upstairs and downstairs, each of which should supply no more than ten fittings.

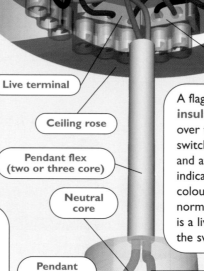

Lighting circuit cables

Earth terminal

PVC sleeving for earth

Switch cable

Neutral terminal

Red PVC tape 'flag'

Live terminal

Switch terminal

Ceiling rose

Pendant flex (two or three core)

A flag of **red PVC insulating tape** is placed over the black wire of the switch cable at the switch and at the fitting. This indicates that the wire coloured black (the colour normally used for neutral) is a live conductor when the switch is on.

Neutral core

Pendant lampholder

Live core

Strain loops

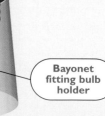

Bayonet fitting bulb holder

Bulb

Filament

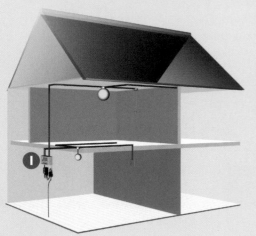

Lighting circuits

Each lighting circuit is wired as a radial circuit, starting at the consumer unit ❶ and terminating at the last light fitting on the circuit.

Replacing a switch

Lighting cable is twin-core-and-earth, with live, neutral and earth cores. The bare earth cores are covered in slip-on green-and yellow **PVC sleeving** when exposed. This cable carries the power for all the lights on the circuit. The flex to each fitting is of a lower rating and only needs an earth core if the lampholder is metal. Switches are connected to each light fitting. When the switch is turned on, a circuit is completed between the light and the live and neutral supply.

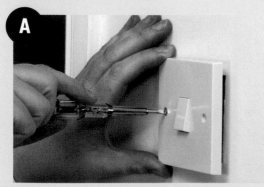

A

1 Turn off the power as in the safety warning (above). Undo the two screws holding the switch in place. There will be a red and a black wire connected to the old switch. The cable earth wire will be connected to the earth terminal in the mounting box. Undo the retaining screws in the terminals and release the wires so you can remove the switch.

2 Reconnect the wires the same way as before. In a 2-way switch used for 1-way switching, connect the red wire to 'common' and black (flagged with red PVC insulating tape) to 'L1' or 'L2'. If the switch is metal, fit a short length of earth core (with green and yellow PVC sleeving) to link the earth terminals on the faceplate and metal mounting box to the earth.

Switches and dimmers

Whether a switch or dimmer unit is being fitted, the cable to the light fitting is the same. Make sure that a dimmer is wired correctly, with red attached to the positive terminal and black (with the red 'flag') connected to the neutral. The earth core should be connected to the earth terminal on the metal box, and linked to the faceplate with an earth link if the switch or dimmer is made of metal.

Fault diagnosis

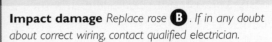

Sparking light switch	**Worn or dirty contacts** Replace switch. **A**
Broken ceiling rose cover	**Impact damage** *Replace rose* **B** *. If in any doubt about correct wiring, contact qualified electrician.*
Broken or brittle lampholder	**Impact damage or heat from lamp** Replace lampholder. **C**
Cracked switch faceplate	**Impact damage** *Replace switch.* **A**

Replacing a ceiling rose

1 Turn off the power at the consumer unit, remove the lighting circuit fuse or switch off MCB. Restore the power to the other circuits and test that the light is no longer working. Then unscrew the ceiling rose cover.

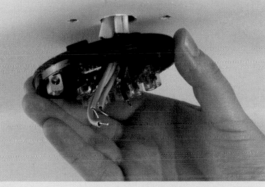

2 Make a drawing to show positions of the wires. Use an electrician's screwdriver to loosen the terminal screws. Disconnect the flex and cable cores, then unscrew and remove the rose baseplate. Remove 'knock-outs' from the base of the new ceiling rose, thread it over the cables and screw it to the ceiling.

3 Reconnect the cores as shown in your drawing, or following the manufacturer's instructions if the new rose is slightly different from the old unit. Feed the flex through the rose cover and reconnect the pendant flex wires. Screw on the cover and test the light.

Replacing a lampholder

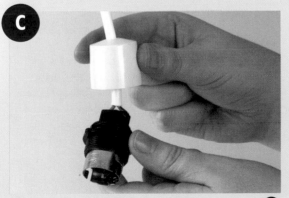

1 Turn off the power for the lighting circuit as in **B** above. Test the light to make sure the power is off. Remove the bulb and unscrew the shade ring. Remove the shade and unscrew the top cover.

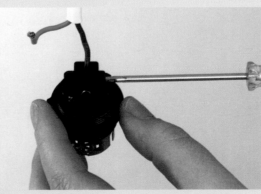

2 Using an insulated screwdriver, unclip the flex wires from the strain loops at the top of the fitting and disconnect from the terminals. Remove the lampholder and the cover from the flex.

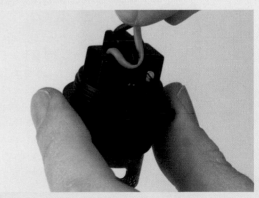

3 Slide the new cover on to the flex and attach the flex cores to the terminals. Hook the cores over the strain loops and screw on the upper cover. Refit shade, shade ring and bulb.

Outdoor electricity

Many electrical items, such as lawnmowers, hedge trimmers, pond pumps and garden lights are used outdoors. Water and electricity are a dangerous combination, so special switches and sockets with hinged weatherproof covers are essential for outdoor installations.

Test button

On/off switch

RCD (residual current device)

Spur from ring main

1 The outdoor socket or switch is connected to the ring main (see Domestic wiring, page 26) via an **RCD** on a **spur** running from an indoor socket outlet circuit. If the new outlet has an integral RCD, it can be connected directly to the ring main at a socket outlet or junction box.

2 **PVC cable** is run to the desired location indoors, then routed through a hole drilled in the wall and wired straight into back of the new box. **Conduit** protects the cable where it runs exposed outdoors. If the cable is to provide power for a pump or to a shed, then armoured cable is preferable (see left).

3 Drain holes in the base of the **mounting box** allow condensation build-up to escape.

PVC insulated cable

Conduit and PVC cable

Outdoor electrical cabling

There are two options for running power outside your home. One is standard PVC insulated cable **1** run through a protective conduit **2**. The other is armoured cable (shown left). Twin core armoured cable has two insulated conductors **3** in a PVC inner sheath surrounded by steel wires **4**, which act as the earth, and by a tough outer PVC sheath to protect the cable from damage **5**. This type of cable is suitable for sockets that are exposed, on a patio, for example, or for running to pond pumps. Because the earth connection is made with the steel wires, the gland nut **6** must be tightened firmly.

Armoured cable

5 When a power supply is being run to an outbuilding, it must not be fed from a spur, but must have a dedicated circuit wired from the consumer unit.

Safety warning ⚠

To avoid digging through cables, outdoor cabling to a shed or outhouse should be buried at least 60cm underground. Armoured cable needs no further protection, but twin core cable must be run through PVC conduit (left).

4 The spring-hinged **weatherproof cover** prevents rainwater from entering the terminals of the socket outlet, depending on its IP rating (see right).

Weatherproof cover

Outdoor socket outlet

Mounting box

Conduit (covering cable)

Index of protection (IP)

The IP system rates outdoor fittings according to their enclosure's ability to protect against entry of solid objects and water. A fitting will have the letters IP followed by two numbers. For an outdoor socket, the IP rating should be 54 or 55.

First number	Protection against solid objects	Second number	Protection against water
0	No protection	0	No protection
1	Solid objects exceeding 50mm	1	Dripping water
2	Solid objects exceeding 12mm	2	Dripping water when tilted up to 15°
3	Solid objects exceeding 2.5mm	3	Spraying water, rain
4	Solid objects exceeding 1mm	4	Splashing water
5	Dust protected	5	Water jets
6	Dust tight	6	Heavy seas
		7	Effect of immersion
		8	Immersion

Maintenance

Before each use	**Press test button on RCD to check it is operating correctly** Then press reset or move switch to 'on' position to restore the power.
Once a year	**Clean mounting box and cover** Ⓐ

Fault diagnosis

No functions	**Power off** Check RCD has not tripped. Then check MCB (or fuse) serving the circuit. Reset or repair.

Cleaning the socket

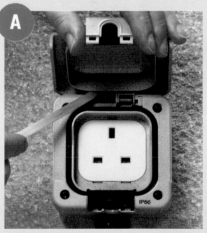

Ⓐ

Turn off the outdoor extension by switching the RCD to 'off'. Using a clean, damp cloth, wipe the exterior surfaces of the socket and cover. Restore the power.

Apply a small amount of grease to each of the spring hinges (above). This will keep the action free and displace water to prevent rusting.

Solar panel

Individual solar cells grouped in a solar panel harness energy from electric light or the sun and convert it into a form suitable for powering low-wattage appliances, from calculators to outdoor lighting. Another type of solar panel simply collects heat from the sun's rays and uses it to heat water.

6 In a solar panel, a number of PV cells are connected together in parallel (side by side) or series (end to end), to create a strong enough current to power electrical equipment.

5 The current flows to an external circuit via the **metallic contact grid**. The contact grid is designed to provide maximum contact with the silicon layer so that hardly any of the current is lost, while also letting as much light energy as possible pass through it and into the silicon layers beneath.

1 A **PV (photovoltaic) cell** is built around two layers of silicon. Each layer has been impregnated or 'doped' with a different element to give it specific electrical properties.

Light

2 The upper layer is known as **n-type silicon** because it has more negatively charged electrons than normal; the lower layer is called **p-type silicon** and has more '**holes**' where negatively charged electrons should be, giving it a positive charge.

Solar (PV) cells

Glass or transparent plastic covering

Solar (PV) cells

Metallic contact grid

pn-junction

Hole

N-type silicon layer

Electron

P-type silicon layer

3 When these differently charged layers are sandwiched together, a few **electrons** and **holes** drift across the **pn-junction**, creating a balanced electrical field at the junction, which stops further flow of electrons and holes.

4 When **light** hits the solar cell, it knocks electrons loose. These are pulled from the n layer to the p by the positive charge there. Electrons from adjoining atoms move to fill the holes left by the migrating electrons. This creates a current flow between the two layers.

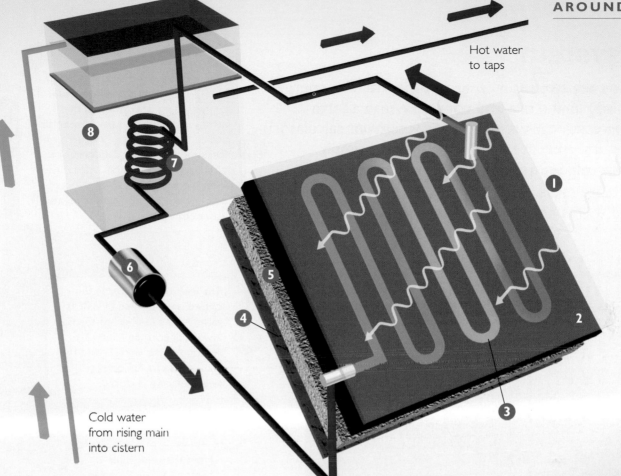

Hot water
to taps

Cold water
from rising main
into cistern

How solar heating panels work

Many roof or ground mounted solar panels are not electrical; they absorb the heat of the sun to warm water for use in the house or in swimming pools. Sunlight passes through a glass layer **①** and is absorbed by a black material **②**, which surrounds copper pipes **③** . Because copper is a good heat conductor, the heat is transferred from the material to the pipes, which contain water. The pipe zigzags backwards and forwards across the panel to occupy the maximum possible surface area for absorbing heat. Aluminium foil **④** and a layer of insulation **⑤** reflect back any heat not already absorbed by the copper pipe. As the pipe is heated, the heat is conducted to the water inside.

A pump **⑥** slowly circulates the water through a heat exchanger **⑦** in a water cistern **⑧** . The water in the solar panel circuit never comes into contact with the water being heated, in the same way as the water in a hot water tank heating coil never mixes with the water in the tank (see Central heating, page 66).

Even on cloudy days, an array of solar heating panels can warm water enough to make an outdoor swimming pool comfortable, or augment domestic hot water supplies enough to reduce bills. Because the pump runs relatively slowly, it is quiet and efficient and, with well insulated pipes and tanks, the heated water should stay warm overnight. If being used to heat swimming pools, the collectors can be at ground level so there is no restriction on the number of panels, unlike on a roof.

Fault diagnosis

Solar cells should last at least 20 years and will often come with a long-term guarantee. There is little you can do to repair them.

Electrical output reduced (PV panel)	**Check no part of panel is in shade** *In a basic PV panel, if just one of its cells is shaded, power production is cut dramatically.*

Maintenance

Once a year (heating panels)	**Remove obstructions** *Remove anything in vicinity that might obstruct sunlight, such as tree branches.* **Make visual external inspection** *Make sure glazing seals are in place and sound. Check insulation is attached correctly. Look for signs of corrosion.* **Check panels** *Make sure there is no air in system (noisy pump or air visible in flow meter window). Check system pressure – consult manual. Ensure insulation and fixings tightly fixed. Look for signs of leaks.*

Water system

In the UK, there are two main types of household water system: direct and indirect. In an indirect system, all the toilets and cold-water taps are fed from a cold-water storage cistern, normally in the roof space, except for the kitchen sink cold tap and, possibly, the washing machine, which are mains fed. In a direct system, all cold-water taps and toilets are fed directly from the mains.

Getting water into your home

Mains water is carried from water treatment centres in underground cast iron or plastic pipes, which connect with domestic water systems. Outside your home, a pipe, called the communication pipe ❶, runs from the water mains ❷ to a stoptap ❸, which is set within a stoneware or plastic pipe about 1m underground. From the stoptap, a service pipe ❹ brings water to your house via a rising main ❺. The indoor stoptap ❻, usually found under the kitchen sink, can be used to cut the water supply to the house.

Householders are responsible for the service pipe from their property to the external stoptap and for all the piping on their property. Some properties share a service pipe, which can lead to fluctuations in water pressure when demand on the shared supply is high.

Two thirds of the UK's drinking water comes from surface water, such as reservoirs and rivers, and the remainder comes from underground supplies. From these sources the water passes through clarification, filtration and disinfection systems to remove contaminants such as agricultural chemicals and treated effluent. Water quality and mineral content varies from area to area. However, everyone is entitled to a copy of the water analysis for their area from the local water company – check the phonebook for details.

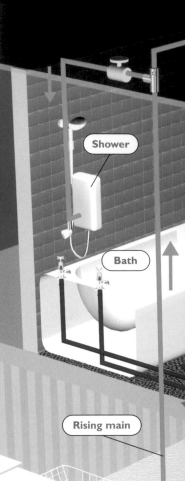

1 In an indirect water system (shown here), water from the **rising main** is connected via a **stoptap** to the **kitchen sink**, the **washing machine** and to the **cold water cistern**, which feeds the rest of the cold taps. In a direct system, the water is fed directly from the rising main to all the cold taps and the **toilet**. There is no cold water storage cistern.

2 The level of the water in the cistern is maintained by a float valve. As the level drops the float lowers, opening an inlet valve. As soon as the water – and the float – rises to the correct level, the valve is closed.

3 From the cold water cistern, an **overflow pipe** leads to the outside in case the float valve fails and the cistern overfills.

4 The cistern is fitted with a securely fixed access cover. This must prevent light and insects entering the cistern. The whole cistern, apart from the base, is insulated.

Overflow pipes

Shower

Bath

Rising main

Service valve

Hot and cold feeds to washing machine and dishwasher

Drain valve

Indoor stoptap

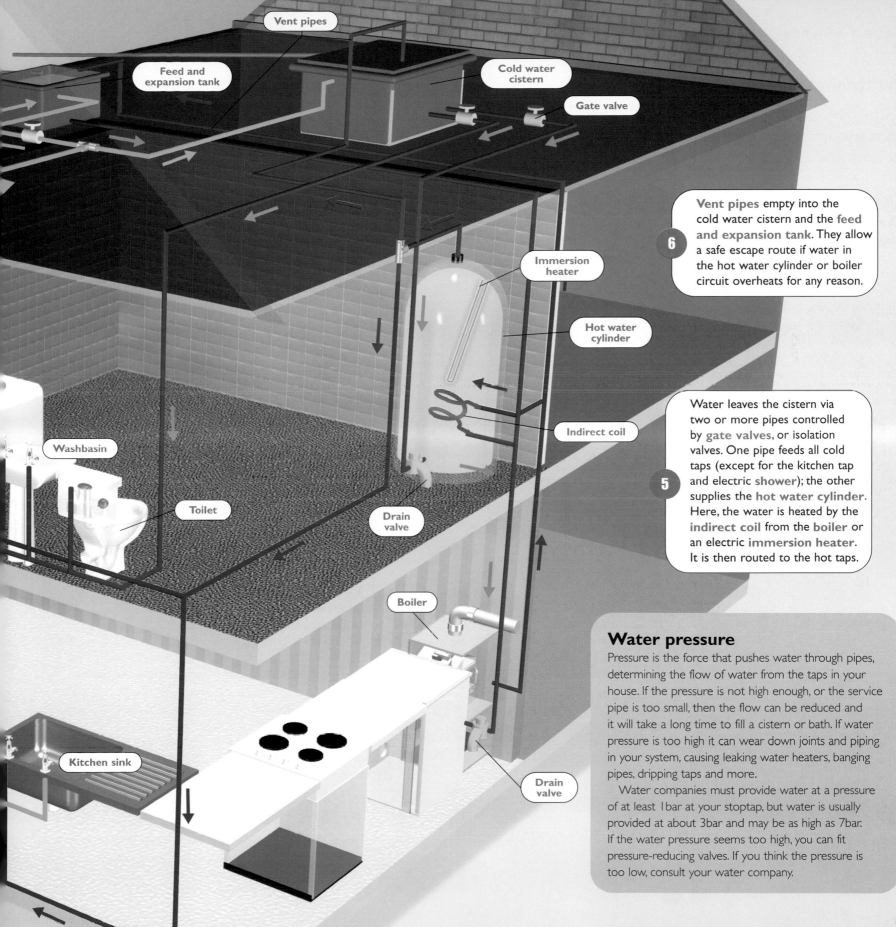

Vent pipes

Feed and expansion tank

Cold water cistern

Gate valve

6 Vent pipes empty into the cold water cistern and the feed and expansion tank. They allow a safe escape route if water in the hot water cylinder or boiler circuit overheats for any reason.

Immersion heater

Hot water cylinder

Indirect coil

5 Water leaves the cistern via two or more pipes controlled by gate valves, or isolation valves. One pipe feeds all cold taps (except for the kitchen tap and electric shower); the other supplies the hot water cylinder. Here, the water is heated by the indirect coil from the boiler or an electric immersion heater. It is then routed to the hot taps.

Washbasin

Toilet

Drain valve

Boiler

Drain valve

Kitchen sink

Water pressure

Pressure is the force that pushes water through pipes, determining the flow of water from the taps in your house. If the pressure is not high enough, or the service pipe is too small, then the flow can be reduced and it will take a long time to fill a cistern or bath. If water pressure is too high it can wear down joints and piping in your system, causing leaking water heaters, banging pipes, dripping taps and more.

Water companies must provide water at a pressure of at least 1 bar at your stoptap, but water is usually provided at about 3 bar and may be as high as 7 bar. If the water pressure seems too high, you can fit pressure-reducing valves. If you think the pressure is too low, consult your water company.

Softening and purifying your water

The water delivered from the mains supply contains a certain amount of chlorine and various other dissolved minerals. There are also traces of metals, nitrates, insecticides and herbicides, although these amounts are controlled by regulations.

There is a range of methods by which water may be treated to remove the chlorine, minerals and contaminants. The simplest and most convenient of these is the jug filter, which sits on the worktop and is filled by hand. These use an activated carbon filter, similar to that in a recirculating cooker hood (see page 128) to remove chlorine and pesticides, and an ion-exchange system (see below) to remove metals and reduce hardness.

The most common plumbed-in system is attached to the incoming water supply so that water used for bathing and washing clothes is softened, but drinking water remains untreated. This is especially important for babies and people on a sodium-restricted diet. This type of system works by passing the water **1** through resin beads **2** that replace the scale-forming magnesium **3** and calcium **4** ions with harmless and taste-free sodium ions **5**. The beads are regenerated by periodically flushing through with salt water, to replenish the supply of sodium ions and remove the magnesium and calcium ions.

1 Water molecules
2 Resin beads
3 Magnesium ions
4 Calcium ions
5 Sodium ions

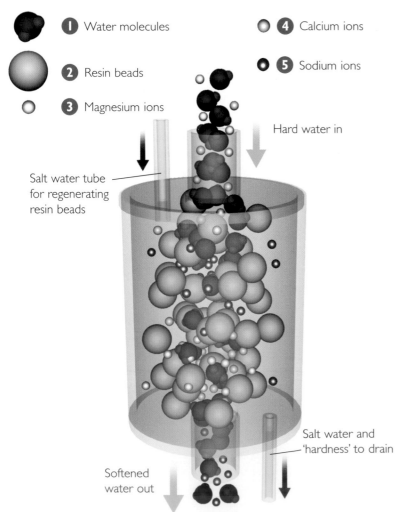

Salt water tube for regenerating resin beads

Hard water in

Salt water and 'hardness' to drain

Softened water out

Positioning a water treatment unit

Any permanently-fitted device that removes hardness from mains water must be fitted close to the incoming service pipe, stoptap and a drain (for the used salt water). Some units contain an electrical system to control when the salt water regenerates the filter, and these require a nearby power source.

Immediately after the stoptap **1** there must be a feed **2** to the mains drinking water tap, usually at the kitchen sink, and there should be a non-return valve **3** to prevent water being drawn back through the unit when the drinking water tap is turned on. Service or isolation valves **4** allow water to be routed through the treatment unit **5**, or enable the system to be bypassed for repair.

Maintenance

Once a month	**Turn rising main stoptap on and off several times to prevent from seizing** *Spray small amount of aerosol lubricant onto spindle. Open tap fully and close by a quarter turn.*
Before winter	**Lag all cold pipes with preformed pipe insulation** *Remember not to insulate under cold water cistern. This allows heat from the house to reach cistern and helps keep it from freezing in very cold weather.* **A** **Drain any outside taps** *Turn off isolating stoptap and undo drain screw underneath tap, (or leave the tap open).* **Leave the heating on low if you go away**
Before you go on holiday	**Turn off the water at indoor stoptap on rising main, and drain cistern by opening all cold taps** *This means that there is no stored water in the system to cause damage if pipe bursts or other problem occurs.*

Insulating pipes

1 Cut the preformed insulation with a knife to the correct lengths, and trim the ends at a 45° angle at elbows and tees. Fix with PVC tape.

2 Where the pipe curves, cut v-shaped notches out of one side of the insulation.

3 Then bend the insulation around the curve, with the cuts on the inside of the bend, and tape it on.

Fault diagnosis

Leaking pipe	**Burst or leaking pipe** *Turn off water at indoor stoptap and put bowls under leaks. Then turn on cold taps to drain cold water cistern. Contact qualified plumber.*
No water from taps	**No supply from rising main** *Check whether water company is working close to your property. If not, check stoptap is open. If water is on, contact water company.* **Jammed float valve in cistern** *Check whether cistern is filling. If not, depress the float arm to free the valve and fill the cistern. If this fails, replace the float valve.* **A** **Check for frozen pipes** *Defrost pipes.* **B** **Check for air locks** *Clear by linking affected tap to kitchen cold tap with garden hose and turn both taps on.*
Overflow dripping	**Faulty float valve** *Service or replace float valve.* **A** **Float arm too high** *Adjust or bend arm downwards to lower water level in cistern.* **A**
Banging noise from rising main	**Water hammer caused by float valve bouncing** *Fit dampening device to the float valve.* **C** **Bracing plate loose** *If cistern has a bracing plate, check it is securely fitted.* **Loose, unclipped pipework** *Secure with pipe clips.*
Frozen pipes	**No lagging or temperature dropped too far** *Defrost pipes* **B** *and insulate* **A** .
Low flow rate	**Partially closed stoptaps** *Check internal and external stoptaps are fully opened.* **Leaking pipe** *Check for signs of a pipe leaking in house. Replace piping if necessary.* **Too much demand** *Pressure varies during day depending on demand for water placed on supply system. When demand is high (for example in the morning and early evenings), pressure can be lower than during rest of day. There can also be problems during dry spells when people are using sprinklers and hosepipes to water gardens. Wait two or three hours and try again. If low pressure persists, contact local water company.* **Damaged service pipe** *Householders are responsible for service pipe from their property to external stop tap. Contact the local water company – they can take pressure and flow measurements and determine whether problem lies with service pipe, or whether it lies with communication pipe or water mains, for which they are responsible.* **Cold water tank empty** *If a lot of water has been taken from the cold water cistern in the loft, it may be empty. It will take a short while to refill, during which time water pressure from indirect-fed taps will be low. Wait for the cistern to fill — it is usually possible to hear it filling up. If the pressure is still low once it is full, check that gate valves on supply pipes from cistern are fully open.*
Build-up of limescale	**You live in hard water area** *Install a water treatment unit (see opposite).*

Replacing a float valve

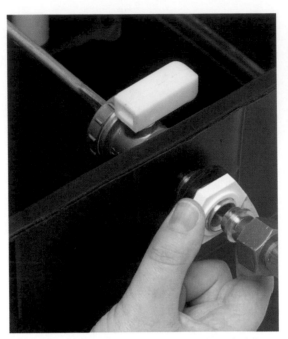

1 Turn off the main indoor stoptap. Use an adjustable spanner to undo the tap connector attaching the supply pipe to the valve at the cold water cistern, and then disconnect the supply pipe. Keep a towel handy to mop up any drips.

2 Use the spanner to loosen the back nut holding the valve to the outside of the cistern. then unscrew the nut by hand and remove the valve. Remove the back nut from the new valve and put it safely to one side.

3 Put a new flat plastic washer over the valve tail (and an inner locking nut if supplied) and fit the new valve to the cistern making sure it is orientated correctly (in the same position as before).

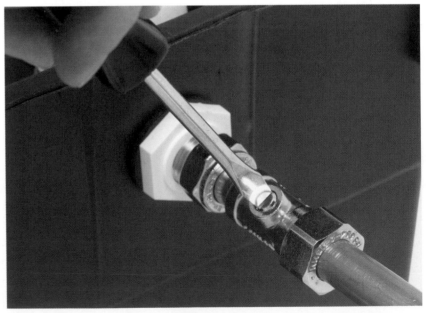

4 Put another plastic washer over the outside of the valve tail and screw on the back nut by hand, before tightening it half a turn with the adjustable spanner. Disconnect the existing tap connector and in its place fit a service valve that has a tap connector at one end and a 15mm compression fitting at the other.

5 Use a screwdriver to fully open the service valve – the screw slot will be in line with the pipe – and then turn the water back on at the main indoor stoptap.

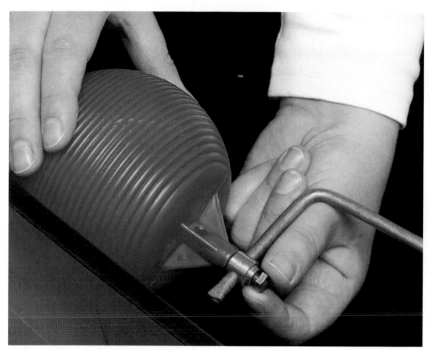

6 Check the water level of the cistern when the valve shuts – it should be 25mm below the level of the overflow. Adjust the water level if necessary by loosening the float nut and sliding the float up or down the arm. Slide it up to raise the water level or down to lower it, and then tighten the float nut. On older, piston-type valves, the only way to adjust the float height is to bend the arm.

Defrosting pipes

First check the pipe has not burst and have towels and bowls to hand in case of leaks. Locate the frozen section of pipe by checking which taps have stopped working. Then, turn off the indoor stoptap. Remove any insulation from the frozen pipe and open the nearest tap to allow water to escape as it expands. Wrap a hot water bottle around the pipe, or use a hairdryer to heat the pipe.

Never use a blowlamp or heat gun to defrost a pipe. Replace the insulation or fit some if none was present before. Close the tap and then open the main stoptap and check for split pipes or parted joints.

Fit a frost thermostat to the central heating to maintain an ambient temperature above 0°C, or leave the heating on constantly at a low setting during winter breaks.

In case of a leak
Make sure everyone in the house knows where the main indoor stoptap is located and how to turn it off.

Making a dampening device

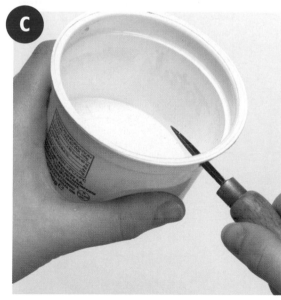

1 Purpose-made dampening devices are sold but it is easy to make your own. Thoroughly clean a small plastic pot and make a hole on either side at the top to attach a wire handle.

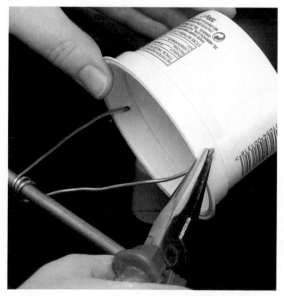

2 Attach a loop of wire to one of the holes, wrap the wire twice around the float arm and then attach it to the hole on the other side of the pot.

3 Suspend the pot in the water making sure it doesn't obstruct the movement of the float arm. Finally, make sure that the rising main pipe is clipped to a ceiling joist near to where it enters the cistern.

Taps

All taps work in more or less the same way – a rotating handle opens and closes a valve inside the body of the tap. Traditional taps, such as the shrouded head rising spindle tap, use a system of nuts and screws to open the valve. However, in some modern taps, one ceramic disc is rotated against another until openings in the discs line up, and water can flow through (see page 48).

Index disc

Capstan head

Retaining screw

Spindle

Gland nut

Headgear

Metal shroud

Headgear nut

Jumper

Washer

Tap body

Seat

Outlet

Backnut

Tail

Retaining screw

Head

Top plate

Index ring

O-ring nut

Headgear

Headgear nut

Spindle

Jumper

Washer

Seat

Backnut

Tail

Shrouded head rising spindle tap

This is one of the oldest designs of tap, with its familiar cross-head shape. It is a simple design, but reliable. Water is fed into the tap through the **tail** from below, normally through a hole in a sink. When the tap is closed, a **washer** is held down to close the hole in the **seat**.

The washer is mounted on a **jumper**, which is screwed via a **spindle** up into the **headgear**. The headgear is mounted in the body of the tap, secured by the **headgear nut**, and protected by a **metal shroud**.

As the **capstan head** is turned anti-clockwise, the spindle rises, lifting the washer away from the seat, so allowing water to flow through and out of the tap's **outlet**. The spindle screws up and down within a **gland nut**, which is filled with watertight packing to prevent water leaking up past the spindle when the tap is turned on.

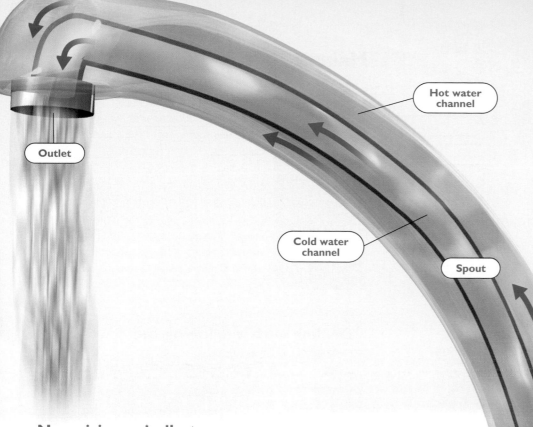

Outlet

Hot water channel

Cold water channel

Spout

Top plate

Head

O-ring seal

Headgear

Headgear

Outlet

Mixer taps

The only difference between a mixer tap and a non-rising spindle tap is that the hot and cold water share the same **outlet**. In a kitchen mixer, shown here, the spout has two separate **water channels** for hot and cold water. The two jets of water mix only as they leave the outlet because it is against water regulations to mix cold water from the mains (as it is on all kitchen taps) with hot water from a water cylinder. This is because the pressure on the mains supply can vary and under certain conditions could draw back non-drinking water from the cylinder into the mains supply.

Mixer units for use on baths and basins can merge water supplies within the tap body as long as the cold water is coming from a water tank, not directly from the rising main supply. If the cold water is mains-fed, a back-flow prevention device must be fitted on the cold water supply pipe.

Non-rising spindle tap

The non-rising spindle tap is a more modern design than the shrouded head tap. It has a more compact **head**, which helps to protect the lubricant in the tap mechanism from water and detergent entering via the **spindle**. Instead of a separate casing and handle, the two are combined into one head and cover. In the centre of the head and cover is a protective **top plate**, which usually indicates whether the tap is a hot or cold one, and clicks into place over a **screw** holding the head in place.

When the head is turned anti-clockwise, it turns a spindle which has a thread allowing it to keep turning without rising up inside the body of the tap. Instead, the **washer** rises up the lower shaft of the spindle, so allowing water to flow through and out of the tap **outlet**. Usually this sort of tap does not use a gland nut to maintain a watertight seal around the spindle: instead, it may have a nut or a split pin retaining a pair of rubber O-rings.

Ceramic disc taps

This type of tap operates on a different principle from conventional taps with washers and spindles. Positioned within the body of the tap is a **cartridge** containing a pair of **ceramic discs**, each with two holes in it. One disc is fixed in position; the other rotates when the handle is turned. As the movable disc rotates, the holes in it line up with the holes in the fixed one and water flows through them and out through the **spout**.

When the tap is turned off, the movable disc rotates so that the holes no longer align. A rubber seal at the bottom of the cartridge helps keep the tap watertight when it is closed. Unlike conventional taps that go round and round several times, these discs move a quarter turn only from closed to fully open.

Maintenance

Once a year

Check taps for hard water damage *If you live in a hard water area, turn off mains supply and supply from the tank (usually found in the airing cupboard or loft). One at a time, check headgear on each tap unscrews easily. Use penetrating oil to release stiff nuts and use spanner and wrench wrapped in cloth to hold body of tap. Soak parts in vinegar or limescale remover if limescale is present. Smear thread and washer with silicone lubricant before reassembling.*

Dealing with a dripping tap

Fix dripping taps immediately. In conventional taps this usually means replacing the washer, although turning over and refitting the old washer may temporarily fix the problem. If a scratched ceramic disc is causing the leak, the entire cartridge must be replaced: left-handed for a hot tap or right-handed for a cold tap. Remove the old cartridge and take it with you when buying a replacement to make sure it is the correct size and 'hand'. Ceramic taps can also drip if the seal at the base of the cartridge has perished. Replace it if necessary **(see page 50)**.

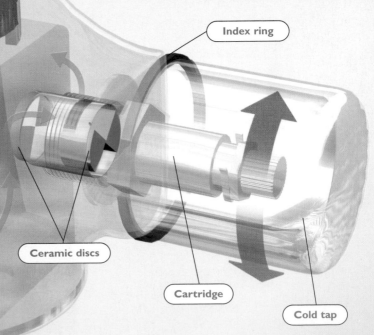

Spout

O-ring seals

Hot tap

Index ring

Ceramic discs

Cartridge

Cold tap

Fault diagnosis

While working on taps, put the plug in the plughole to stop small parts being lost, and protect the unit with a towel to avoid scratches or chips. Fault diagnosis and repair will vary depending on type of tap you have: traditional or ceramic disc, rising or non-rising spindle, gland nut or O-ring.

Dripping tap	**Non-rising spindle tap: worn washer** *Replace washer.* **A** **Ceramic disc tap only: worn rubber seal** *Replace.* **Ceramic disc tap only: faulty cartridge** *Clean inside or replace cartridge.* **B** **Rising spindle tap: worn washer** *Replace washer.* **C** **Traditional tap only: damaged valve seat** *Cover seat with nylon liner, sold by plumbing suppliers with matching jumper and washer. Follow manufacturer's instructions.*
Leaking spindle	**Non-rising spindle tap: worn O-ring** *Replace.* **D** **Rising spindle tap: loose gland nut or gland packing faulty** *Tighten nut and check. packing.* **E** **Mixer tap: worn O-ring on spout** *Replace.* **F**
Tap 'screams' when open	**Worn jumper. Replace washer and jumper** *Open body of the tap and replace the entire washer and jumper assembly.* **Rising spindle tap only: loose spindle** *Open the body of the tap and tighten gland nut.* **E**
Tap thudding and banging when turned off	**Loose washer** *A loose washer can flutter in water stream, sending minor shockwaves through system, creating what is known as 'water hammer'. Replace washer.* **A C** *If problems persists, consider installing water hammer arrestor, which is an air-filled chamber connected to plumbing that lets pressure dissipate harmlessly into cushion of air.* **Worn or cracked ceramic discs** *Replace cartridge.* **B**
Tap stuck or difficult to open	**Hard water damage** *Dissemble and clean (see Maintenance, left).* **Worn or cracked ceramic discs** *Replace cartridge.* **B**

Non-rising spindle tap: replacing worn washer

 **A**

1 Turn off the water supply, make sure the tap is turned on fully and wait until water stops flowing. Unscrew or lever off the top plate with a screwdriver.

2 Remove the retaining screw and pull off the head, putting the screw in a safe place.

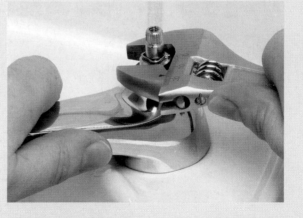

3 Use a spanner to undo the headgear nut. Do not force the nut if it is stiff. Brace the tap body by hand or with a pipe wrench wrapped in cloth, to prevent the tap from turning and fracturing pipework supplying it.

4 Unscrew or lever off the old washer and replace with the correct size for your tap. Reassemble the tap by following the steps in reverse order.

Cleaning or replacing ceramic discs cartridges

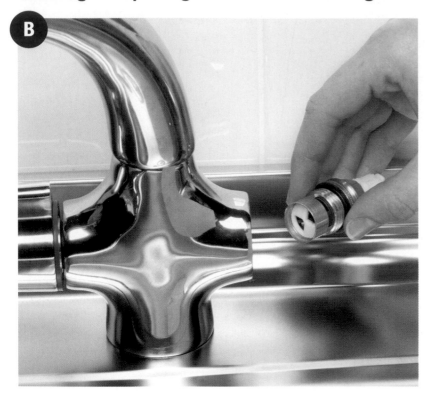

B

1 Turn off the water supply, pull off the tap handles (it may be necessary to unscrew a small grub screw on each) and use a spanner to unscrew the headgear section. Carefully remove the ceramic cartridges, keeping hot and cold separate. Check both cartridges for dirt and wear and tear. If they are worn, replace with identical parts for the tap unit. Make sure the hot and cold cartridges are fitted in the correct taps.

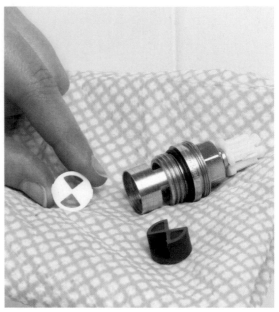

2 If the cartridges are dirty, clean them with a damp cloth. Replace rubber seal, if worn. Replace cartridge in the tap unit, fitting the hot and cold in the corresponding taps.

Rising spindle: replacing washer

C

Remove small screw to release the capstan from the spindle. Use a wrench wrapped in cloth to unscrew the metal shroud and lift it away from the headgear nut. Then, follow steps for non-rising spindle tap: replacing worn washer (see **A**, page 49).

Non-rising spindle tap: replacing O-rings

D

1 Follow **A** steps 1–3 (see page 49) to remove the headgear. Turn the spindle clockwise, lever out the circlip (above) or unscrew the nut to release the spindle.

2 Lever the O-rings from the spindle and fit same size replacement. Smear with silicone grease before reassembling the tap.

...ng leaking spindle

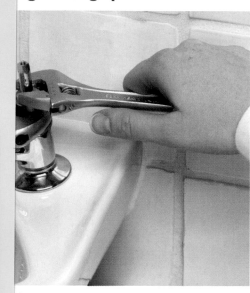

...o the screw to release capstan handle. Then ...ift the handle off and then remove the metal ...r nut with a spanner. Then, use another spanner ...rn. Slip the handle back on and check the tap. ...by another half turn and check again.

2 If the spindle still leaks, remove the gland nut completely and lift it out. Make a note of the packing used – it could be string, hemp, graphite or a rubber O-ring. Replace string packing with fibre string or PTFE tape, and reassemble tap.

...bout O-rings

...d twist the spout to align it with the body of ...screw behind the unit in the tap body, unscrew ...e it from the body of the tap.

2 Make a note of the position of the O-rings and prise them off using a flat head screwdriver. Smear the replacement O-rings with silicone grease before fitting, and reassemble the tap.

Waste disposal unit

There are two types of under-sink waste disposal unit: continuous feed and batch feed. Both grind organic kitchen waste so that it can be washed away. Continuous feed disposers, like the one shown here, spin all the time once switched on, as waste and running water are fed through a rubber protective shield. Switched on and off at the wall, batch feed disposers work only when a magnetic stopper is inserted in the plughole and turned to the 'on' position.

1 An **electric motor** mounted vertically under the unit directly turns a rotating **disc**, on the edge of which are two metal **pivoting blades** and two sharp **fixed blades**.

2 The disc spins inside a chamber, lined with a **shredder ring**, which has sharp **slots** on its inner wall. Waste material is washed into the unit with running water. It hits the disc, is spun outwards by centrifugal force and sliced by the fixed blades, then ground between the pivoting blades and the shredder ring.

3 The water and mashed up waste material pass through the slots in the shredder ring and into the drainage system through an **outlet pipe**.

Sink

Plughole

Rubber protective cover

Shredder ring

Slot

Pivoting blades

Fixed blade

Disc (turntable)

Outlet pipe

Waste material

To drains

Electric motor

Trap

Reset button

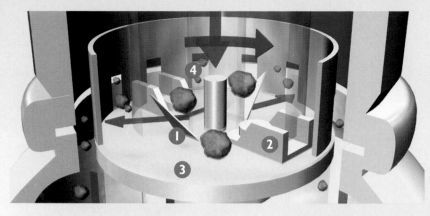

How the blades work

The fixed blades ❶ work like those in a liquidiser (see page 131). The pivoting blades ❷ spin out as the disc ❸ turns. Waste material is also forced outwards towards the shredder ring by centrifugal force. Small pieces pass easily through the slots ❹. However, large bits stick at the edge where they are hit by the pivoting blades and broken into smaller pieces. If a lump is too solid to break, the blade pivots out of the way, avoiding damage.

Waste water

Make sure the waste disposal unit routes directly into a soil stack or back inlet gully. Otherwise, waste products from the unit can collect around drain cover grids or hoppers.

Safety first

Always unplug, disconnect or isolate any appliance when carrying out cleaning or maintenance.

Maintenance

Once a month	**Clean disposal unit** *Use proprietary cleaning product to remove food, grease and odours. Put lemon peel through unit to mask unpleasant odours.*

Fault diagnosis

No functions	**No power** *Check mains lead, plug fuse and wiring, and wiring at socket outlet.* **Overload device cut out** *Press red reset button. If it pops out again, unit is jammed.*
Disposer hums	**Foreign object jammed inside** *Cutlery, bread ties, can pulls and other hard objects can jam between the blades and the shredder ring. Check that water is running freely through unit. Remove blockage.* ⓐ
Disposer leaking	**Leaking outlet pipe** *Remove drain pipe and replace rubber gasket. Contact qualified repairer if unsure.* **Leak from body of unit** *Contact qualified repairer.*
Waste thrown back into sink	**Torn rubber cover** *Get this part replaced immediately. Contact qualified repairer.*

Removing blockages

Ⓐ

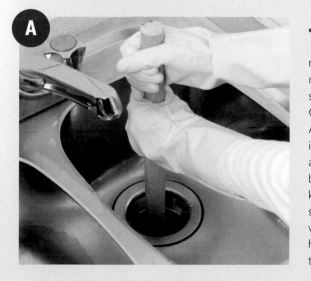

1 Turn off the disposer and unplug from the mains. Use the special release tool, if one was supplied with the unit. Otherwise, insert an Allen key into the recess in the base of the unit and try to free the blades by twisting the key. If there is no Allen socket, use a solid wooden stick, such as a hammer handle, to turn the disc from above.

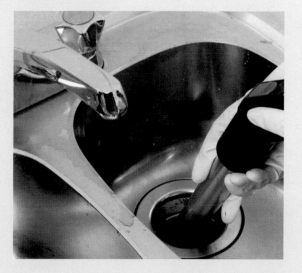

2 If this does not work, check again that the disposer is turned off and unplugged, then attempt to free the object carefully by sucking with a wet-and-dry vacuum cleaner, if you have one. Do not use your hands. If you cannot find the blockage, or if the disc will not turn, contact a qualified repairer.

Toilet

The basic design of the one-piece ceramic toilet has changed little in more than 100 years. Clean water is stored in a cistern above the bowl until the lever arm is pressed down to flush the toilet. The water is channelled around the rim, rinsing waste matter out of the bowl and into the drainage system (see Waste water, page 60).

Inlet valve

U-pipe

Cistern

Float

Overflow pipe

Lever arm

Dome

Flushing plate

1 The flush action of a toilet **cistern** works by siphoning the water from the cistern into the toilet bowl. An upside down **U-pipe** is connected at one end to the **flush channel**. At the other end is a wider **dome** with a **flushing plate** and **flap valve**.

Flap valve (also known as cistern diaphragm or siphon washer)

Flush channel

Flushing rim

Soil pipe

Bowl

Outlet pipe

Supply pipe

Trap

2 When the toilet is flushed, the **lever arm** rotates and lifts the perforated flushing plate and the flap valve. This lifts water over the bend in the U-pipe, creating a siphon and emptying the cistern. As the flushing plate falls, the flap valve flexes upwards, allowing the siphonic action to continue.

3 Water siphons from the cistern through the flush channel, and is distributed around the bowl under the **rim**. It then flows quickly down the sides of the bowl, washing the surface clean before exiting through the **trap**.

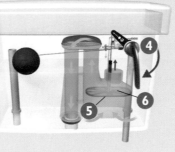
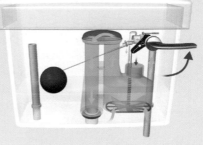
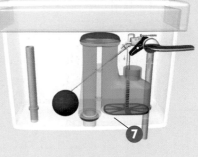

How the flush mechanism works

Under normal circumstances, water cannot flow from the cistern into the bowl because of the inverted U-pipe **1**. The inlet valve **2** is held shut by the float **3** pushing upward.

When the lever **4** is pressed, the flushing plate **5** is lifted. Because the flexible flap valve **6** lies on top of the plate, the water pressure holds it flat. The plate acts as a piston, forcing water over the U-pipe.

When the lever is released, the flushing plate drops. However, the flap valve lifts allowing water to siphon over the inverted U-pipe and into the bowl. As the water level drops, the float lowers, opening the inlet valve.

The siphon effect continues until air enters the U-pipe under the rim **7** of the dome. Water stops flowing out of the cistern and the tank fills until the float closes the inlet valve.

6 As the water level rises in the cistern, the **float** lifts the **inlet valve** arm. When the arm reaches the top of its travel, the inlet valve closes off the flow of water entering through the **supply pipe**. Some cisterns use a quieter Torbeck valve which has a small cylinder in place of the ball float.

5 When the cistern is empty, air passes under the edge of the dome and breaks the siphoning effect. The cistern refills from the cold-water cistern (or from the rising main in a direct system).

4 The last few litres of fresh water stay in the trap to prevent foul gases from entering the house up the **outlet pipe**. This is the same principle that is used in the plug outlets of sinks, baths and washbasins.

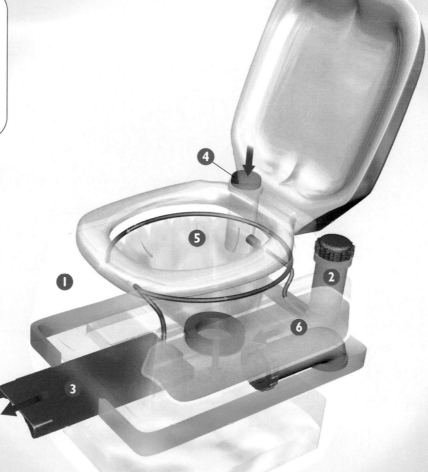

Alternative design

Commonly used at temporary outdoor sites where plumbing is limited, the **chemical toilet** is simply a seat over a removable holding tank **1**, which is filled with a mixture of water and disinfectant through the filler pipe **2**. This mixture converts waste into a 'sludge' which can be emptied into the sewer after a period of use and the drum replaced. A dyestuff and perfume are added to the mixture to colour it and neutralise odour. In a flush chemical toilet (shown here) a sliding plate **3** is pulled out of the way then water is pumped by a hand pump **4** into the bowl **5**, from a tank **6** positioned to the side of, or around, the bowl. The water carries the waste with it down into the holding tank or drum where it mixes with disinfectant.

Removing limescale from bowl

1 Hold a small mirror under the rim of the bowl to check for limescale deposits. Clean with toilet descaler and brush.

2 If the limescale is difficult to remove, pass a descaling product through the cistern several times. Also, squirt it under the rim and leave to dissolve the deposits.

Maintenance

Once a month	**Descale toilet bowl under the rim** *Squirt proprietary toilet cleaning product around rim and leave for a short time, according to manufacturer's instructions. Flush toilet and brush away residue with a toilet brush.*
Once a year	**Check for flakes of limescale inside cistern** *This can block siphon valve. Cut off water supply to cistern, flush toilet and scoop out any flakes of limescale.* **Check with handheld mirror for hidden limescale under rim of the bowl** *This can inhibit flow of water.* **A**

Safety first

Do not mix toilet descalers or rim cleaners with bleach. This can produce chlorine, which is a poisonous gas.

Clearing a blockage

To increase the force when freeing a blockage, stand on a chair and pour a bucket of warm water in one go into the bowl.

Levelling the bowl

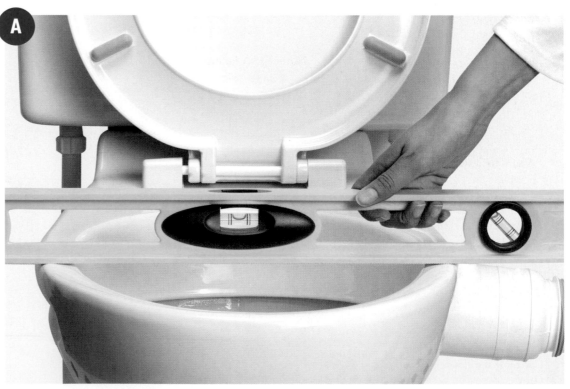

Use a spirit-level to check whether the rim of the toilet is level from side to side and front to back. If it isn't, loosen the nuts or screws holding the bowl down and level the bowl using strips of vinyl tile, shims or sealant. Screw down firmly.

Fault diagnosis

Toilet doesn't flush properly	**Bowl not level** *Check and correct if necessary.* **A** **Flap valve (cistern diaphragm) failing** *Call plumber to replace flap valve.*
Toilet doesn't flush at all	**Cistern not refilling properly** *Check height of ball valve and adjust if necessary.* **Flap valve (cistern diaphragm) failed** *Call plumber to replace flap valve.*
Water coming from overflow	**Inlet valve arm closing at wrong height** *Adjust level of float arm.* **Inlet valve faulty** *Replace valve.* **Float punctured** *Replace float.*
Continuous siphoning	**Debris or limescale in cistern** *Turn off water supply to toilet, empty cistern and scoop out flakes of limescale and grit.* **Toilet filling too fast.** *If cistern fills too fast, siphoning effect may not be interrupted by air entering siphon dome, and water entering from inlet valve will continue to be drawn into bowl. If an isolating valve is fitted on supply pipe, close it slightly to reduce supply pressure. If no valve is present, fit smaller orifice seating on inlet valve*
Broken or swivelling seat	**Seat broken** *Replace seat.* **B** **Loose nuts** *Tighten wing nuts under the back of bowl.*
Handle turns (or button pushes down) but no flush	**Broken link** *Make temporary repair with coat-hanger wire. Then replace link.* **(See C, page 58)** **Flap valve (cistern diaphragm) failed** *Call plumber to replace valve.*
Leaking behind toilet	**Toilet worked loose** *Make sure bowl is screwed down firmly.* **Faulty bowl connector** *Check seals on bowl connector. Replace if necessary.*
Leaking on inlet to ball valve	**Loose nut** *Tighten with adjustable spanner. If this fails, turn off water supply to toilet and flush. Then unscrew external nut on ball valve, clean threads and re-wrap with PTFE tape (thread seal tape). Tighten nut again.*
Noisy refill	**Portsmouth ball valve fitted** *Replace with diaphragm valve. (See Water system, page 40.)*
Water rising up bowl when flushed	**Toilet outlet pipe blocked on washdown bowl** *Unblock toilet using plunger. See Waste water, page 60.)* **Toilet outlet blocked in siphonic bowl** *Pour bucket of warm water into bowl. If this fails, use auger to dislodge blockage. (See D, page 58)*
Condensation on cistern	**Inadequate ventilation** *Make sure bathroom is ventilated and fit an extractor fan (see page 162), if necessary. Condensation is a problem primarily for cisterns supplied by water directly from rising main (see Water system, page 40) because this water is colder than that supplied from water tank in loft.*

Replacing the seat

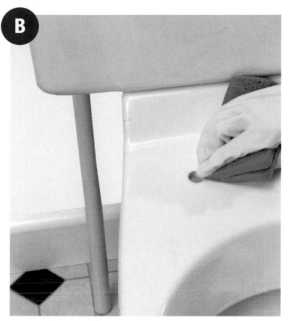

1 Undo the plastic wing-nuts under the rear of the toilet bowl and remove the broken seat. Clean around the bolt holes and make sure the area is rinsed properly and dry. Place the new seat in position.

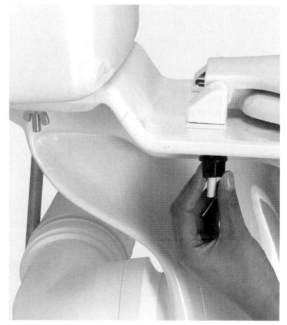

2 Make sure the supplied washers are fitted above and below the bowl, on both bolts. Finger-tighten the wing-nuts. Then check the seat is centred on the bowl. Tighten the nuts fully.

Replacing a broken link to the ball valve

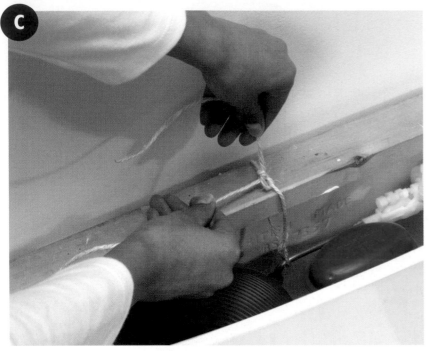

1 Turn off the water supply to the toilet and flush by pulling up on the rod protruding from the dome of the siphon. If you cannot turn the water off, place a wooden batten across the cistern and tie the ball valve arm up.

2 Remove the broken sections of link from the ends of the rods and discard. Then fit the new link between the siphon rod and the nylon connector bar.

Clearing a blocked trap and outlet pipe

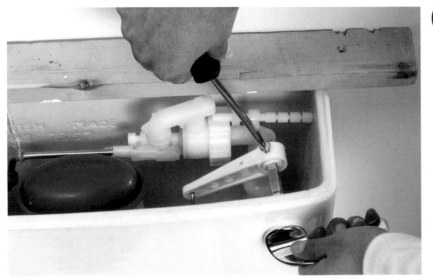

3 Push the other end of the bar onto the lever arm rod. Make sure the lever arm is in the correct 'rest' position, and tighten the retaining screw. Then untie the float from the wooden batten and allow the cistern to fill.

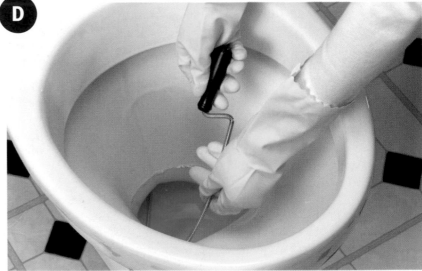

Use a flexible drain auger to remove a blockage in the outlet or trap. As you insert the auger, turn it slowly. If you meet hard resistance, turn the auger back and forth to move it past the trap. When you meet soft resistance, push and pull gently to dislodge the blockage. Flush the bowl with a bucket of water.

Bidet

Although it looks like a toilet bowl, a bidet is more like a washbasin. Over-the-rim bidets with a mixer tap are the most common, and the simplest to fit. Vertical spray bidets must be fitted by a plumber.

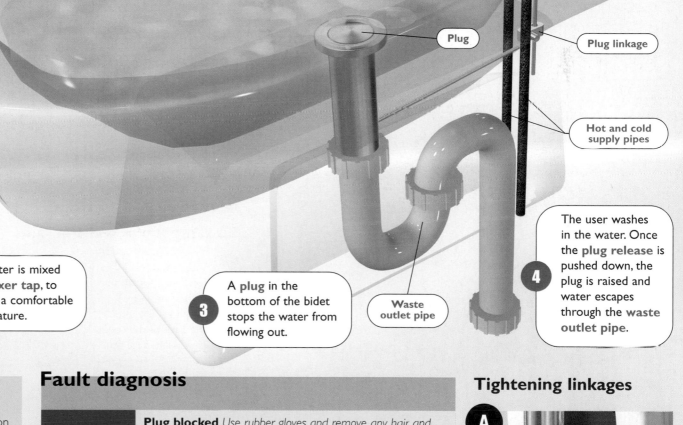

Plug release

Mixer tap

Ceramic bowl

Plug

Plug linkage

Hot and cold supply pipes

1 When the tap of the bidet is opened, hot and cold water is drawn from the **supply pipes**.

2 The water is mixed in a **mixer tap**, to achieve a comfortable temperature.

3 A **plug** in the bottom of the bidet stops the water from flowing out.

Waste outlet pipe

4 The user washes in the water. Once the **plug release** is pushed down, the plug is raised and water escapes through the **waste outlet pipe**.

Maintenance

Much of the maintenance for a bidet is the same as for the taps on a washbasin. See Taps, page 46.

After each use	Wash the bidet out with hot water
Once a month	Keep bowl free from limescale using descaler

Fault diagnosis

Water not draining	**Plug blocked** *Use rubber gloves and remove any hair and debris blocking plug hole. If this does not work, use sink plunger to unblock the outlet. See Waste water, page 63.* **Pop-up waste failing to pop up** *Linkages have slipped. Tighten or refit linkages.* **A**
No water	**Taps seized up from lack of use** *Lubricate tap. See Taps, page 46.*
Dripping	**Tap leaking** *See Taps, page 46.* **Trap leaking** *Tighten connections.*

Tightening linkages

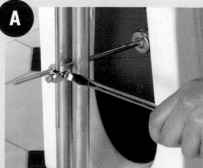

A

Realign the linkages and tighten the screws locking the arms together.

Waste water

Houses have either a single-stack or two-pipe drainage system. Homes built since the mid 1960s have a single-stack system like the one shown here: water from all sinks, baths, toilets and appliances flows into one waste pipe. Older homes use a two-pipe drainage system separating the toilet and other waste water.

Vent pipe

1 Waste water from a **bath**, **sink** or **wash basin** passes through the plug hole into a **trap**, which holds enough water to prevent foul air from the drain passing back into the house.

Bath

Wash basin

Connecting pipe

2 Waste water from a **toilet** also passes into a trap, which is built into the base of the toilet (see Toilet, page 54).

Toilet pipe direct into soil stack

Soil stack

Sink

Waste disposal unit

Sink trap

Connection to drains

Alternative design

In older houses, with a **two-pipe system**, the waste water from an upstairs bath or sink runs through narrow pipes into a hopper head **1** on the side of the house, then into a gully linked to the drains **2**. The soil and vent pipe **3** is used solely for toilets. The downstairs waste water is fed directly into the gully.

Septic tank (not nearer than 15m to house)

Perforated effluent distribution pipes

Drain field (area of land required depends on percolation value of ground)

4 From the trap, the waste water passes into the **soil stack**, which is open at the top to allow gases to escape, and down into the underground **drain** to the sewer (or septic tank). Gravity carries the water through the sewers.

Toilet

How a septic tank works

A septic tank is, in effect, a private sewerage system, used in rural areas that don't have access to a communal sewerage system. A septic tank is usually made of fibreglass-reinforced plastic, metal or concrete and is buried in the grounds of a house. Typically it holds 4000 litres of water. Tanks are vented through the roof through pipes. The waste water passes into the tank through an inlet pipe **1**. In the septic tank, matter that is lighter than water (scum) floats to the top **2**, while matter that is heavier than water (sludge) falls to the floor **3**. Water, rich in bacteria, nitrogen and phosphorus, occupies the middle area **4**. As new water enters the tank, some of the existing water is displaced through the exit pipe **5** into a series of perforated pipes in the drain field (above). This is an area of gravel trenches covered in soil where the water soaks away. Special care must be taken if you have a septic tank as non-biodegradable products, such as tampons, can block the system, and household chemicals can interfere with the bacteriological action of the tank.

3 The plastic traps are either 'U', 'P' or bottle-shaped. As water fills up past the bend in the 'U' it spills over the edge and drains away through a **connecting pipe**.

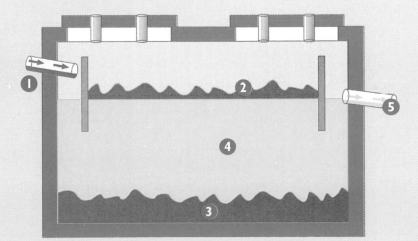

Maintenance

Every two or three months	**Check washing machine and dishwasher non-return valves for blockages** Ⓐ
Once every six months	**Clean waste pipes and traps** *Add small amount of chemical drain cleaner (not with septic tanks). Pour down plugholes of sinks and basins. Take care as these chemicals can be poisonous. Use a product designed to break down fats and grease.* **Check outside grates over gullies** *Clear blockages of leaves, dirt and garden debris.*
Once a year	**Have septic tanks emptied and cleaned** *The proportion of effluent, sludge and scum must be carefully balanced for the tank to work efficiently.*

Avoid and clear blockages

Put only waste water down a drain. If possible, keep grease, ground coffee, hair and fluff out of the drain. Try to remove any build-up of hair in basin or shower wastes before it becomes a blockage. A wet and dry vacuum cleaner is a good tool for this job. Do not flush tampons or nappies down the toilet.

Never pour fat down a sink in case the fat solidifies when it returns to room temperature. If you do so accidentally, immediately squirt in some washing up liquid and flush with very hot water. Hot air from a hair dryer applied around the trap will also melt congealed fat. To clear a blocked waste disposal unit, see page 52.

Check non-return valves

1 Locate the non-return valve behind or near the washing machine or dishwasher. The drain hose will be attached to it. Unscrew the plastic retaining collar, which holds the hose coupling to the valve.

2 Lift out the valve and remove any dirt or fluff which is blocking the valve. Retighten the retaining collar firmly by hand.

Fault diagnosis

Water not draining from sink or bath	**Blocked waste pipe** *Clear blockage with plunger. If no plunger is available, undo trap connections and clear blockage manually.* Ⓐ
Water draining slowly from sink or bath	**Partially blocked plug hole or waste pipe** *Pick out dirt and debris from plug hole or use a chemical drain cleaner. Chemical drain cleaners should not be used with septic tanks. Never use a plunger after using chemical cleaner in case the chemicals splash.* Ⓑ
Toilet blocked	**Blockage in pipe** *Use toilet plunger to clear the blockage. Make sure rim of plunger is below surface of the water and pump 10 times before removing abruptly. If this fails, use a closet auger to dislodge the obstacle. Turn the handle slowly clockwise as you push towards the blockage.*
Bad smells	**Leak in system** *Check under sinks and bath for leaks. Try tightening trap nuts. Replace O-ring seals if worn.* **Blockage farther down system, beyond house** *Contact drain and pipe cleaning company to rod the drains.* **Trap seal losing water** *Consult qualified plumber or fit deeper traps.*
Sulphurous smells from washing machine (see page 100)	**Waste water entering washing machine** *Incorrectly fitted outlet pipe. Some washing machines and dishwashers are fitted with a non-return valve to prevent waste water being drawn back into machine. Some washing machines will not take a non-return valve but will lock out if they detect too much resistance in the waste pipe.* **Waste hose at wrong angle** *This should be higher than sink overflow to stop water from the sink flowing back into washing machine. It also prevents siphonage.* **Blocked non-return valve** *Unscrew plastic collar and remove fluff and debris clogging valve.* Ⓐ

Clearing a blocked waste pipe

1 Block the overflow with a wet cloth and fill the sink to cover the rim of the plunger. Allow any air to escape. Then pump the plunger up and down 10 times.

2 If this does not work, place a bucket under the trap and remove its plug, or unscrew the bottom of a bottle trap. If necessary, remove the whole trap.

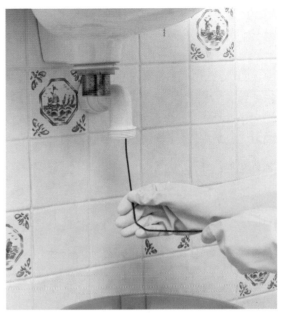

3 Allow water to drain, and probe using bent wire inside the pipe to remove any clogged material. Clean and replace trap.

Cleaning a waste pipe

4 Another method is to feed an auger through the plug hole. Turn the handle clockwise to get past the trap. When you feel soft resistance, work the auger back and forth. Flush with hot water.

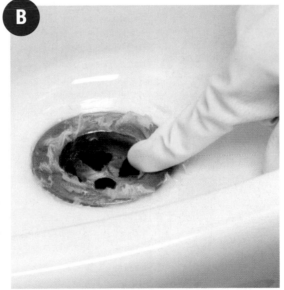

1 Allow remaining water to drain, then smear petroleum jelly on the rim of the plug hole. This is to protect the finish against the harsh chemicals required to clear a drain.

2 Pour chemical cleaner (caustic soda or enzyme) down the plug hole according to manufacturer's instructions. Rinse with fresh water. Never use a plunger immediately after cleaning with chemicals.

Electric shower

Most electric showers are fed directly from the rising main (see Water system, page 40), heating water as it passes through the unit. Heavy power usage means they must be connected to a dedicated circuit from the consumer unit (See Domestic wiring, page 26). They must also have a double-pole isolating switch that is out of reach of the person using the shower.

Shower head

1 The double-pole pull-cord switch is clicked on to allow power to reach the unit.

2 Mains water flows into the shower when the shower **control knob** is turned on. Current is supplied to the **heating elements** and as the water passes through the **heating unit** it is warmed in the same way as water in a hot water tank is heated by contact with the heating coil (see page 66).

3 The temperature of the water is controlled by adjusting the **flow rate**: the faster the water runs past the heating elements, the cooler it will be. The shower may have a two-stage heating setting as well.

Inlet for cold water (from rising main)

5 It is possible to adjust the type of water flow on some showers. Turning the head can change the water stream from a fine spray to powerful jets, and even to massaging bursts.

Heating unit

Heating element

Temperature and flow rate control knob

4 As the heated water exits the unit through the **shower hose**, it is forced through the jets in the **shower head**.

Shower hose

Alternative design

Where the mains water pressure is low, or a high flow rate is desirable, a **power shower**, which has an internal or external electric pump **1**, will boost the flow. These units mix hot and cold water from your hot water cylinder **2** and cold water cistern **3**.

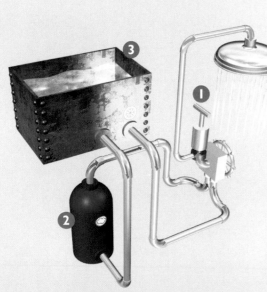

Maintenance

Once a month	**Descale shower head**  *Also clean shower unit using a non-abrasive sponge and a mild detergent. Make sure limescale isn't building up around knobs and fittings. Wipe down with white vinegar or descaler.*
Every year	**Clean shower pump filters** *If shower is a power shower, clean the plastic filters located within the hot and cold pump inlet connections.*

Descaling the shower head

1 Unscrew the shower head. There may be a tool supplied with your shower; use a screwdriver if there is a central screw. If the rose does not unscrew, remove the whole head from the hose. Pour white vinegar or descaler through or over the head.

2 Scrub the rose with an old nailbrush or washing-up brush. If the holes are badly blocked, soak the head in a proprietary descaler according to the manufacturer's instructions or leave it overnight in undiluted distilled white vinegar.

3 Reattach the shower head to the hose, and turn the shower on for a few minutes on its cold setting to rinse out the limescale and remaining descaler or vinegar. Repeat this process several times to make sure all the cleaning product has been thoroughly rinsed away.

Fault diagnosis

Water keeps going cold	**Faulty thermostat** *Contact qualified repairer.* **Water pressure dropping below normal atmospheric pressure** *This may be due to people flushing toilet or local variations. Fit pumped shower.*
No hot water from instant unit	**Thermal safety cut-out tripped** *Allow shower to run cold until cut-out is reset. If this happens repeatedly, water pressure is too low.* **Elements overheating** *This could be caused by build-up of scale on elements. Contact qualified repairer.* **Thermostat faulty** *Contact qualified repairer.* **Element burned out** *Contact qualified repairer.* **MCB tripped** *Check consumer unit.*
No hot water from power shower	**No hot water left in hot water cylinder** *Heat water.* **Blocked pump inlet filters** *Clean or replace.* **Pump drawing in air** *See 'noisy pump' below.*
Leaks from unit or hose	**Internal valves worn** *Contact qualified repairer.* **Washers worn or damaged** *Replace washers in ends of hoses with identical parts. (Many manufacturers sell a spares kit with a full diagram on how to fit parts.)*
Flow from shower head is low	**Limescale build-up** *Check showerhead. Descale.* **Local mains pressure down** *Check pressure from taps. Try again when pressure restored.* **Stopcock not open fully** *Locate main stoptap and open to one quarter turn less than fully open.* **Pump not functioning** *Check power supply.*
Pump noisy (if fitted)	**Limescale or debris in mechanism** *Descale and clean pump if possible. If not, contact qualified repairer.* **Air being drawn into pump** *If pressure on inlet is not sufficient and water is very hot, a problem known as cavitation can occur. Water under low pressure boils at a lower temperature than at normal pressure but, as it is not possible to pump boiling water because of the steam, the water remains in the pump, swishing around noisily. The shower goes cold until thermostatic control cuts the flow rate of the cold water. The pump will then return to normal and the cycle will repeat until water temperature is lowered or the pressure increases. To solve problem permanently, increase size of pipes (22mm diameter for inlet and 15mm for outlet is best).* **Bearings worn** *Contact qualified repairer.*

Central heating

Most central heating systems burn gas to heat water, which is pumped through a system of pipes and radiators to warm rooms. The same water can be pumped to a special coiled heat exchanger inside the hot water tank, which in turn heats the water in the tank to supply the hot taps. The system is controlled by an electronic timer and thermostats. The timer determines when the heating operates, and thermostats maintain the room or hot water tank temperature at the selected level. Some boilers are variations on this system, with the hot water for taps being heated directly as it passes through a 'combination' boiler, rather than being stored in a tank.

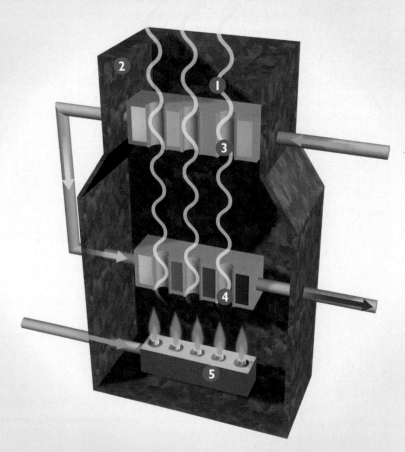

Water from rising main

1 Cold water flows into the boiler's heat-exchanger, and is heated by burning gas. The hot water passes through the pump and then is routed by a motorised valve to either the radiators, or to a **heater coil** inside the **hot water cylinder** where it heats water for the taps. The valve is controlled by the **room thermostats** and **cylinder thermostats**.

Cold water from cistern keeps the system topped up

2 The pressure in the system is generally maintained from a **feed and expansion cistern** in the loft. If the pressure drops, water from the cistern passes into the system. If the pressure rises, water passes back into the cistern via the **vent pipe**. A float valve keeps the cistern topped up from the **rising main**.

3 The **programmer** has a clock and stores two on and off times for a day. There are settings to turn the heating on continuously, once, or twice a day. Once a day turns the heating on at the first 'on' time and off at the second 'off' time. There will also be advance or over-ride buttons. These move the program on to the next stage in the cycle when pressed.

Programmer

4 When the first on time is reached, the programmer starts the **boiler**. The gas supply is turned on and the jets are ignited by a pilot light. Water is pumped through the **heat exchanger** where it is heated up. The boiler temperature is monitored by a high-temperature safety cut-out.

Alternative design

Although reliable, older boilers are not as fuel-efficient as modern **condenser boilers**, which use heat from the escaping gases **1** in the flue **2** to begin warming the water **3** before it passes through the heat-exchanger **4**. This maximises the heat energy extracted from the burning gas **5**.

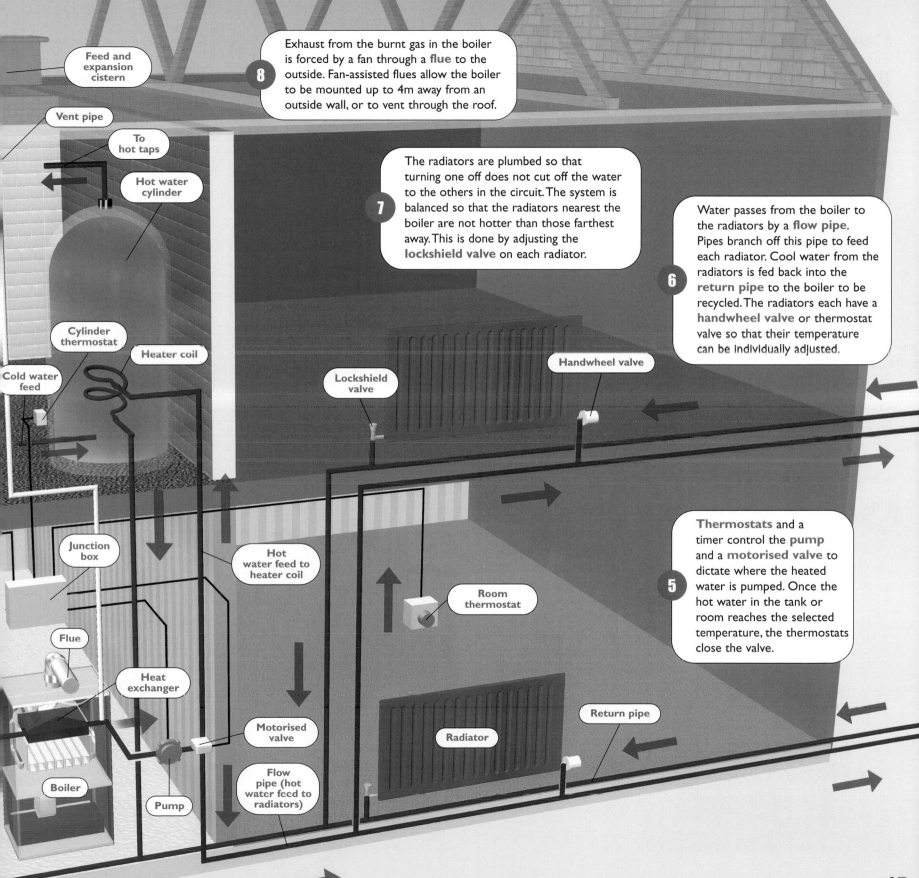

Feed and expansion cistern

Vent pipe

To hot taps

Hot water cylinder

Cylinder thermostat

Heater coil

Cold water feed

8 Exhaust from the burnt gas in the boiler is forced by a fan through a **flue** to the outside. Fan-assisted flues allow the boiler to be mounted up to 4m away from an outside wall, or to vent through the roof.

7 The radiators are plumbed so that turning one off does not cut off the water to the others in the circuit. The system is balanced so that the radiators nearest the boiler are not hotter than those farthest away. This is done by adjusting the **lockshield valve** on each radiator.

6 Water passes from the boiler to the radiators by a **flow pipe**. Pipes branch off this pipe to feed each radiator. Cool water from the radiators is fed back into the **return pipe** to the boiler to be recycled. The radiators each have a **handwheel valve** or thermostat valve so that their temperature can be individually adjusted.

Lockshield valve

Handwheel valve

Junction box

Hot water feed to heater coil

Room thermostat

5 **Thermostats** and a timer control the **pump** and a **motorised valve** to dictate where the heated water is pumped. Once the hot water in the tank or room reaches the selected temperature, the thermostats close the valve.

Flue

Heat exchanger

Motorised valve

Radiator

Return pipe

Boiler

Pump

Flow pipe (hot water feed to radiators)

Maintenance

Monthly	**Check and bleed radiators if required** *If radiators are hot at bottom and cold at top, they need bleeding.* **A**
Every year (preferably before switching on heating for the winter)	**Test the water in a central heating system for corrosion** *Internal corrosion can be extremely expensive to repair.* **B** **Check the lagging** *Make sure all the pipes in the loft are covered before winter. If you're taking a short break leave the heating on a low setting while you are away.* **Have the boiler serviced**

Bleeding a radiator

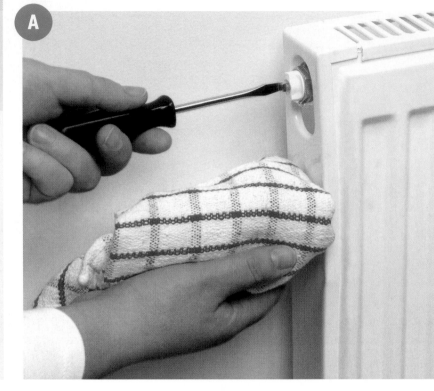

A

Use a radiator drain key – obtainable from any hardware store – to release air from the system. On some radiators, a flat tip screwdriver may be required instead of a key. Turn the key anticlockwise (no more than a quarter turn), and hold a cloth directly under the valve to stop dirty water dripping. Air should vent from the valve, making a hissing noise. When water starts to come out, close the valve and wipe the area dry.

Checking and inhibiting corrosion

B

1 Drain off some water from the drain valve at the boiler into a glass jar. Place two bright (non-galvanised) nails in the jar. Put the lid on and leave for a week or so. If, after a week, the nails are badly corroded and the water has changed to a rust orange colour, then there is corrosion in the system. Some black deposits are acceptable.

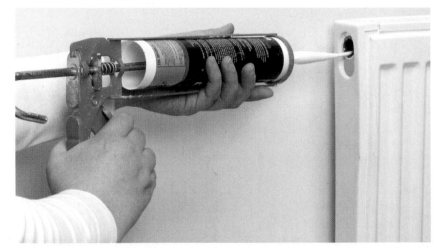

2 Corrosion inhibitors can be injected directly into the valve at the top of each radiator – follow the manufacturer's instructions carefully. Otherwise, add a corrosion inhibitor/antifreeze to the feed and expansion cistern in the loft. Tie up the ball valve arm, drain off some water from the system, and add antifreeze to the tank (make sure you only add the mixture to the central heating feed and expansion tank). Then release the ball valve arm. Refer to the manufacturer's instructions for the correct amount and specific details.

Fixing a leaking radiator valve

1 Turn off the valves at each end of the radiator. Make a note of the number of turns of the lockshield valve. Put a towel and a bowl under the valve to catch water, and have a bucket and a second bowl ready.

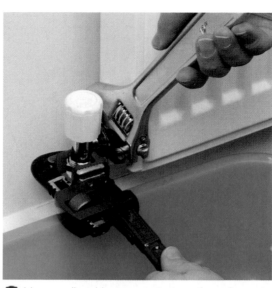

2 Use an adjustable spanner to turn the union nut (attached to the radiator) anticlockwise (when looking from the radiator to the valve) until the joint is loose. To prevent bending the pipe, counterbalance the force by holding the nut just below the valve with a Stilson wrench.

3 Open the air vent using a flat tip screwdriver or the radiator key (depending on the make of valve). This will allow the rest of the water to flow out into the bowl.

4 Wind PTFE tape (see Basic toolkit, page 12) tightly around the thread on the valve tail to prevent water seepage. Start at the end and make a 50 per cent overlap on each turn. Then, retighten the nut firmly over the tape. Open the lockshield and handwheel valves and allow the radiator to fill with water. When water starts to run out of the bleed valve, close it.

Fault diagnosis

No heat or water

Timer and thermostats set incorrectly *Make sure that programmer is on, that all thermostats are set high enough and that any heating controls on the boiler are turned up.*
No power *Check power supply and MCB in the consumer unit. If they are both on, call a heating engineer.*
Problem in valve motor *Check motorised valve by sliding the manual lever. If difficult to move, call heating engineer.*
Jammed pump *Tap pump gently with a mallet. If this doesn't work, try to start pump manually by turning the screw on the front of the pump housing. If neither works, call heating engineer.*
Pilot light gone out *Re-ignite pilot light following the instructions in boiler manufacturer's manual.*
No gas *Check other gas appliances, such as cooker. If no supply, call gas company. If gas is just not reaching boiler, call heating engineer.*

Central heating working but no hot water

Check thermostat on hot water cylinder is set to 60°C *If too low, then valve will not open to route hot water through heater coil in cylinder.*
Bleed air release valve next to hot water cylinder *This can usually be found on pipe which feeds hot water to heater coil.*
Manually open and close motorised valve *If it sticks or is difficult to move, call heating engineer.*

Leak in system

Leaking pipe joint *Most pipe joints are compression fittings. This means they can be tightened slightly. This will stop most leaks.*
Leaking radiator valve *If leak is from beneath valve, call plumber. If between valve and radiator, then use PTFE tape to seal the joint.* **A** *If leak is from under cap, repack the gland.* **(See B, page 70)**
Leaking bleed valve *Tighten bleed valve using Allen key. If this doesn't work, turn off both radiator valves and replace the bleed valve.* **(See C, page 70)**

Repacking a radiator gland

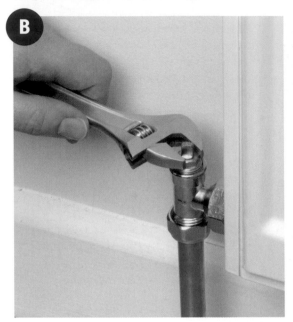

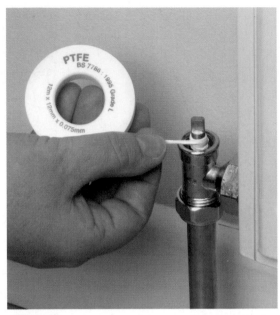

1 Turn off the handwheel valve and close the lockshield valve at the other end of the radiator. Remove the cap from the leaking valve and use an adjustable spanner to undo the small gland nut.

2 Slide the nut up out of the way. Pull a length of PTFE tape into a string and wrap this around the spindle four or five times.

3 Use a small screwdriver to push the tape down firmly into the valve body.

Curing a leaking bleed valve

4 Smear on silicone grease using a wooden spatula, and retighten the gland nut using the adjustable spanner. Replace the head and turn the valve back on.

Use a radiator bleed valve key to tighten the valve. If the leak continues, turn off the handwheel and lockshield valves at the bottom of the radiator where the water pipes enter and leave. Then unscrew the leaking valve and replace it with the correct part for your radiator.

Protect against frost damage

An anti-corrosive antifreeze can be added to the feed and expansion cistern to prevent heating pipes freezing. You can also fit a frost thermostat to the heating system. This overrides the system's programs and turns the heating on if the air temperature approaches zero.

Immersion heater

An immersion heater is used where there is no central water heating via the heater coil in the hot water cylinder (see page 66) or when a boost is required. The water temperature is controlled by a thermostat, which turns the elements on and off according to the temperature setting.

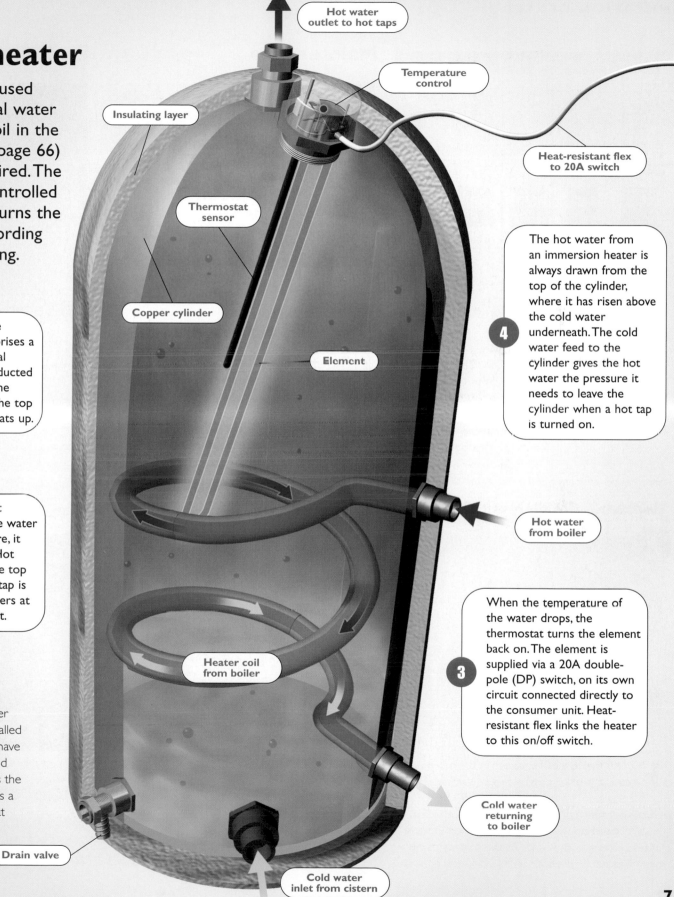

Hot water outlet to hot taps

Temperature control

Insulating layer

Heat-resistant flex to 20A switch

Thermostat sensor

Copper cylinder

Element

1 Mains power heats the **element**, which comprises a wire encased in mineral insulation. Heat is conducted from the element to the water, which rises to the top of the cylinder as it heats up.

4 The hot water from an immersion heater is always drawn from the top of the cylinder, where it has risen above the cold water underneath. The cold water feed to the cylinder gives the hot water the pressure it needs to leave the cylinder when a hot tap is turned on.

2 When the **thermostat sensor** detects that the water is at the set temperature, it turns the element off. Hot water is drawn from the top of the cylinder when a tap is turned on, and cold enters at the bottom to replace it.

Hot water from boiler

3 When the temperature of the water drops, the thermostat turns the element back on. The element is supplied via a 20A double-pole (DP) switch, on its own circuit connected directly to the consumer unit. Heat-resistant flex links the heater to this on/off switch.

Heater coil from boiler

Alternative design

Where there is no gas or oil-fired central heating, the hot water cylinder does not have a heater coil. This is called a **direct water cylinder** and will have two elements, one at the bottom and one at the top. The lower element is the main heater and the upper is used as a 'top-up' element to heat the water at the top of the tank quickly.

Cold water returning to boiler

Drain valve

Cold water inlet from cistern

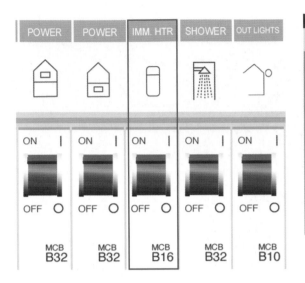

POWER	POWER	IMM. HTR	SHOWER	OUT LIGHTS
MCB B32	MCB B32	MCB B16	MCB B32	MCB B10

Supplying the power

Because of its wattage and the proximity of water, the heater element in an immersion heater must be powered by its own circuit direct from the consumer unit. This must have a dedicated circuit fuse or MCB (see Domestic wiring, page 26), marked with a symbol and text identifying the immersion heater circuit (see above). The circuit is rated at 15 or 16A, and should run from the consumer unit to a double-pole switch and possibly a timer, near the hot water cylinder.

Replacing the element

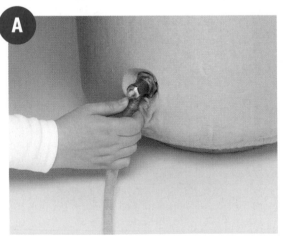

1 Turn off the cold water supply to the hot water cylinder. If your immersion heater is on top of the cylinder, turn on a hot tap until no more water comes out then go to step 3. Otherwise, attach a hose to the drain valve (which is either on the side of the cylinder as shown, or on the cold water inlet pipe) and run it to a drain.

Maintenance

When required	**Remove sediment** *Turn off the cold water supply to the cylinder, disconnect the hot feed pipe and add a descalent chemical to cylinder and leave for 24 hours, then drain cylinder fully, turn on the cold water supply and refill. See* **A** *steps 1, 2 and 7 to drain cylinder.*

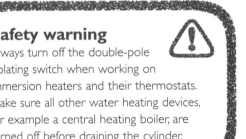

Safety warning

Always turn off the double-pole isolating switch when working on immersion heaters and their thermostats. Make sure all other water heating devices, for example a central heating boiler, are turned off before draining the cylinder.

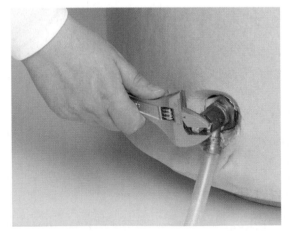

2 Turn on a hot tap or open the drain valve until no more water comes out. If the nut is tight, grip the body of the tap with an adjustable spanner.

Fault diagnosis

No heat	**Faulty element** *Replace immersion heater.* **A** **Faulty thermostat** *Turn off power at local switch, then remove immersion heater's top cover, as in* **A**. *Disconnect cables and replace thermostat.*
Water not hot enough	**Thermostat set too low** *Adjust temperature to around 60°C.* **B** **Faulty thermostat** *See above.* **Sediment in cylinder** *See Maintenance (above left).*
Noise when heating	**Mineral deposits on element** *Replace immersion heater.* **A** **Sediment in cylinder** *See Maintenance (above left).*

3 Turn off the power to the element at the local switch. Remove the element's top cover and disconnect the flex cores.

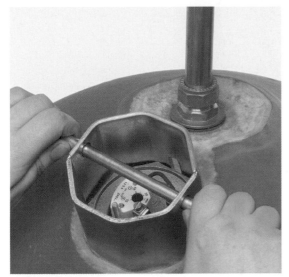

4 Use an immersion spanner to unscrew the element, taking care not to split the cylinder. Then pull the element out. If it is stuck, either apply penetrating oil and wait ten minutes or, if the cylinder has no insulation moulded round it, use a gentle flame from a blowlamp.

5 Make sure the area around the hole is clean. Wrap PTFE tape around the threads on the new element.

6 Insert the element into the cylinder and tighten it fully with the immersion spanner. Reconnect the flex and ensure the element is properly earthed.

Adjusting the temperature

7 Replace the element's top cover. Close the drain valve and hot tap and refill the cylinder, watching carefully for any leaks, which will happen as soon as refilling starts. If you have opened the drain valve, close this as soon as clear water runs out. When the cylinder is full, turn the power back on and check for heat.

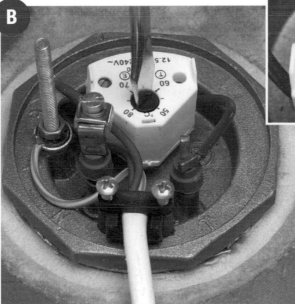

B

Turn off the power to the immersion heater at the double-pole isolating switch and remove the outer cover. Use a small screwdriver to adjust the desired water temperature to 60°C (see above right). If the temperature of the water is still not correct, contact a qualified repairer to replace the thermostat.

Economical heating

The element of an immersion heater may be wired to the mains electrical supply via a timer, which enables you set the times you wish to have the water heated. If your property has access to Economy 7 power during the night, it is possible to set the timer to heat the water during these times, when electricity rates are at their cheapest. Some cylinders can have two heaters, one for off-peak and one for daytime supply.

Night storage heater

A cost-effective home heating option is to install night storage heaters, which heat special bricks in a metal case at night using off-peak cheap-rate electricity, then release the heat throughout the day.

The off-peak electricity is measured using a special meter and controlled by a timer. This makes storage radiators cheaper to run than heaters running on peak-rate electricity. They require virtually no maintenance.

1 A timer switches the heater on during low-cost off-peak periods and its electricity consumption is measured on a secondary electric meter.

2 The off-peak electricity passes through a central **element**. This heats **heat-retaining bricks** made of magnetite, within the radiator, to temperatures of around 600–700°C at the heart of the **storage core**. Special **insulation** prevents the heat from escaping too quickly.

Top flaps to control convected heat

Storage core

Electric elements

Insulation

Heat-retaining refractory brick

Bottom air inlet

3 A **thermostat** controls the level of heat supplied to the bricks. Some radiators have temperature sensors, which allow the amount of stored heat to be controlled more accurately. The surface temperature of the **metal cabinet** must not exceed 90°C.

Maintenance

Once a month

Vacuum bottom air inlet under heater *Also, make sure nothing is blocking outlet vents.*
Clean under control flap *Keep knobs free from dirt.*
Clean any fan inlets *If your storage heater has a fan to assist heating, keep inlet and outlet vents clear of dirt and obstruction.*

Most heat is convected through **vents** at the top of the unit, drawing cool air in at the bottom.
5 **Flaps** at the top can be opened to control the ventilation and, therefore, the amount of convected heat released into the room.

Vents

Flap control knob

Metal cabinet

4 As the bricks are warming through, the radiator heats the room. The bricks then release heat during the day.

Control

Thermostat

Dedicated 20A double-pole switch

Night and day

During the night (and, on some tariffs, mid-afternoon) electricity heats an element which in turn heats the bricks inside the radiator (above left). During the day, the element is switched off and the accumulated heat gradually leaves the bricks and heats the room (above right). The timer and off-peak meter are fitted near the consumer unit. Other circuits may be controlled by the timer as well, such as a secondary immersion heater in the hot water cylinder. In some cases, the entire electrical supply for the property switches over – the power is controlled and measured by a single multirate meter – allowing the occupants to use appliances, such as tumble-dryers, at off-peak times to save money.

Fault diagnosis

No heat	**Control knob set too low** *Make necessary adjustments.* **Fuse blown/MCB tripped** *Check consumer unit (see Consumer unit, page 28).* **Element failed** *Call qualified engineer. Do not open unit.*

Portable gas heater

The fuel used in a portable gas heater is liquefied petroleum gas (LPG), also known as propane. This is stored in a cylinder within the body of the heater and is piped to the elements via an ignition system.

Safety warning ⚠

If your heater is not working properly, it can produce highly poisonous carbon monoxide (CO) gas. This is difficult to detect as it has no colour, smell or taste. Symptoms of CO poisoning are similar to that of a viral infection (headache, weakness, dizziness, nausea) and severe exposure can lead to depressed heart action, slowed respiration and, in extreme cases, death. It also affects mental ability, causing a person to become confused. Install a CO detector (see page 97) in your home and check heater regularly for faults.

1 Before the heater is used, the valve on the **regulator** must be turned to the 'on' position. When the **control knob** is turned to the 'ignition' position and held down, a piezoelectric crystal generates a spark, which lights the **pilot light**.

2 After a few seconds, the knob is turned to the heat setting and the main gas supply to the **ceramic elements** ignites.

Control knob and ignition switch

Tubing

Regulator

LPG cylinder

Fireguard

Heat reflectors

Pilot light

Ceramic elements

Piezoelectric ignition

Pressing the ignition knob causes a small hammer device **1** to hit, and therefore compress, a piezoelectric crystal **2**, generating an electric current between its faces **3**. The current sparks across a gap **4** in front of the pilot light outlet and ignites the gas. A safety device will cut the gas supply to the pilot light until it heats up, so the gas knob must be kept depressed for a few seconds after ignition.

Maintenance

If you are in any doubt about your ability to follow the instructions below, contact a qualified repairer.

Immediately	**Check your heater to see if it uses a screw-on regulator** *If so, you should replace it with a more reliable click on regulator.* **A**
Once a month	**Inspect hoses for wear and tear or signs of damage** *Make sure connections are secure and that there are no tears in hose. Keep hoses away from hot spots.* **Keep appliance clean** *Remove dust and dirt from behind the fireguard because this can impair heat reflection and also pose a fire risk.*
Every two years	**Have appliance serviced** *Always use a CORGI (Council for Registered Gas Installers) registered engineer.*
Every five years	**Have hose changed** *Ask CORGI-registered engineer to carry this out.*

Fault diagnosis

Hazy burning, noisy burning, or soot on elements	**Carbon monoxide emission** *If heat elements are dull and burn with blue haze, if there are soot deposits on the elements, or they are broken, heater may be producing CO. Switch off heater immediately and have it checked by a CORGI-registered repairer.*
Smell of gas	**Possible gas leak** *Extinguish all naked flames and ignition sources. Turn off all other gas appliances. Do not switch on or off any electrical equipment. Open all doors and windows to increase ventilation. Turn off gas supply at cylinder. Contact CORGI-registered repairer immediately. Do not use gas heater until it has been made safe and tested.*

The control knob regulates the amount of gas fed to the elements and, therefore, heat radiated. If the flame or pilot light goes out, the reduction in temperature is detected by a thermostatic device, which cuts off the gas.

4

The compressed LPG expands as it exits the cylinder and becomes a gas. This gas is ignited by the pilot light. The heat generated warms the hard **ceramic elements**, which glow orange.

3

Changing the regulator

A

1 Unscrew the clip to disconnect the hose from the existing regulator and slide the clip down the hose. Cut 3cm off the end of the hose that you just disconnected, taking care to make a clean square cut.

2 Push the newly cut hose end onto the new regulator and tighten the clip. Don't over-tighten the clip, as it may cut the hose. Turn off all the taps on the heater and then, following the manufacturer's instructions, clip the new regulator onto the cylinder.

3 Turn on the regulator and brush the hose connection with soapy water to check for leaks. If bubbles form, turn the regulator off and contact a qualified repairer. If no bubbles form, dry the hoses and the appliance is ready to use.

Air conditioner

Some air conditioners work exactly like fridges (see Fridge-freezer, page 114), with coolant flowing through a circuit of condenser and evaporator coils. Other units, like the one shown here, work by spraying water droplets onto coils containing a coolant liquid. The water evaporates and heat passes from the coils; sweating keeps the body cool in a similar way.

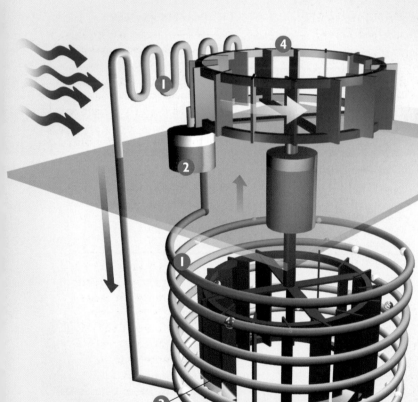

Cooling by evaporation

The coolant in a water air conditioner passes through a simple circuit of two coils **1** and a pump. **2** Water is sprayed onto the lower coils by a fan and stirrer **3** and the moving air from the fan causes the droplets to evaporate. The evaporated water demands energy and therefore draws heat out of the coils and coolant inside. The cold coolant then flows to the upper coils, where the upper fan **4** draws in warm air from the room. The heat from the air is transferred to the coolant, which flows back to the lower coils, and the cooled air **5** is blown into the room.

Cooling fins

Upper coils

Filter

Safety warning ⚠️

To prevent transmission of potentially fatal disease, always use a disinfectant when cleaning an air conditioner unit – the odourless type used for home brewing is ideal for portable units.

1 A central **electric motor** drives two fans via a **drive shaft**. Attached to the top of the **lower fan** is a **stirrer unit**.

2 The **upper fan** draws warm air from inside the room into the unit at the top rear, over the **cooling fins** and **upper coils** and out through the front. The **lower fan** draws air from the room, blows it over the **lower coils** and out through the vent pipe.

Vent pipe

3 The speed of the motor can be selected using a **control switch** on the front of the unit. A **timer switch** selects the length of time the air conditioner should run for, and also has a continuous setting.

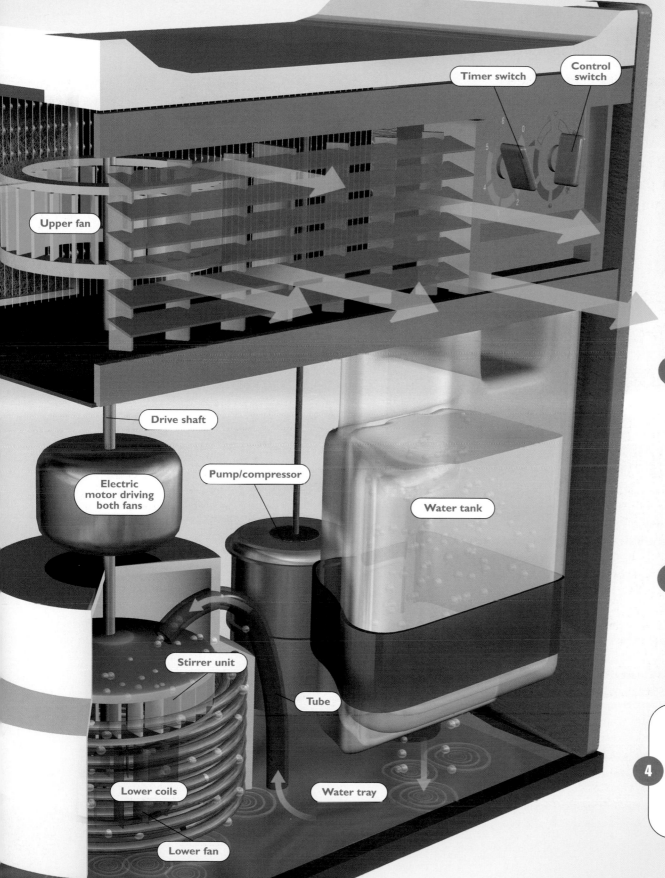

Timer switch

Control switch

Upper fan

Drive shaft

Electric motor driving both fans

Pump/compressor

Water tank

Stirrer unit

Tube

Lower coils

Water tray

Lower fan

7 The warm coolant then passes back to the lower coils, where it is cooled again by the evaporating water. The tank must be regularly topped up with water, and periodically cleaned.

6 The warm damp air is blown through a **vent pipe** to the outside. A **pump** moves the cooled liquid from the lower coils to the **upper coils** and to the **cooling fins**, where warm air from the room flows over them. Heat is transferred from the air to the coolant and the cool air is blown into the room.

5 The droplets of water hit the **lower coils** and evaporate as the air from the fan passes over them. This causes heat energy to be transferred from the lower coils to the evaporating water, thereby lowering the temperature of the coolant in the lower coils.

4 As the lower fan turns, water is drawn up a **tube** from the **tray** at the bottom of the unit. This tray is kept topped up by the **water tank**. The water then drips onto the top of the stirrer and is flung out by centrifugal force as droplets.

Cleaning the filters

Unplug the unit and slide out the filters. Carefully vacuum dust from the filter plates (replace if disposable) and fins. Use a proprietary refrigeration coil cleaning product (or car degreaser) on stubborn dirt – but check the product is suitable for aluminium first. Straighten bent fins with a fin comb.

Cleaning the water system

1 Unplug the air conditioner, open the front of the unit and lift out the water bottle. Take off the cap and drain and rinse the bottle over a sink.

2 Unclip the hose from the rear of the unit and pull it down over a washing up bowl. Allow the water from the tray to drain out completely.

Maintenance

Once a month (while in use)	**Clean filters** *Vacuum dust from filter plates.* **A** *Wash foam and metal filters in soapy water, if necessary, then rinse and leave to dry before refitting. Replace disposable filters with same type.* **Clean and straighten evaporator and condenser coil fins** *When refitting filters, clean dust from fins and vents. Straighten vent fins with a fin comb.* **If not in use, regularly change water** *Water can become contaminated when standing.* **B**
Every six months	**Lubricate fan motor** *If the motor has oil ports, they will be covered with caps or fitted with screws. Put a few drops of SAE 20 motor oil in each port. Check manufacturer's instructions first.* **Drain unit and clean tray** *Dirt and limescale can accumulate in the tray. Remove the tank. Drain and clean the tray.* **B**
During winter	**Empty water tank and drain system** **B** **Cover external condenser coils (external unit only)** *This should be done to prevent weather and frost damage.* **Run car air conditioning unit periodically** *Turn on once every few weeks for about 10 minutes to keep the system in good health.*

Fault diagnosis

The compressed gas in the cooling coils of an air conditioner means it is dangerous to tamper with them. For any repairs not listed below, consult a qualified engineer.

Bad smells	**Dirty evaporator fins**. *Clean with proprietary product.* **Clogged drain hole** *Unblock hole with wire and pour in one teaspoon of household ammonia. Wash water tray in disinfectant.*
Cools badly	**Clogged filter** *Clean or replace filter.* **A** **Dirty evaporator fins** *Clean fins.*

Stopping and starting

If you have just turned off an air conditioner, wait 5 minutes before turning it back on to avoid putting undue strain on the compressor.

Thermometer

Bulb thermometers work on the principle that liquids change in volume depending on their temperature. Mercury or alcohol is generally used. Digital thermometers use a thermistor, whose resistance changes according to temperature.

1 Ambient temperature changes affect the temperature of **mercury** (or red alcohol), which expands as it heats up and contracts as it cools.

2 Because the **tube** in a bulb thermometer is so thin, a small change in the volume of the liquid in the **bulb** is reflected by a visible rise or fall in the level of the liquid in the tube.

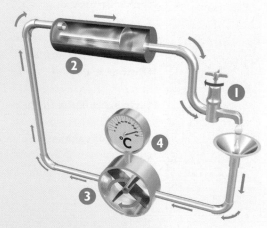

Alternative design

A **digital thermometer** uses a special resistor called a thermoresistor, or thermistor, which changes its resistance in response to temperature. The thermoresistor acts like a tap **1**. As the temperature rises, the thermistor becomes less resistant and so allows more current to flow from the battery **2** around the circuit. Electronic circuitry **3** measures the flow of the current and converts it to a temperature value, which is displayed on an LCD **4**.

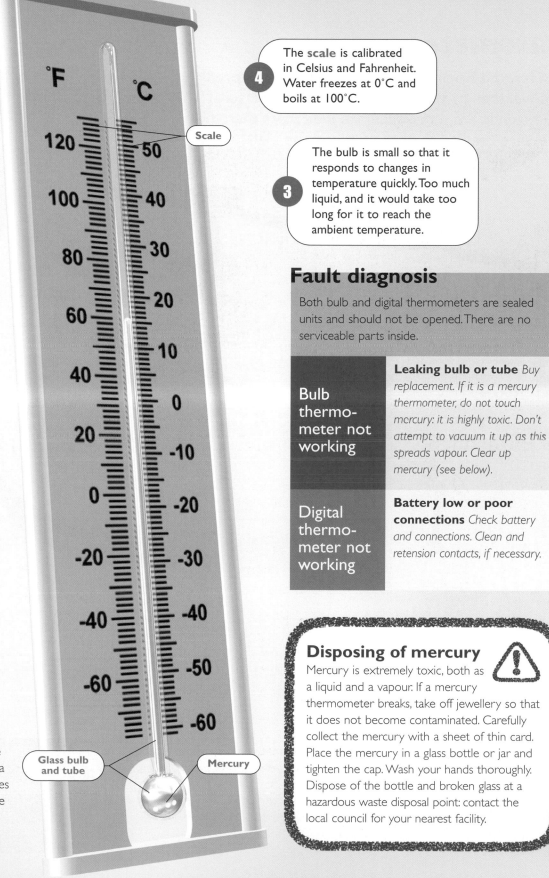

Scale

Glass bulb and tube

Mercury

4 The scale is calibrated in Celsius and Fahrenheit. Water freezes at 0°C and boils at 100°C.

3 The bulb is small so that it responds to changes in temperature quickly. Too much liquid, and it would take too long for it to reach the ambient temperature.

Fault diagnosis

Both bulb and digital thermometers are sealed units and should not be opened. There are no serviceable parts inside.

Bulb thermo-meter not working	**Leaking bulb or tube** *Buy replacement. If it is a mercury thermometer, do not touch mercury: it is highly toxic. Don't attempt to vacuum it up as this spreads vapour. Clear up mercury (see below).*
Digital thermo-meter not working	**Battery low or poor connections** *Check battery and connections. Clean and retension contacts, if necessary.*

Disposing of mercury ⚠

Mercury is extremely toxic, both as a liquid and a vapour. If a mercury thermometer breaks, take off jewellery so that it does not become contaminated. Carefully collect the mercury with a sheet of thin card. Place the mercury in a glass bottle or jar and tighten the cap. Wash your hands thoroughly. Dispose of the bottle and broken glass at a hazardous waste disposal point: contact the local council for your nearest facility.

Barometer

An aneroid barometer makes it possible to predict the weather by tracking changes in air pressure. The trends are more accurate indicators than the pressure reading or the words on the dial.

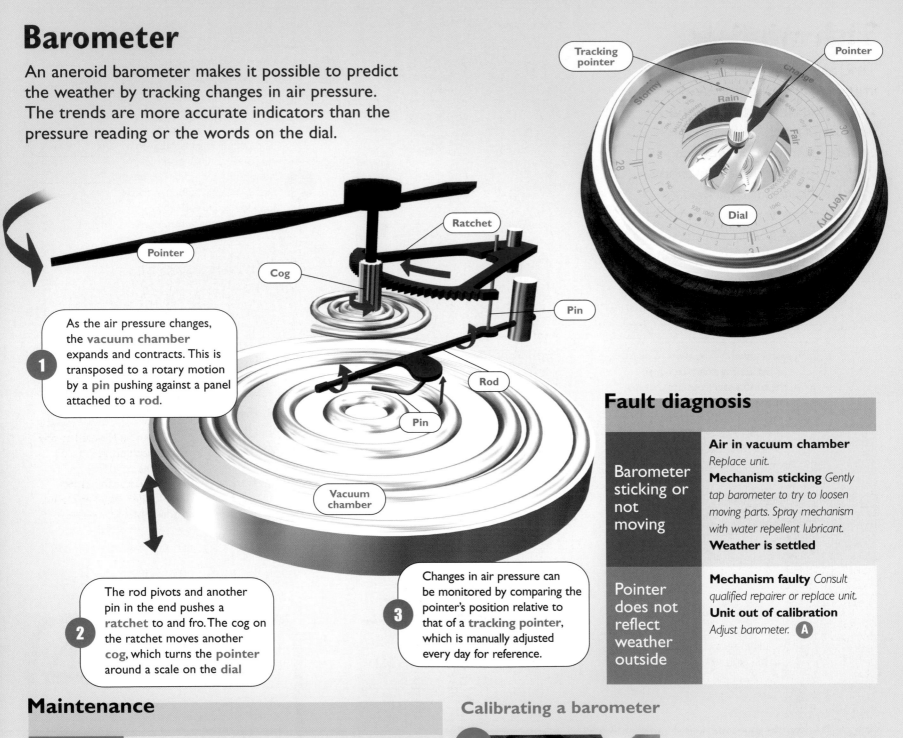

Tracking pointer

Pointer

Dial

Ratchet

Pointer

Cog

Pin

Rod

Pin

Vacuum chamber

1 As the air pressure changes, the **vacuum chamber** expands and contracts. This is transposed to a rotary motion by a **pin** pushing against a panel attached to a **rod**.

2 The rod pivots and another pin in the end pushes a **ratchet** to and fro. The **cog** on the ratchet moves another **cog**, which turns the **pointer** around a scale on the **dial**

3 Changes in air pressure can be monitored by comparing the pointer's position relative to that of a **tracking pointer**, which is manually adjusted every day for reference.

Fault diagnosis

Barometer sticking or not moving	**Air in vacuum chamber** *Replace unit.* **Mechanism sticking** *Gently tap barometer to try to loosen moving parts. Spray mechanism with water repellent lubricant.* **Weather is settled**
Pointer does not reflect weather outside	**Mechanism faulty** *Consult qualified repairer or replace unit.* **Unit out of calibration** *Adjust barometer.* **Ⓐ**

Maintenance

Once a year	**Check indicated pressure against weather report air pressure for your area** *Turn adjustment screw on back, if necessary, to obtain an accurate reading.* **Ⓐ** **Have older barometers serviced** *Aneroid barometers believed to be more than 25 years old should be cleaned and adjusted by a qualified repairer.*

Calibrating a barometer

Ⓐ Call the Met Office to get an accurate reading or consult the Met Office web site, which has isobar maps. Then use a small screwdriver to turn and set the barometer to the appropriate pressure for your area.

Sash window

The traditional sash window has two vertically sliding wooden sashes, or window units, in a wooden frame. Each one is counterbalanced by weights in the frame, which are attached by cords. Some modern sash windows use a spring lift system, which is easier to maintain, and may have metal or plastic sashes.

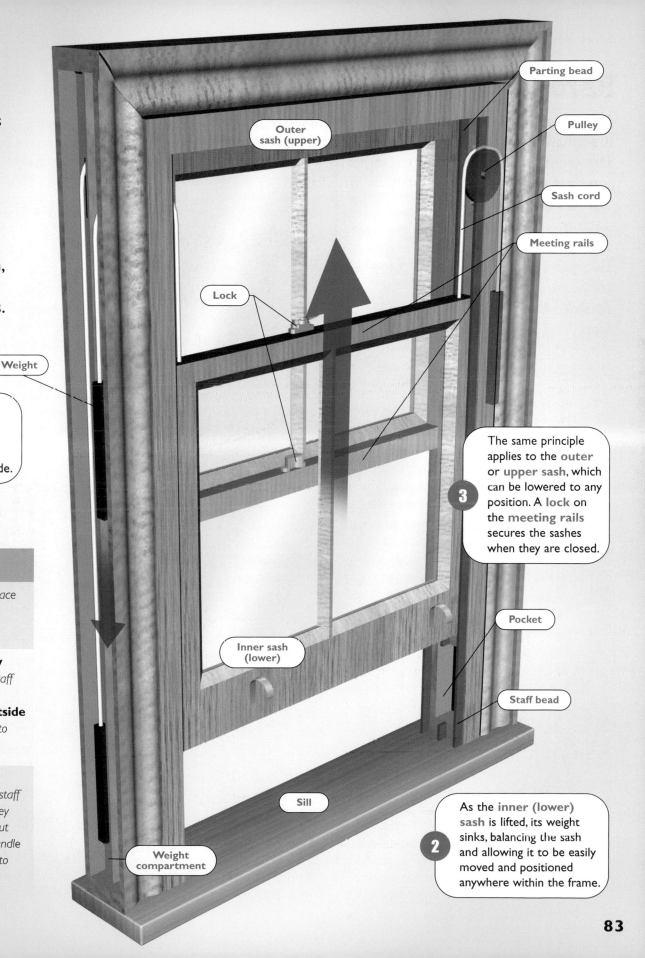

Parting bead

Pulley

Sash cord

Meeting rails

Outer sash (upper)

Lock

Weight

1 Each sash is attached to two **weights**, which together are equal in weight to the sash, and act as a counterbalance. The weights are hidden inside the frame at each side.

3 The same principle applies to the **outer** or **upper sash**, which can be lowered to any position. A **lock** on the **meeting rails** secures the sashes when they are closed.

Pocket

Staff bead

Inner sash (lower)

Sill

Weight compartment

2 As the **inner (lower) sash** is lifted, its weight sinks, balancing the sash and allowing it to be easily moved and positioned anywhere within the frame.

Fault diagnosis

Window won't stay in position	**Sash cords broken** *Replace sash cords.* **Ⓐ**
Rattling windows	**Staff bead too far away from sashes** *Reposition staff bead closer to sashes.* **Air coming in from outside** *Fit brush-type draught strip to sides of sashes.*
Sticking windows	**Staff beads nailed too close to sashes** *Prise off staff beads and re-nail so that they touch edges of sashes without impairing movement. Rub candle wax on inside of staff bead to lubricate.*

Replacing sash cords

Never attempt to remove a sash window on your own – the sashes and weights are extremely heavy, and certain tasks, such as cutting and tying the sash cables, will need two pairs of hands. Make sure you have all the right tools to hand before you start, and put a sheet down on the floor to protect it.

A

1 Prise off the staff beads using a chisel or large screwdriver. Start in the middle and work towards the ends. Pull out any nails with pliers, taking care not to split the wood.

2 Once the staff beads are loose, pull them away from the window. Watch out for nails sticking out from the inside edge. If you're replacing just one cord, you may only need to remove the staff bead on one side of the window in order to slide the sashes out. Otherwise, remove both beads and set them aside for re-fitting later.

3 Once the staff beads have been removed, lift the lower sash out of the window as far as it will go, and ask somebody to hold it in position for you.

4 Firmly tie the end of a long piece of string around the top of each sash cord (unless the cord is broken).

5 Hold the cord very tightly near the pulley and cut it near the sash with a sharp knife. Make sure someone is holding the window firmly before you start and be careful not to damage the window frame.

Gradually feed the cord and length of string over the pulley, allowing the weight to drop slowly to the bottom of the box. The string will be used later to thread the new sash cord. Once both cords are cut (if they were unbroken), detach the remnants of cord from the side of the lower sash and set it aside.

6 Use a chisel to prise the parting beads from the grooves. Then lift out the upper sash, tying string around each unbroken cord and cutting it as before (step 5).

7 Prise out the pocket covers with a chisel. They may be screwed in place. Reach into the pockets and pull the weights into the room, making sure the string stays over the pulley. Then measure the distance from the top of the window to the sill and cut four lengths of sash cord to this measurement.

8 Where the cords have broken, tie a screw to a length of string then thread it over the pulley and into the pocket. Tie the new cord to the other end of the string and pull it over the pulley, into the pocket. Knot the end of the cord so it won't pull right through.

9 Tie the other replacement cords to the strings left dangling in step 5, and pull them over the pulleys and through the weight compartment. Untie the old cords from their weights then tie the replacement cords to the weights with a double knot. Slide the weights back in the pockets and refit the pocket covers.

Do not glue the covers, they should sit securely in the holes. Make sure the correct pocket cover is fitted in each side of the frame. Rest the upper sash on the window ledge and get a helper to pull down a cord so its weight is just touching the pulley.

10 Screw (or nail) the cord into the groove on the side of the sash using galvanised screws or clout nails. Repeat the procedure with the other cord. Fit the sash in place and check it runs smoothly.

11 Refit the parting beads, tapping them firmly into the grooves. Fit the lower sash as before. Refit the staff beads on each side of the frame, making sure the ends match up correctly.

Burglar alarm

The simplest type of burglar alarm has detectors built into door and window frames that sense when the door or window is opened and sound a siren or bell. The more complex systems combine these sensors with infrared detectors, and may also call an emergency telephone number when an intruder is detected.

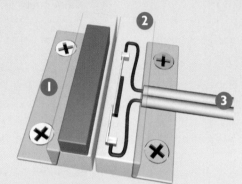

Magnetic circuit breakers

This type of sensor is simple yet effective. A magnet **1** mounted on the door or window aligns with a switch **2** on the frame or jamb. When the door or window is closed, the magnet holds the switch closed, maintaining a circuit. If the magnet is moved or the wires **3** cut, the switch opens and the alarm sounds.

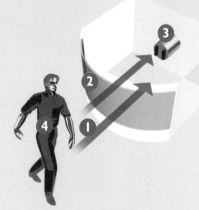

Passive infrared (PIR) detector

PIR detectors are usually positioned at ceiling height in the corners of rooms. They work by detecting changes in infrared radiation, **1** which is emitted by heat-generating objects, such as a human body. The infrared radiation is focused through a lens **2** onto two sensors **3** within the detector. These sensors cancel each other out unless an object emitting heat moves in front of them **4** and triggers first one and then the other. This type of detector would be triggered by the body heat of a person moving across a room, but not by something that's stationary, such as a radiator.

> **Magnetic circuit breakers on upstairs window**

> **Magnetic circuit breakers** have a small magnet in the door or window aligned with a magnetic switch in the frame. When the door or window is opened, the circuit is broken and the alarm system is triggered.

> **Magnetic circuit breakers on downstairs window**

> The **control unit** is the brains of the system, monitoring the output from the PIR detectors and the magnetic circuit breakers in the doors and windows. The sensors may send signals by wire, or may communicate with the control unit using radio waves (a wire-free system). If an intruder is detected, the alarm system is enabled and a siren or bell housed in the **external alarm box** sounds.

External alarm box

Panic button

Passive infrared (PIR) detector

The control unit may also dial a telephone number to notify a security company or nominated neighbour of illegal entry. Pushing a **panic button** will trigger the alarm, even if the system is not enabled.

Passive infrared (PIR) detector

Control unit with keypad

Passive infrared (PIR) detectors watch for changes in the position of infrared radiation emitted by the human body. Even if a person moves very slowly across a room, the detectors will pick up his or her body.

Magnetic circuit breakers on door

The control unit has a numeric **keypad** so that occupants can enable and disable the alarm with a personal code number, and turn it off in case of a false alarm. It can also be used to alarm specific zones, such as upstairs or downstairs.

Maintenance

On installation	**Rehearse turning alarm off** *Make sure everyone in household can quickly access control unit and knows how to disable alarm. Include all key-holders in this routine.*
Once every six months	**Check batteries (if any) in system** *Wire-free detectors run on batteries. Some control units may also have back-up batteries. Make sure they are fresh or charging if rechargeable. Consult manufacturer's instructions for details.*
Once a year	**Have system tested and serviced** *Call security company who supplied alarm to have system checked.*

Fault diagnosis

Repeated false alarms	**Fault in system** *Have alarm checked as soon as possible.* **Window or door switch open** *Check all protected doors and windows are closed properly.*
Alarm fails to trigger	**Fault in system** *Have alarm checked as soon as possible.*
Warning lights on control panel	**Call alarm installer immediately**

Stay secure

Make sure your burglar alarm and locks comply with the Association for Chief Police Officers (ACPO) standards.

Security lighting

A PIR (passive infrared) detector provides the trigger to turn on security lights, which have a range of uses, from illuminating domestic entry ways, to providing illumination for security cameras.

1 When a person moves within the field of view of the **PIR detector**, the infrared radiation given off by their body hits two infrared sensors (see Burglar alarm, page 86).

2 The signal from the PIR detector is sent through an amplifier and then activates a switch. This switch completes the larger circuit that incorporates the power source and **light bulb**, causing the light to switch on.

3 A **dusk sensitivity screw** determines when it is dark enough for the PIR detector to operate, while a **timer screw** determines how long the light bulb stays on. On some models, a PV solar cell (see Solar panel, page 38) charges a battery during the day, which then provides power for the light during the night.

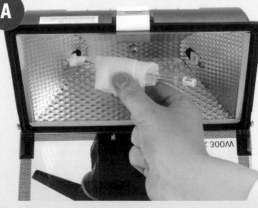

Reflector

Light bulb

Glass cover

Timer screw

Dusk sensitivity screw

PIR (passive infrared) detector

Fault diagnosis

Light won't come on	**Bulb dead** *Replace bulb.* 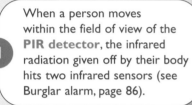 **Detector obstructed** *Relocate detector.* **Battery flat (rechargeable models)** *Check that solar panel is working and in direct sunlight during the day. Check that battery charging circuit isn't broken at some point.*
Light triggered during day	**Dusk sensor incorrectly set** *Adjust dusk sensitivity screw.*
Light on too long	**Timer incorrectly set** *Adjust timer screw.*

Changing the bulb

Turn off power to unit and allow unit to cool. Open glass. Replace bulb with correct part for the model. Never touch the surface of a halogen bulb – use a clean dry cloth to hold it.

Cylinder door lock

Nearly every front door is fitted with this type of lock. It has an ingenious mechanism, and one that is easy to put right if the familiar flat key fails to turn.

Two-part pins

Key entering keyhole

1 As the key is pushed into the keyhole, its notched edge pushes up a series of **two-part pins**, the ends of which are held against each other by springs.

Shear line

Key turning

2 When the key is fully in, the breaks in the tops of the pins will all coincide with the **shear line** between the case and cylinder, allowing the cylinder to turn with the key.

Interior knob

Latch case

5 The **interior knob** also operates a double-sided cam to push on the spring-loaded bolt and depress the latch into its case, allowing the door to be opened.

Double-sided cam

Cylinder case

Cylinder

Latch

Connecting bar

Spring-loaded bolt

3 The connecting bar sticking out from the end of the cylinder turns a **double-sided cam**, which operates a spring-loaded bolt to depress the latch.

4 Releasing the key reverses the sequence: the spring-loaded bolt pushes the latch out; the cam, connecting bar and cylinder turn; and the ends of the pins line up.

Replacing a cylinder

A

1 Remove the latch case on the inside of the door and undo the two screw-headed bolts securing the cylinder to the mounting plate. Use the other hand to support the lock on the outside of the door, so that it does not fall out.

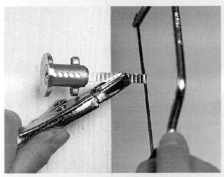

2 Hold the connecting bar of the replacement cylinder with molegrips or pliers and cut with a junior hacksaw to same length as that on old cylinder. File the end smooth.

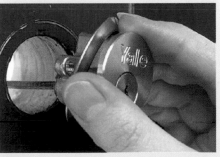

3 Slide the replacement cylinder into place and connect it to the mounting plate with the bolts, checking that the maker's name on the lock face stays upright as you tighten the bolts. Refit the latch case and make sure the new key turns smoothly to operate the lock.

Maintenance

| Whenever required | **Lubricate cylinder and latch case** *Moisture and dust can enter lock through keyhole, making it difficult to insert and turn the key. Use lubricant spray or powdered graphite (stocked by locksmiths) to lubricate cylinder, squirting it down keyhole. Then turn interior knob to depress latch and lubricate latch case through latch cut-out. If lock is still stiff, it is a sign that cylinder is worn and needs replacing.* **A** |

Fault diagnosis

| Key sticks in lock or won't turn | **Worn cylinder** *In time, the ends of the pins become worn, making it increasingly difficult to turn the key. However, as long as interior knob is not operated by a key, you can buy just a replacement cylinder, together with new keys.* **A** |

Mortise door lock

A mortise deadlock is commonly used as a second lock on a front door that already has a cylinder lock. It is recessed into a slot cut in the edge of the door, and shoots a bolt into a hole in the door frame. The more levers a mortise lock has, the harder it is to pick. Choose a lock with a minimum of five levers (shown right). One with seven is better still.

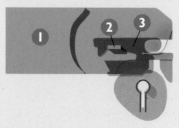 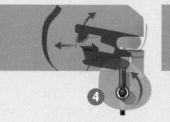 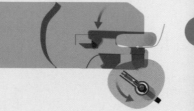

> **A mortise key** has a series of notches. When the key is inserted into the keyhole and turned, these notches align with the **levers** inside the lock casing, which are held in place by **springs**. ❶

Opening the gate

When the lock is not locked, the bolt ❶ is held in place because the stump ❷ is gripped by the levers ❸ (only one lever shown in the diagrams above).

When the key is turned, the notches in the key match the shape of the levers and lift them. The bolt thrower ❹ turns with the key and pushes the bolt out.

Once the bolt has moved into the locked position, the levers move back into position, making it impossible to push the bolt back into the lock.

Maintenance

Whenever required	**Lubricate mechanism** *Use aerosol lubricant or powdered graphite (stocked by locksmiths) to lubricate the levers by squirting it in through the keyhole. Operate the lock a few times to dispense the lubricant.*

Key combinations

The key is a solid piece of metal with a bow ❶ at one end, which can be hooked onto a key ring. At the other end of the shank ❷ is the shoulder ❸, which prevents the key from sliding right through the keyhole. The post ❹ and bit ❺ are the parts that fit inside the lock. Each notch ❻ in the bit can be cut to one of seven different positions. There will be five notches in a key for a five-lever lock (shown above). Despite security restrictions on the relative position and depth of notches, a five-lever lock will have more than 1000 possible combinations.

Home security

A lock is only as strong as the door and frame in which it is fitted. Replace fragile wood before fitting new locks. Also, one lock may not be enough to secure against determined force. Fit a mortise and cylinder lock (see page 89) at different heights on the door. This spreads the load of any blows to the door. Buy only locks that conform to British Standard BS 3621.

Steel pins

Bolt

Keeper

Door frame

Strike plate

5 To unlock the door, the key is turned in the opposite direction. The notches on the key raise the levers to free the bolt, which is moved back towards the lock by the bolt thrower.

4 **Steel pins** embedded in the bolt roll under a hacksaw blade, making it impossible to saw through the bolt. The casing is made of drill-resistant hardened steel. The keeper in the **door frame** is a steel box, which prevents an intruder forcing the bolt back into the lock.

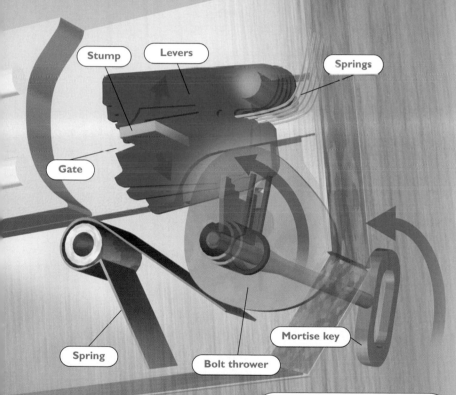

Stump

Levers

Springs

Gate

Spring

Mortise key

Bolt thrower

2 As the key is turned, the notches raise each lever to the height of its **gate**. Only at this position can the **stump** pass the gate, freeing the **bolt**.

3 The key also turns the **bolt thrower**, which is kept in place by a **spring**. The bolt thrower has a ridge (shown in blue), which pushes the bolt out into the **strike plate** and **keeper**. The springs push the levers back down into a locked position when the bolt is fully extended. The door is now deadlocked.

Replacing a mortise lock

A

1 Open the door to expose the bolt and the strike plate. Unscrew the strike plate, then turn the key to operate the bolt.

2 Remove the key and then slide out the lock by gripping the projecting bolt with pliers and pulling outwards.

3 Push a matching replacement lock into the door, and secure the lock and strike plate with the screws.

4 Make sure the new key turns smoothly to operate the lock.

Fault diagnosis

Key turns but bolt doesn't move	**Grime between levers** *This prevents them from moving freely. Lubricate levers.* **Worn levers** *During years of use, levers can become worn, so their gates won't properly free the stump. Replace lock.* **A** **Broken springs** *Replace lock.* **A**
Key doesn't turn	**Worn or damaged key** *Get a new key cut from an unworn spare.*

Window locks

There are many different types of lock but they all have the same function – to prevent a burglar from being able to open the window frame after smashing through the glass. Like other home security features, clearly visible window locks act as a deterrent to would-be intruders.

Locks for sash windows

Outer plate

Sash window press locks are two-part locks mounted on top of the meeting rails of the upper sash and lower sash, in place of the standard interlocking catch. A simple **push bolt** locks the **inner plate** and **outer plate** together and is released with a **key**.

Key

Inner plate

Push bolt

Dual screws (also known as sash locks) consist of a long, steel, key-operated screw **1** that passes through a metal sleeve **2** set in the top rail of the inner sash and into a threaded sleeve **3** set in a hole in the bottom rail of the outer sash. This locks together the top and bottom sashes, preventing either from being opened. Screw locks are usually fitted in pairs (one near each side of the sash rail).

Realigning a press lock

A

1 Before starting, make sure nothing else is blocking the lock.

2 Remove the screws holding the lock and plate in place.

Sash stops are also fitted in pairs but, unlike screw locks, they can allow the window to be slightly opened for ventilation. A removable lock nut **1**, operated with a key **2**, is fastened to a mounting plate **3** on each side of the upper sash to prevent the lower sash from sliding up. A second pair of plates may be fitted further up the sides of the upper sash to provide a ventilation position.

3 Refit the lock. If necessary, move both units away from old holes.

Security tip
Window locks are only as secure as their fixing screws, and those supplied can sometimes be too short. For maximum security, replace all screws with screws of the same gauge, the same material and as long as the casement or frame will accept.

Locks for casement windows

Locking handles can be fitted in place of the existing window handle, and are locked and unlocked using a security key **1**. Some allow the window to be locked slightly ajar for ventilation.

Cam locks are operated with a key that turns a cam **1**, or notched rotating shaft, locking two components together to secure the window to the frame.

Swing-bar locks have a D-shaped bar **1** fixed to the window, that swings over a locking plate **2** on the frame to prevent the window from opening. The bar can be locked in place with a removable key **3**.

Fault diagnosis

Any lock is stiff to operate

Components rubbing
Apply lubricating oil to moving parts.
Reciprocal parts of lock no longer line up
Move one half of lock so that two parts line up. **A**
Window frame slightly warped or damaged
Reposition the lock. Otherwise, replace the window.

Window security bolts (also known as mortise rack bolts) are designed for larger framed wooden windows. A simple key **1** engages with a gear and, as it is turned, drives the bolt **2** into a hole in a plate **3** in the window frame. This type of lock is not visible from the outside.

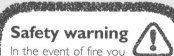

Safety warning ⚠️
In the event of fire you may need to exit via the windows and will need to be able to undo the locks quickly. Keep the keys for each window easily accessible but beyond arms-reach for a burglar who has smashed the window glass. Make sure the whole family knows where the keys are and how to use them.

Doorbell and entry system

Whereas a doorbell is a simple circuit between a button at the door and a chime in the house, an entry system consists of a camera, microphone and speaker at the door, and a screen and telephone-type handset inside.

Solenoid release catch

Camera

Light

Speaker

Call button and microphone

Handset

Fault diagnosis

It is not possible to repair a video entry system yourself. Use this panel to help diagnose the problem before consulting a qualified repairer.

1 When a visitor presses the **call button**, the **camera** and **light** are turned on. At the same time, a buzzer sounds inside the property and the **monitor** displays the image from the camera.

No picture	**No power to camera** **Camera failed** **Poor connection to camera** **No power to monitor**
No sound	**No connection to microphone**
Open button does not work	**No connection to solenoid release catch**
Doorbell does not work	**Flat battery** *Replace.* **Faulty bell push** *Replace.* **Bad connection in bell wire** *Replace wire.* **A** **Jammed chimes** *Reposition bars.*

Alternative design

A basic **door chime** consists of a switch, a power supply and a bell. When the button **1** is pushed, metal contacts **2** meet and form a circuit between the power supply **3** and a solenoid **4** (see Nail gun, page 268). This pushes a rod **5** towards a chime bar **6**. When the circuit is broken, the magnet releases the bar. A spring **7** forces it to bounce back and hit the second chime **8**, making the second tone of the bell. Other systems use an electromagnet to pull a hammer back, at which point the circuit is broken and the hammer hits a bell.

3 To admit the visitor, the **entry button** is pressed. This activates a **solenoid release catch**, which pulls back a catch in the door lock mortise allowing the door to be opened.

Monitor

Microphone

Entry button

2 When the occupant lifts the **handset** a two-way audio connection is established between the **microphone** and **speaker** at the door and the handset through a wire. The monitor displays the moving picture taken by the camera.

Fixing a doorbell wire

A

1 If the doorbell is mains powered, turn off the power first. If it is battery powered, remove the bell unit cover and take out the batteries. Then unscrew the bell push from the door frame. Remove the terminal screws retaining the old wire and connect a new length of wire. You may have to route the cable through a hole in the door frame first. Replace the bell push.

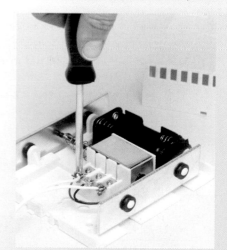

2 Cut the new wire to the length of the old one. Make a note of the position of the connections, then remove the old wire from the bell unit, and attach the new wires to the terminals. Fix the new wire to the wall and door frame. If the bell is mains powered, replace the cover and turn on the mains power. Otherwise, replace the batteries and reattach the cover. Then test the bell push.

Smoke detector

A battery-powered smoke detector is inexpensive, easy-to-fit and can be a life-saver. There are two types of smoke detector: ionising (shown here) and photoelectric.

Test button

Horn

Sensing chamber

Transducer

1 Smoke particles rise from the source of the fire to the unit. These are detected in the **sensing chamber**.

Battery

3 The alarm is triggered when an electrical current is fed to a **transducer**. Its noise is amplified by a conical **horn**. Detectors that flash or vibrate are available for houses with deaf occupants.

Safety warning ⚠

Smoke detectors must now be fitted, by law, in all new houses. Detectors should be fitted within 7.5m of the doorway to every habitable room in the house. They should be fixed to the ceiling, 30cm or more from any wall. Make sure all smoke detectors comply with safety standards.

2 Depending on the type of detector used, the smoke particles either deflect a beam of light, or affect an electrical current (see below).

Fault diagnosis

Beeps regularly	**Battery going flat** *Replace immediately.*
Alarm fails to sound when tested	**Battery flat** *Replace at once.* **Faulty alarm** *If, after replacing battery, alarm fails test then replace alarm immediately.*

Maintenance

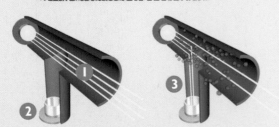

Once a month	**Clean alarm** *Gently vacuum outside and inside detector.* **Check alarm** *Press test button to check battery is not flat. Some detectors can be tested with a torch beam – check your manual.*
Annually	**Replace battery** *This does not apply if model has a ten-year lithium battery.*

Deflecting a light beam

Photoelectric detectors are ideal for kitchen use. Smoke particles are detected using a beam of light **1** and a photoelectric sensor **2**. These are mounted at right-angles to one another. Normally the light travels in a straight line, bypassing the sensor. When smoke enters the detector it deflects some of the light towards the sensor **3**. Circuits in the detector react to the light and set off the alarm.

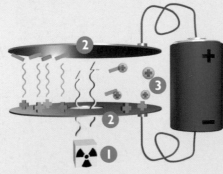

Changing a current flow

Ionising detectors use an alpha radiation source **1** to ionise the oxygen and nitrogen atoms in the air between two charged metal plates **2**. This causes a current to flow across the air between the plates. If positively charged smoke particles **3** enter the space between the plates, they attract the negatively charged ions causing a reduction in the current flow. This is detected by a microchip, which switches on the alarm.

Carbon monoxide detector

A carbon monoxide (CO) detector is not the same as a smoke detector. It detects dangerous, odourless and invisible CO gas, which can be produced by faulty fuel-burning appliances.

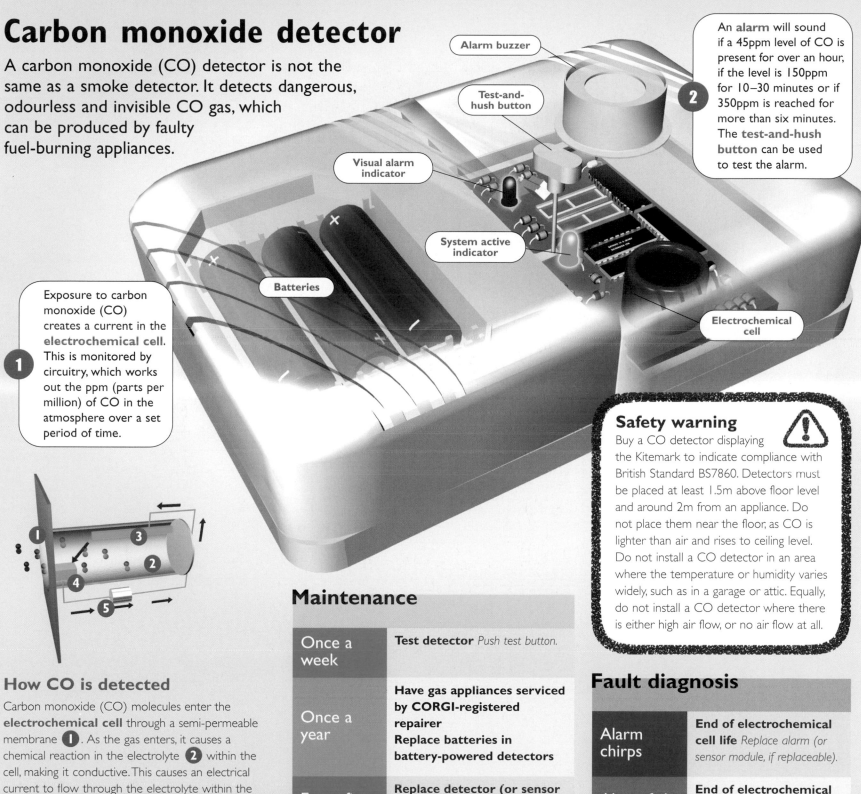

Alarm buzzer

Test-and-hush button

Visual alarm indicator

Batteries

System active indicator

Electrochemical cell

2 An **alarm** will sound if a 45ppm level of CO is present for over an hour, if the level is 150ppm for 10–30 minutes or if 350ppm is reached for more than six minutes. The **test-and-hush button** can be used to test the alarm.

1 Exposure to carbon monoxide (CO) creates a current in the **electrochemical cell**. This is monitored by circuitry, which works out the ppm (parts per million) of CO in the atmosphere over a set period of time.

Safety warning ⚠

Buy a CO detector displaying the Kitemark to indicate compliance with British Standard BS7860. Detectors must be placed at least 1.5m above floor level and around 2m from an appliance. Do not place them near the floor, as CO is lighter than air and rises to ceiling level. Do not install a CO detector in an area where the temperature or humidity varies widely, such as in a garage or attic. Equally, do not install a CO detector where there is either high air flow, or no air flow at all.

How CO is detected

Carbon monoxide (CO) molecules enter the **electrochemical cell** through a semi-permeable membrane **1**. As the gas enters, it causes a chemical reaction in the electrolyte **2** within the cell, making it conductive. This causes an electrical current to flow through the electrolyte within the cell from the positively charged anode **3** to the negatively charged cathode **4**. A sensor **5** detects the current and triggers the alarm.

Maintenance

Once a week	**Test detector** Push test button.
Once a year	**Have gas appliances serviced by CORGI-registered repairer** **Replace batteries in battery-powered detectors**
Every five years	**Replace detector (or sensor module)** Certain models have a 10-year guarantee on sensors.

Fault diagnosis

Alarm chirps	**End of electrochemical cell life** Replace alarm (or sensor module, if replaceable).
Alarm fails test	**End of electrochemical cell life** Replace alarm (or sensor module, if replaceable).

Appliances

Washing machine

All washing machines have the same basic parts: a watertight container called the tub; a drum, which fits inside the tub, to hold the washing; electrically operated valves to allow water into the tub; a heating element to raise the water temperature; an electric motor to turn the drum; a pump to drain the water; and a programmer to control the switching of the various components. Once you understand how the different parts work in the washing process, maintaining and repairing your machine is much easier.

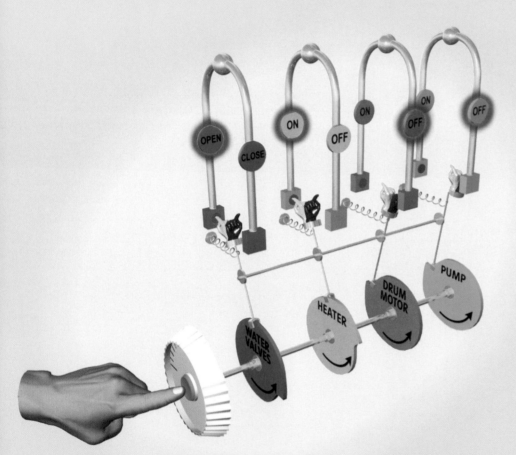

Door

1 Setting the **programme controller** and switching on the machine activates the door interlock: once the **door** is shut, it cannot be opened until the programme is finished.

2 As soon as the door is locked, the programme begins. The **inlet valves** are opened, allowing water to flow into the **drum**. On the way it passes through the **detergent tray**, collecting powder or liquid.

How a programmer works

The programmer is the brain of the washing machine: once you choose the desired setting for the types of fabrics in the wash load, the programmer takes over. Every programme is a permutation of the same factors: the amount of water taken in via the inlet valves (which dictates how far the clothes fall when they drop off the top of the drum – and so how hard they hit the water); the temperature of the water and detergent solution; how long the drum turns for during the wash and spin sequences and how fast it turns. The programmer also controls the operation of the pump to drain the machine at various points in the wash cycle.

3 The water entering the drum compresses air in a **pressure chamber**. This pressure is relayed along a flexible **pressure tube** to a **pressure switch**, which shuts the inlet valves at the programmed water level.

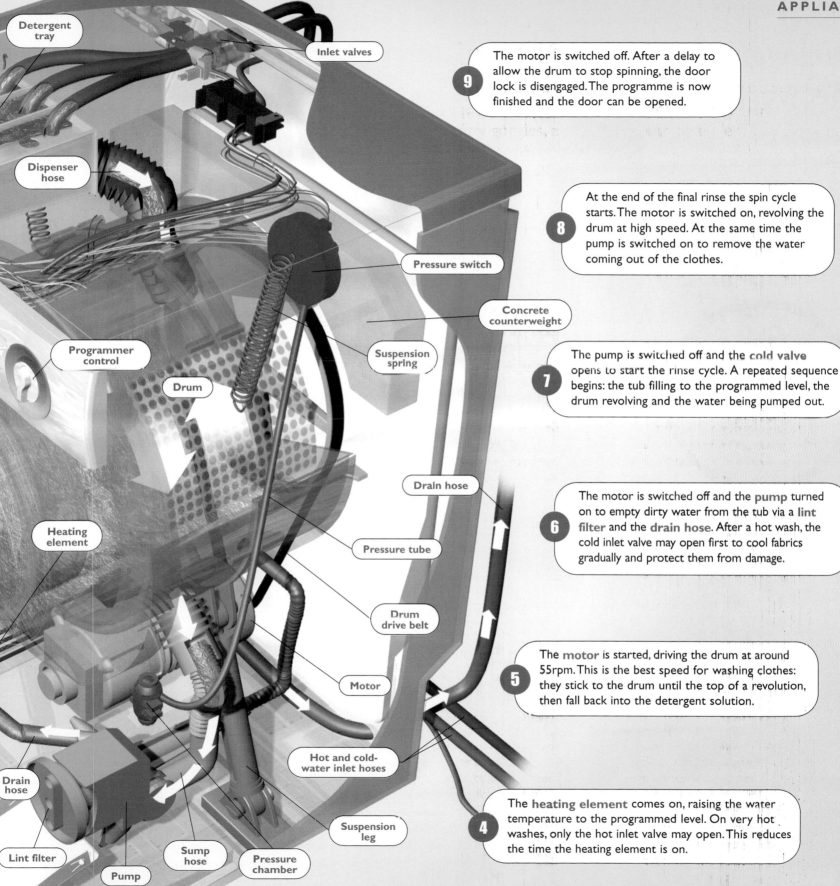

Detergent tray

Inlet valves

Dispenser hose

Pressure switch

Concrete counterweight

Programmer control

Suspension spring

Drum

Drain hose

Heating element

Pressure tube

Drum drive belt

Motor

Hot and cold-water inlet hoses

Drain hose

Suspension leg

Lint filter

Sump hose

Pressure chamber

Pump

9 The motor is switched off. After a delay to allow the drum to stop spinning, the door lock is disengaged. The programme is now finished and the door can be opened.

8 At the end of the final rinse the spin cycle starts. The motor is switched on, revolving the drum at high speed. At the same time the pump is switched on to remove the water coming out of the clothes.

7 The pump is switched off and the **cold valve** opens to start the rinse cycle. A repeated sequence begins: the tub filling to the programmed level, the drum revolving and the water being pumped out.

6 The motor is switched off and the **pump** turned on to empty dirty water from the tub via a **lint filter** and the **drain hose**. After a hot wash, the cold inlet valve may open first to cool fabrics gradually and protect them from damage.

5 The **motor** is started, driving the drum at around 55rpm. This is the best speed for washing clothes: they stick to the drum until the top of a revolution, then fall back into the detergent solution.

4 The **heating element** comes on, raising the water temperature to the programmed level. On very hot washes, only the hot inlet valve may open. This reduces the time the heating element is on.

Unclogging the works

Washing machines can quickly become clogged up with undissolved detergent, limescale and fluff from dirty laundry. Regular cleaning can keep your appliance fully operational.

Safety first
Keep the disconnected plug in view while you work to make sure that no one puts it back into the socket.

Maintenance

Every month	**Inspect detergent tray** *If washing powder clogs tray because of insufficient water pressure or using too much detergent, clothes won't be properly cleaned.* **A** **Clean door glass** *Limescale and other debris can allow water to escape between glass and seal.* **B** **Test door seal** *If seal feels tacky, it's a sign that it is perishing and needs replacing* **(see D, page 105)**. **Operate hose taps** *A flood can result if either tap seizes in the open position and there's a leak in hoses between taps and inlet valves.*
Every six months	**Clean lint filter** *This coarse sieve catches bits of fluff, small coins and other objects. If it gets blocked, water can remain in machine and leak may occur.* **C** **Empty catchpot** *Machines with no lint filter have one of these to trap items left in pockets and other debris. If not emptied, their contents can be drawn into pump.* **D** **Examine inlet hose connections** *Because these are on the back of machine, a leak from one of them can go undetected, causing damage to floor and machine* **(see A, page 104)**.

Cleaning a catchpot

Disconnect inlet hoses and unplug. Then, with another person's help, lay the machine face-down, first positioning a support on the floor to prevent damage to the control panel and provide hand space. Remove the clip securing sump hose to catchpot, pull off the catchpot, empty and refit.

Cleaning the detergent tray

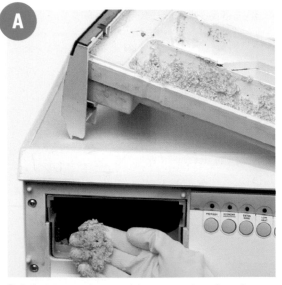

Pull the tray or drawer right out to clean it and examine the recess too; on some machines, this can also become clogged with detergent.

Cleaning the glass door

Dip an abrasive pad in warm water, without any detergent in it, and rub debris off glass, concentrating on the area that touches the seal.

Cleaning the lint filter

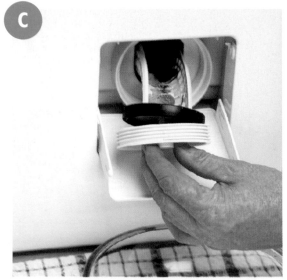

Open the access hatch on the front of the machine, undo the filter cap and pull out the filter assembly. Remove fluff and other debris, rinse and refit.

Look for clues in the water

Once you know the sequence of operations involved in the wash cycle, it is often possible to identify the cause of a fault by noting when it occurs. With a leak, the water itself provides an added clue. If it's clear without any sign of detergent in it, you know the leak must be occurring before the water gets to the detergent tray. If the water is soapy, the door seal, sump hose or pump could be leaking. And if it's dirty, the blame could lie with a defective drain hose.

Best place to grip

The door opening is the safest place to hold the machine when you want to move it. First tilt the appliance backwards and slide a piece of hardboard underneath to protect the floor; then drag it away from the wall, making sure your fingers are wrapped around the inside edge of the shell. Take care not to dislodge the water inlet if it comes through the top of the door seal.

Fault diagnosis

Appliance won't start	**Door not shut** Check door is properly shut. **Faulty interlock won't allow door to shut** Contact qualified repairer. **No power** Check flex, plug wiring, fuse and mains supply for faults. **Faulty on/off switch (check power light if fitted)** Contact qualified repairer.
No water entering	**Inlet hose kinked** Free trapped hose. **Taps turned off** Open taps **Inlet valve filter blocked** Clean valve filter (see **A**, page 104). **Pressure system blocked in pressurised state** This causes appliance to think that it is full of water. Contact qualified repairer.
Machine overfills and floods	**Inlet valve staying open or pressure switch not operating** Disconnect from power supply. If water continues to flow in, hot or cold inlet valve is faulty. Discover which by turning off each tap in turn. Replace valve (see **B**, page 104). If water stops flowing in, pressure system is at fault. Contact qualified repairer.
Drum won't rotate	**Loose or worn drive belt** Adjust or replace belt (see **C**, page 105). **Worn motor brushes** Contact qualified repairer. **Faulty timer** Contact qualified repairer. **Faulty spin control unit** Contact qualified repairer.
Stuck on wash cycle	**Faulty timer** Advance programme to spin cycle. Contact qualified repairer. **Faulty heater** Contact qualified repairer. **Faulty thermostat** Contact qualified repairer.
Door won't open at end of programme	**Worn door seal** Old door seals can become sticky with age and adhere to glass. Carefully ease door open, then replace seal (see **D**, page 105). **Water still in machine** Repeat spin cycle to operate pump again. Inspect filter and clean if necessary. Inspect outlet hoses for kinks or blockages. **Door interlock faulty** Contact qualified repairer. **Door handle broken** Replace handle (see **E**, page 105).
Clothes damaged	**Water overheating due to faulty programmer** Contact qualified repairer. **Water overheating due to faulty thermostat** Contact qualified repairer. **Drum damaged or metal object in machine** Contact qualified repairer.
Clothes still dirty	**Detergent dispenser clogged** Clean dispenser. **A** **Loose or broken belt** Adjust or replace belt (see **C**, page 105). **Worn motor brushes** Contact qualified repairer.

Servicing inlet hoses

Safety first

Always unplug, disconnect or isolate any appliance when carrying out cleaning or maintenance.

Turn off the water supply and undo the hose connections at both ends – they should never be more than handtight. Remove the washers from the connections and replace if they appear worn or there is water staining around the connection points on the back of the machine.

Using pliers, carefully draw the hose filters out of the back of the valve bodies. Rinse filters under running water and, before refitting, remove any debris lodged in the valve inlet, making sure none of it gets pushed into the valve itself.

Replacing an inlet valve

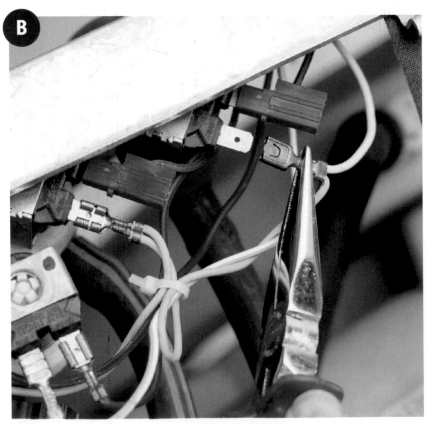

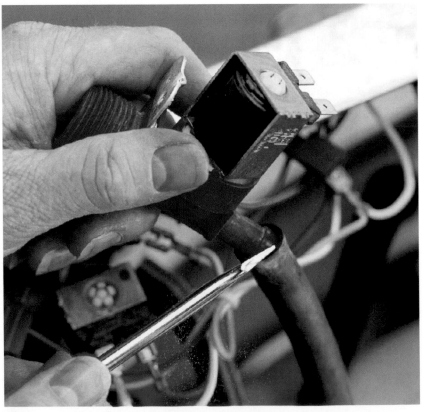

1 Unplug the machine, turn off the water supply and disconnect the inlet hoses. Next, remove the top panel to gain access to the valves. Disconnect the electrical connections to a valve by gripping the terminals, not the wires, with a pair of long-nosed pliers. Then ease them apart.

2 Remove the screws securing the valve to the back of the machine. Don't try to pull the hose to the detergent tray off the valve outlet – a ridge on the end of the outlet resists force. Instead, use a flat-bladed screwdriver to lever the hose off. Fit the new valve in the reverse order.

Replacing a drum drive belt

1 Test the tension of a drive belt by pressing it midway between the pulleys; it should have about 15mm of play. On some machines, one of the motor mounting bolts passes through a bracket with a slot in it, allowing the motor to be moved and belt tension adjusted. If a glance at the bolts shows no slots, your machine has an elasticated belt, which has to be replaced if it stretches.

2 To remove a belt, twist it so that its wearing surface faces out and start to rotate it, making sure you don't pinch your fingers between belt and drum pulley; the belt will flip off the drum pulley. Loop the new belt over the motor pulley, then stretch it onto the drum pulley by rotating it. The drum pulley is slightly crowned to enable the belt to centre on it; slide the belt in or out on the motor pulley until it is correctly aligned vertically between the two pulleys.

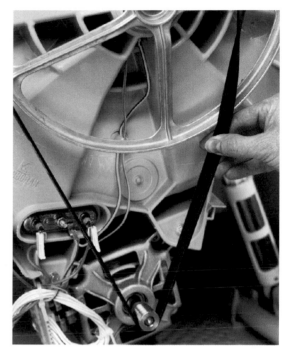

Replacing a door seal

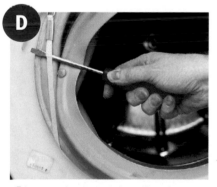

1 Locate the outer clamp band securing the seal to the shell of the machine and examine it carefully. Many can be carefully prised off with a flat-bladed screwdriver, but some have a tensioning arrangement that has to be loosened. After removing the outer clamp band, locate the inner one securing the seal to the drum and establish how this is secured. It may be necessary to loosen a clip, or you may be able to prise the band off with a flat-bladed screwdriver.

2 Once the clamp bands have been removed, use both hands to pull the seal away from the locating lips on the shell and drum.

Rubbing a smear of fabric conditioner into the groove that locates on the drum makes fitting the new seal easier. If the clamp band has no tensioning adjustment, locate it on the bottom of the seal first, then push it on with both hands working in opposite directions towards the top.

Fitting a new handle

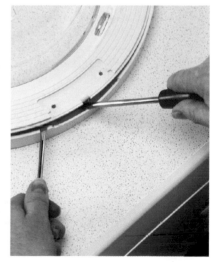

1 Replacement door handle kits are available for most models. To remove the faulty handle, you must first take the door off the machine by undoing the hinge fixings. This often reveals a small cut-out, normally hidden by the hinge, in the door inset.

2 Starting at the cut-out, use two flat-bladed screwdrivers to carefully lever the inset away from the outer rim, stepping one screwdriver over the other until the two parts click apart. With the inset removed, dismantle the handle mechanism and use the replacement kit to fit the new one.

Toploading washing machine

An older design than front loading washing machines, toploading machines tend to use more water and electricity. They have much in common with front loading washers but there are some important differences in their operation, maintenance and repair.

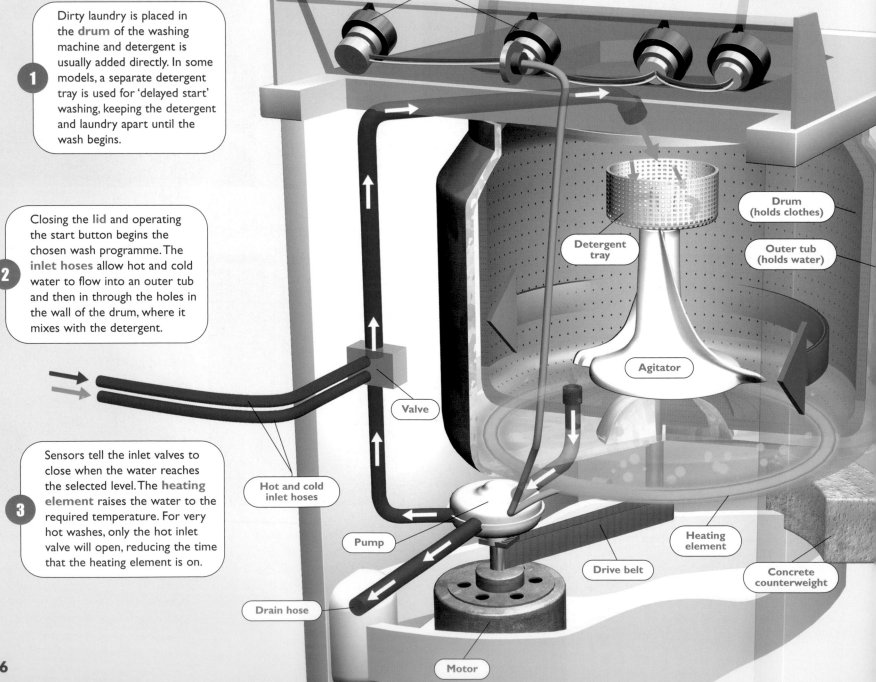

1 Dirty laundry is placed in the **drum** of the washing machine and detergent is usually added directly. In some models, a separate detergent tray is used for 'delayed start' washing, keeping the detergent and laundry apart until the wash begins.

2 Closing the **lid** and operating the start button begins the chosen wash programme. The **inlet hoses** allow hot and cold water to flow into an outer tub and then in through the holes in the wall of the drum, where it mixes with the detergent.

3 Sensors tell the inlet valves to close when the water reaches the selected level. The **heating element** raises the water to the required temperature. For very hot washes, only the hot inlet valve will open, reducing the time that the heating element is on.

6 The drum then refills with cold water, via the cold inlet **valve**, to rinse the clothes. The motor drives the agitator, then the pump drains the water and the motor spins the drum again to extract water from the clothes. The number of repeats of this process depends on the rinse programme selected.

Lid

Timer and selector switches

Detergent tray

Drum (holds clothes)

Outer tub (holds water)

Agitator

Valve

Hot and cold inlet hoses

Pump

Drain hose

Drive belt

Heating element

Concrete counterweight

Motor

5 When the initial wash stage is completed, the agitator stops and a **pump** drains the water from the machine, via the **drain hose**. The motor spins the inner tub at high speed so that water drains from the clothes through the small holes in the wall of the drum.

4 A motor drives an **agitator** at the centre of the drum, making repeated three-quarter turns back-and-forth. This moves the clothes through the water and cleans them with a rubbing motion. During the wash, water is pumped from the bottom of the drum up and out through the **detergent tray**.

Maintenance

Every month	**Operate hose taps** *Flood and water damage can result if either tap seizes in the open position and a leak occurs in hoses between taps and inlet valves. Hoses may leak or split over time and need replacing.* **Clean lint filter** *Some machines have a lint trap through which the water is pumped as the machine washes. Clean this periodically to stop lint and small items being drawn into pump.* **Clean out agitator** *Some machines trap lint in the agitator. Remove it periodically for cleaning.* **A**

Fault diagnosis

No functions	**No power to unit** *Check mains lead, plug wiring, fuse and mains outlet for faults.* **Lid switch defective** *Contact qualified repairer.*
No water entering	**Taps off or hose kinked** *Check taps and hose.* **Inlet filter blocked** *(see Washing machine, page 100).*
Agitator movement restricted	**Loose or worn drive belt** *Replace drive belt (see Washing machine, page 100).* **Worn clutch (if fitted)** *Contact qualified repairer.* **Motor burnt out** *Contact qualified repairer.* **Worn agitator** *Contact qualified repairer.*
Noisy running	**Clothes unbalanced** *Stop washer, lift lid, redistribute clothes evenly round agitator and restart.* **Machine not level** *Adjust legs (if fitted) to correct imbalance.*
Drum will not spin	**Loose or worn drive belt** *See above.* **Worn clutch (if fitted)** *Contact qualified repairer.* **Motor burnt out** *Contact qualified repairer.* **Transmission (gearbox) faulty** *Contact qualified repairer.* **Lid switch open** *Check lid is closed. Contact qualified repairer if this fails to resolve problem.*
Washer slow to drain	**Drainage hoses blocked** *Check for blockages.* **A** **Pump blocked** *Contact qualified repairer.* **Pump drive or pulley broken** *Contact qualified repairer.*

Cleaning the agitator

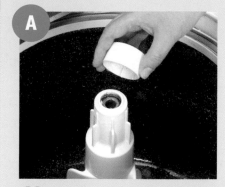

1 Remove the cap covering the top of the agitator (and the detergent tray, if fitted) and clean the area. Pull the agitator off the spindle.

2 Lift the agitator from the drum and clean with detergent and hot water. Make sure the area around the spindle in the tub is clear of debris.

Unblocking the outlet

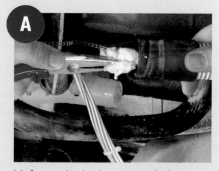

Unfasten the back cover and place a tray under the machine to catch water. Locate the pump and unclip the drain hose. Remove any foreign objects, then refasten the hose and replace back cover.

Washer dryer

Combining the washer features of a washing machine and the drying function of a tumble-dryer in one unit saves space, and is also usually more economical than running two dedicated units. With a condenser dryer, there is also no need for external air venting. The disadvantages are that the machine's dryer capacity is usually only half that of its washer capacity, and laundry takes longer than with a separate washer and dryer.

Maintenance

After each use	**Leave the door slightly ajar** *This prevents stale odours from forming in the machine.*
Every three months	**Flush and clean the machine** *Put the machine on a hot cycle using normal washing machine detergent but no clothes. Clean lint filter.*

Fault diagnosis

No functions	**No power** *Check mains lead, plug fuse and wiring, and mains outlet for faults.* **Door not closed correctly** *Washer dryer will not work if door is open or catch has not engaged properly.* **Water supply disconnected or off** *If washer dryer cannot load water it cannot start a wash cycle. Check supply.*
Washer doesn't fill with water	**Hoses not correctly connected** *Check water supply is properly connected to machine.* **A** **Rubber hose constricted** *Ensure hose supplying water is as straight as possible and isn't bent or squashed.*
Washer keeps filling	**Drain hose positioned too low** *Make sure hose is at height recommended in manufacturer's instructions.* **B**
Does not dry	**No water supply to condenser unit** *Check water supply is properly connected.*

1 The washing and drying programmes are set using the **programme selector knob**. Extra positions on the knob allow the choice of high or low drying temperature settings.

Electric motor

Cold water supply to condenser unit

Hot and cold water inlet valves

2 The washing mechanism works in exactly the same way as in a front loading washing machine (see page 100).

Drain pipe

Programme
selector knob

Heating
elements

Water
pipes for
detergent tray

Detergent
tray

Door

Cooling fins

Drum

Condenser unit

Checking connectors

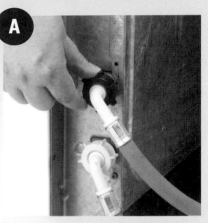

A

Make sure the water inlet connectors are tight and the hoses are as straight as possible, and not bent or squashed.

Checking the drain hose

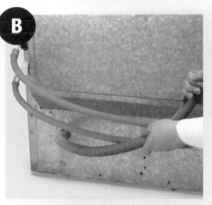

B

Make sure the drain hose is at the height recommended in the manufacturer's instructions. If it is connected lower than the fill level of the machine, the water can siphon out as it fills. Waste pipes should be either connected to the waste system via a non-return valve (see Waste water, page 60) or hooked into a standpipe which should be 600–900mm above floor level.

4 The warm wet air then passes into a **condenser unit**. Here, the air comes into contact with, and is cooled by, a series of **cooling fins** over which cold water from the water supply trickles. As cooler air can hold less moisture than hot air, the excess is deposited onto the cold surface, drips down and is pumped out through the same **drain pipe** as the water from the wash.

3 Once the clothes have been washed and spun, the machine switches into drying mode. A fan draws cold air over **heating elements** and passes the dry heated air into the drum. The clothes are turned in the drum and moisture evaporates.

Tumble-dryer

Much like a combination of a washing machine and a hairdryer, a tumble-dryer rotates wet laundry inside a drum while blowing hot air through it to dry it. The resulting damp hot air is piped outside or vented into the room.

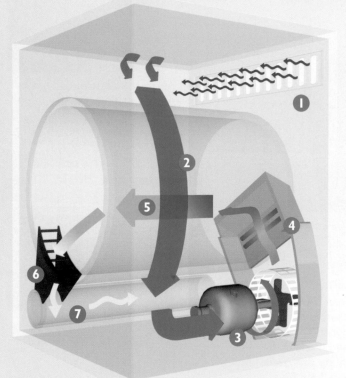

1 Clean, washed and spun clothes are placed in the **drum** and the heat setting selected. The dryer will not start until the door is shut and the **door catch** engaged.

2 Turning the **timer knob** starts the **electric motor**. This powers a **drive belt** to turn the drum, and directly drives the **blower**.

3 After a few revolutions to allow the damp clothes to separate around the drum, the **heating element** is turned on.

Flow of air

Cold air is drawn in at the top rear of the unit **1** and passes over the drum **2** and motor **3** before being blown by the fan over the heating elements **4**. The hot air then flows through the drum and rotating clothes **5** and out through a filter **6** into a vent pipe **7**. On some models, the user can choose for the air to exit from the front or the rear of the vent pipe depending on the location of the tumble-dryer.

Alternative design

Condenser dryers blow the evaporated moisture from your laundry over a cool surface, causing the moisture to condense to water. This is either collected in a container that must be emptied, or is pumped away through the waste water system. For more on condenser dryers, see Washer dryer, page 108.

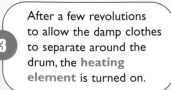

Heat control switch

Door catch

Lint filter

Exhaust tube to vent at rear

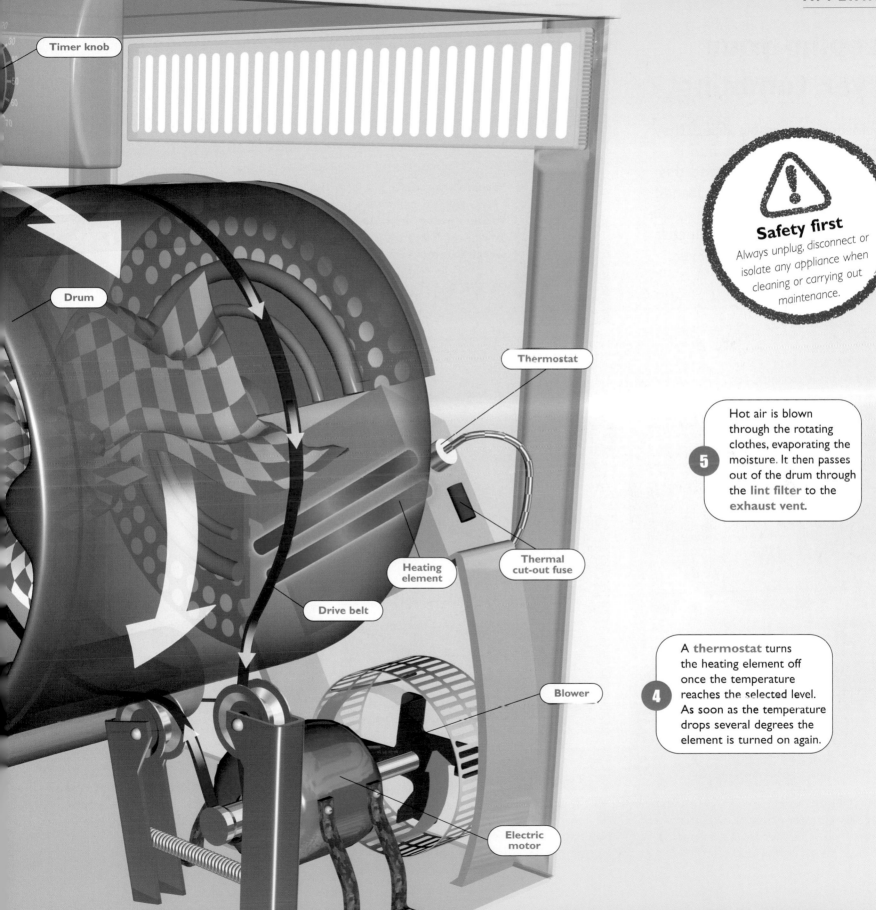

Timer knob

Drum

Thermostat

Safety first
Always unplug, disconnect or isolate any appliance when cleaning or carrying out maintenance.

5 Hot air is blown through the rotating clothes, evaporating the moisture. It then passes out of the drum through the lint filter to the exhaust vent.

Heating element

Thermal cut-out fuse

Drive belt

Blower

4 A thermostat turns the heating element off once the temperature reaches the selected level. As soon as the temperature drops several degrees the element is turned on again.

Electric motor

Keeping your dryer tumbling

As clothes are tumble dried, they drop fibres. Most of this fluff is trapped by the lint filter and this needs to be checked and cleaned regularly. Lint also builds up in the vent pipe and around the electric motor in the rear of the dryer.

Maintenance

If the dryer continues to operate when the door has been opened the door switch may well be faulty. Turn it off immediately. Unplug it, make sure everyone knows not to use it, and contact a qualified repairer.

After each use	**Clean lint filter** *Dryer designs vary but the lint filter should lift or slide out easily. Clear screen and reinstall, making sure it is seated properly.* **A**
Every six months	**Vacuum area where lint filter sits** *Remove filter and use a narrow vacuum nozzle to remove dust and lint from fitting.* **Vacuum heater area, blower housing and vent pipe connection** *Unplug dryer, remove back, making sure you do not catch or dislodge any wires or connections.* **B** **Check external vent (if fitted)** *Make sure there are no obstructions in the vent.*
Once a year	**Remove and check entire vent pipe for lint** *Make sure there are no snags or sharp turns on the pipe, which can collect dust or moisture.* **C**

Cleaning the lint filter

Wait until the dryer cools, open the door and lift out the lint filter. Gently brush off lint using your fingers. On many models, the filter may also be washed. Check your manual for instructions.

Cleaning inside the dryer

1 Make sure the dryer is cool, switch it off and unplug it. Unscrew the retaining screws on the back panel, and lift it off. Vacuum the blower area.

2 Also vacuum around the vent pipe connection. Replace the back panel and refit all the screws.

Checking the vent pipe

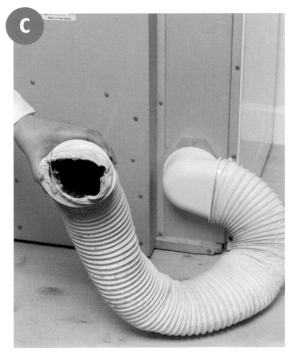

Wait for the dryer to cool. Unplug the vent hose and inspect its entire length for snags in the pipe. Make sure the vent is not obstructed on the outside wall, and fit a flap or screen to keep out small animals.

Avoiding dryer problems

Make sure the dryer is level and does not rock, and consult the manufacturer's instructions for the maximum weight of clothing to dry at one time. Also, make sure clothes have been spun-dry before putting them into the dryer.

Fault diagnosis

Nothing functions at all	**No power to appliance** *Check mains lead, plug fuse and wiring, and mains outlet.* **Door switch faulty** *Verify nothing is blocking door catch. If not, contact qualified repairer to replace switch.* **Timer switch faulty** *Reset timer and try again. If the symptom persists, contact qualified repairer to replace switch.* **Delay timer faulty** *If a delay timer is fitted, check that it has not been reset. If the symptom persists, contact a qualified repairer to replace switch.*
Timer turns, but no drum rotation	**Drum motor faulty** *Contact qualified repairer.* **Drum belt snapped** *Contact qualified repairer.* **Timer switch faulty** *Reset timer and try again. If the symptom persists, contact qualified repairer to replace switch.* **Reversing timer faulty (if fitted)** *Reset timer and try again. If the symptom persists, contact qualified repairer.*
Clothes not drying but drum and timer both turn	**Thermostat faulty** *Contact qualified repairer.* **Heating element faulty** *If there is some heat when a high setting is selected, the element may be faulty. Contact qualified repairer.* **Thermal cut-out fuse has operated** *Wait 15 minutes and try again. If the symptom persists, replace thermal fuse if accessible. Refer to manual and replace with manufacturer's recommended thermal fuse. Otherwise, contact qualified repairer.*
Clothes slow to dry	**Heating element faulty** *Contact qualified repairer.* **Heat control switch faulty** *Contact qualified repairer.* **Restricted air flow** *Clean the lint filter* *and the vent pipe.* **Machine overloaded** *Consult manufacturer's instructions for correct loads.* **Over-wet clothes** *Make sure clothes are spun dry before tumble drying.* **Thermostat faulty** *Contact qualified repairer.*
Clothes overheat or burn	**Thermostat faulty** *Contact qualified repairer.* **Cut-out faulty** *Contact qualified repairer.*
Clothes tangled or creased	**Reversing timer faulty** *Turn machine off and on again. If symptom persists, contact qualified repairer to replace timer.* **Timer switch faulty** *Reset timer and try again. If symptom persists, contact qualified repairer to replace switch.*
No delay operation (if fitted)	**Delay timer faulty** *Contact qualified repairer.*
Odours	**Blocked lint filter** *Clean lint filter.*
Noisy operation	**Object in drum** *Open and remove.* **Worn bearings** *Contact qualified repairer.*

Fridge-freezer

Refrigerators and freezers work by taking heat from inside the appliance and transferring it to the outside. This is achieved by the repeated evaporation and condensation of a substance called a refrigerant. The heat required to make the refrigerant evaporate (change from liquid to gas) is taken from inside the compartments. Then, when the refrigerant is condensed (changed from gas to liquid), it gives out heat, which is released outside the appliance.

1 An **electric motor** drives the **compressor**, which pressurises the **refrigerant** gas and pumps it round the system. Compressing the gas causes energy to be released in the form of heat.

2 The gas then passes through small radiators on the back of the appliance called the **condenser coils**, which give off heat into the room. Cooling the pressurised gas condenses it into a liquid.

3 The cooled liquid refrigerant then passes though a **dryer** to remove particles of dirt. Immediately after that, it enters a very narrow **capillary tube** under pressure.

4 The liquid flows to the evaporator coils where it passes through an **expansion chamber**, causing the pressure, and therefore the boiling point, to immediately drop. The liquid expands rapidly and boils, turning into a cold gas

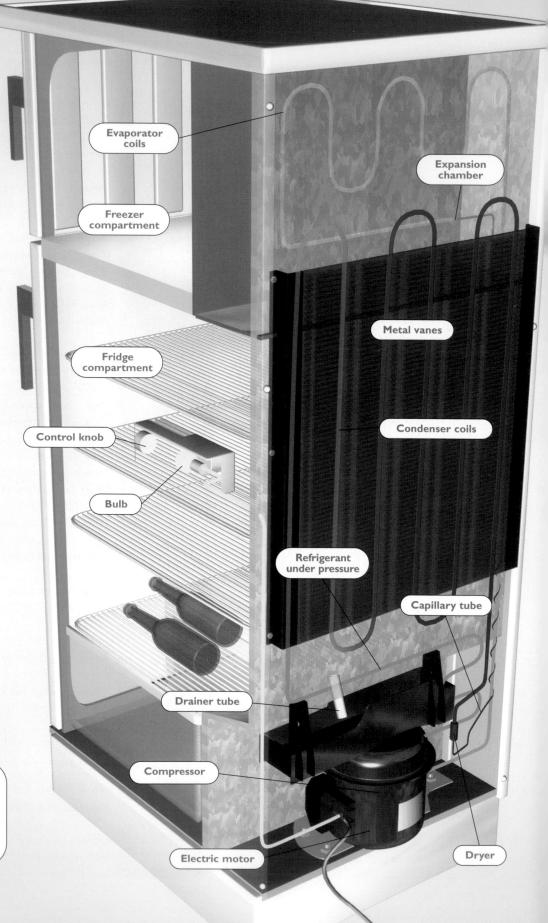

Evaporator coils

Expansion chamber

Freezer compartment

Metal vanes

Fridge compartment

Condenser coils

Control knob

Bulb

Refrigerant under pressure

Capillary tube

Drainer tube

Compressor

Electric motor

Dryer

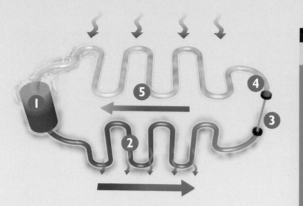

The cooling process

A fridge, like a pressure cooker (see page 135) alters the pressure within a sealed unit to change the boiling point of a liquid. The fridge lowers the pressure to lower the boiling point of a liquid refrigerant; the pressure cooker raises the pressure so that a liquid (water) boils at a higher temperature.

A refrigerant gas is compressed by a pump **1**. The compression forces it to lose some of its energy because the molecules cannot move so freely and thus collide in the reduced space. This energy, in the form of heat, is dissipated by a radiator called the condenser **2**. Here the gas condenses into a warm liquid, which then passes into a narrow tube **3**. When it exits this tube **4** its pressure drops, lowering its boiling point and causing it to boil as it draws heat energy from its surroundings: the evaporator and inside of the fridge **5**.

> **7** A thermostat connected to the **control knob** case maintains the fridge or freezer's temperature by switching the compressor on and off according to the selected temperature setting.

> **6** The gaseous refrigerant then flows at low pressure from the evaporator coils down to the compressor to begin the cycle again.

> **5** The cold gas passes through the **evaporator coils**, or plate, which pass through the walls of the freezer and fridge. Heat is conducted through the interior walls from the compartments into the cold gas, warming it.

Maintenance

Every 4–6 months

Defrost freezer *Frost build-up reduces freezer efficiency. If there is not an automatic defrost system, turn the thermostat to 'Off' or 'Defrost'. Remove all food from freezer compartment, wrap in newspaper or blankets and store in cool place or in coolbox. Then unplug fridge and carefully scrape away frost and ice from inside freezer using plastic tool. When defrosting is complete, clean compartment with baking soda solution, rinse and allow to dry before turning unit back on.*

Clean interior of fridge *Remove all food, racks and drawers. Make sure drain hole is clear.* **A**

Clean door gasket *Dirt can ruin seal between door and compartments, allowing cool air to escape.* **B**

Vacuum around back of fridge-freezer *Be careful near condenser coils.* **C**

Cleaning the gasket

Clean the rubber door seal of both the fridge and freezer compartments with detergent solution. Make sure all the dirt is removed from between the grooves. Then rinse and wipe dry.

Moving a fridge-freezer

Open the door and place one hand inside to lift the front. If possible, place your other hand on a worktop to give you support. Then wiggle the appliance gently from side to side as you pull it forwards. Always allow a fridge-freezer to settle for a couple of hours with the power switched off before and after moving it.

Cleaning the fridge interior

Remove glass and plastic shelves and allow them to reach room temperature before washing in warm detergent solution. Rinse and wipe dry. Wash the fridge compartment with a baking soda solution. Use coat-hanger wire to carefully remove food or mould from the drain hole at the back of the compartment.

Cleaning the back

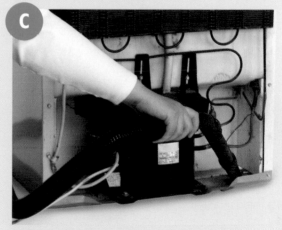

Gently vacuum around the condenser coils and motor to remove any accumulated dust and dirt.

Keeping cool

Refrigerators keep food at temperatures that slow down the growth of bacteria. Freezers stop bacterial activity altogether. If a fridge-freezer is not maintained properly, bacteria can breed.

Checking the thermostat

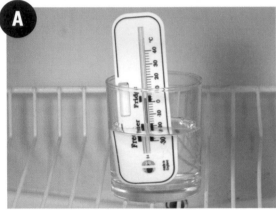

1 Set the thermostat to its lowest setting (usually called '1'). Put a glass of water in the centre of the fridge for 24 hours, then check its temperature with a fridge thermometer. The temperature should be between 0°C and 5°C.

2 If the temperature is not within the safe range, make sure the thermostat sensor (a small metal tube with a thin tube running to the thermostat) is not covered with anything – spilt food for example. If it is clean, the thermostat may be faulty, so contact a qualified repairer.

Fault diagnosis

Fridge too cold or too warm	**Thermostat tube blocked or covered** *Check thermostat accuracy.* **A** **Thermostat control loose or slipping** *Check and replace control knob.* **Frost build-up** *Defrost fridge.* **Door seal ineffective** *Check seal is clean and has no tears in it. Clean or replace if possible* **(see B , page 115)**. **Faulty thermostat** *Contact qualified repairer.*
Fridge-freezer not cooling and interior light off	**Faulty power supply** *Check mains lead, wiring inside plug, and plug fuse for faults. Replace fuse if necessary.* **Faulty mains supply** *Check mains supply to wall socket by plugging in another appliance that you know is working.*
Fridge-freezer not working but light on	**Thermostat off or set to 'defrost'** *Adjust to normal setting.* **Faulty thermostat** *Contact qualified repairer.* **Faulty compressor** *Contact qualified repairer.*
Light not working	**Bulb blown** *Replace with correct type and wattage.* **Door switch faulty** *Clean away any dirt around switch. If it still doesn't work, contact qualified repairer.*
Compressor motor runs continuously	**Faulty thermostat** *Contact qualified repairer.* **Loss of refrigerant** *Contact qualified repairer.* **Faulty compressor** *Contact qualified repairer.*
Freezer often needs defrosting	**Faulty door seal** *Clean or replace if possible.*
Water accumulates in the base of the fridge	**Blocked drainer tube** *Remove debris with a bent coat-hanger, taking care not to puncture tube. Drainer tube is small rubber cylinder in the back wall of fridge compartment. Two water channels converge, making a 'V' shape. Drainer tube can be found at the bottom edge of the 'V'.*
Freezer makes a noise when it clicks off	**Faulty compressor** *Compressor pump mounting may be loose, allowing it to bang against side of unit. Disconnect from mains supply and tighten mounting bolts or screws. If this is not possible, contact a qualified repairer.*

Dishwasher

A dishwasher uses two rotating arms to spray water and detergent over the dishes and utensils before pumping away the dirty water and rinsing the dishes clean.

8 The dishwasher regenerates the water softener by rinsing it with salt solution delivered from the **salt container** (see Water system, page 40).

7 The hot rinsing water is pumped away leaving very hot dishes that dry quickly.

6 The timer activates a cool or cold rinse and then a second heated rinse. Rinse-aid is released from the **rinse-aid dispenser** on the second rinse to help to prevent streaks and marks being left during the drying process.

1 Detergent is placed in the **soap dispenser**. The timer and selector switches on the door set the washing programme by controlling the timing, temperature and sequence of events.

5 The water sprays from angled nozzles in the **sprayer arms**, turning them in the same way as a garden sprinkler. When the wash cycle ends, the dirty water is pumped away from the sump.

2 A switch starts the washer as soon as the **door** is closed and stops the machine at any point in the washing cycle if the door is opened.

4 An **electric pump** draws the water through a **strainer**, over a **heating element** and supplies it under pressure to the **sprayer arms**. A thermostat controls the element to maintain the correct washing temperature.

3 Hot water enters through the **inlet valve** and passes through a **water softener** to the **sump**. Here it mixes with the **detergent**, which falls into the machine when a **catch** releases the cover of the **soap dispenser**.

Upper tray

Rinse-aid dispenser

Soap dispenser

Catch

Detergent tablet

Door

Sprayer arms

Mains water inlet

Water softener

Salt container

Strainer

Inlet valve

Sump

Heating element

Electric pump

Outlet valve

Keeping it clean

Loading your dishwasher correctly and using the correct detergent and rinse-aid can help to prolong the operating life of your machine. It is also essential to use the correct type of salt to keep the water softener working properly, unless your house has softened water already. This, in turn, ensures that there is no harmful build-up of limescale within the dishwasher.

Safety first
Be careful when you open the door – hot steam can escape from the dishwasher when first opened.

Maintenance

Every week	**Remove, clean and rinse main strainer** *There may be a secondary filter inside.* 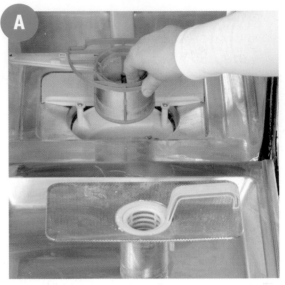 A **Check sprayer arms for blocked holes** *Clean if blocked.* B **Check sprayer arms rotate freely** *If not, remove and clean pivot.* **Check rinse-aid level** *Refer to small glass window on rinse-aid dispenser inside door. Top up when required.* **Check salt level** *Undo cap and check level if your dishwasher has no warning light.*
Every six months	**Check and clean door seal** *Use non-abrasive detergent.* **Check condition of hoses** *Clean out any deposits from hoses and inlet filter.* **Run cleaning programme using proprietary cleaner** *Follow manufacturer's instructions and rinse through after cleaning.*

Correctly loading the dishwasher

Make sure nothing protrudes from the racks. Any items that can stop the sprayer arms turning, such as saucepan handles and knives (below left) will prevent the machine from washing properly. You should also be careful that no item will stop the soap dispenser opening once the door is closed.

Cleaning the main strainer

Remove lower basket. Unscrew retaining screws, if any, and lift out filter. Some dishwashers may have two-part filters (above). Wash under running water using household detergent. Rinse thoroughly and then refit.

Cleaning the sprayer arms

The sprayer arms are held in place either by a simple clip or a locking nut. Remove each sprayer arm separately to clean. Rinse through under the tap and make sure no flakes of limescale or food are blocking the holes. Use a toothpick to clear the sprayer holes of debris if necessary.

Replacing an inlet valve

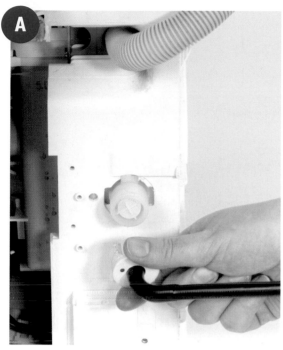

1 Drain the dishwasher and disconnect or isolate it from the mains supply. Turn off the water supply and disconnect the hose from the supply tap. Pull the dishwasher out and then disconnect the water inlet hose at the back of the unit. To do this, you may need to turn the dishwasher onto its side.

Fault diagnosis

Machine does not function	**No power to dishwasher** *Check flex, plug wiring, fuse, and mains supply for faults.* **Door switch not closed** *Check loading of items and that door is properly closed.* **No water** *Ensure water supply is present and turned on. Check for hose filter blockages.*
No water present	**No water supply** *Ensure water supply is present and turned on.* **Inlet valve blocked or faulty** *Check for blockages. Continuity test the valve's operation with a multimeter (see Basic toolkit, page 12). If it is not, replace valve.* **Ⓐ**
Does not wash clean	**Incorrect quantities of detergent** *Refer to manual.* **Machine incorrectly loaded** *Refer to manual.* **Sump filter blocked** *Clean filter.* **Ⓐ**
Does not empty	**Sump strainer or filter blocked** *Clean filter.* **Ⓐ** **Blocked sump or drain hose** *Check and clear.* **Faulty drain pump motor** *Consult qualified repairer.*
White streaks on dishes	**No or insufficient salt** *Check salt dispenser (see manual).* **Machine not rinsing properly** *Consult qualified repairer.* **Softener unit faulty** *Consult qualified repairer.*
Ring marks on glass items	**Too little rinse-aid** *Check level and setting (see manual). Top up if necessary.*
Glass items sticky	**Too much rinse-aid** *Check setting (see manual) and alter as necessary.*

2 Remove the retaining screws or clips holding the dishwasher casing together. Remove the top, side and back panels, and turn the dishwasher onto its side. Then pull out the retaining pins at the rear that lock the base hinges closed.

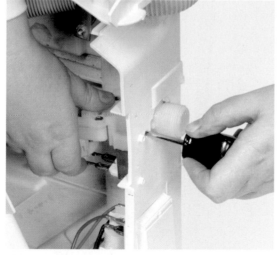

3 Carefully pivot the base away from the body of the dishwasher. Use a blunt object, such as a cross-head screwdriver, to push the locking pin that secures the inlet valve to the back of the machine and turn the valve to free it.

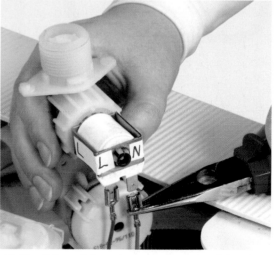

4 Carefully pull the valve away from the dishwasher base. Label the connectors on the inlet valve and disconnect the cables and pipes. Then, referring to the tags on the old valve, connect up the new valve before reassembling the dishwasher.

Microwave oven

The cooking capability of the microwave oven is provided by the heating effect of high-frequency radio waves on food. The oven only produces microwaves at intervals during the cooking process – the number and length of the pauses is dictated by the power level chosen.

Safety warning ⚠️

Unlike conventional heat, which can be felt on the surface of the skin, microwaves cook by agitating particles in the food. This means their heating effects are harder to detect before damage is done. If the door does not latch properly or the door seals appear loose, do not use the oven and contact a qualified repairer. Because of the high voltages inside, you should never remove the main cover of a microwave oven.

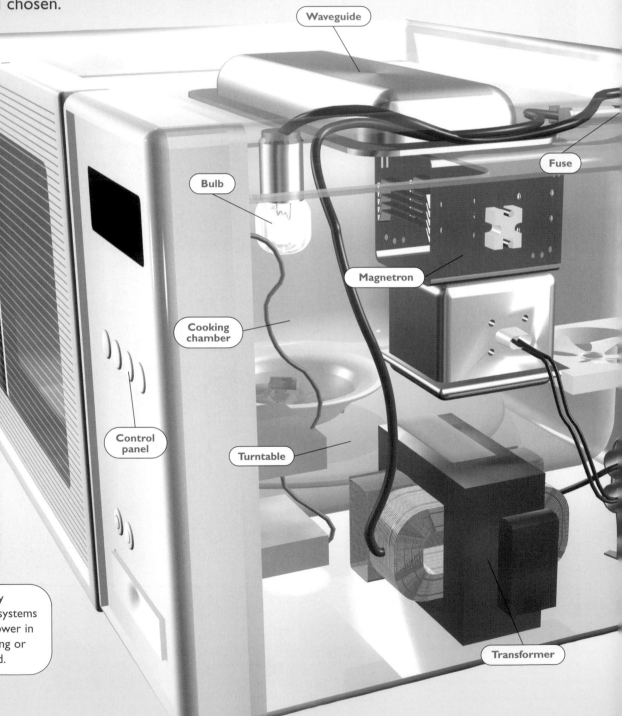

Waveguide

Fuse

Bulb

Magnetron

Cooking chamber

Control panel

Turntable

Transformer

1 The cooking time and power level are set using the **control panel**. There may also be presets for common tasks such as defrosting and reheating.

2 The 230V mains supply passes through safety systems designed to cut the power in the event of overheating or the door being opened.

How microwaves cook food

Microwave ovens cook using high-frequency radio waves (microwaves), oscillating at approximately 2.5GHz. At this frequency, microwaves are absorbed by water, certain fats and sugars – the primary constituents of most foods. In a water molecule **1**, the two hydrogen atoms (red) carry a small positive charge and the oxygen atom (blue) carries a negative charge. The oscillating electric field of the microwave **2** interacts with these charged atoms to cause the molecule to twist. This rotation causes friction, producing heat to cook food or boil fluids.

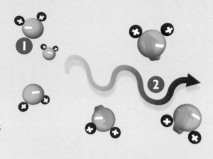

Cleaning the oven

A

1 Use a non-abrasive cleaning product to remove dirt and grease from the cooking chamber. Make sure the door seal, control panel and exterior panels are clean. Check that nothing is clogging the ventilation slots, either under or on top of the unit.

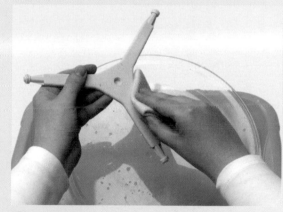

2 Remove the turntable and wash it with warm water and washing-up liquid. Clean the rotating ring (or spider) and turntable area thoroughly.

5 A **turntable** rotates the food slowly to give even cooking. Some ovens achieve this by using a microwave stirrer instead. This is positioned inside the roof of the chamber.

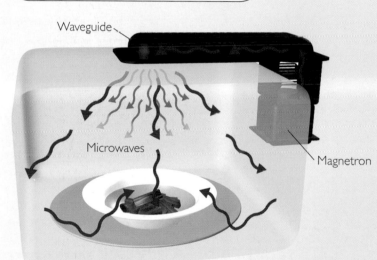

Waveguide

Microwaves

Magnetron

Cooling fan

Capacitor

4 The microwaves are conducted through the **waveguide** into the **cooking chamber**. Here they are reflected from the walls and door, and penetrate the food from the sides and above.

3 The mains voltage is stepped up by a **transformer** and a **capacitor** to around 3000V, to power the **magnetron**, which generates the microwaves.

Maintenance

Regularly	**Keep cooking chamber and outside clean** *Unplug unit. Do not use abrasive products as they may damage surfaces. Make sure turntable and rotating ring are clean.* **A**
	Check door not damaged or misaligned *If door damaged, or gap uneven, microwave radiation may escape. Contact qualified repairer.*
	Check door lock mechanism *Oven should not operate while door is open. If it does, turn off and unplug oven immediately. Then contact qualified repairer.*

Safe microwave servicing

Undercooked food can be a serious health hazard, so the turntable in a microwave must rotate freely to ensure food is heated evenly during cooking. The turntable motor is one of the few parts of a microwave that can be repaired by the user.

Replacing a turntable motor

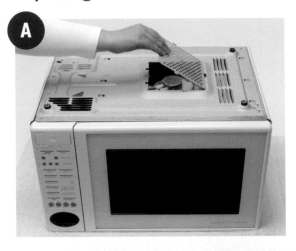

A

1 Unplug the microwave oven from the mains, and remove the turntable and ring. Place a towel on a flat work surface, and carefully turn the microwave oven upside down. Remove the retaining screws from the motor housing and lift it off.

2 Mark the positions of the wires with tags, unscrew the motor and replace it with an identical part for your model of microwave. Reconnect the wires as marked, and refit the motor housing and screws. Set oven upright, plug in, switch on and test motor operation is now satisfactory.

Fault diagnosis

Microwave ovens are one of the most dangerous appliances to repair. Under fault conditions, the high-voltage capacitor can store a potentially lethal charge for an indefinite period. Specialised equipment and knowledge are needed to discharge it safely because simply shorting it out may cause it to explode. Also, any components or wiring connected to the capacitor may present the same danger. Only the tasks suggested here can be performed safely.

Microwave oven appears completely inoperative	**Faulty power supply** *Check mains lead, plug fuse and wiring, and mains outlet for faults.* **Time not set** *Built-in clock may need to be set in order for oven to run. Follow manufacturer's instructions.* **Internal safety device faulty** *Stop using unit immediately. Contact qualified repairer.* **Door not closed** *Open and close again. If this fails, stop using oven and call qualified repairer.*
Food heats up but interior light is out	**Interior bulb faulty** *Replacing bulb involves working in dangerously close proximity to capacitor and parts connected to it. Contact qualified repairer.*
Food heats unevenly and turntable doesn't rotate	**Dirt under turntable** *Remove and clean turntable and rotating turntable ring* **(see A, page 121)**. **Faulty coupling between motor and turntable** *Ensure turntable is sitting correctly on holder.* **Turntable motor faulty** *Check motor with multimeter (see Basic toolkit, page 12) and replace motor if necessary.* **A**
Food does not heat up but interior light and turntable working	**Magnetron and associated circuitry faulty** *Contact qualified repairer.* **Incorrect power setting or cooking time selected** *Alter as necessary.*
Food takes too long to cook	**Control system or components associated with magnetron faulty** *Contact qualified repairer.*
Sparks arcing in cooking chamber	**Exposed metal edges** *Metal foil, food bag ties, containers and utensils should never be used in microwave ovens. Remove any metallic objects. Don't use crockery decorated with metallic paint or glazes.* **Carbonised food in cooking chamber or on door** *Clean cooking chamber and door.* **Small holes in cavity lining** *Sand down area around burn spots and repair with specialist microwave interior paint.*

Electric fan oven

Fan-assisted ovens differ from standard electric ovens only in that a fan distributes the heat around the cooking compartment. This means that food is cooked evenly and cooking times are reduced.

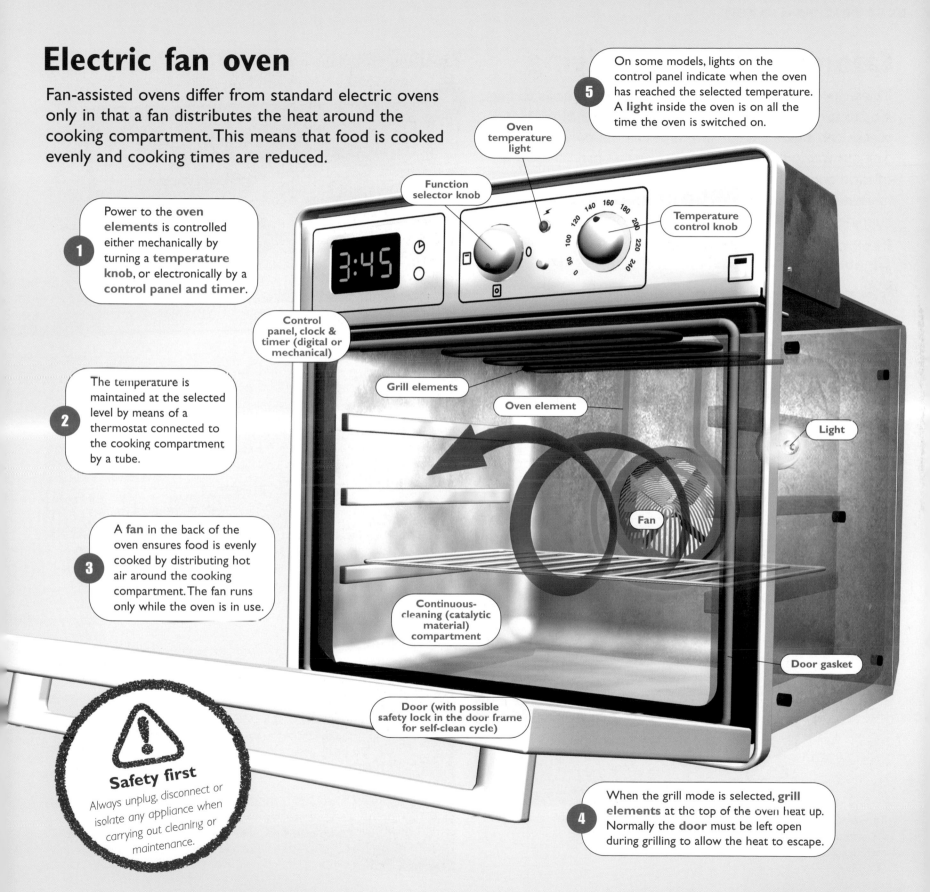

5 On some models, lights on the control panel indicate when the oven has reached the selected temperature. A **light** inside the oven is on all the time the oven is switched on.

Oven temperature light

Function selector knob

Temperature control knob

1 Power to the **oven elements** is controlled either mechanically by turning a **temperature knob**, or electronically by a **control panel and timer**.

Control panel, clock & timer (digital or mechanical)

Grill elements

Oven element

Light

2 The temperature is maintained at the selected level by means of a thermostat connected to the cooking compartment by a tube.

3 A **fan** in the back of the oven ensures food is evenly cooked by distributing hot air around the cooking compartment. The fan runs only while the oven is in use.

Fan

Continuous-cleaning (catalytic material) compartment

Door gasket

Door (with possible safety lock in the door frame for self-clean cycle)

Safety first
Always unplug, disconnect or isolate any appliance when carrying out cleaning or maintenance.

4 When the grill mode is selected, **grill elements** at the top of the oven heat up. Normally the **door** must be left open during grilling to allow the heat to escape.

Cleaning the oven

The main maintenance task for an electric oven is to keep it as clean as possible. Otherwise, a build-up of spills and grease can cause smoke and fumes. Some ovens have a 'self-clean' mode, which you can use to burn off splashes of food and fat from the oven walls. Some have 'continuous cleaning' interiors, which can be cleaned by running the oven at high temperature for an hour or so.

Cleaning the oven walls

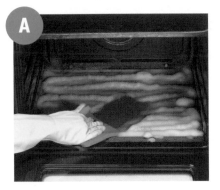

Spray a proprietary oven cleaner inside your oven and leave it to work for the time specified in the manufacturer's instructions. Then use a clean sponge to wipe off the foam residue. Wear rubber gloves to prevent the cleaner coming into contact with your skin and make sure the kitchen is well-ventilated to disperse the fumes produced by the cleaner. Repeat if necessary.

Changing the door gasket

Turn off the oven at the mains supply and allow it to cool. Open the oven door and carefully peel away the worn rubber gasket from the door frame. Then press in the replacement gasket.

Cleaning the glass door

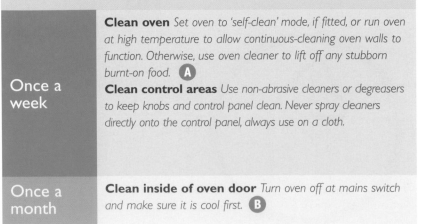

If possible, remove the oven door glass following the manufacturer's instructions. Use warm water with a little detergent to clean the glass sections of the door. Burned-on dirt can be removed with a mild abrasive cleaner.

Maintenance

Once a week	**Clean oven** *Set oven to 'self-clean' mode, if fitted, or run oven at high temperature to allow continuous-cleaning oven walls to function. Otherwise, use oven cleaner to lift off any stubborn burnt-on food.* **A** **Clean control areas** *Use non-abrasive cleaners or degreasers to keep knobs and control panel clean. Never spray cleaners directly onto the control panel, always use on a cloth.*
Once a month	**Clean inside of oven door** *Turn oven off at mains switch and make sure it is cool first.* **B**

Changing the light bulb

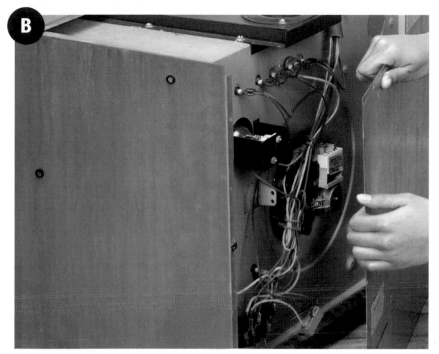

1 To replace a light bulb on some ovens, it is necessary to remove the back panel. Allow oven to cool. Disconnect or isolate from the mains supply. Carefully slide oven out from cabinet and place on floor, or worktop if cable is not long enough. Then remove the retaining screws and take off the back panel.

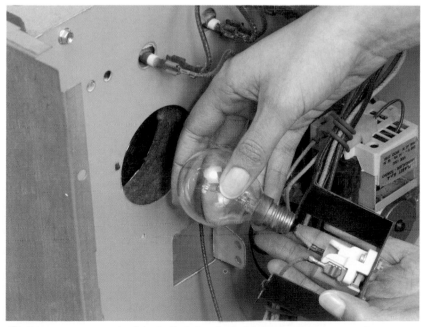

2 Prise or unscrew the light bulb fitting from the back of the oven and remove the blown bulb. Clean out any grease or dirt from the fitting before inserting a replacement bulb.

Fault diagnosis

Apart from peripheral items such as the door seal and bulb, most repairs should not be undertaken by an unqualified person. If you are unsure about any repair, contact a qualified repairer.

No functions	**No power** *Check wall switch is on and MCB in consumer unit has not tripped off. If it has, reset it to 'on'. If you cannot, call an electrician to trace and rectify the fault.*
One or more elements does not heat up	**Thermostat tripped** *Turn off oven and wait until it has fully cooled down before trying again.* **Timer set to Auto** *Make sure timer is set to Manual.* **Element failed** *Contact qualified repairer.* **Control thermostat faulty** *Contact qualified repairer.*
Thermostat trips when using grill	**Grill overheating** *This will trip the thermal cut-out. Make sure oven door is left open by the recommended amount during grilling.*
Oven not cooking evenly	**Faulty or jammed fan** *Check and clean. Consult qualified repairer.* **Incorrect shelf positions** *Make sure temperatures and shelf positions are correct.*
Door won't close properly	**Hinge spring or latch defective** *Replace, following manufacturer's instructions.* **Gasket worn** *Replace door gasket – the rubber or plastic seal on interior door edge or on body of cooker.* **(A)**
No light	**Bulb blown** *For many ovens, it is possible to change bulb from inside oven compartment, although burnt-on grease can make the glass cover difficult to remove. If this isn't possible, change the bulb by removing the back of the oven. Follow manufacturer's instructions and replace bulb with correct rating and type.* **(B)** *Otherwise contact a qualified repairer.*
Sparks or burning smell	**Loose connections or poor contacts** *Turn off immediately and contact qualified repairer.*
Noisy fan	**Dirt or grease inside motor** *Contact qualified repairer.*

Gas cooker

Natural gas is a colourless gas that burns very efficiently with a blue flame. Gas cookers have several advantages over conventional electric models as they provide heat instantly, the heat can be adjusted accurately, and they do not retain heat for as long after they are switched off.

Controls

Electric ignition

Metal gauze

Central grill pipe

Gas pipe to oven burner

Oven burner

Igniter

1 Natural gas from the gas mains is piped to a connection on the the back of the cooker. When a **control** is turned, it opens a valve regulator, allowing the gas to flow through the jets of the burners.

2 When the **ignition** is pressed (or, on automatic models, when the action of turning a control sets off the automatic ignition) a battery or mains-powered electronic circuit produces a spark.

3 This spark ignites the natural gas, which is evenly distributed by the **burners** (see facing page).

4 When the **oven** is required, the control is turned to the desired temperature. Gas flows through a burner at the lower back of the oven and its flow is regulated by a simple thermostat. The top of the oven tends to be hotter than the bottom, which can be useful when cooking different dishes.

5 The **grill** works in a similar way to the hob, except the gas flames flow outwards from tiny holes in a **central pipe** across a **metal gauze** or grid. As the gauze heats up, it evenly cooks the foodstuffs positioned below.

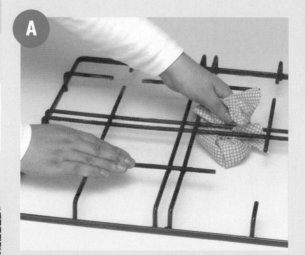

How the burners work

When the valve is turned to the on position, gas flows through the supply pipe to the jet **1** under the burner **2**. From here, it is distributed evenly in a circle by the slots **3** in the edge of the burner. The burner cap **4** protects the burner from food spills, and is removable for easy cleaning. It also forces the gas to flow out through the slots. When the ignition switch is pressed, or on some models any knob turned, a spark jumps from the igniter **5** to the burner, and the gas starts to burn as it exits the burner slots. The rigid metal pan supports **6** keep the pan level and away from the flame during cooking.

Maintenance

After each use	**Clean cooker** *Make sure the hob has cooled down first.*
Once a week	**Clean oven and hob** *Clean hob and burners.* **A** *Thoroughly clean oven.*

Safety warning

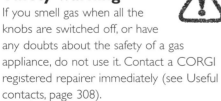

If you smell gas when all the knobs are switched off, or have any doubts about the safety of a gas appliance, do not use it. Contact a CORGI registered repairer immediately (see Useful contacts, page 308).

Cleaning the hob

A

1 Lift off the pan supports and wash in warm, soapy water. Use a cloth soaked in warm water, with a little cream cleaner to remove caked-on food, and wash the surface of the cooker, taking care not to get water into the burners.

2 Wipe down the burner caps, and replace them and the pan supports. Turn the burners on for a short while to evaporate any excess water.

Cooker hood

A cooker hood removes cooking odours and droplets of grease from the air above a hob using nothing more than a fan and a filter. It either draws air through a grease filter then a charcoal filter and recycles it back into the kitchen, or just through a grease filter then a vent to the outside.

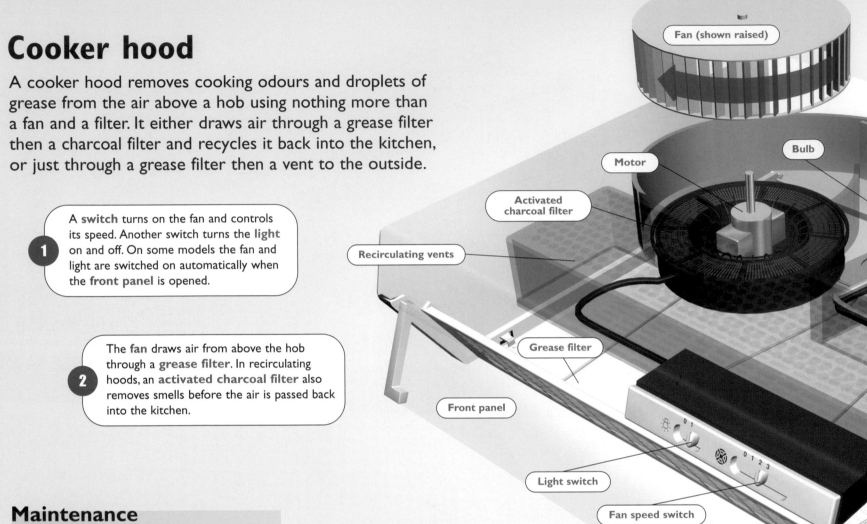

Fan (shown raised)

Bulb

Motor

Activated charcoal filter

Recirculating vents

Grease filter

Front panel

Light switch

Fan speed switch

1 A **switch** turns on the fan and controls its speed. Another switch turns the **light** on and off. On some models the fan and light are switched on automatically when the **front panel** is opened.

2 The **fan** draws air from above the hob through a **grease filter**. In recirculating hoods, an **activated charcoal filter** also removes smells before the air is passed back into the kitchen.

Maintenance

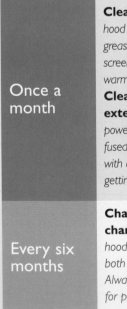

Once a month

Clean grease filter *If cooker hood only vents air, then soak grease filter, which looks like fabric screen, in degreasing agent, then warm soapy water.* **A**

Clean interior and exterior of hood *Turn off power at local socket outlet or fused connection unit and clean with a non-abrasive cleaner. Avoid getting liquid in lamp socket.*

Every six months

Change grease and charcoal filters *If cooker hood is recirculating type, replace both grease and charcoal filters. Always use recommended parts for particular model.* **B**

Cleaning the filter

A

Remove the filter by pressing the release switches and lowering the panel. Unclip the filter and soak it in a degreasing agent, then clean with warm soapy water. If you have a dishwasher, wash the filter in the upper rack.

Replacing the filters

B

If the cooker hood recycles air, the filters cannot be cleaned. Replace both the grease filter and the activated charcoal filter every six months, depending on usage.

If a cooker hood is the type that only vents the air to the outside, then the grease filter will be thicker and the air is pumped through a **vent pipe** leading to a vent in the wall.

Vent pipe

Vent panel

From recirculating to venting

Most cooker hoods have a switch to select either recirculating or venting mode: the first mode is necessary if there is no wall vent to outside. In recirculating mode, a vent panel (in green below) **1** covers the vent pipe, routing the filtered air back into the kitchen through holes in the top of the hood **2**. In venting mode, the panel is moved **3** and the air routed through the wall to the outside **4**.

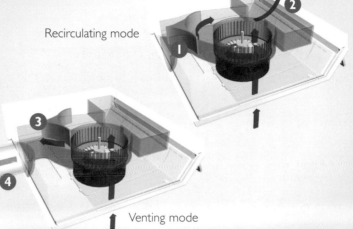

Recirculating mode

Venting mode

Cleaning the fan

A

1 Switch off the cooker hood and turn off the power at the local socket outlet or fused connection unit. Unclip the activated charcoal filter, if fitted, and remove it.

2 Locate the circular motor and fan unit. Remove the fan mounting screws. Then carefully slide out the motor unit and fan assembly.

3 Unscrew the central retaining screw and remove the fan blades. Soak in warm water and washing-up liquid or a degreasing agent. Clean and dry thoroughly, then refit.

Fault diagnosis

Light works but fan does not turn	**Fan switch faulty** *Contact qualified repairer.* **Motor burnt out** *Contact qualified repairer.* **Jammed fan blades** *Remove fan blades and clean with degreasing agent.* **A**
Light does not work	**Bulb blown** *Turn off power at fused connection unit, or disconnect hood from mains supply. Then open hood and replace bulb.* **Faulty switch or wiring** *Contact qualified repairer.*
Nothing works	**No power** *Check for blown fuse in plug or fused connection unit, or tripped circuit breaker in consumer unit.*
Fan noisy	**Greasy fan blades** *Remove fan blades and clean with degreasing agent.* **A** **Blocked filters** *Clean.* **A** **Worn motor or fan bearings** *Lubricate with light oil, or call qualified repairer.*

Replacing the bulb

To replace the bulb, turn off the power and unclip the hood. The replacement bulb will usually have a screw fitting.

Food processor

A food processor is a versatile kitchen appliance. Using interchangeable metal and plastic tools it can chop, slice, shred, grate and mix a wide range of foodstuffs. Some models also include a liquidiser, although it is possible to buy one as a separate unit.

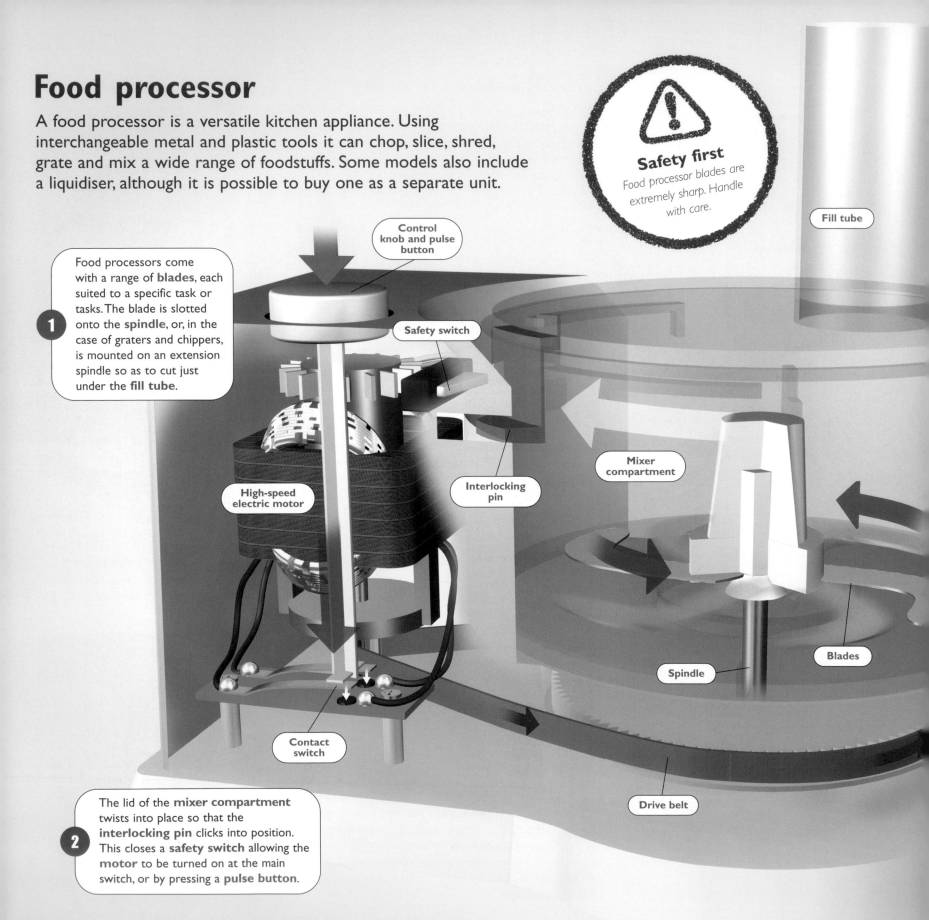

Safety first
Food processor blades are extremely sharp. Handle with care.

Fill tube

Control knob and pulse button

1 Food processors come with a range of **blades**, each suited to a specific task or tasks. The blade is slotted onto the **spindle**, or, in the case of graters and chippers, is mounted on an extension spindle so as to cut just under the **fill tube**.

Safety switch

High-speed electric motor

Interlocking pin

Mixer compartment

Contact switch

Blades

Spindle

Drive belt

2 The lid of the **mixer compartment** twists into place so that the **interlocking pin** clicks into position. This closes a **safety switch** allowing the **motor** to be turned on at the main switch, or by pressing a **pulse button**.

Liquidiser

The blades in a liquidiser cannot be removed. They have four angled cutting edges, which spin more quickly than the blades in a food processor. This results in a more aggressive chopping action, reducing foodstuffs to a finer, more liquid consistency than can be achieved in a processor.

4 Ingredients are fed through the fill tube and are chopped, shredded, mixed or diced by the spinning blades. Blunt plastic blades are used to knead dough.

3 The motor drives the spindle via a rubber **drive belt** and reduction gear. This means that the spindle and blades spin at a lower speed than the motor, but they have greater torque (rotational force) allowing them to chop raw vegetables or mix thick fluids without stalling the motor.

Maintenance

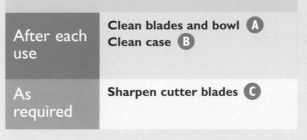

After each use	Clean blades and bowl Ⓐ Clean case Ⓑ
As required	Sharpen cutter blades Ⓒ

Fault diagnosis

No functions	**No power** *Check flex, plug wiring, fuse and mains supply for faults.* **Safety switch not closed** *Check that lid is fitted correctly and that interlock pin on the lid engages safety switch.* **Thermal cut-out tripped** *Wait a few moments to see if it resets. If it cuts out again, make sure you have not overfilled processor.* **Motor burned out** *Contact qualified engineer.*
Bowl leaks	**Bowl overfull** *Do not fill bowl above specified maximum line.* **Bowl cracked** *Buy new bowl.*
Solid food sticks on the blades	**Blades blunt** *Sharpen cutter blades.* Ⓒ **Chunks of food too large** *Cut food into smaller pieces before filling.* **Wrong cutting option** *Use push button pulse mode.*
Blades do not turn but motor running	**Broken or worn drive belt** *Fit new drive belt as specified by the manufacturer.*

Cleaning the bowl

A

Fill the bowl half full of hot water with a little washing up liquid, then run the processor at top speed. Make sure the spindle and inside of any plastic parts are clean. Rinse and dry.

Cleaning the case

B

Clean case with a mild detergent, keeping away from vents. Remove debris from vents with a soft brush.

Sharpening the blades

C

Push the edge of the blade away from you along a wet sharpening stone (available from DIY shops). Repeat the process for each blade which needs to be sharpened.

Breadmaker

A programmable sequence of mixing, proving and baking in a breadmaker means that the process of cooking bread can be fully automated. On some models, you can set a delay so that the breadmaker starts working in time for you to enjoy freshly made bread for breakfast.

1 The raw ingredients are placed into the removable stainless steel **non-stick pan** and the program is set using the **control panel**. Shutting the **lid** starts the cooking sequence, which may begin immediately or, in some models, with a delay to finish at a pre-set time.

2 First the motor-driven **kneading blade** mixes the ingredients for a specified time. An audible signal lets you know when to add further ingredients, such as raisins, if desired.

Lid

Steam vent

Non-stick pan

Heating elements

Kneading blade

Blade shaft

Drive belt

The cooking cycle

Once the ingredients have been mixed together, the kneading blade stops and the element is switched on to warm the mixture **1**, a process known as 'proving'. This causes the mixture to rise, which takes about an hour, depending on the type of loaf. After the proving period, the timer switches the elements to the higher heat necessary to bake the loaf **2**, which can take another 2–3 hours.

4 — The elements turn on and off periodically after cooking so that the bread remains warm. After approximately an hour, the elements turn off completely.

Display

Control panel

Motor

3 — Elements around the pan then heat the mixture to a warmer temperature for a period of proving and then to a higher temperature to cook It for a number of hours, depending on the selected program. After the cooking period is over, a beeper sounds and the elements switch off.

Maintenance

| Once every six months | **Lubricate blade shaft** *Rub a little vegetable oil on kneading blade shaft.*
Clean inside of breadmaker |

Fault diagnosis

No functions	**No power** *Check mains lead, plug wiring, fuse and socket outlet for faults.*
Dough doesn't cook	**Faulty heating element** *Contact qualified repairer.*
Cannot select cooking programme	**Faulty circuitry** *Contact a qualified repairer or buy a replacement unit.*
Blades jamming	**Clogged blades** *Remove pan and blades and soak.*
Cannot remove bread	**Bread sticking to pan** *Try tapping gently on sides of pan. If this does not work, remove pan from breadmaker and wrap pan in a damp cloth. Allow pan to cool and bread should drop out. If this does not work, turn nut attached to kneading blade under the pan slightly from side to side to loosen bread.*
Dough doesn't mix	**Bread pan not inserted correctly** *Remove the pan and reinsert.* **Kneading blade not inserted** *Always make sure that blade is fitted before ingredients are put in pan.* **Faulty motor or drive** *Contact a qualified repairer.*
Smoke or smell of burning from steam vent	**Ingredients spilled on heater element** *Switch off, unplug and allow breadmaker to cool. Clean inside machine with damp cloth.* **Thermostat faulty** *Contact qualified repairer.*

Electric kettle

Most kettles have an exposed element in the jug, but in some units it is sealed in the casing. Many kettles come with a base unit that plugs into the mains supply. The jug can be lifted off the base for filling and pouring.

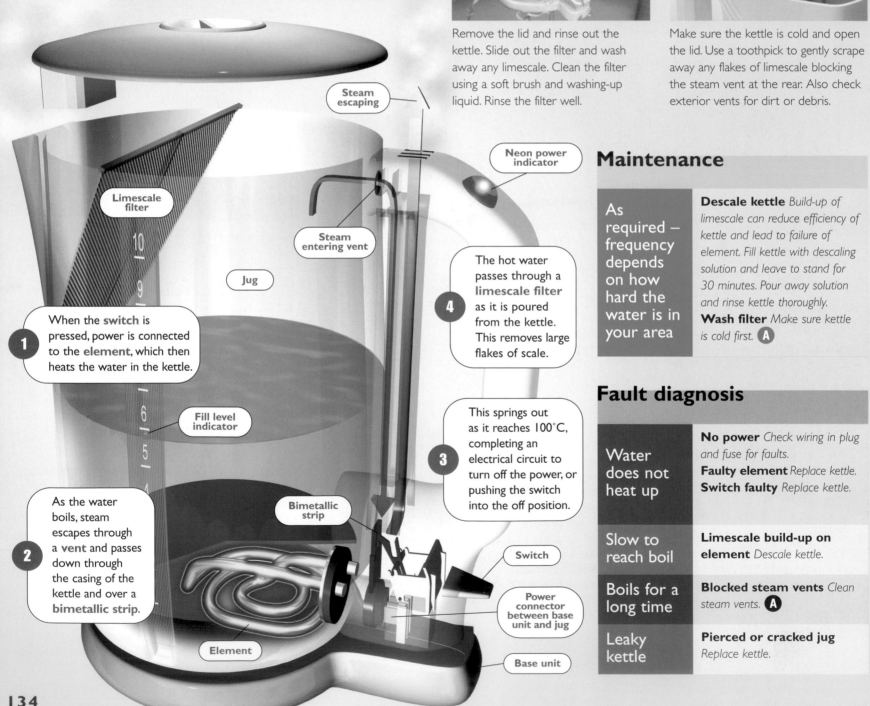

1 When the **switch** is pressed, power is connected to the **element**, which then heats the water in the kettle.

2 As the water boils, steam escapes through a **vent** and passes down through the casing of the kettle and over a **bimetallic strip**.

3 This springs out as it reaches 100°C, completing an electrical circuit to turn off the power, or pushing the switch into the off position.

4 The hot water passes through a **limescale filter** as it is poured from the kettle. This removes large flakes of scale.

Labels: Steam escaping · Neon power indicator · Limescale filter · Steam entering vent · Jug · Fill level indicator · Bimetallic strip · Switch · Power connector between base unit and jug · Element · Base unit

Washing the filter

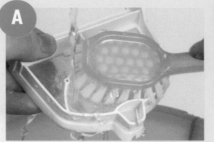

A

Remove the lid and rinse out the kettle. Slide out the filter and wash away any limescale. Clean the filter using a soft brush and washing-up liquid. Rinse the filter well.

Cleaning steam vents

A

Make sure the kettle is cold and open the lid. Use a toothpick to gently scrape away any flakes of limescale blocking the steam vent at the rear. Also check exterior vents for dirt or debris.

Maintenance

As required – frequency depends on how hard the water is in your area	**Descale kettle** *Build-up of limescale can reduce efficiency of kettle and lead to failure of element. Fill kettle with descaling solution and leave to stand for 30 minutes. Pour away solution and rinse kettle thoroughly.* **Wash filter** *Make sure kettle is cold first.* **A**

Fault diagnosis

Water does not heat up	**No power** *Check wiring in plug and fuse for faults.* **Faulty element** *Replace kettle.* **Switch faulty** *Replace kettle.*
Slow to reach boil	**Limescale build-up on element** *Descale kettle.*
Boils for a long time	**Blocked steam vents** *Clean steam vents.* **A**
Leaky kettle	**Pierced or cracked jug** *Replace kettle.*

Pressure cooker

A pressure cooker confines the steam given off by boiling water, causing a rise in pressure inside the cooker. This raises the boiling temperature of the water to around 120°C, ensuring that the food cooks more quickly than by conventional methods.

Weight

Safety plug

Vent pipe

4 A **safety plug** protects against over-pressurisation. It pops out to release the pressure if the pan overheats or the vent gets blocked.

1 A thick **metal pan** with a **rubber seal** and **locking lid** seals the food and a little water inside. This is heated on a hob.

Heat-resistant handle

Rubber seal

Locking lid

Cover interlock – to prevent the cooker being opened while pressurised

2 Steam builds up inside the cooker and escapes at a controlled rate via a **vent pipe** with a **weight** on top. This keeps the pressure constant within the cooker.

3 The weight can be altered to increase or decrease the pressure (and hence the temperature) within the cooking chamber to suit different foodstuffs. See the manufacturer's instructions for which weight to use.

Trivet

Metal (aluminium or steel) pan

Maintenance

Once a month	**Rub a little vegetable oil on seal to keep it flexible** *This makes it easier to remove lid and keeps seal from becoming hard and brittle.* **Check that handle is tight** *If there is any play, use screwdriver to tighten screw that holds handle to the body.* **Keep vent pipe clean** *If vent pipe gets blocked safety plug will blow out.* **A**

Fault diagnosis

Pressure does not build up	**Seal dirty** *Allow pan to cool, remove and clean seal.* **A** **Hardened seal** *Rub in a little vegetable oil to soften. Otherwise buy and fit a replacement.* **Weight not closing valve** *Check valve and weight are clean.* **Safety plug popped out** *Refer to manufacturer's instructions.*

Cleaning the valve

A

Remove the weight by lifting it off, and rinse it out. Clean around the vent pipe and make sure it is clear of obstruction. Wipe and rinse thoroughly.

Washing the seal

A

Carefully prise the rubber seal from the lid using a plastic spatula. Wash by hand using a mild detergent, and rinse several times. Refit the seal.

Ice cream maker

An electric motor provides the power to churn ice cream while it freezes in a special container. Some are chilled by an integral miniature freezer, others (shown here) require the bowl to be frozen in advance.

Maintenance

Before each use	**Freeze bowl** *Wash and dry bowl thoroughly. Wrap dry bowl in a clean plastic bag – this prevents frost from forming on steel surface when bowl is put in freezer.* **A**
After each use	**Clean appliance thoroughly** *Wash bowl and paddle in warm, soapy water.*

1 The **ice cream bowl** must be frozen in advance for at least 18 hours. It is a double walled bowl, plastic on the outside and steel on the inside. Between the bowl walls is a **refrigerant fluid**.

Cover

Paddle

2 When the ice cream mixture is prepared, the bowl is removed from the freezer and attached to the **motor support**.

Ice cream bowl

3 The **paddle** is fitted to the **cover**, which is attached to an **electric motor**. When the unit is switched on, the motor drives the paddle, which starts to rotate.

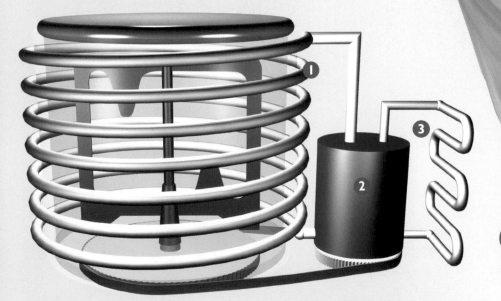

Alternative design

More expensive ice cream makers use their own **miniature freezer** to chill the bowl and freeze the ice cream. The bowl is cooled by evaporator coils **1** that surround it. An electric motor **2** doubles as a refrigerant pump and ice cream stirrer. Heat generated by the cooling process (see Fridge freezer, page 114) is radiated by small condenser coils **3**. Take care when moving and cleaning these units because the refrigeration mechanism is very delicate. Also, the refrigerant needs to settle overnight before use if the machine has been moved.

When the ice cream is thoroughly frozen, the paddle stops moving and the user switches off the motor. **6**

As the mixture hits the cold bowl it starts to freeze. The paddle keeps the mixture moving so that it freezes slowly. This creates the small ice crystals, and air pockets, that give ice cream its texture. **5**

Electric motor

On/off switch

Motor support

Refrigerant fluid

The ice cream mixture is poured into the bowl through the top. **4**

Health and safety

Many ice creams contain raw eggs and fresh fruit, both of which are potential causes of food poisoning. The bowl and paddle must always be kept scrupulously clean, and all fresh produce should be washed thoroughly before use to minimise the chances of bacterial infection.

Fault diagnosis

No functions	**No power** Check mains lead, plug fuse and wiring, and mains outlet for faults.
Paddle stops	**Ice cream ready** Serve ice cream or freeze for later. **Paddle dislodged from motor** Replace paddle.
Mixture remains runny	**High alcohol content** High alcohol content in ice cream mixture can prevent it from freezing. **Bowl not thoroughly frozen** Decant ice cream mixture to plastic container and refrigerate. Thoroughly clean and dry bowl and replace in freezer, wrapped in plastic bag.

Freezing the bowl

A

Wrap the bowl in a large plastic food bag before freezing it. This prevents condensation forming on the inside of the bowl during the freezing process, which can spoil the flavour of the ice cream and slow the blades.

Iron

The three factors required to produce crease-free clothes are heat, pressure and moisture. Modern irons maintain a constant temperature, deliver steam at a controlled rate and can pump water through a nozzle to tackle stubborn creases.

How a mercury switch works

Mercury, a liquid metal that conducts electricity, is housed in a cylinder containing two electrical contacts. When the iron is moved to the horizontal position (below right), the mercury flows down so that it touches both contacts, completing a circuit that activates a timer. If the circuit remains unbroken for a fixed period the timer switches off the heating element.

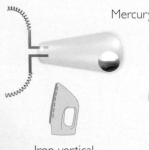

Mercury

Contacts

Iron vertical   Iron horizontal

1 The iron is filled with cold water through the **filler funnel** on the front of the iron. This may have a removable or sliding cover.

2 Once the iron is plugged in, a **heating element** warms the **soleplate** to a temperature determined by a **control knob** and an adjustable thermostat.

3 Water drips through a valve into a **steam chamber** where it is quickly heated to boiling point. The steam then passes out of the iron through the holes in the soleplate.

Pump button

Temperature control knob

Jet nozzle

Filler funnel

Steam control

Steam chamber

Heating element

4 The amount of steam is adjusted by a variable **steam control** and a button for a concentrated burst.

Replacing a damaged flex

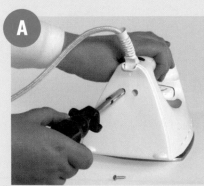

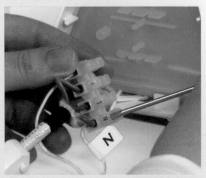

1 Unplug the iron and make sure it is cool. Unscrew the back plate. If your iron has tamper-proof screws, you may need a special screwdriver. Gently prise off the plate and unclip the flex. Make a note of the flex route.

2 Unscrew the terminal block screws. Remove the old flex and replace. Reassemble the iron, being careful not to trap any wires. Before use, with a multimeter test for continuity between the soleplate and the earth pin of the mains plug (see Basic toolkit, page 12).

Power indicator

Water tank

Thermal fuse

Soleplate

6 A **thermal fuse** cuts the power if the iron overheats. Some irons have a mercury switch, which switches the element off if the iron is left in the horizontal position for too long.

5 Cold water can be sprayed through a **jet nozzle** on the front of the iron by pushing the manual **pump button**.

Maintenance

After each use	**Wipe the soleplate with a damp cloth while it is still warm to remove any deposits** *Do not use an abrasive cleaner on the plate.* **Empty residual water according to manufacturer's instructions**
Once a month or as advised	**Clean out iron according to the manufacturer's instructions** *Fill iron to the full mark with cold water. Plug it in and turn thermostat to full (or select 'auto clean' setting). Once iron has heated fully, unplug and hold over an empty sink. Press steam burst (or auto clean) button to force steam through holes and blow out any mineral deposits.* **Check for damaged flex** *Replace if necessary.* **A**
As advised	**Descale iron** *Carry out descaling procedure according to manufacturer's instructions.*

Fault diagnosis

Iron doesn't heat	**No power** *Check flex, plug wiring, fuse and mains supply for faults.* **Control knob set at cold** *Adjust.* **Element or thermostat faulty** *Replace iron.*
No steam	**Not enough water in reservoir** *Add water.* **Wrong steam valve setting** *Adjust.* **Steam valve blocked** *Activate steam valve button a few times to clear blockage.* **Wrong thermostat setting** *Adjust.*
Soleplate leaks water	**Soleplate not hot enough** *Increase setting.* **Variable steam control set too high** *Reduce setting.* **Bursts of steam too frequent** *Allow more time between bursts.*
Iron sticks to or stains fabric	**Burned material stuck to soleplate** *Clean soleplate. Use recommended cleaning fluid.* **Mineral deposits in the chambers and tubes** *Clean all vents and holes.* **A**

Cleaning an iron

1 Gently clear steam vents with a toothpick or pipe cleaner. Keep the iron angled so that dislodged deposits fall away from the holes.

2 Use a very fine sewing needle to clean the spray nozzle. Be careful not to enlarge the opening by pressing too hard.

3 Flush the iron out with a proprietary cleaning product. Place the iron on a metal rack over a large pan and set to steam until the tank is empty. Repeat with clean water.

Filter coffeemaker

Simple paper filter coffeemakers were first introduced at the beginning of the 19th century and the basic principle hasn't changed since. Water is heated and passed through ground coffee beans into a carafe.

Drip head

Mesh filter

Safety first
Always unplug, disconnect or isolate any appliance when carrying out cleaning or maintenance.

Ground coffee

1 Ground coffee beans are placed in a paper or **mesh filter** and the **water reservoir** is filled with cold water.

Riser tube

One-way valve

Glass carafe

2 Cold water flows from the reservoir down through a **one-way valve** into a curved **aluminium tube** attached to a **heating element** in the base of the machine.

Heating element

Tube connectors

3 The **carafe** is placed under the filter and the power is turned on at the **switch**. This heats the element.

Switch

Aluminium tube

Thermostat

Metal plate

The boiling water then passes through the coffee and into the carafe. The heating element also warms a **metal plate** beneath the carafe, which keeps the brewed coffee hot.

7

Case with water reservoir

The drip head releases the water through many small holes, in a similar way to a shower head, so that it drips evenly onto the ground coffee.

6

Heat is conducted from the element to the **aluminium tube** causing the water to boil. Since the one-way valve prevents it flowing back into the reservoir, the hot water is forced up the **riser tube** and into the **drip head**.

5

The heating element is regulated by a **thermostat**. When the thermostat detects the temperature has reached a certain level, it cuts off the power to the element until it cools slightly.

4

Maintaining the temperature

The thermostat **1** works in the same way as a kettle thermostat (see Kettle, page 134) to regulate the temperature of the element. A bimetallic strip bends as the temperature increases, eventually cutting off the power to the element **2**. As the temperature drops, the strip bends back.

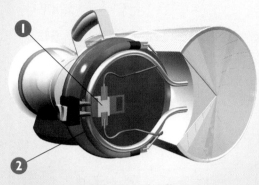

Underside of coffeemaker

Descaling the coffeemaker

A

1 Mix a solution of commercial descaler in a jug. Pour the solution into the reservoir and place the carafe under the filter basket. Turn on the heating element and allow approximately half the liquid to pass through the coffeemaker. Then turn the power off and leave for 30 minutes.

2 Add the solution in the carafe to the reservoir and then turn the coffeemaker back on. Allow all the solution to pass through the machine. To clean out any residue, pass two carafes of clean water through the machine, letting it cool between cycles.

Maintenance

As required	**Flush mineral deposits from the system using commercial descaler** *Limescale builds up rapidly in small tubes, especially if you live in a hard-water area.* **A**
Once a month	**Check carafe for cracks and chips** *Replace it if you find any damage; it could leak or break when heated.*

Fault diagnosis

Your ability to repair certain faults will depend on the availability and cost of parts for your particular model. In some cases, replacing the machine will be more cost-effective.

No heat	**Faulty element** *Check and replace if necessary* **(see A, page 142).** **Thermostat not working** *Check and replace if necessary.* **No power** *Lead damaged or on/off switch faulty. Switch off coffeemaker and unplug from mains supply. Remove retaining screw from plug to check plug wiring and fuse.*
Weak coffee	**Drip holes blocked** *Empty coffeemaker, remove carafe, and unclog holes using a toothpick* **(see B, page 142).**
Little or no hot water coming from drip head	**One-way valve clogged or jammed** *Clean valve unit or replace if broken.* **Tubes blocked with mineral deposits** *Flush out using a commercial descaler.* **A** **Drip holes blocked** *See above.*

Keep the coffee flowing

Regular descaling should keep a coffeemaker running smoothly. However, the most common repair job is replacing the element.

Safety first

Always allow the coffeemaker to cool for at least 30 minutes before attempting repairs.

Replacing the element

1 Remove the carafe and filter basket and unplug the appliance. Unscrew the base-plate and gently lever it away from the housing with a screwdriver.

2 Unscrew the heating element and aluminium tube assembly, and pull it away slightly from the warming plate. There may be a tensioned metal bar holding it in place.

Clearing the drip holes

 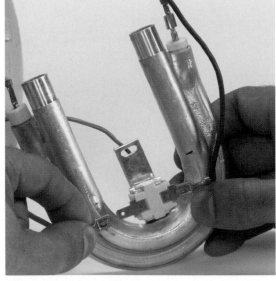 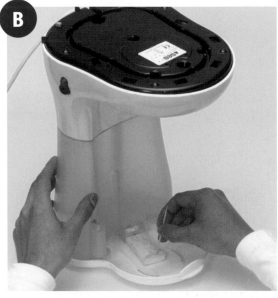

3 Disconnect the tube connectors that link the aluminium tube to the one-way valve and riser tubes. Leave them connected to the tubes.

4 Unclip the cores from the thermostat (as shown here) and unscrew it. Then, remove the cores from the ends of the element. Replace the assembly with the recommended part for the model.

Unplug the coffeemaker and remove the carafe and filter basket. Turn the unit upside down (over a sink to catch any water left inside) and unblock the holes with a toothpick. Rinse with clean water before use.

Espresso maker

The pressure required to make an espresso maker work can simply be derived from the water as it boils in a confined space. However, some models, such as the one shown here, create a higher pressure by using a pump.

Heating chamber

Dial

Elements

Filter

Filter cup filled with ground coffee

Reservoir

Steam wand

Pump

Drip tray

Switch and indicator light

1 The **reservoir** is filled with cold water and the power turned on. **Elements** in the **heating chamber** start to heat up.

2 An **indicator light** shows when the elements are at operating temperature. The **filter cup** is then inserted and a **dial** is turned to the 'coffee' position.

3 This starts the **pump**, which pumps a small amount of water from the reservoir into the heating chamber at high pressure.

4 The hot water passes through the coffee grounds into the cup.

5 If the dial is moved to 'steam', the pump pulses, pushing a much smaller amount of water over the elements. This immediately boils and the steam is routed through the **steam wand** for frothing milk in a separate container.

Maintenance

After each use	**Clean filter** *Use dishwasher or rinse under tap. Empty and clean drip tray.*
As required	**Descale** *Remove limescale that has collected in the machine.* **Ⓐ** *This is especially necessary in hard-water areas.*

Fault diagnosis

Before making any repairs, turn off the machine, unplug it and allow it to cool.

Leaks from around filter cup	**Ground coffee breaking seal** *Remove metal filter assembly and clean cup thoroughly.* **Filter assembly not screwed on properly** *Remove and refit filter cup correctly.* **Coffee packed too tightly** *Refill with less coffee.*
Pressure cap leaking (steam models)	**Cap loose** *Tighten cap.* **Thread dirty** *Remove cap and make sure threads are clean.* **Gasket worn** *Replace gasket with new one if this part is readily available for your model. Remove lid of water reservoir and prise out worn gasket with screwdriver. Then press new gasket into place.*

Descaling the machine

Ⓐ

Remove the filter cup and the filter from beneath the heating chamber. Prepare a commercial descaler and load it into the coffeemaker. Heat as normal but without the filter cup or filter in place. Collect the descaling solution in a pot then pass distilled water through the system two or three times to rinse out the solution. Clean the filter and refit it.

Toaster

Modern toasters rely increasingly on electronic rather than mechanical controllers. This means there are fewer maintenance and repair tasks that you can perform yourself. However, a modern toaster is also likely to be more reliable than earlier models.

1 Once the bread has been inserted into the slots, the **lever** is pressed down to lower the **bread carriers** into the toaster. As they are lowered they press against a **contact switch**, which closes the contacts to activate the toaster's circuits.

Alternative design

Some toasters use a **bimetallic strip** to trigger the release mechanism, rather than an electromagnet. This strip is made from two bonded metals, usually brass **1** and steel **2**. The strip bends as its temperature changes **3** because brass expands more quickly and by a different amount than the steel. At a point determined by the browning control setting, the strip makes a connection inside the toaster **4** or trips a mechanism. This causes the toast to pop up and the elements to turn off.

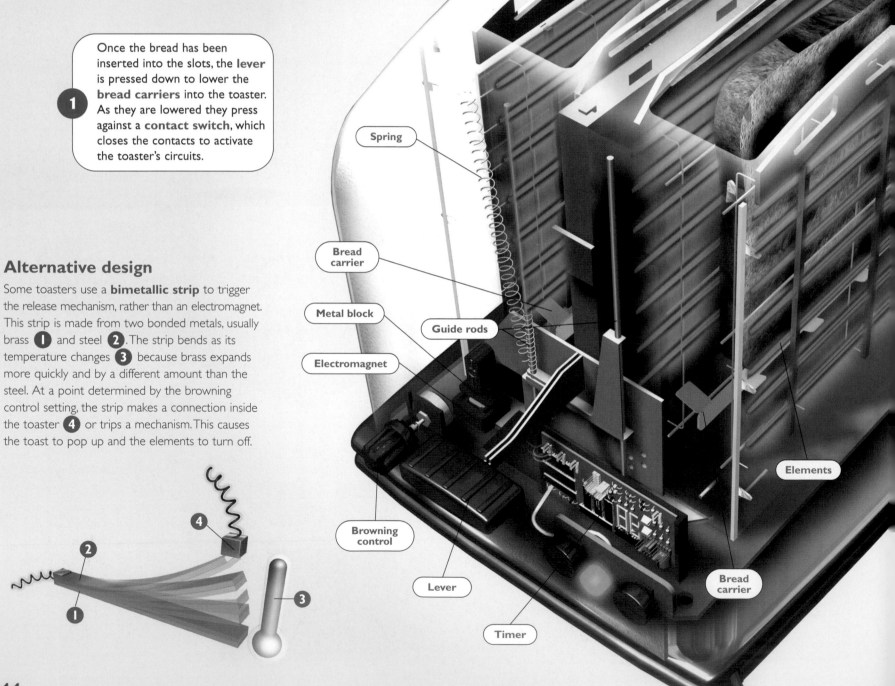

Spring

Bread carrier

Metal block

Guide rods

Electromagnet

Elements

Browning control

Bread carrier

Lever

Timer

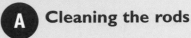

Safety first

Always unplug, disconnect or isolate any appliance when carrying out cleaning or maintenance.

Contact switch

The **elements** heat up and begin to brown the toast. After a set period, regulated by the **browning control**, the **timer** switches off the power to the electromagnet. This releases the bread carriers, which are pulled upwards by the **spring**, releasing the contact switch and turning off the elements.

3

2 Most toasters now use an electromagnetic latching mechanism. A **metal block** attached to the carrier comes into contact with an **electromagnet** at the base of the toaster. The electro-magnet then holds the bread carriers in position.

Maintenance

Every week	**Clean out crumb tray** *This usually pulls out from underneath toaster.*
Whenever required	**Dislodge trapped pieces of bread with non-metallic object** *Unplug toaster and wait for it to cool before attempting this. Take great care not to touch heating element wires, which are fragile and easily broken. In stubborn cases, it may be necessary to remove casing to complete job without damaging appliance.*

Fault diagnosis

Symptoms and repairs will depend upon the type of latch your toaster uses, mechanical (**M**) or electromagnetic (**E**). The ability to resolve these problems depends upon availability of spare parts for your particular model.

Carrier will not latch down	**M only** *Unplug toaster, allow it to cool and remove cover. Check bread carrier latch mechanism. Remove obstructing debris.* **E only** *Check mains supply, plug fuse and wiring for faults.* **E only** *Electromagnet or timer circuit faulty. Replace toaster.*
Carrier down, but no heat	**M only** *Check mains supply, plug fuse and wiring for faults.* **M only** *Switch contacts may be faulty. Replace toaster.* **M or E** *Faulty elements. Replace toaster.*
Carrier does not pop up	**M or E** *Bread trapped. Turn off toaster and use non-metallic object to free bread. Take care not to damage elements.* **M only** *Bimetallic switch or latch faulty. Replace toaster.* **E only** *Faulty timer module. Replace toaster.* **M or E** *Dirt on guide rod mechanism. Clean guide rods.* **A** **M or E** *Lift spring faulty. Check spring is still attached.* **B**
Bread under-cooked – even set at maximum	**M only** *Bimetallic switch or latch faulty. Replace toaster.* **E only** *Faulty timer module. Replace toaster.*
Bread only cooked on one side	**M or E** *Element on one side broken. Replace toaster.*
Sparks from toaster	**M or E** *Loose connections. If heating element wires break or any other connection becomes loose, sparks may come from toaster. Stop using toaster immediately, and replace it.*

A Cleaning the rods

1 Unplug the toaster and unscrew the base. Remove the lever handle and lift or slide off the cover and/or the end plates.

2 Check the guide rods for dirt. These are the two vertical steel poles, which ensure the carriage moves vertically. Clean the rods and carriage with a wire brush or a dry scourer. If this does not solve the problem, replace the toaster.

Reattaching the spring

B

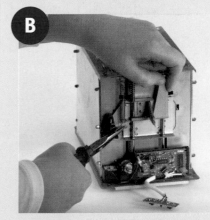

Unplug the toaster and remove the casing. Make sure the spring is attached to both the bread carrier and the top of the toaster. Reattach if necessary.

Toasted sandwich maker

Two hot non-stick metal plates press together when a toasted sandwich maker is clipped shut, cooking the bread and its contents. The plates are often moulded, to crimp the sandwich into triangular shapes.

1 When the switch is turned on power flows to the **elements** and a **LED** is illuminated to indicate that the machine is in operation. A second LED indicates when cooking temperature is reached.

LEDs

Moulded top plates

Diagonal divider

4 On some models, a timer turns off the elements and the LED when the sandwich is ready.

Moulded base plates

Elements

2 The sandwich, buttered on the outside, is placed on the **moulded base plate**. Then the sandwich maker lid is closed.

3 The elements heat the plates, cooking the sandwich. As it cooks, the bread shrinks slightly, and is crimped into triangles around the edges and along the **diagonal divider**.

Maintenance

After each use	**Clean plates** *Turn on empty unit and heat until LED turns off. Then clean cooking plates.* **A**

Fault diagnosis

Nothing works	**No power to unit** *Check mains lead, plug wiring, fuse and mains outlet for faults.*
Bread sticks to plates	**Not enough butter on sandwich or low-fat spread has been used** *Thoroughly spread outside of sandwich with butter or margarine only.* **Cooked-on debris** *Turn on empty unit and heat until LED turns off. Then clean cooking plates.* **A**
Sandwich not cooked through	**Heat escaping from unit** *Ensure catch is in place.*

Cleaning the plates

A

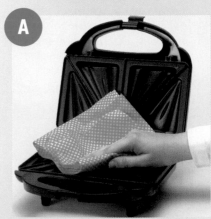

Unplug the unit and allow it to cool down for a while. Moisten a cloth with warm water. Wipe the cloth across the plates to remove food debris. Cleaning is easier while the plates are still warm, but be careful not to touch hot metal.

Deep fat fryer

Conventional deep fat frying means having a pan of oil on the hob, with the potential for a 'chip pan fire'. Modern, electrically powered, deep fat fryers virtually eliminate the risk of fire thanks to sophisticated thermostatic controls.

1 Cooking oil is poured into the **aluminium bowl**. The bowl sits above an electric heating **element**. When the **lid** is closed and the **on/off switch** is switched on, the elements heat the bowl to the temperature selected by the **temperature control**.

2 While the oil is approaching the operating temperature, a **neon indicator** comes on. When the required temperature is reached, a thermostat (see Toaster, page 144) turns off the element and the neon indicator. The fryer is now ready for use.

6 When the food is cooked, the unit is switched off, the lid opened and the basket lifted from the oil to allow it to drain.

5 The heat causes the water molecules in the food to boil. Steam from the bowl passes through a filter in the lid, to remove cooking odours and oil vapour, and exits through ventilation holes in the lid.

4 The thermostat monitors cooking temperature and turns the elements off or on, as required, to keep the oil hot.

3 The lid is opened, using the **lid release button**. The food is placed in the **basket**, which is then lowered into the hot oil. The **handle** is removed and the lid closed. Some models have a **window** so the cooking process can be viewed.

Window

Lid

Aluminium bowl

Basket handle

Basket

Lid release button

Element

On/off switch and temperature control

Neon indicator

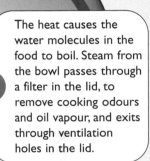

Maintenance

After each use	**Filter oil** *Unplug and allow cooker to cool for at least 30 minutes. Pour oil into sealable container through culinary filter paper and a funnel. Store for future use.* **Wash basket and bowl** *Wait until cool. Use warm, soapy water.*

Fault diagnosis

No functions	**No power** *Check mains lead, plug fuse wiring, and mains outlet for faults.*
Food overcooks	**Temperature too high** *Try reducing temperature or cooking time slightly.*
Smoke from unit	**Food residue burning** *Turn off unit and wait for oil to cool. Filter oil and clean out bowl.*

Vacuum cleaner

There are two varieties of vacuum cleaner: pull-along cylinder cleaners and push-along uprights. Apart from the shape, a major difference between the two is that the upright version has a rotating brush, called a beater, to loosen dust and dirt from the carpet, where the cylinder relies on suction.

Upright cleaner

1 In a simple upright cleaner, the **motor** drives both the **suction fan** and a **rubber belt** to drive the **brush roller**.

2 The brush roller dislodges dirt and dust in the carpet under the cleaner. The suction fan draws this over the fan and into the **dust bag**.

3 Clean air is drawn over the motor by the **cooling fan**. This air keeps the motor temperature down and then exits through vents in the top cover.

5 A mechanism detects the decrease in air pressure caused by blockages in the bag and the vents, and warns when the bag is full.

4 Dirt and dust is trapped and settles in the dust bag while the air passes through the twin surfaces of the bag, which act as a filter.

Dust bag

Dirt inlet

Electric motor

Suction fan

Brush roller

Cooling fan

Rubber belt

Cylinder cleaner

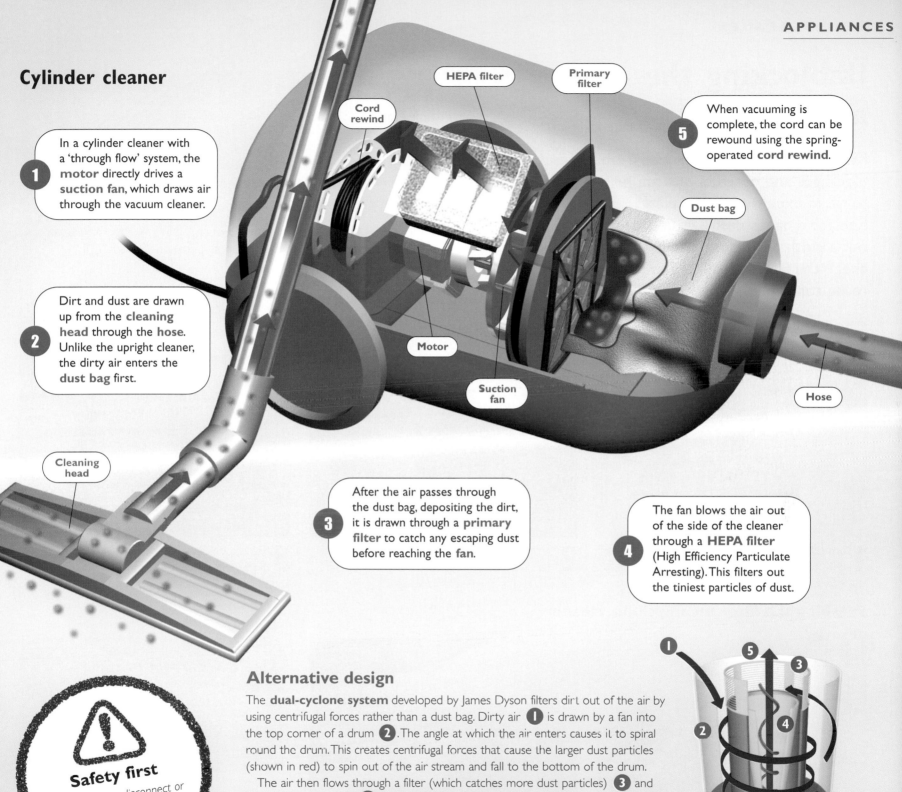

1 In a cylinder cleaner with a 'through flow' system, the **motor** directly drives a **suction fan**, which draws air through the vacuum cleaner.

2 Dirt and dust are drawn up from the **cleaning head** through the **hose**. Unlike the upright cleaner, the dirty air enters the **dust bag** first.

Cord rewind

HEPA filter

Primary filter

5 When vacuuming is complete, the cord can be rewound using the spring-operated **cord rewind**.

Dust bag

Motor

Suction fan

Hose

Cleaning head

3 After the air passes through the dust bag, depositing the dirt, it is drawn through a **primary filter** to catch any escaping dust before reaching the **fan**.

4 The fan blows the air out of the side of the cleaner through a **HEPA filter** (High Efficiency Particulate Arresting). This filters out the tiniest particles of dust.

Safety first

Always unplug, disconnect or isolate any appliance when carrying out cleaning or maintenance.

Alternative design

The **dual-cyclone system** developed by James Dyson filters dirt out of the air by using centrifugal forces rather than a dust bag. Dirty air **1** is drawn by a fan into the top corner of a drum **2**. The angle at which the air enters causes it to spiral round the drum. This creates centrifugal forces that cause the larger dust particles (shown in red) to spin out of the air stream and fall to the bottom of the drum.

The air then flows through a filter (which catches more dust particles) **3** and into a conical cylinder **4**, which is housed within the drum. The angle at which the air enters and the sloping walls of the cylinder combine to cause the air, containing the smallest dust particles (shown in blue), to spin down to the bottom of the cone at an increasing speed. Centrifugal forces acting on the air stream increase, forcing the dust particles against the sides of the cone and through the hole in the bottom of the cone, while the air escapes up the centre **5**.

Dual-cyclone system

149

Unblocking the airways

Keeping a vacuum cleaner free from blockages and obstructions can help to avoid expensive repair bills. Replace a paper dust bag, or clean out a cloth bag before it is full and check the filters regularly. Do not reuse paper bags.

Maintenance

Every three months	**Test bag full indicator** *Put hand over end of hose to reduce air pressure and simulate 'bag full' conditions.* **Check hose for blockages** *Unscrew and examine ends of tubing for fluff obstructions. Drop coin through hose to locate internal blockages.* **Clean roller on upright cleaners** *Also, check for threads or hair wrapped around shaft or belt and remove by cutting carefully.*
Every six months	**Change filters and bag on 'through flow' systems** *Over time, filters get blocked and this reduces vacuum cleaner efficiency and can cause motor to overheat.* **A** **Wash filters on a cyclonic cleaner** **B**
Every six bag changes	**Replace exhaust filters** *If cleaner has an HEPA (High Efficiency Particulate Arresting) exhaust filter, change it regularly.*

Changing filters and bag

1 Turn off the cleaner and unplug it. Then open the HEPA filter compartment and replace the filter. You may have to undo a retaining screw.

2 Replace the primary filter with a new one. If the filters were badly clogged, check the tubes and ducts leading to the bag for blockages.

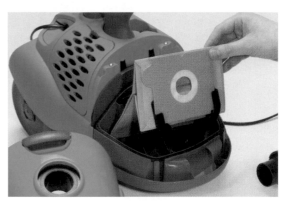

3 Replace the bag with the correct type for your model. Make sure it is clipped in place properly and that the hose fits snugly when the lid closes.

Washing the filter on a cyclonic cleaner

1 Unplug the vacuum cleaner. Then unclip and open the filter cover, and carefully lift out the circular filter container.

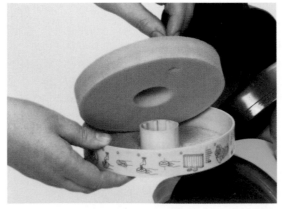

2 Grip the tab and lift out the foam filter from the container. Wash with a mild detergent then rinse and dry thoroughly before replacing.

Use the correct parts

Never use a vacuum cleaner component, bag or filter which is damaged.

Also, avoid low-cost alternative replacement bags and filters as these may not perform as well as the original manufacturer's parts.

Listening for warning signs

Upright cleaners can suffer from damage to the fan blades, since the dirt and debris passes directly from the floor over the fan.

Avoid vacuuming coins or hard objects, which could cause problems. If the cleaner is labouring or making an unusual noise, switch it off and unplug it immediately, then check the bag, filters and tube for blockages.

Fault diagnosis

No functions	**No power to appliance** *Check flex, plug fuse and wiring, and mains outlet for faults.* **Flex worn** *Make sure vacuum cleaner flex is not damaged. Replace if it is.*
Brush roller not turning	**Wrong setting** *Check that brush is in carpet mode.* **Wrong brush height** *Change setting.* **Hair or threads wrapped around brush** *Use a comb to remove hair and lint from brush. Use a sharp knife to cut threads and hairs wrapped around the shaft.* **Broken drive belt** *Replace drive belt with the correct part, and check for obstructions.*
Poor or no suction	**Bag full** *Replace bag.* **Blocked pipes** *Check all tubes for obstructions. Remove as necessary.* **Clogged filters** *Check and replace. (See manufacturer's manual for specific details).* **A** **Leaky hose** *Check and replace.*
Flex won't rewind	**Flex tangled** *Pull out all the way and untangle flex.* **Spring broken** *Contact qualified repairer.*
Noisy operation	**Faulty drive belt** *Replace drive belt.* **A** **Motor dirty** *Contact qualified repairer.* **Fan broken** *Contact qualified repairer.* **Obstruction** *Check fan area, tubes and ducts for clogging. Clean if necessary.*

Replacing the drive belt

1 Turn off and unplug the vacuum cleaner. Remove the front panel to give access to the motor spindle (this may unclip or have retaining screws).

2 Unclip the drive belt from the motor spindle. Lift out the roller brush, clean the bearings, replace the belt and reassemble.

Carpet cleaner

Designed to deep-clean carpets and remove stains, carpet cleaners pump a mixture of water and detergent into the carpet, and immediately draw the dirty water out for disposal.

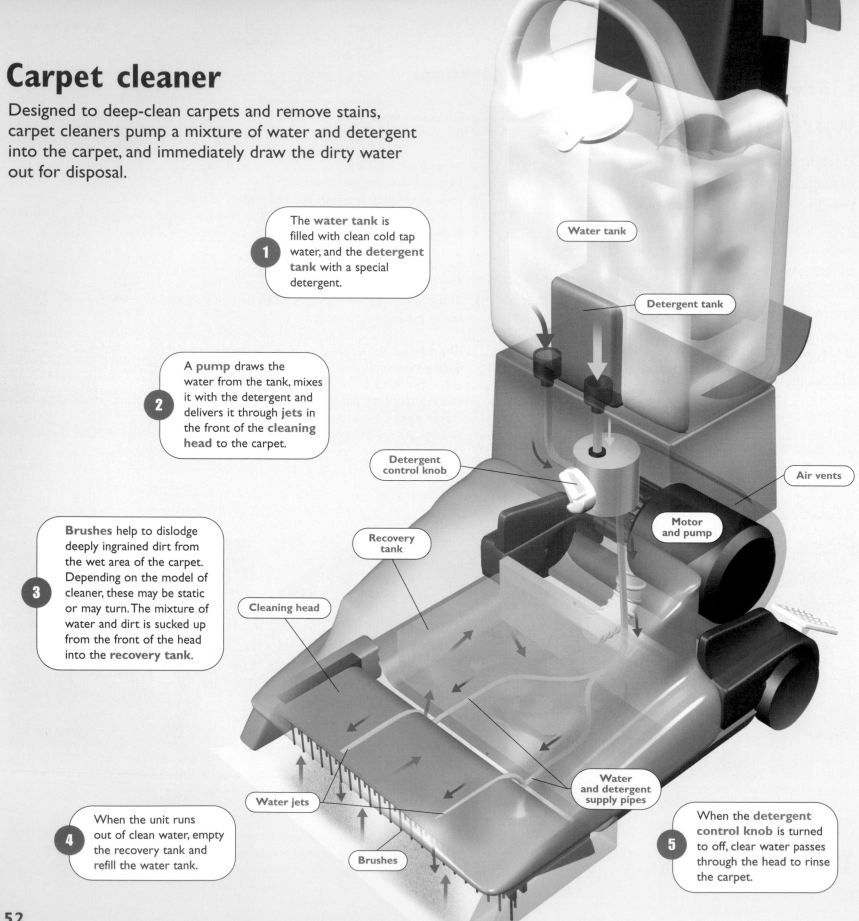

1 The **water tank** is filled with clean cold tap water, and the **detergent tank** with a special detergent.

2 A **pump** draws the water from the tank, mixes it with the detergent and delivers it through **jets** in the front of the **cleaning head** to the carpet.

3 **Brushes** help to dislodge deeply ingrained dirt from the wet area of the carpet. Depending on the model of cleaner, these may be static or may turn. The mixture of water and dirt is sucked up from the front of the head into the **recovery tank**.

4 When the unit runs out of clean water, empty the recovery tank and refill the water tank.

5 When the **detergent control knob** is turned to off, clear water passes through the head to rinse the carpet.

Water tank

Detergent tank

Air vents

Detergent control knob

Motor and pump

Recovery tank

Cleaning head

Water and detergent supply pipes

Water jets

Brushes

Alternative design

Cylinder carpet cleaners work on the
same principle as upright models. Cold water
and detergent are mixed and poured into a
storage tank **1**. As the carpet is cleaned,
this mixture flows down a thin pipe **2** to a
wide cleaning head **3** and into the fibres,
and is immediately drawn back **4** up and
into the body of the unit **5**. Once inside
the unit, the air stream enters a wider area,
which causes it to slow down. The drop in
speed causes the dirt and liquid droplets to
fall out of the air stream and into the tank.
A float **6** blocks a hole when the tank is
full, and so protects the motor **7** from
water. The motor blows the air out of vents
on the top on the unit **8**. To empty the
tank, you have to remove the lid and tip its
contents down the drain. Some newer
models have drain valves or spouts to make
them easier to empty. Cylinder carpet
cleaners can be larger than upright models
and have wide set wheels to prevent them
tipping over.

To cleaning head

From cleaning head

General precautions

With any type of carpet cleaner, always
test a carpet cleaning solution on a
hidden area of carpet before using.
Protect damp carpet from rust stains by
standing furniture with metal legs on
aluminium foil or plastic bags.

Vacuuming with a carpet cleaner

Some carpet cleaners can be used for conventional 'dry'
vacuum cleaning. For dry cleaning they are fitted with a finer
filter to remove dust and dirt. This will usually need to be
removed for wet cleaning. Some models are fitted with a
washable, reusable filter, which doesn't need to be changed
for small spills, although this must still be removed for larger
jobs such as cleaning an entire carpet.

Cleaning the brushes

Hairs and dirt can collect on the brushes and drag across the carpet. Clean with a stiff-haired brush.

Emptying the recovery tank

Remove the recovery tank and unscrew the plug from the back. Empty the tank and flush out with warm water.

Clearing the filters

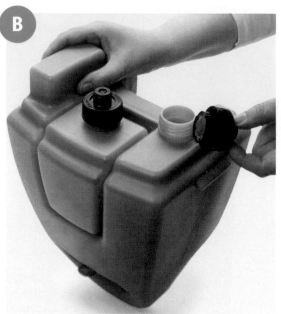

Remove the water tank and unscrew the inlet plug. The filter is behind the plug. Clean the filter with a washing up brush.

Unblocking the pipe

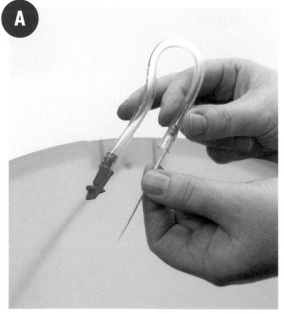

Poke out any debris with a toothpick or pipe cleaner, being careful not to puncture the pipe. Clean with warm water and a little mild detergent.

Maintenance

After each use	**Clean head and brushes** *Check brushes regularly, as long hairs and fibres can collect in head.* **A** **Check and clear filter** **B** **Detach and clean recovery tank** *Rinse tank thoroughly and check no debris or hair is left inside.* **C**

Fault diagnosis

No functions	**No power** *Check mains lead, plug fuse and mains supply.*
No water flow	**Pump failure** *Contact qualified repairer.* **Pump belt broken or drive shaft clogged with carpet fibres or hair** *Make sure unit is turned off, disconnected from mains and cool. Remove any debris, or replace belt if broken.* **Blockage in pipe or filters** *Check and clean filters. Disconnect pipes and flush.* **A** *Use descaler if mineral deposits are a problem in your area.*
Brushes not turning	**Dirt, hair or fibres wrapped around spindle** *Turn unit off and disconnect from mains. Check for dirt, hair or objects wrapped around spindle. Remove brush if possible. If not, use a scrubbing brush to clean.*
Detergent not getting to carpet	**Detergent tank empty** *Fill with recommended detergent.* **Unit on wrong setting** *Make sure detergent control knob on cleaner is in 'on' position setting to clean and not rinse.*

Electric heater

A portable electric heater employs a basic fan to blow air over heated elements and out into the room, creating up to 3kW of heat. The heater can be controlled by a thermostat to maintain a constant temperature in a small area.

Thermostat control knob

5 When the thermostat detects the room temperature has reached the set level, it turns the heater off until the temperature drops.

Air inlet grille

Heat level knob and on/off switch

Heating elements

Fan blades

Fan motor

Air outlet grille

1 When the power is turned on and the **thermostat knob** set at a temperature higher than that of the room, power is supplied to the **heating elements** and the **fan motor**.

4 As air is blown over the elements, it is heated, then vented via an **air outlet grille** at the front of the heater. The degree of warming is controlled by a **heat level knob**, which varies the amount of current supplied to the elements. The air near the motor is not heated and keeps the motor cool.

3 The heating elements are made of NiChrome (an alloy of nickel and chromium), which is a poor conductor of electricity. When an electrical current is passed through the elements, resistance to the current makes them heat up and glow.

2 The motor directly turns the **fan blades**, drawing air through an **air inlet grille** in the housing and blowing it over the heating elements.

The dangers of dust

Air is constantly moving around heaters, even those without fans, so dust and dirt can build up quickly. This can affect the efficiency of the heater and cause it to generate unpleasant smells when first turned on. It is also a potential fire risk.

Safety warning

If incorrectly used, electric heaters can be a fire hazard. As well as keeping the heater free of dust, you must be careful not to cover either the inlet or outlet grille of the heater, or position the heater too close to any flammable items such as curtains or bedspreads. Avoid plugging the heater into a mains multi-plug adaptor.

Maintenance

Once every six months

Clean radiant heater reflectors *Dust or dirt on reflector affects heater's efficiency, and poses a fire risk.* **A**

Clean convection heater vents and filters *Make sure dust does not accumulate around air intake and outlet. Keep possible obstructions well clear.*

Lubricate motor *Apply a drop of light machine oil to motor spindle and bearings as recommended by manufacturer.* **A**

Alternative design

An **oil-filled radiator** is better for heating a large area than a bar fire. This is a sealed unit, filled with a diathermic oil ❶, a liquid that transmits heat easily. The oil is heated by an element ❷, which is controlled by a thermostat and controller ❸ so that a comfortable temperature can be maintained. Hot oil rises, setting up a circulation within the columns of the radiator and heating its surfaces.

Cooler ceramic

Some fan heaters use ceramic elements. These can operate at lower temperatures while still producing ample heat, and are therefore safer because they do not get as hot.

Cleaning radiant heaters

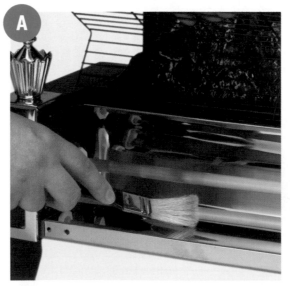

1 Unplug the heater and allow it to cool down. Unscrew and take off the protective metal grille. Remove any dust from the heater elements with a clean soft brush.

2 Clean both the grille and the reflective plate with a non-flammable metal polish – do not spray it directly onto the elements and make sure no polish residue is left anywhere on the heater. Carefully reassemble the grille and heater, and tighten the retaining screws.

Allow it to cool

Before attempting any repair or maintenance tasks on an electric heater, you should first switch it off and unplug it from the mains supply. Then leave it to stand for at least half an hour to allow it to cool.

Fixing a noisy fan

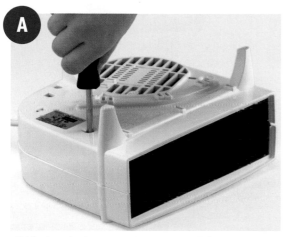

A

1 Unplug the heater and make sure it has cooled down. Screws to retain the top or bottom should be underneath the heater. Unscrew the casing and open it carefully.

Fault diagnosis

No heat, fan not turning	**No power to appliance** *Check flex, plug wiring, fuse and mains outlet for faults.* **Faulty control switches** *Contact qualified repairer.* **Faulty thermostat** *Contact qualified repairer.* **Loose connections** *Open casing and check connections are secure.*
No heat, fan turning	**Controls set for 'Cold Air'** *Select a heat setting.* **Heating element faulty** *Contact qualified repairer.* **Faulty control switches** *Contact qualified repairer.* **Thermostat tripped** *Reset if possible, or allow fan to cool.*
Heat for short period, fan not turning	**Fan blades obstructed** *Clean fan blades and remove obstruction.* **Faulty fan motor** *Contact qualified repairer.*
Low heat	**Faulty control switches** *Contact qualified repairer.* **Faulty thermostat** *Contact qualified repairer.* **One or more heating elements broken** *Contact qualified repairer.*
Fan noisy and running slowly	**Motor bearings dry** *Disassemble fan heater and lubricate moving parts with suitable lubricant.* **A** **Dust and dirt on bearings or blades** *Clean interior (see **A**, step 3).*
Burning smell	**Dirty elements, grille and reflector on radiant heater** *Clean heater.* **A** **Dust on coiled element** *Clean interior (see **A**, step 3).*

2 Remove the fan and add one drop of lubricating oil to the shaft of the motor. Turn the shaft back and forth a few times to distribute the oil.

3 Clean any dust off the fan blades with a soft clean brush, and use a vacuum cleaner on low power to clean inside the heater. Do not touch the elements.

Shaver

Modern shavers use a reciprocating or rotating action to cut hair, and run on mains power or rechargeable batteries. Both types of shaver cut by trapping the hair between a moving and fixed blade (the foil).

5 A **battery indicator** on the shaver's casing shows how much charge is left in the battery.

4 The flip-out **beard trimmer** is used for longer hair, such as sideburns. This works in the same way as a hair trimmer (see page 160).

3 Hairs pass through tiny perforations in the fixed **foil** and are sheared off by the blades on the moving **blade head**.

Blade head

Blades

Foil

1 The power **switch** is moved to the 'on' position or to an appropriate speed setting. This connects the **electric motor** to the **battery** or mains.

Electric motor

NiCad battery

Beard trimmer

Sliding on/off and speed selector switch

Battery indicator

Alternative design

Rotating head shavers cut with two or three steel discs with radial blades **1**, like the spokes of a bicycle wheel, that rotate under circular protective housings **2**. The housings have radial slots **3**, through which beard hairs poke **4**. Because the angle of each blade is slightly different from that of the slot, a shearing action snips the hair neatly.

Maintenance

After each use	**Open shaver head and shake out shavings** *Clean blade head with dry brush.* **A**
When necessary	**Lubricate** *Apply light machine oil or proprietary shaver lubricant to foil and blade head.*

Cleaning the blades

A

2 The motor drives a cam and eccentric crank mechanism, similar to that in an electric sander (see page 262), which moves the blades rapidly from side to side.

Unplug the shaver. Remove the foil section by squeezing the buttons on either side of the unit. Place somewhere safe. Use the brush supplied with the unit to brush hairs from between the blades. Replace foil carefully.

Fault diagnosis

Shaver does not work	**No power** *Check mains flex, plug, adapter fuse and socket outlet for faults.* **Battery discharged** *Recharge battery.*
Poor shave	**Dirty shaving head** *Clean head.* **A** **Foil worn or damaged** *Replace.*
Slow action	**Low battery** *Recharge battery.* **Worn motor** *Contact qualified repairer.*

Hair dryer

The most common problems with hair dryers are caused by dust and hair clogging the air intakes and motor bearings.

Motor

Heating elements

Inlet grille

Intake filter

Fan

Insulated case

Switches

1 A small **motor** drives a **fan** directly. This draws air through an **intake filter** and blows it over **heating elements**.

2 Many hair dryers have **switches** to change motor speeds and heat settings.

3 If the dryer gets too hot, a thermal cut-out switches it off.

4 The cut-out resets when the hair dryer cools. On some models it must be reset manually.

Unjamming the motor

A Unplug the hair dryer and allow it to cool. Unclip the inlet grille and remove the casing screws. Note the position of screws and parts for reassembly. Using a toothpick or tweezers, remove hair and debris around motor and fan bearings. Gently clean dust from the elements with a clean paintbrush and reassemble.

Unclogging the filter

1 Unplug the dryer and allow to cool. Twist off the rear grille (there may be a retaining screw).

2 Take out the air intake filter and use fingers or a soft brush to gently remove hair, lint and debris.

Maintenance

Once a month	**Clear intake screen** If filter becomes clogged, motor cannot draw sufficient air through to cool elements and thermal cut-out will trip. **A**
Every six months	**Check flex and plug for damage** Pay attention to where lead enters dryer and plug. Movement of dryer makes these areas susceptible to damage. Repair as necessary.

Fault diagnosis

No heat but fan running	**Thermal cut-out tripped** Clean air intake. **A** Reset manual cut-out, if necessary, or wait for automatic reset. **Element broken** Replace or contact qualified repairer.
Dryer keeps cutting out	**Thermostat faulty** Replace or contact qualified repairer. **Blocked intake filter** Check and clean.
Nothing works	**Fuse blown** Open plug and change fuse. **Faulty flex** Check flex and connections for damage.
Element hot, no air	**Motor or fan jammed** Open dryer and check motor and fan bearings for threads or lint. **A**

Hair trimmer

A hair trimmer uses a solenoid similar to that in a simple doorbell (see page 94) to move the blades back and forth.

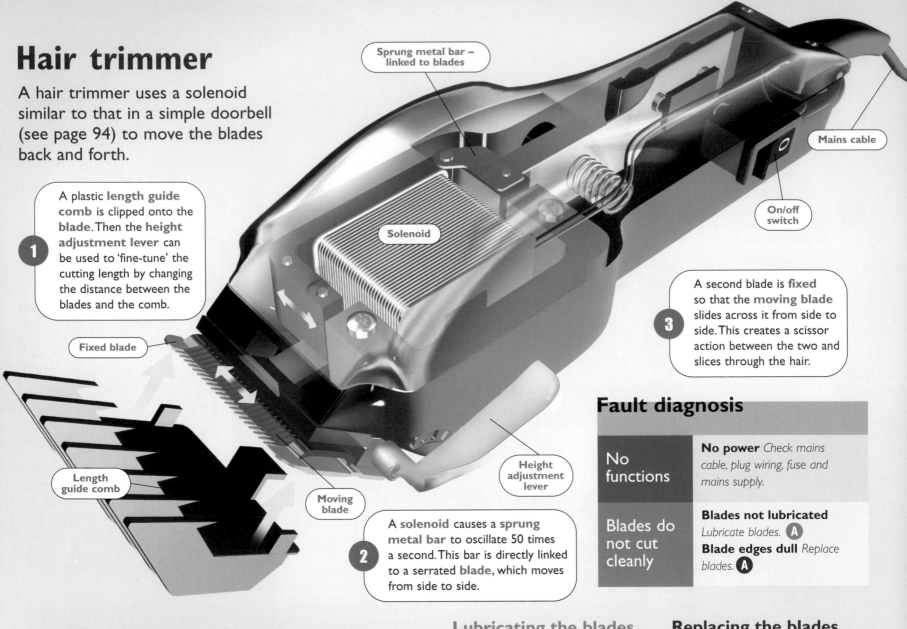

Sprung metal bar – linked to blades

Mains cable

Solenoid

On/off switch

① A plastic length guide comb is clipped onto the **blade**. Then the **height adjustment lever** can be used to 'fine-tune' the cutting length by changing the distance between the blades and the comb.

Fixed blade

Length guide comb

Moving blade

Height adjustment lever

③ A second blade is fixed so that the **moving blade** slides across it from side to side. This creates a scissor action between the two and slices through the hair.

② A solenoid causes a **sprung metal bar** to oscillate 50 times a second. This bar is directly linked to a serrated **blade**, which moves from side to side.

Fault diagnosis

No functions	**No power** *Check mains cable, plug wiring, fuse and mains supply.*
Blades do not cut cleanly	**Blades not lubricated** *Lubricate blades.* **A** **Blade edges dull** *Replace blades.* **A**

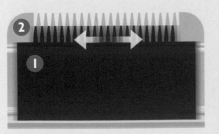

The cutting action

The upper blade **①** moves from side to side 50 times a second. As it slides against the lower blade **②**, hairs are trapped between the two cutting edges and neatly severed.

Maintenance

After each use	**Clean comb and blades** *Gently brush all hair and debris from comb and blades with soft, clean brush, and wipe down case.*
Every few uses	**Lubricate blades** **A**

Lubricating the blades

A

Using a lubricant recommended by the manufacturer, apply a few drops across the blade edges. Let the trimmer run for a few seconds to disperse the oil.

Replacing the blades

A

Undo the blade retaining screw and remove the blunt blades. Fit the correct blades for the model, and replace the retaining screw.

Bathroom scales

Mechanical bathroom scales employ a simple mechanism to translate the downward force of a person standing on the platform to the rotary motion of a dial, which has a printed scale.

Spring and spring plate

Pivot

4 An **adjusting knob** enables the user to set the dial at zero. This moves the spring plate up and down, and so adjusts the starting position of the rack when the scales are at rest.

Receiving levers

Adjusting knob

1 The **platform** rests on four **receiving levers**, which distribute the weight evenly. Two of the levers are pivoted, with one end resting on the outer edge of the case and the other on the **spring plate**.

Dial

Window on dial

Receiving levers

Rack

Pinion

Alternative design

Although they look much like their mechanical counterparts, **electronic bathroom scales** have a liquid crystal display instead of the mechanical dial. Electronic bathroom scales work using a device which converts force into a change in an electric current. A microprocessor calculates the weight based on the amount of electricity conducted.

Rack spring

2 The platform rests in notches very near the pivots of the levers, reducing the pressure on the **spring** holding the spring **plate** to around a twelfth of the weight on the platform.

Platform

3 As the spring plate moves down, a **pivot** converts the vertical motion into the horizontal motion of the **rack**. This engages a cog, called the **pinion**, which turns the **dial**.

Maintenance

To ensure accurate measurement, keep scales on a firm, level surface and not on a rug or carpet.

As required	**Recalibrate scales** *Repeated use or jarring of scales can lead to inaccuracy. Use adjusting knob to reset the scales to zero.*

Lubricating the scales

Remove the top cover and apply light lubricating oil to the rack and pinion and pivot. Check that no dirt or debris is obstructing the mechanism.

Fault diagnosis

Digital scales cannot be repaired. If the spring or a lever breaks in a mechanical scale, replace the unit.

Scales sticking	**Moving parts jammed** *Lubricate moving parts.* Ⓐ
Inaccurate measuring	**Faulty spring** *Reset scale to zero and check with heavy kitchen weights. If weight is not accurately displayed, replace unit.*
Scale will not zero	**Faulty adjustment mechanism** *Buy a new set of scales.*

Extractor fan

Installed in kitchens for removing cooking smells, or in bathrooms to expel moist air, extractor fans are simple devices that create an airflow to the outside.

Piping air to the outside

Extractor fans can be mounted in walls, windows or ceilings. Fans in bathrooms are often fixed in the ceiling **①** directly above the shower **②** , and the air exits through a duct (wide pipe) **③** in the loft, terminating in an outlet grille **④** . Regulations state that extractor fans must be positioned where they draw the replacement air (usually from the doorway of the room) over the source of the moisture or smells. There must be no socket outlets in bathrooms, so an extractor must be wired via an FCU, which must not have a switch if it is within reach of the bath or shower – a ceiling switch is used to control the fan if it has no built-in cord pull switch. Where a bathroom does not have an openable window, the extractor must be wired to come on automatically when the light is turned on, and stay on for at least 15 minutes after it is turned off.

① When the **cord switch** is pulled, electricity is supplied to the **motor**. In some bathroom versions, when the light switch is pulled, a power line from the switch turns the fan on. The fan has its own power supply and turns off after a period set by a timer.

② The electric motor directly spins the **fan blades**. These are angled so that air from the room is directed outside through a vent in a wall, window or ceiling.

Electric motor

Shutters

Cord switch

Safety warning

With all electrical devices that work near water, such as heated towel rails and extractor fans fitted in bathrooms, installation must comply with electrical safety rules. All appliances must be wired via an unswitched fused connection unit (FCU), which in turn is connected to a ceiling switch inside the bathroom. For more information on electricity, see Safety, page 20.

3 The airflow through the vent as the motor turns causes internal **shutters** to open. Air flows from the room through the **outside grille**.

Outside grille

Fan blades

Maintenance

Once a week	**Kitchen fan** *Wipe blades and vents to remove grease and dust build-up.*
Once a month	**Bathroom fan** *Clean blades and vents to prevent mould build-up.*

Fault diagnosis

Although fans should be connected via an FCU to the mains supply, in some cases this may not have been done in accordance with regulations. If you are in any doubt about isolating the fan, turn off the MCBs (or remove the fuses) for all circuits, then test that the fan has no power before starting any repairs.

Broken pull cord	**Replace cord** *Some models don't have a cord.*
Fan time wrong	**Trimmer out of adjustment** *Turn unit off and adjust trimmer screw.* **A**
Noisy operation	**Blades catch or shutters rattle** *Adjust.* **Motor bearings worn** *Have unit replaced.*

Adjusting the trimmer screw

A

Extractor fans in enclosed bathrooms should run for 15 minutes before turning off automatically. To adjust the fan operating time, turn off the power, and locate and adjust the trimmer screw according to the manufacturer's instructions.

Ventilation regulations

The most important issue when fixing an extractor fan is a source of replaceable air. If a fan is to be fitted in a room with a fuel-burning appliance, building regulations must be adhered to, and wiring must be done in accord with IEEE (Institute of Electrical & Electronics Engineers) regulations. Ducting must be insulated if it passes through a roof space. If in doubt on any of these issues, consult a professional.

Electric toothbrush

Dentists recommend electric toothbrushes over conventional fixed head types. The regular movement of the brush head is perfectly suited to removing plaque and bacteria. Some versions even use ultrasonic waves to remove plaque and reduce gingivitis.

How the brush charges up

When any electrical item is used in close proximity to water, there is an electric shock hazard. For this reason, neither the toothbrush nor its charger unit can have exposed metal connections. Instead, power is transferred to the rechargeable battery in the brush by electromagnetic induction. This is the same process by which transformers work. A small alternating current derived from the mains supply is passed through a coil in the charger unit **1**. This energises the bar protruding from the charger unit's base with an alternating electromagnetic field. When the toothbrush is placed onto the charger unit, a small coil in the base of the brush **2** fits over the charger unit's bar, and receives energy from the alternating electromagnetic field.

1 The **rechargeable battery** drives a small electric **motor**, which is controlled by a **switch**. Some models have a timer that turns the toothbrush off, or gives an audible indication, after a recommended brushing period, typically 2–3 minutes.

2 The motor turns a **drive shaft** and gears which transfer the motion to the brush head. This may be a back-and-forth rotary motion or the head may vibrate or oscillate.

3 The brush heads are removable, so that different members of the family can use the same electric toothbrush unit, and so that the heads can be replaced regularly.

Switch

Motor

Charger coil

Rechargeable battery

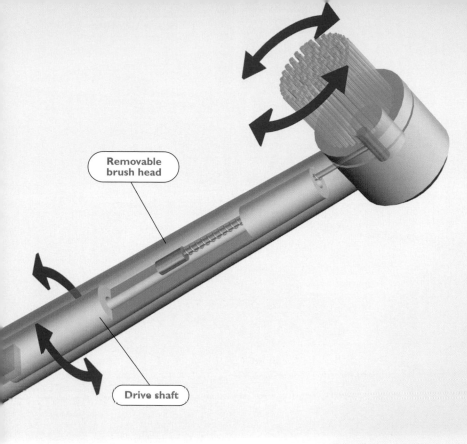

Removable brush head

Drive shaft

Alternative design

The principle behind a **sonic toothbrush** is similar to a musical tuning fork. The head of the toothbrush is not moved by mechanical parts such as gears, drive shafts, or levers. Instead it is 'tuned' or balanced so that it will resonate from side to side when it is exposed to vibration. This is generated by an extremely high-speed motor spinning at 250 revolutions per second. The vibration of the toothbrush head creates 31,000 cleaning strokes a minute, more than ten times that of a standard electric toothbrush. This high speed scrubbing disintegrates plaque and bacteria, even between teeth and below the gum line.

Rinsing the brush head

A

Toothbrush head designs vary, but all have holes to allow excess toothpaste and debris to be rinsed away. Hold the head under a running tap to clean it.

Electricity in the bathroom

The charger unit for an electric toothbrush is designed to plug into a shaver socket. The supply from this type of socket is isolated from the mains, making it safe for use in the bathroom. Only sockets that conform to British Standard BS3535 are suitable for bathroom use.

Maintenance

After each use	**Wash head** *Flush warm water through the cleaning holes on the toothbrush head to remove debris.* **A**
Every week	**Recharge toothbrush's battery**
Every month	**Clean charger post** *If post is covered with debris, brush will not sit correctly on base unit and charging will be impaired. Clean with water, detergent and a cloth.* **Clean charger port** *Keep charger port on toothbrush base clear of dried toothpaste.*
Every three months	**Replace brush heads** *Do this frequently if they are worn.*

Fault diagnosis

Battery not charging	**No power** *Check mains lead, adapter plug and mains outlet for faults.* **Dirt on charger or brush port** *Clean with water and mild detergent.* **Rechargeable battery faulty** *Replace unit.*
Nothing functions	**Battery not charging** *See above.* **Charger unit faulty** *Replace unit.* **Brush motor or battery faulty** *Replace unit.*

Sewing machine

The modern sewing machine is capable of hundreds of types of stitches and embroidery. However, the sewing mechanism still works by simply looping the needle thread around a thread from a bobbin below.

Needle tightener

Presser foot

Needle

Needle plate

Feed dogs

Shuttle hook

Bobbin

Shuttle

Rotating cam

1 All motorised sewing machines are controlled by a sprung foot pedal. The position of the pedal precisely controls the speed of the **motor** inside the sewing machine using an electronic circuit.

2 The motor drives all the mechanical parts of the machine via a rubber **drive belt**. The rotating motion is transferred through a series of levers and gears to the up-and-down and side-to-side motion of the **needle** and the operation of the **feed dogs** and **bobbin**. The **presser foot** holds the material flat while the feed dogs move it along.

The thread path

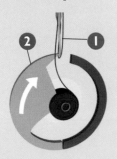

Each stitch starts with the needle pushing a loop of thread **1** through the material and below the needle plate. This loop is grabbed by the shuttle hook **2**.

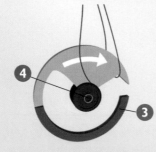

The shuttle is pushed round by a cam **3**, driven from the motor. As the shuttle rotates, it drags the loop of thread over the shuttle and bobbin **4**.

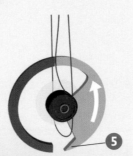

When the shuttle completes half a turn **5**, the cam reverses direction. The loop slips off the hook and is pulled up around the bobbin and thread.

The shuttle and bobbin start to turn back. The thread-tightening arm pulls the looped needle and bobbin threads **6** tightly together into a stitch.

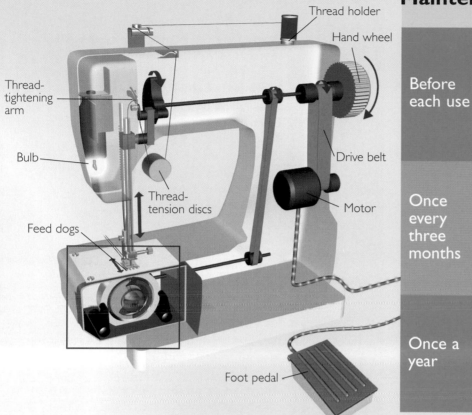

Thread holder

Hand wheel

Thread-tightening arm

Bulb

Thread-tension discs

Feed dogs

Drive belt

Motor

Foot pedal

Maintenance

Before each use	**Check needle is correct type for job** *Test on a scrap of the fabric you intend to use at appropriate tension. Make sure needle is not bent, blunt or scratched. Using an incorrect or worn needle can impair efficiency and even damage the sewing machine's timing.* **Check power cables** *Check that power flex, foot pedal and main unit are correctly connected.*
Once every three months	**Remove lint and dust from thread-tension discs** *A sewing machine is precisely engineered and, without regular cleaning, can quickly start to run badly* **A**. *Keep feed dogs and shuttle clean of lint.* **(see B, page 168)** **Run sewing machine for a short time** *If you don't use your sewing machine regularly, run it for a few minutes to keep the parts lubricated.*
Once a year	**Oil moving parts** *Sewing machines contain many moving metal cams and gears, and these need to be lubricated. Make sure you use correct oil and grease, and that you apply only where indicated. Some sewing machines don't need lubrication so check manual first. Sew a few stitches afterwards to remove any excess oil.* **(see C, page 168)**

5 The type of stitch is normally selected by a dial or buttons. In a computerised sewing machine, there may be individual motors for the needle and feed dogs, and a touch-sensitive colour screen to program patterns.

4 A **bobbin** under the needle plate contains a separate thread. The **shuttle hook** grabs the loop of thread from the needle and passes it over the bobbin to form the stitch.

3 Thread passes from a reel on top of the sewing machine through the **thread-tightening arm** and a tensioning device to the **needle**. The needle lowers as the arm releases the tension, pushing the thread through the fabric. This allows a loop to form under the needle plate (see left).

Cleaning thread-tension discs

A

1 Unplug the machine and remove the front casing around the thread-tension assembly.

2 Slide a small piece of paper or a toothpick between the discs of the thread-tension assembly to clean out any lint or dust.

Cleaning the feed dogs

Raise the presser foot and remove the needle and needle plate. Brush out lint from the shuttle and use tweezers to remove debris from the feed dogs. If necessary, remove the feed dogs by unscrewing the retaining screws.

Changing the drive belt

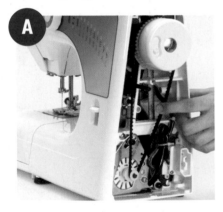

Unplug the sewing machine, then unscrew and take off the rear panel. Remove the broken or worn drive belt and discard. Replace the belt with the correct part for your model of sewing machine. Check that the teeth are engaged in the cogs and reassemble the unit.

Oiling the moving parts

Clean lint and dust from the moving parts. Then remove the access panels and apply a few drops of high-quality sewing machine lubricant to the lubrication points. Check your manual for specific details.

Fault diagnosis

Does not function	**Power fault** *Check plug fuse, wiring and mains lead.* **Internal component fault** *Contact qualified repairer.*
Motor working but needle not moving	**Worn drive belt** *Replace drive belt with identical part.* **A** **Loose drive belt** *Reposition motor to tension drive belt.* **Mechanism too stiff** *Try cleaning and lubricating as directed in manual.* **C**
Motor not working	**Power fault** *Check plug fuse, wiring and mains lead.* **Problem with foot pedal** *Check pedal is correctly plugged in. In older models, clean contacts.* **C** **Lack of lubrication** *Lubricate as directed in manual.* **C** **Faulty motor** *Consult qualified repairer.*
Bulb not lit	**Bulb blown** *Replace.*
Skipping stitches or needle-thread breaking	**Needle worn** *Change needle, making sure you use the correct needle and thread for the material being sewn.* **Needle thread tension too high** *Reduce by adjusting the tension dial.* **Rough edges on shuttle hook** *Use emery cloth to smooth edges, Replace if badly worn.*
Breaking bobbin thread	**Shuttle installed incorrectly** *Remove and refit with shuttle hook pointing upwards. Check manual for details.* **Rough edges on needle plate** *Rub down with fine emery cloth or replace the plate.* **Shuttle dirty** *Lift plate and brush out lint.* **Shuttle thread tension too high** *Adjust.* **B**

Testing and adjusting shuttle tension

1 Without removing the bobbin from the shuttle, suspend it by the thread. The shuttle should drop 5–10cm. If it drops more, the tension is too low; less and the tension is too high.

2 Adjust the tension by turning the screw on the side of the shuttle. Make tiny adjustments one at a time and test. Clockwise increases tension, anti-clockwise decreases tension.

Cleaning the foot pedal

Unplug the sewing machine and the foot pedal cable. Unscrew the pedal cover and open the unit (taking note of how it is assembled). Brush out lint and clean the contacts or sliders with contact cleaner.

Electric blanket

The modern electric blanket detects the room and bed temperature, and automatically adjusts the heat accordingly. Some advanced models will even increase the temperature in colder areas of the bed.

3 The temperature is regulated by a **controller** unit that has a range of heat selections. If the blanket is double bed-sized, it may have two controllers and two elements.

2 The heat is conducted through the plastic and fabric of the blanket to warm the bed.

Flex

Element

Controller

1 Electric blankets generate heat using an **element**. As electricity is passed through the element, resistance causes it to heat up. In most models the element consists of a NiChrome wire wound into a tiny coil around 2mm in diameter, encased in a plastic tube.

Checking the blanket

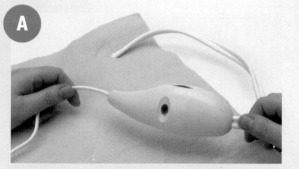

A

Check that the connections to the plug, controller unit and blanket are not loose or worn. Examine the cable for signs of wear and tear. Make sure none of the stitching on the blanket has come loose, and that the elements are in position and do not touch each other.

Safety warning ⚠

If in any doubt about the condition of an electric blanket, do not use it and contact a qualified repairer immediately.

Maintenance

Once a month	**Check the blanket** Check the flex and switch for damage or poor connections. **A**
Every three years	**Have the blanket serviced** Some local authority Trading Standards offices will check blankets that are over five years old free of charge. Otherwise, contact qualified repairer.

The controller unit

A knob **1** turns a connector onto different metallic contacts. Each selects a different heat setting. When the blanket is on, a neon or LED indicator **2** lights.

Do not overheat

Make sure your electric blanket has overheat protection and is covered by the BEAB certification mark or similar. If a blanket is over ten years old, replace it.

Clocks and watches

The majority of household clocks and watches use a quartz crystal oscillating 32,768 times per second as a timing device. Another common type of clock is the battery-powered quartz clock, which displays time using light emitting diodes (LEDs) or a liquid crystal display. Clockwork clocks are purely mechanical, and use a wound spring to drive carefully regulated cogs, which turn the clock hands.

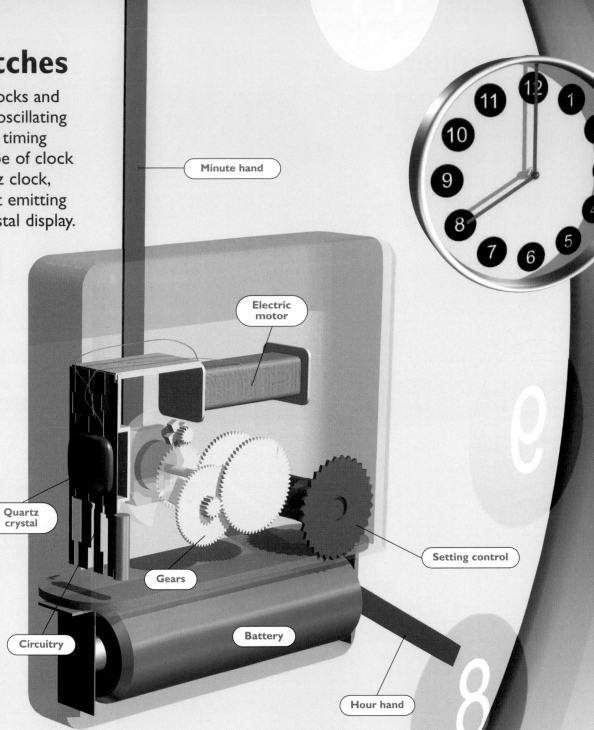

Minute hand

Electric motor

1 Electricity from a **battery** is passed through a **quartz crystal**. The current causes the crystal to vibrate at exactly 32,768 times per second.

Quartz crystal

Setting control

Gears

2 A counter measures the vibrations and sends a pulse after every 32,768 vibrations to turn the tiny **electric motor** that moves the hands.

Circuitry

Battery

Hour hand

3 A series of **gears** ensures that on each full rotation of the **minute hand**, the **hour hand** moves one hour.

Maintenance

| Once a month | **Keep case clean** *Use mild detergent on a damp cloth.* |
| Every two years | **Lubricate mechanical clocks** *Use a light lubricating oil.* **Have mechanical clocks cleaned ultrasonically** *Contact a qualified repairer.* |

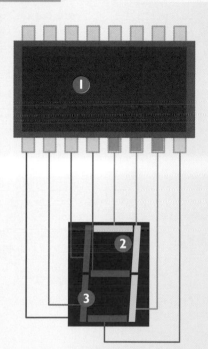

Alternative design

Many devices, including some clocks, use seven segment **light emitting diodes (LEDs)** to display the numbers. Each of the separate bars of the device will light up when powered from the chip **1**. In the diagram, three bars are lit **2** and four are not **3**. This creates the number 7.

Refitting hands

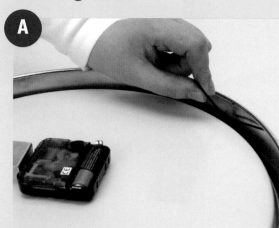

1 Prise the cover stays from the back of the case using a screwdriver if necessary.

2 Gently remove hands and replace on the stem, making sure the hands are in the correct sequence. Point both hands at the number 12 to check that they are aligned correctly.

Handling watch batteries

Be careful when replacing the battery on a watch – the contacts can be easily dislodged or broken. Never touch watch batteries with your bare fingers because the grease from your skin may reduce the life of the battery. Instead handle the battery with plastic tweezers. Take waterproof watches to a qualified repairer to have the batteries changed.

Fault diagnosis

No functions	**No power** *Check and retension battery contacts by pulling them inwards. Or, check flex, plug fuse and mains supply.* **Flat battery** *Replace battery. If the problem persists, contact qualified repairer.*
LED clock controls erratic	**Switch contacts dirty** *Clean electrical contacts with small amount of switch cleaner.*
LED/LCD display corrupted	**Faulty LED/LCD** *Contact qualified repairer or replace clock.*
Clock running slow/fast	**Wrong speed level** *(mechanical clock). Turn the speed control towards the '+' sign if clock is running too slow, or towards '–' if running too fast.* **Battery running low** *Replace if necessary.* **Trimmer capacitor on wrong setting** *Some older quartz clocks have an adjustable screw inside, which can be turned to speed up or slow down clock. If clock does not have this screw or problems persist, contact qualified repairer.*
Watch stopping	**Flat battery** *Replace battery if possible. Otherwise, contact qualified repairer.* **Hands misaligned** *If face cover can be removed, check hands are not touching each other as they pass. Otherwise, contact qualified repairer.*
Hands jammed or fallen off	**Faulty fitting** *Refit hands.* **A** *If case cannot be opened to access the hands, contact qualified repairer.*

Electric lamp

Simple electric lamps use light bulbs in different wattages to achieve various levels of brightness. Halogen bulbs give more light output for the same power.

Light fitting

Light head

Tungsten coil

Sealed glass bulb

4 As the filament heats up, it releases energy in the form of visible light. Nitrogen and/or argon gas within the bulb prevent the tungsten filament from oxidising and burning out.

1 The **switch** is moved to the 'on' position, completing an electrical circuit. Power is delivered from the mains to the **light fitting**.

2 When power enters the **sealed-glass bulb** it passes into a thin **tungsten coil**. The coil is very short, but if uncoiled would stretch to around 2m.

3 As the current passes through the filament, it excites the tungsten atoms, causing a vibration that creates heat.

Power cable

Switch

Base

Alternative design

Halogen light bulbs are longer lasting and produce a brighter and whiter light than a standard light bulb. In a halogen bulb, the tungsten filament is encased in a tiny quartz case filled with a gas from the halogen group, such as iodine. As current flows through the filament, the tungsten glows white hot, producing light and tungsten vapour **1**. The vapour reacts with the iodine gas at the bulb surface to form tungsten iodide **2**. When the tungsten iodide contacts the hot filament, it reverts to tungsten and iodine **3**.

Maintenance

Every three months	**Clean base** Unplug lamp and remove bulb. Wipe inside and outside light head, with dry cloth.

Fault diagnosis

Nothing works	**No power** Check mains lead, switch and bulb. Then check plug wiring, fuse and mains outlet for faults. **Bulb blown** Replace bulb. **A**
Light flickers	**Intermittent connection** Check bulb and plug wires are fitted securely.

Replacing a halogen bulb

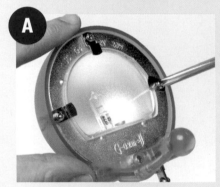

A

1 Make sure the lamp is unplugged. Check that the light head is cool by placing the back of your hand close by. Unscrew the protective glass plate. Remove the halogen bulb.

2 Never touch a halogen bulb surface with bare fingers; use a clean cloth to hold the bulb as it is fitted. Then replace the glass plate.

172

Torch

The battery-powered torch is the simplest application of an electrical circuit. Current flows from batteries via an on/off switch to a bulb.

3 On many models, a **focus collar** can be tightened or loosened to provide a wide, diffuse beam or a bright, concentrated beam.

1 When the **on/off switch** is pushed into the 'on' position it completes an electric circuit, allowing current from the **batteries** to flow through the bulb.

On/off switch

Batteries

Coiled spring contact

2 Resistance in the filament of the light **bulb** creates heat and light (see Electric lamp, page 172).

Bulb

Lens

Focus collar

Fault diagnosis

Doesn't light up	**Batteries flat** *Replace.* **Battery contacts loose** *Retension contacts.* **A** **Bulb loose** *Tighten bulb in socket.* **Bulb blown** *Replace bulb.* **B**

Retensioning contacts

A

Remove cap and take out batteries. Cut a length of string roughly twice the length of the battery chamber. Create a loop and hook it under the spiral spring contact. Pull the spring upwards.

Changing the bulb

B

Unscrew the cap. Carefully unscrew the blown bulb from the cap, replace it with a new one and reassemble the torch. Avoid touching the glass of halogen bulbs.

How a simple electric circuit works

Electrons flow from negative to positive. This is because they are negatively charged and are therefore attracted to their opposite charged terminal: positive. In an electric circuit such as a torch, electrons flow from the negative terminal **1** of the battery (see Batteries, page 174) through the switch **2** to the outer case **3** of the bulb. From here electrons flow through the filament **4** and back to the positive terminal **5** of the battery via the connector on the base of the bulb. If the switch is moved to the 'off' position, the circuit is broken.

Batteries

Whatever its shape and size, a battery generates power by using a chemical reaction. This produces electrons, which flow from a negative terminal to a positive one through the connecting wires and provide the current to power an attached device. Although different chemical combinations are used to achieve different battery characteristics and some batteries are rechargeable, the basic principle is the same.

1 A battery is lined with a chemical **paste** that acts as a **positive electrode**. Inside this is another combination that acts as a **negative electrode**.

2 The two layers are kept apart by a **separator** and are saturated in an electrolyte gel. The chemical properties of the outer layer mean that it has a lack of electrons while the inner layer has extra electrons.

Alternative designs

Button cells are either filled with silver oxide (used to power watches), or lithium (used for small appliances with long-term, low current needs). They are not rechargeable.

Lithium Ion or Lithium Polymer batteries are commonly used for devices where weight and size are an issue, such as mobile phones and laptop computers. They produces power for a relatively long period, are rechargeable and can be made very light and thin. The battery design is usually unique to each particular brand or model of phone.

NiCad (Nickel Cadmium) batteries are used for heavy-duty cordless power tools, such as drills and jigsaws. They produce a strong current, but run down relatively quickly, take time to recharge and are heavy. Their design is usually unique to the particular manufacturer.

Sealed Lead Acid batteries (typically 6 volt or 12 volt) are used in cars. They are rechargeable.

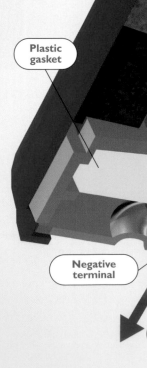

Positive terminal

Top plate

Steel case

Paste acting as negative electrode

Electrons

Collector nail

Paste acting as positive electrode

Plastic gasket

Separator (paper or fabric)

Negative terminal

3 When metal contacts are attached to the terminals of the battery cell, the **negative terminal** (attached to the **collector nail** in the inner layer) 'pumps' the extra electrons into one end of the circuit, while the **positive terminal** (attached to the outer layer) 'sucks' them from the other end. The flow of electrons around the circuit is an electrical current.

Bottom plate

5 As the active ingredients in the two layers become depleted, the chemical reactions slow down, meaning that fewer extra electrons are pumped into the circuit and fewer drawn from it. The cell has run flat when all of the active ingredients in the two paste layers have been used up.

4 The **electrons** 'sucked' into the positive terminal are absorbed by the outer layer, where they cause a chemical reaction called 'reduction'. This sends negatively charged ions through the electrolyte solution from the outer layer to the inner layer. Here, they cause a chemical reaction in the inner layer called 'oxidisation', which creates additional electrons to flow into the circuit.

Safe storage

To avoid battery leakage, remove batteries from any device that won't be used for long periods.

Maintenance

Once a month	**'Deep discharge' NiCad rechargeable batteries** *Use device until battery is completely flat and then recharge overnight.*

Recharging batteries

A

If no recharger was supplied with the batteries, obtain one from an electrical store. Make sure it is the right rating for the batteries to be recharged. Place the batteries in the unit and leave until the LED indicates they are fully charged.

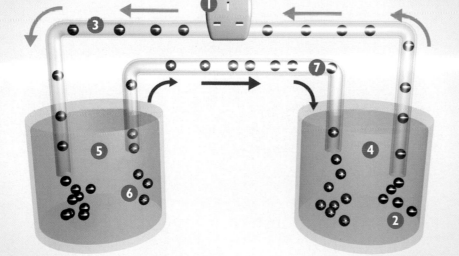

Recharging a battery

The difference between a standard and a rechargeable battery is that power can be 'put back' into a rechargeable cell by restoring the active materials that have been depleted. Most rechargeable batteries can be re-used up to 1000 times. Attaching the batteries to a mains transformer **1** reverses the normal current. This means that the electrons **2** flow through the wire **3** from the positive electrode **4** to the negative electrode **5** and the positive ions **6** flow through the electrolyte **7** from negative to positive.

When the battery is fully recharged and in use, the flow changes. The electrons flow from negative to positive through the device to be powered, such as a bulb. The positive ions flow through the electrolyte from positive to negative. However, the chemical reactions in a rechargeable cell take place even when it's not connected to a circuit, so it constantly loses power and needs to be regularly charged. This makes rechargeable batteries unsuitable for smoke detectors and other low-drain devices, but ideal for high drain devices that use a lot of power, such as cordless power tools.

Fault diagnosis

Battery needs recharging more regularly	**'Memory' problem** *Deep discharge several times (see Maintenance).* **Battery worn out** *Replace.*
Battery leaking	**Seal broken** *Throw away immediately.*
Battery running down quickly	**Incorrect battery for unit** *Check manual and replace with correct type.*

Audio-visual

Portable radio

Even the smallest portable radio employs a sophisticated circuit design that can filter out and decode a specific AM or stereo FM station from the myriad signals it receives.

1 Radio stations transmit their programmes as high frequency radio signals (electromagnetic waves). There are many radio transmitters around the country and each one is allocated a different transmission frequency.

2 Radio receivers typically have two aerials: an external **telescopic aerial** to receive frequency modulated (FM) signals and an internal **ferrite rod** aerial for amplitude modulated (AM) signals.

Telescopic aerial

Built-in ferrite rod aerial

Tuner

Tuning scale

Demodulator

FM/U

88 92 96 100

M/W/M

53 60 70 80 100

LW/L

46 18 20 2

Speaker

Amplifier

F

Band switch

From transmitter to speaker

A mixture of radio frequencies sent out by transmitters is received by the aerial **1**. All these frequencies are sent to the tuner **2** from the aerial. The tuner resonates at the frequency selected on the tuning dial and filters out all the other frequencies. The demodulator **3** then extracts the audio (AF) information from the filtered signal. Finally the audio signal is amplified **4** so it can drive the speaker or speakers **5** in the radio set.

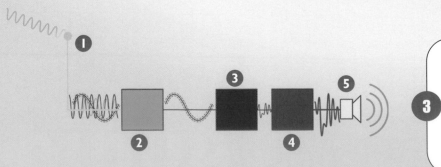

3 Radio frequency (RF) waves induce tiny electrical signals in the aerial. These are passed to the **tuner**, which acts as a variable filter, and outputs only the frequency for the desired station selected with the **tuning control**.

Maintenance

As required	**Clean telescopic aerial** *This prevents it sticking.* **Clean controls** *Use switch cleaner to clean volume, tone and band switches.* 

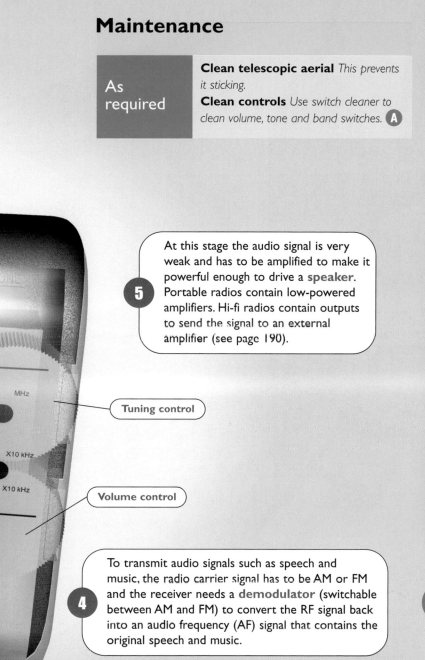

Tuning control

Volume control

08 MHz
10
60 X10 kHz
10
X10 kHz

LW

5 At this stage the audio signal is very weak and has to be amplified to make it powerful enough to drive a **speaker**. Portable radios contain low-powered amplifiers. Hi-fi radios contain outputs to send the signal to an external amplifier (see page 190).

4 To transmit audio signals such as speech and music, the radio carrier signal has to be AM or FM and the receiver needs a **demodulator** (switchable between AM and FM) to convert the RF signal back into an audio frequency (AF) signal that contains the original speech and music.

Fault diagnosis

No functions	**Flat batteries** *Replace batteries.* **No power** *Check plug fuse, wiring and mains supply.* **Radio faulty** *Contact qualified repairer.* **Poor battery connections** *Clean and retension battery contacts.*
Poor-quality signal or interference	**Check aerial orientation** *Adjust the position or alignment of the telescopic aerial for FM stations and adjust the position or orientation of the whole radio for AM stations.* **Proximity to electrical interference** *Move radio away from other devices.* **Broken aerial** *Replace.* 
Sound distorted	**Batteries low** *Replace or use mains power.* **Radio not tuned in correctly** *Adjust tuning.* **Faulty speaker or internal circuitry** *Contact qualified repairer.*
Tuner will not pick up any stations	**Aerial not extended** *Fully extend aerial and rotate for best signal.* **Faulty internal aerial connection** *Consult a qualified repairer.* **Faulty tuner circuit** *Contact qualified repairer.*
Noise when turning volume control	**Dirty control** *Use switch cleaner to clean.* 

Cleaning the switches

If the radio is mains powered, switch off and disconnect. Locate position of switches and volume control – try to identify any access hole. Sparingly spray switch cleaner into the component and operate the control mechanically several times to help to clean the contact.

Replacing the aerial

If the radio is mains powered, switch off and disconnect from the mains supply. Open case if necessary. Remove the screw holding the aerial. Slide new aerial into place and reattach any screws. Attach cables and reassemble the case, if required.

Alternative design

Analogue transmissions are set to be gradually taken over by 2015 by **digital radio** (also known as Digital Audio Broadcasting or DAB). The sound quality is near that of CDs with no hiss or distortion, and the format allows for transmission of extra data, such as traffic information, song titles and even images. The signal is sent as the ones and zeros of computer data and decoded by a digital to analogue converter (see Digital cordless telephone, page 246).

179

Personal cassette player

Miniature motors, tiny integrated circuits and powerful batteries make it possible to shrink the mechanism of a standard cassette deck (see page 188) and fit it into a portable unit. In fact, the only difference between the two is size.

Auto-reverse heads

The tiny mechanism in some personal cassette players can play both sides of the tape without the user having to open the case and turn the tape over. These units have auto-reverse heads, each having four pick-up coils instead of two (see Cassette deck, page 188). In effect the head is reading all four tracks at once – side A left and right, and side B left and right. However, only one side ❶ is being routed to the headphone amplifier. When the tape reaches the end, the direction is reversed and the heads play the second side ❷.

Maintenance

Once a year	**Clean heads and rollers**
	Even though cassette tape is coated with a dry lubricant, deposits build up on heads and rollers as they get used. This can eventually cause sound problems and slipping tape. Ⓐ

Use good-quality cassettes

If you make your own recordings, use quality branded cassettes – avoid using C120 tapes, which are prone to stretch and snap.

❶ Pressing the 'open' button releases a catch, which holds the sprung hinged door closed. A cassette tape is inserted.

Supply reel

Cassette

Tape spool

Operating buttons

Play head

Capstan shaft

Pinch roller

❷ Batteries provide the power for a tiny motor. This turns a spindle to drive the sprockets in the cassette tape. When the 'Play' button is pressed, the **pinch roller** presses the tape against the **capstan shaft** and the **play head** moves into place.

❸ The motor drives the capstan to move the tape past the head at 4.763cm/second. The motor also drives the **take-up reel**, which gathers the tape as it is driven between the capstan shaft and the pinch roller.

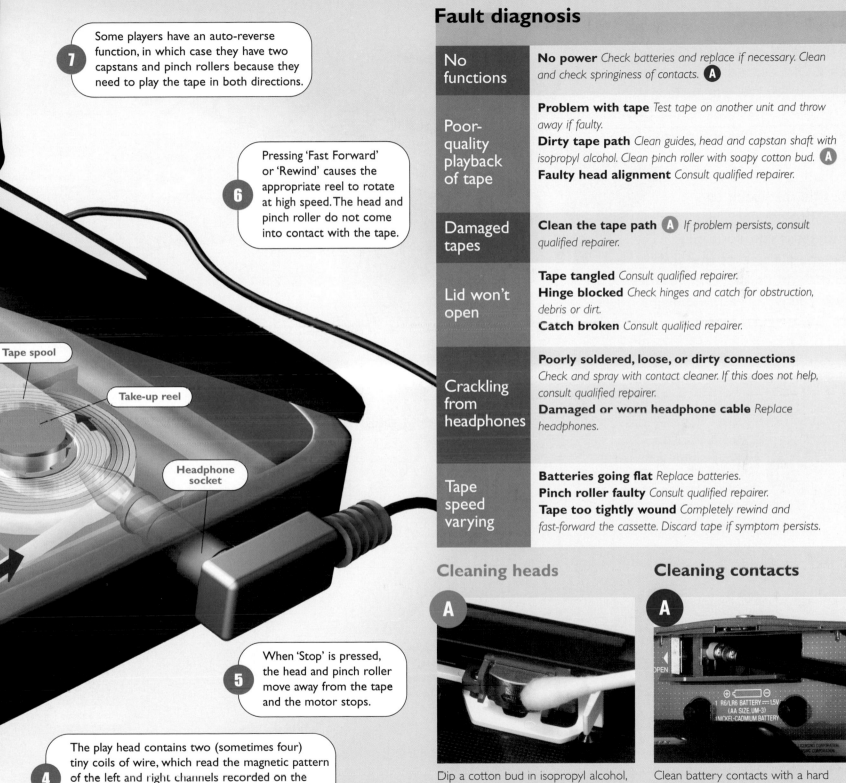

7 Some players have an auto-reverse function, in which case they have two capstans and pinch rollers because they need to play the tape in both directions.

6 Pressing 'Fast Forward' or 'Rewind' causes the appropriate reel to rotate at high speed. The head and pinch roller do not come into contact with the tape.

Tape spool

Take-up reel

Headphone socket

5 When 'Stop' is pressed, the head and pinch roller move away from the tape and the motor stops.

4 The play head contains two (sometimes four) tiny coils of wire, which read the magnetic pattern of the left and right channels recorded on the tape. The electrical signals from the play head are amplified and fed to a set of headphones.

Fault diagnosis

No functions	**No power** *Check batteries and replace if necessary. Clean and check springiness of contacts.* **A**
Poor-quality playback of tape	**Problem with tape** *Test tape on another unit and throw away if faulty.* **Dirty tape path** *Clean guides, head and capstan shaft with isopropyl alcohol. Clean pinch roller with soapy cotton bud.* **A** **Faulty head alignment** *Consult qualified repairer.*
Damaged tapes	**Clean the tape path** **A** *If problem persists, consult qualified repairer.*
Lid won't open	**Tape tangled** *Consult qualified repairer.* **Hinge blocked** *Check hinges and catch for obstruction, debris or dirt.* **Catch broken** *Consult qualified repairer.*
Crackling from headphones	**Poorly soldered, loose, or dirty connections** *Check and spray with contact cleaner. If this does not help, consult qualified repairer.* **Damaged or worn headphone cable** *Replace headphones.*
Tape speed varying	**Batteries going flat** *Replace batteries.* **Pinch roller faulty** *Consult qualified repairer.* **Tape too tightly wound** *Completely rewind and fast-forward the cassette. Discard tape if symptom persists.*

Cleaning heads

A

Dip a cotton bud in isopropyl alcohol, squeeze out excess drops and then gently rub it across the heads and capstan shaft. Allow to dry.

Cleaning contacts

A

Clean battery contacts with a hard pencil eraser. Make sure the contacts are tensioned so they make a good connection with the batteries.

Compact disc player

The digital data on a compact disc or CD is stored on its underside as variations in the surface contours. A compact disc player works by spinning the disc past a laser beam, which is reflected by the disc back to a photo sensor. This monitors the contours on the surface of the disc and outputs a stream of ones and zeros corresponding to the original music recorded.

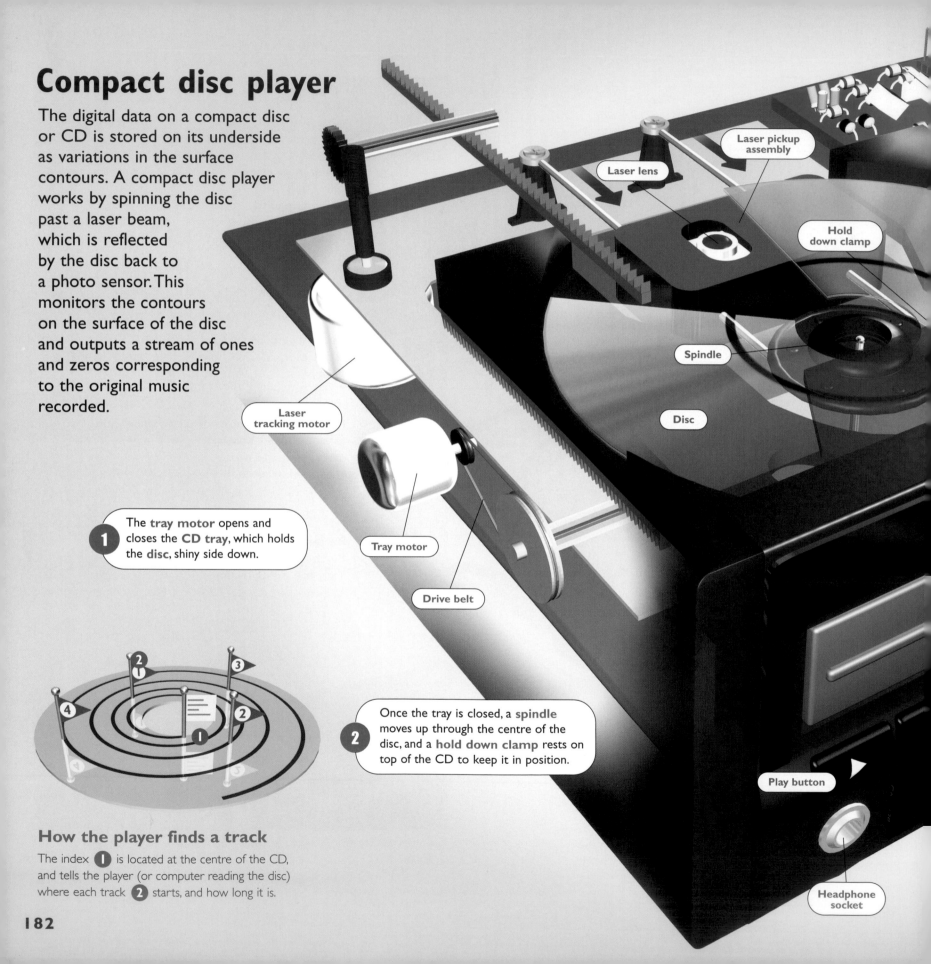

Laser pickup assembly

Laser lens

Hold down clamp

Spindle

Disc

Laser tracking motor

1 The **tray motor** opens and closes the **CD tray**, which holds the **disc**, shiny side down.

Tray motor

Drive belt

2 Once the tray is closed, a **spindle** moves up through the centre of the disc, and a **hold down clamp** rests on top of the CD to keep it in position.

Play button

Headphone socket

How the player finds a track

The index **1** is located at the centre of the CD, and tells the player (or computer reading the disc) where each track **2** starts, and how long it is.

Digital to analogue converter

Pre-amplifier

How the laser assembly works

A laser beam **1** is directed at the underside of the compact disc **2**. The data recorded on the disc is stored as a series of pits and bumps **3**. These correspond to the binary zeros and ones of digital data. The irregularities in the surface vary the reflected laser beam **4**, effectively turning it on and off. The beam is reflected by a one-way mirror **5** to a photo sensor **6**, which 'reads' these variations and feeds the data through a digital to analogue converter to produce an audio signal.

2

3

4

5

6

1

CD tray

5 As the laser assembly reads the disc (see above right), circuits in the unit send an analogue audio signal via the **pre-amplifier** to the CD player's output sockets, and then on to the amplifier and speakers.

4 When the **play button** is pressed, the disc starts spinning again and the laser assembly slowly moves from the centre out, reading the spiral track.

3 The disc spins briefly and the **laser pickup assembly** moves to the centre where it reads the index. This tells the player how many tracks there are on the disc, how long each track is and where it starts. The number of tracks and total play time is usually displayed on an LCD panel on the front of the player.

The speed of the disc's rotation

If a CD rotated at a constant speed, the pits and bumps on the outside track would pass the lens at a greater speed than those at the centre. This principle can be seen on a bicycle, where the wheel rim passes the frame at a greater speed than the centre. For the data to be read at a constant rate, the revolutions per minute of the disc must be decreased to compensate as the laser moves away from the centre.

CD care

Keeping compact discs clean and free from scratches helps to ensure that the laser beam is reflected accurately off the surface of the CD. It also helps to keep the laser lens within a CD player free from dirt.

> **Safety warning** ⚠️
> Never open the CD player case when the power is connected. A CD player uses a laser to read the disc, and laser light can cause damage to eyesight.

Maintenance

Once a month	**Clean casing of CD player** Wipe down outside of CD player with dry lint-free cloth. Remove dust and greasy fingerprints. Don't spray furniture polish on unit: use a little on cloth.
Every six months	**Clean laser lens with a good-quality lens-cleaning CD** Follow manufacturer's instructions explicitly. If there are smokers in household, this process may need to be carried out more frequently. (A)

Fault diagnosis

No functions	**No power to appliance** Check flex, mains supply, plug fuse and wiring for faults. If battery-powered, check batteries. Clean and retension contacts.
Disc spins initially but will not play	**Wrong type of CD** Some CDs, such as those recorded on PCs, will not play in many older CD players. If no discs play try cleaning the laser lens – see Maintenance. (A)
Track skipping	**Dirty or scratched disc** Clean disc. (A) **Dirty lens** See Maintenance. (A)
Disc spinning but no sound	**Poor connections** Check connections between player and amplifier, and between amplifier and speakers. **Wrong audio source selected on amplifier** Check CD player input is selected on amplifier (see page 190). **Faulty circuitry** Contact qualified repairer.

Cleaning CDs

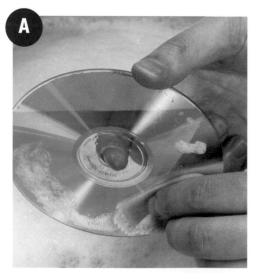

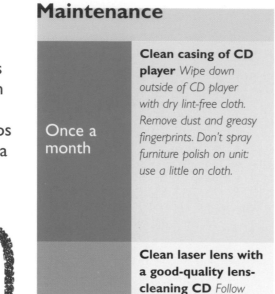

1 Clean gently with water and washing-up liquid and a soft lint-free cloth to remove dirt or fingerprints. Rinse and pat dry with a clean lint-free cloth. Wipe from the centre of the disc outwards in straight lines.

2 Light scratches can sometimes be polished out using a proprietary CD repair kit. Buy a reputable brand and follow the manufacturer's instructions explicitly. Always polish radially outwards from the centre of the disc.

Cleaning the lens

Obtain a reputable make of lens-cleaning disc. Follow the manufacturer's instructions carefully. Place the disc in the drive as instructed and press play. The tiny brushes remove dust and debris from the lens area.

MiniDisc player

The audio MiniDisc format uses two types of media: a recordable magneto-optical disc or a standard optical disc, like a compact disc, for playing pre-recorded material.

5 When recording, data is received from another audio source via an **optical link socket**. The laser and **magnetic head** work together to store the data on the surface of the disc (see below).

4 Finally, the digital signal is converted to an analogue audio signal, amplified and routed to the outputs.

1 When a **MiniDisc** is inserted and the lid closed, a **shutter** on the disc case is pushed back to reveal the **optical disc** inside. Motors spin the disc via a **spindle** and move the **laser assembly** across the disc.

Spindle

Connectors

MiniDisc

Laser assembly and magnetic head

Optical disc

Optical link socket

Shutter

3 The changes in magnetic information affect the reflected laser beam and the signal from the laser pick-up is converted to the original digital information.

2 During playback, the spinning disc is read by the **laser** in the same way as in a CD player (see page 182).

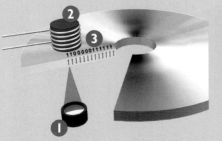

Recording on MiniDisc

When recording on a MiniDisc, one side is heated by a laser **1** while an electromagnetic head **2** on the other side writes data to the heated area. Electrical signals cause the magnet to switch polarity from north to south, changing the polarity of the heated areas of the disc to represent ones or zeros **3** respectively.

Maintenance

Every six months	**Clean optical link sockets and plugs** *Clean sockets with compressed air spray and plugs with lens cleaning fluid.*
Every two years	**Service player** *Take MiniDisc player to qualified repairer to have connectors cleaned, and moving parts lubricated.*

Cleaning the lens

Apply a small amount of fluid to the cleaning disc (according to the maker's instructions) and place the disc in the unit. Close the lid and press the play button.

Fault diagnosis

Unit not operational	**No battery power** *Check batteries. Clean and retension battery connectors.* **Unit may need resetting** *Some players have reset button on back or may be reset by holding a button while powering up. Check manual for details.*
Skipping tracks	**Faulty disc** *Try another disc.* **Dirty or obscured lens** *Clean using proprietary cleaning disc and fluid.* **A** **Faulty laser unit** *Contact qualified repairer.*
Lid stuck	**Case interlock jammed** *Contact a qualified repairer.*

Record deck

The turntable of a record deck rotates a vinyl disc in which is stamped a spiral groove. A tiny needle sits in the groove and is vibrated as the record is turned. The movement of the needle is converted into an audio signal, which is sent to a set of speakers.

Coils

Cantilever

Magnets

Groove

Stylus

Dust cover

1 A rubber **drive belt** runs from the shaft of the **electric motor** to the base of the **platter**, making it turn.

2 The **stylus**, mounted in the **cantilever**, rests in a spiral groove on the record (left). As the disc spins, ridges in the sides of the grooves cause the stylus to vibrate. The shape of the ridges corresponds to the shape of the sound waves of the music when it was recorded. On a stereo record one side of the ridge contains the left channel audio information, the other side, the right.

Spindle

Electric motor

Drive belt

Platter

Headshell

Stylus

Cartridge

3 **Magnets** and **coils** inside the **cartridge** convert the movement of the stylus and cantilever into tiny electrical signals. The electrical signals created are proportional to the original audio signal.

4 These electrical signals are transmitted through wires down the **tone arm**. The signal is very weak and needs to be amplified before it is sent to the speakers to produce sound.

Maintenance

Before each use	**Clean stylus** *Brush gently towards front of cartridge with stylus brush.* **Clean record** *Use cylindrical record brush or antistatic cloth.*
Regularly	**Check stylus pressure** *If required, adjust counterweight to manufacturer's specification.* **A**

Correcting the stylus pressure

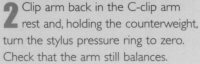

A

1 Take off the stylus protector. While supporting the arm, gently turn the counterweight until the arm floats level. Avoid touching the stylus.

2 Clip arm back in the C-clip arm rest and, holding the counterweight, turn the stylus pressure ring to zero. Check that the arm still balances.

3 Check your manual for the correct pressure and turn the counterweight so that the indicated amount appears on the pressure ring.

Fault diagnosis

Platter doesn't turn	**No power** *Check mains supply, mains lead, plug and plug fuse for faults.* **Drive belt slipping or broken** *Clean or replace belt.* **Controls or switches dirty** *Spray with switch cleaner.* **Motor faulty** *Check and replace if necessary.*
Poor sound quality	**Dirty stylus** *Clean stylus. See Maintenance section.* **Faulty or worn stylus or cartridge** *Replace.* **Stylus pressure incorrect** *Adjust stylus pressure.* Ⓐ
Constant hum	**Record player too close to another appliance** *Check distance between record player and appliances. Ideally other appliances should be at least a metre from the player.* **Bad connection within cartridge** *Check and clean connections to cartridge.* Ⓐ **Earth wire not connected on amplifier** *Connect earth wire's U-shaped connector to screw fitting next to amplifier's phono inputs.* **Faulty cartridge** *(typically causing hum on one channel). Replace cartridge.*
Arm falls incorrectly	**Mechanism out of adjustment** *Many decks have an adjustment for this. Consult manual for precise method.*
Record skips	**Warped, scratched or dirty vinyl** *Try another record or clean record if necessary* **Stylus pressure incorrect** *Check stylus pressure* Ⓐ *and anti-skating adjustment if fitted.* **Faulty stylus** *Replace stylus.*

Checking connections to cartridge

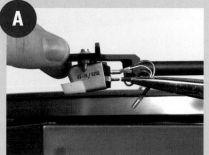

1 Detach the cartridge if possible – consult the manufacturer's manual for the precise method. Note which wire goes where and use long-nosed pliers to unplug each connector.

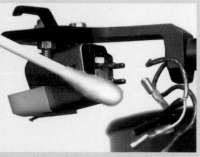

2 Spray switch cleaner onto a cotton wool bud and use it to clean the contacts carefully. Refit connections correctly. Then, refit the cartridge to the tone arm.

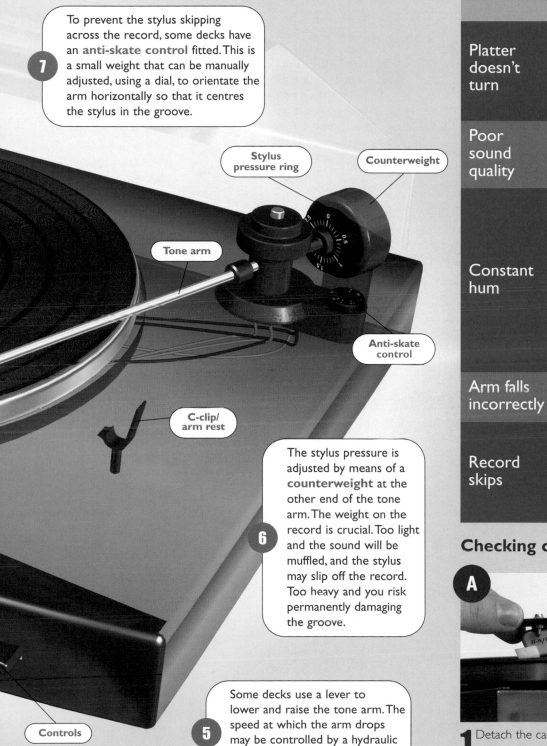

7 To prevent the stylus skipping across the record, some decks have an **anti-skate control** fitted. This is a small weight that can be manually adjusted, using a dial, to orientate the arm horizontally so that it centres the stylus in the groove.

Stylus pressure ring

Counterweight

Tone arm

Anti-skate control

C-clip/ arm rest

6 The stylus pressure is adjusted by means of a **counterweight** at the other end of the tone arm. The weight on the record is crucial. Too light and the sound will be muffled, and the stylus may slip off the record. Too heavy and you risk permanently damaging the groove.

Controls

5 Some decks use a lever to lower and raise the tone arm. The speed at which the arm drops may be controlled by a hydraulic damping system, to avoid damaging the record and stylus.

Cassette deck

The compact cassette revolutionised home recording. It made it possible to record and re-record quickly and simply onto small cassette tapes, which could be played back at home or on the move (See Personal cassette player, page 180).

10 When the 'Fast Forward' or 'Rewind' buttons are pressed, the pinch roller is not in contact with the tape. Instead the supply or take-up reel is driven at high speed.

9 Pressing 'Pause' during record or playback stops all tape movement temporarily. When 'Stop' is pressed, the heads and pinch roller move away from the tape and capstan and take-up reel rotation is stopped. The cassette can now be ejected.

1 Cassette tape is a long thin strip of plastic coated with an iron oxide layer which, when exposed to a magnetic field, becomes magnetised. The tape winds between two **tape spools** mounted in a plastic cassette housing.

2 The cassette has holes that fit over a **capstan shaft** inside the cassette deck, and slots at the bottom that allow access for the **pinch roller** and **heads**.

3 When 'Play' or 'Record' is selected, the **play/record head** moves forward to contact the tape and the pinch roller presses the tape against the capstan shaft.

4 A small **felt pad** inside the cassette ensures the tape is kept in contact with the heads during recording and playback.

Record tab side A

Tape spools

Record tab side B

Supply reel

Tape

Take-up reel

Erase head

Felt pad

Capstan shaft

Play/record head

Pinch roller

Controls

Using electromagnets to record

The play/record head **1** consists of two iron cores – one for the left and one for the right channel – each wound with a coil of wire **2**. These coils carry a current, which varies according to the left and right (stereo) audio input signals. The currents induce a varying magnetic field across the gap in each core, which proportionately magnetises the oxide surface of the tape as it passes the head. The head can record four tracks: side A left **3** and right **4**, and side B left and right when the cassette is reversed.

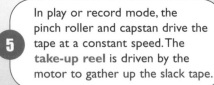

5 In play or record mode, the pinch roller and capstan drive the tape at a constant speed. The **take-up reel** is driven by the motor to gather up the slack tape.

Safety first
To prevent electric shock, unplug a mains powered unit when cleaning pinch rollers.

8 The **record tabs** on the top edge of the tape housing protect recordings you want to keep. If the tab is removed a sprung lever pushes into the gap and disables the cassette deck's record function.

7 During record mode, the tape first passes the **erase head** to clear it of previous recordings. The electromagnets in the record head then write a magnetic pattern on the tape corresponding to the audio signal being recorded (see opposite page).

6 During playback, the play/record head reads the magnetic signals from the tape and converts them into electric signals. These are then processed electronically to give left and right audio outputs.

Maintenance

| Once a year | **Clean pinch rollers and heads** Keep alcohol away from rubber rollers, and water away from electrical circuits. **A** |
| | **Demagnetise heads** Use a proprietary head cleaner to clean heads. **B** |

Cleaning pinch rollers and heads

1 Use isopropyl alcohol to clean the capstan shaft and a cotton bud dipped in soapy water to clean the pinch rollers.

2 To clean the heads, dip a clean cotton bud in isopropyl alcohol, squeeze out any excess drops and then rub it gently across the surface.

Demagnetising heads

Commercially available tape head demagnetisers help to maximise playback and record quality. Always follow the manufacturer's instructions.

Oiling the shaft

Lay the cassette deck on its side and run a single drop of light machine oil down a needle directly onto the shaft of each reel.

Fault diagnosis

Nothing functions	**Fuse or wiring fault** Check plug fuse and plug wiring for faults.
	Flat battery If battery-powered, check and replace batteries. Clean battery contacts and pull contacts slightly forward so they have a firm grip on the batteries (see Batteries, page 174).
Poor playback	**Dirty tape path** Clean pinch roller, capstan shaft and heads. **A**
	Heads magnetised Demagnetise heads. **B**
	Head misaligned Contact qualified repairer.
Noisy winding	**Tape faulty** Try another cassette.
	Reel shafts need lubricating Put a drop of light machine oil onto each shaft. **A**
Damaged tapes	**Tape loose or twisted in cassette** Pull a little slack tape from cassette and then wind reels manually with pen or pencil. Do not put very twisted tape into machine: it could jam.
	Stretched tape C120s are thin and tend to stretch so are unsuitable for repeated use.

Amplifier

The electrical signals produced by CD players, tuners or tape decks are too weak to drive loudspeakers directly. They need to be boosted by an amplifier. Sometimes this is an integral part of another machine or it may be separate, as shown here.

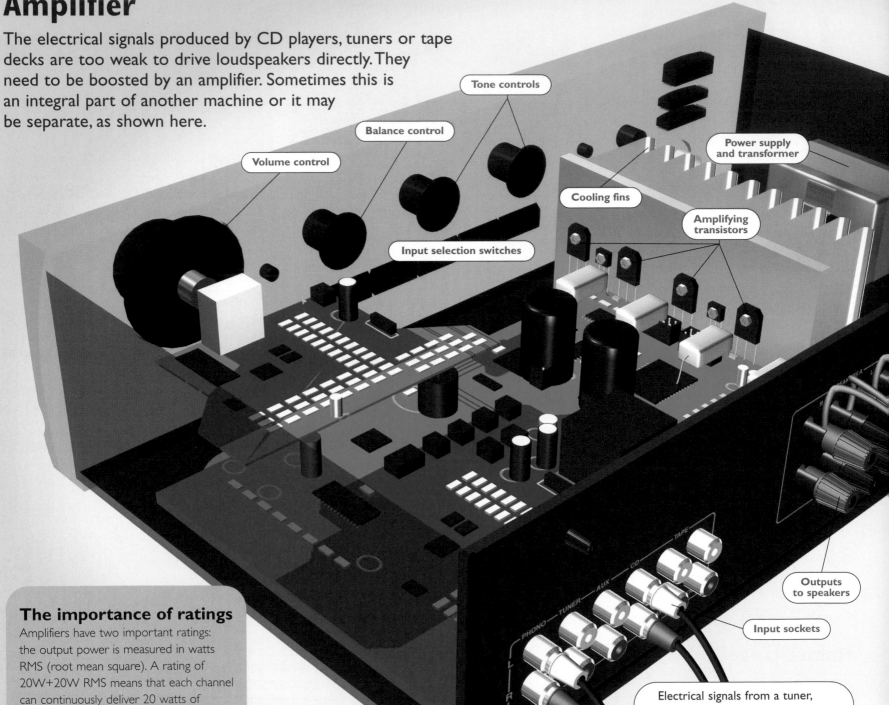

Tone controls

Balance control

Volume control

Power supply and transformer

Cooling fins

Amplifying transistors

Input selection switches

Outputs to speakers

Input sockets

PHONO TUNER AUX CD TAPE

L R

The importance of ratings

Amplifiers have two important ratings: the output power is measured in watts RMS (root mean square). A rating of 20W+20W RMS means that each channel can continuously deliver 20 watts of power to each speaker. The impedance rating refers to the resistance of the speakers that are connected to it. Always make sure that your speakers have the same power and impedance ratings as your amplifier, or damage may occur.

1 Electrical signals from a tuner, CD player or other audio source enter the amplifier via the **input sockets** on the rear panel. A rotary or push button **input selection switch** dictates which input to process. Often a display device indicates the selected input.

③ The signal for each channel is fed to a series of **amplifying transistors**. These transistors amplify the signal in stages until it is powerful enough to drive a set of loudspeakers. This is then delivered as an **output** signal.

② Volume, **balance** and **tone** control is applied to both stereo channels before the signal is amplified.

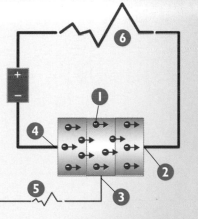

Fault diagnosis

If there is a fault with the sound output from your speakers, check that the symptom is the same when you use headphones. If it is, the amplifier is faulty. If it is not, one or both of the speakers must be at fault.

No functions	**No power** *Check flex, plug fuse and wiring for faults.* **Internal fuse blown** *Fuse must be replaced. Contact qualified repairer.*
No sound from speakers (LEDs lit)	**Wrong audio source** *Switch to correct source.* **Speakers not turned on** *Check speaker switches.* **Speakers not connected** *Check speakers are wired correctly to amplifier.* **Internal fuse blown** *Contact qualified repairer.* **Headphones plugged in** *Unplug.*
No output on one channel	**Balance control offset** *Adjust.* **Faulty speaker connection** *Swap connections.* **Speaker or amplifier faulty** *Swap speakers – if fault persists, contact qualified repairer or replace speaker.*
Crackling when switching source or adjusting volume	**Dirty controls** *Clean with switch cleaner.* **A**
Distorted sound	**Faulty speaker(s)** *Confirm fault by checking with headphones.* **Faulty audio source** *Switch to another input. source. If problem persists, input source is not at fault.* **Faulty internal circuitry** *Contact qualified repairer.*

How transistors work

Most audio amplifiers use **transistors** to amplify the signals. Transistors are made of a sandwich of three silicon layers **①**. Each has chemicals added to make it conductive, and each has an electrode attached: the 'collector' **②**, 'base' **③** and 'emitter' **④**. Even though all three layers are individually conductive, the unique properties of the arrangement mean the transistor will not conduct electricity between the collector and the emitter until the central layer has a small current applied to the base electrode. This causes a change at the boundaries between the layers, allowing electrons to flow, and turning the transistor on like a tap. Because the resulting current is larger than, and directly proportional to the base current, a small varying signal input **⑤** to the base electrode is translated into a proportionally greater signal **⑥** between the collector and emitter.

Cleaning switches

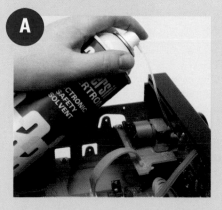

Turn the amplifier off and disconnect it from the mains supply. Remove top cover. Locate position of switches and volume control – try to identify any access hole. Sparingly spray switch cleaner into the component and operate the control mechanically several times to help to clean the contact.

Loudspeaker

The electrical signals generated by an amplifier are turned into sound waves via a loudspeaker. A simple magnet and moving coil are used to transform electrical pulses into the vibration of a thin cone, which moves backwards and forwards to create sound waves.

1 Typically, a small loudspeaker cabinet will have two **speakers** inside the box – a standard speaker, for low and mid-range frequencies, and a **tweeter** for high frequencies. A speaker comprises a paper, carbon fibre or plastic **cone** attached to a moving **coil**, which is positioned inside (as shown here) or around a **magnet**.

2 A varying current from the amplifier passes through the coil inducing a magnetic field. This causes the coil to move backwards and forwards with the amplitude (size) and frequency (timing) of the changes in the current. In turn, the coil pushes the cone back and forth, generating sound pressure waves.

3 In a two-speaker unit, a device called a **passive crossover unit** splits the high and low frequencies. Low and mid-range frequency signals are routed to the main speaker and high frequency signals to the tweeter.

4 The speaker cabinet is designed to minimise unwanted vibration and resonances. In a bass reflex speaker, there is a **tuned porthole** to increase the bass response.

5 Speakers have a rating called impedance (resistance), which is measured in ohms (typically 4–15 ohms). They also have a power rating in watts. Both ratings should match the amplifier that feeds them. If speakers are under-rated, then damage may occur to speakers and amplifier if used at high volume. If speakers are over-rated, then the amplifier may not be able to drive them efficiently.

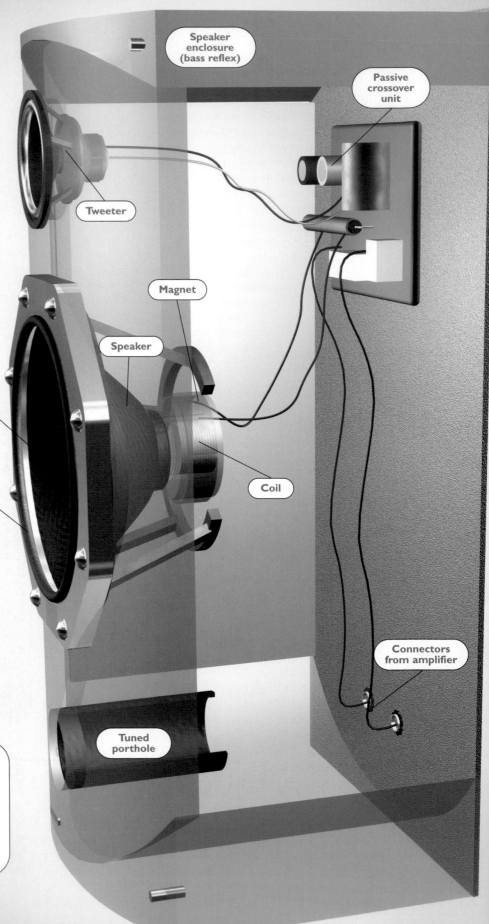

Speaker enclosure (bass reflex)

Passive crossover unit

Tweeter

Magnet

Speaker

Cone

Coil

Rubber suspension ring

Connectors from amplifier

Tuned porthole

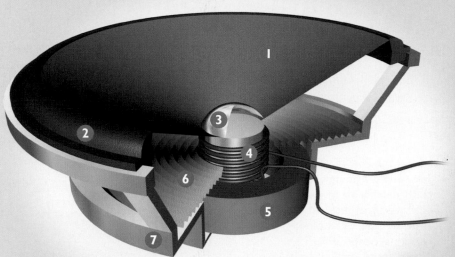

Inside a speaker

The cone ❶ is attached at its outer edge to a suspension ring ❷, which is made of a flexible material such as rubber. At the centre of the cone is the dust cap ❸. This covers the coil ❹, which is attached to the centre of the cone. The coil can move freely back and forth within the magnet ❺. Another flexible mounting called the spider ❻ supports the coil. The outer rim of the spider is attached to the metal or plastic basket ❼, which supports the entire mechanism.

Maintenance

Every six months	**Clean speaker cones and inside of cabinet** Dust can build up, especially on large cones, and eventually cause problems with sound quality. **A**

Fault diagnosis

No sound on one channel	**Balance not centred** Check amplifier balance setting. **Speakers not connected correctly** Check speaker connections and cable. Remake connections as necessary. **One speaker damaged** Swap speakers over to confirm that speaker is faulty. Replace speaker. **A**
Distortion or low sound	**Wrong rating for amplifier** Confirm speakers are correctly rated for amplifier – replace speakers if not. **Speaker fault** Swap speakers. If same speaker still shows symptom, replace speakers with correct rating. Otherwise amplifier may be faulty – consult qualified repairer.
Poor bass response	**Poor-quality cable** Replace. **Speakers not connected correctly** Check speaker connection – reverse one connection if necessary. **B**

Cleaning inside the speaker

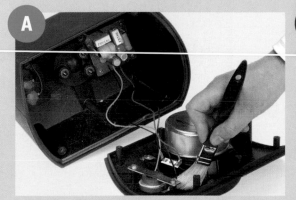

A

Unplug speaker cables and gently prise the cover away from the cabinet, making sure it does not bend too much. Use a soft, dry lint-free cloth to dust the cones and surrounding area carefully. If your speaker is a bass reflex model with a porthole, open the speaker cabinet but remove any dust inside the enclosure with a soft brush. Note that some speaker cabinets are glued together and cannot be opened.

Replacing a speaker

A

Unplug the speaker cables, lay the cabinet on its back and lift off the cover. Unscrew the fastenings to remove the speaker unit and carefully lift it out. You may have to open the case. If so, do this from behind. Note the wire colours. Carefully pull off the connectors using long-nosed pliers. Fit a suitable replacement speaker, reattach the wires correctly, and fit the unit back into the cabinet.

Checking connections

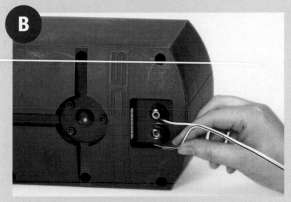

B

Speaker wires may be red and black or one cable may have a stripe (as above). Connect the red or striped wire to the red (positive) connector on the amplifier and the black to the black (negative) connector. Connect the red or striped cable to the red connector on the speaker, and the black cable to the black connector.

Television set

Colour televisions, and computer monitors, rely upon an optical illusion that fools the brain into thinking it sees a moving image in lifelike colours. In fact, the picture is made up from hundreds of thousands of tiny red, green and blue stripes, and a series of still images played in rapid succession to create an impression of continuous movement.

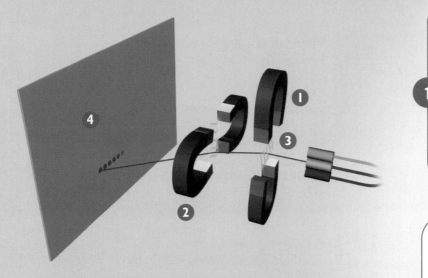

Screen

1 Television programmes reach your TV via an analogue or digital signal received using an aerial, cable or satellite system (see page 208). Regardless of how the **signal** is received, the image is decoded and split into its red, green and blue components, and the sound is separated and routed to an amplifier and speakers.

2 In a conventional TV, three beams of electrons, representing the colours red, green and blue, are fired from heated filaments called **cathodes**. These cathodes form part of three electron guns in a vacuum within a glass container known as the **cathode ray tube** (CRT).

Drawing the picture on the screen

Copper coils wound around the tube neck (scanning coils) work like magnets to deflect the beam of electrons vertically **1** and horizontally **2**, changing its angle **3** like light rays passing through a prism to scan the whole of the screen surface **4**. The beams scan across the screen horizontally, first scanning the even lines 50 times a second, then the odd. This is called interlacing. The whole screen is covered 25 times each second, to create the picture.

3 The beams are focused and accelerated towards the **screen** by an **anode**. The screen is covered in a series of phosphor stripes, which are arranged in groups of three: red, green and blue. When struck by the electron beam, each phosphor stripe glows. The brightness of the emitted light is controlled by the quantity of electrons striking it (current). Just behind the screen is a steel plate with slits in it called the **shadow mask**. This ensures that the electrons from each gun hit only the appropriate **phosphor stripes**.

Shadow mask

Phosphor stripes

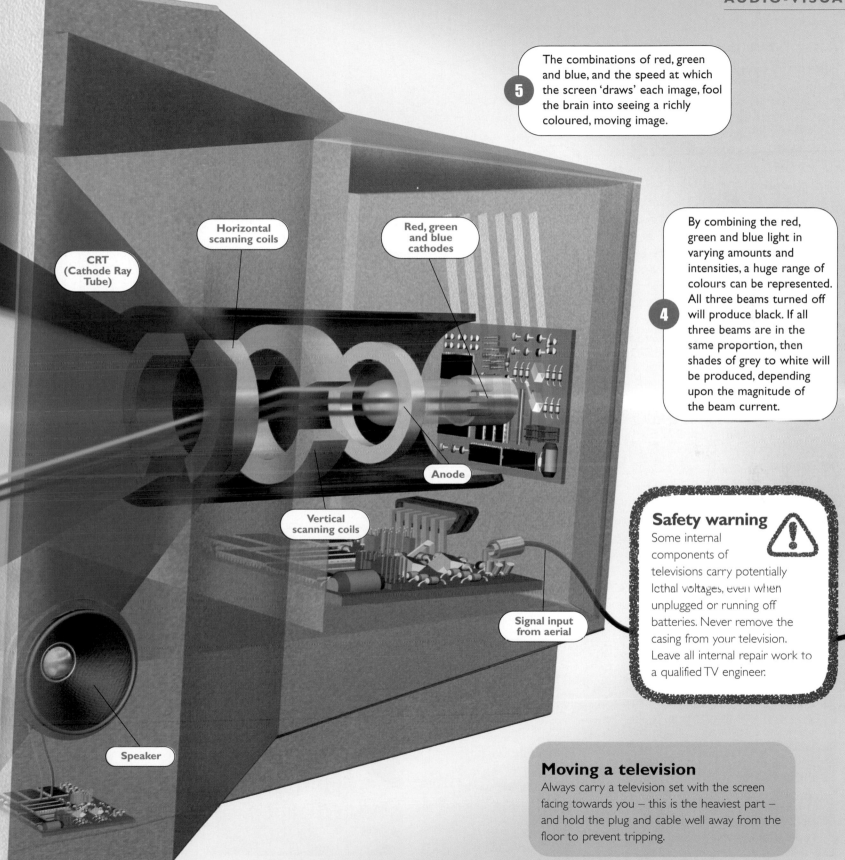

5 The combinations of red, green and blue, and the speed at which the screen 'draws' each image, fool the brain into seeing a richly coloured, moving image.

Horizontal scanning coils

Red, green and blue cathodes

CRT (Cathode Ray Tube)

4 By combining the red, green and blue light in varying amounts and intensities, a huge range of colours can be represented. All three beams turned off will produce black. If all three beams are in the same proportion, then shades of grey to white will be produced, depending upon the magnitude of the beam current.

Anode

Vertical scanning coils

Safety warning ⚠

Some internal components of televisions carry potentially lethal voltages, even when unplugged or running off batteries. Never remove the casing from your television. Leave all internal repair work to a qualified TV engineer.

Signal input from aerial

Speaker

Moving a television

Always carry a television set with the screen facing towards you – this is the heaviest part – and hold the plug and cable well away from the floor to prevent tripping.

195

Alternative design

Flat screen televisions use a **plasma display panel** (PDP) rather than a cathode ray tube (CRT). Each stripe is a tiny sealed cell **1**, which contains a mixture of neon and xenon gas at low pressure, and which is lined with a red, green or blue phosphor coating. A layer of address electrodes **2** sits behind the cells, arranged in vertical rows along a glass plate, and a layer of display electrodes is similarly mounted in front of the cells **3**, but in horizontal rows to form a grid (shown raised from the cells). As current passes from an address electrode to an intersecting display electrode (shown in blue), the gas in the cell between them **4** heats up and emits ultraviolet radiation. This excites the cell's phosphor layer to emit its colour of light **5**. Each cell is triggered individually. The colours blend to create the screen's overall colour. PDP screens are relatively light, thin and presently very expensive compared to CRTs.

Digital television

Many broadcasters are now transmitting digital television signals. Rather than transmitting the programs as analogue waves, they are transmitted as a digital signal of ones and zeros. These are then turned back into an analogue signal by a set-top box or a decoder built into an integrated digital television. The television then displays the programs as normal.

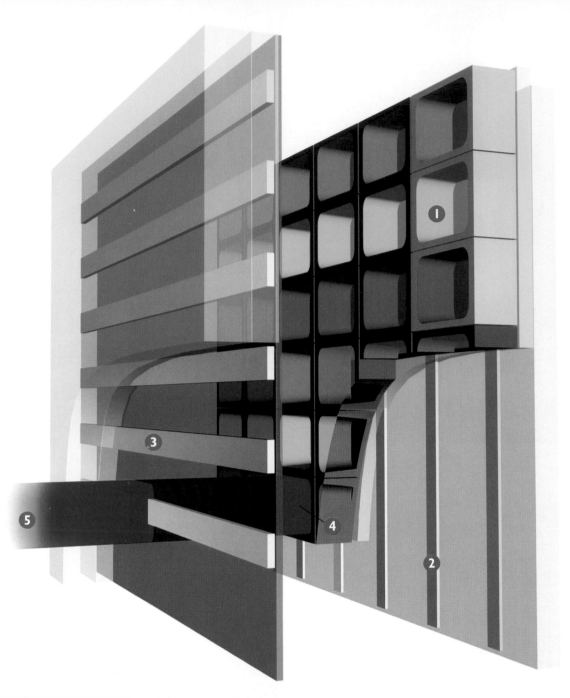

Maintenance

Always use a television as indicated in the manufacturer's manual, and never attempt to connect it in any way other than instructed.

Every week	**Clean the screen and rear of the unit** *High static charge on screen attracts dust.* **A** **Clean the remote control with a slightly damp cloth** *Make sure no moisture is left on the remote control. Do not use abrasive cleaning products. (See Remote control, page 202.)*

Cleaning the set

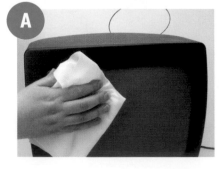

Wipe the television screen gently with an anti-static cleaning cloth or computer monitor cleaning product. Also remove any dust from around the vents and rear of the television. To prevent the set from overheating, it is very important that the cooling vents at the top and back of the television are not blocked or covered.

Fault diagnosis

Simple problems with televisions can usually be resolved by following a few steps. However, if electrical problems or serious faults with the picture or sound occur, switch the set off immediately and contact a qualified repairer.

Coloured patch on the screen	**Shadow mask is magnetised** *A magnetic source such as a loudspeaker has magnetised the shadow mask. Move speakers away from the TV, and demagnetise (degauss) the screen* **A***. Also, keep piles of video cassettes away from the screen and rear of the set.*
No functions	**No power to TV** *Check plug wiring, fuse, and mains socket outlet for faults.*
No picture	**Transmitter failure** *Check on another TV set.* **Aerial or other input cable disconnected** *Check aerial, SCART, S-Video and other connectors.* **B** **Wrong input selected** *Make sure TV is set to correct Input.* **Un-programmed channel selected** *Make sure correct programme number is selected.* **TV not tuned in** *Tune in according to manufacturer's instructions.* **Ancillary equipment not turned on** *Check VCR, satellite, DVD etc.*
Weak signal causing 'snow' on picture	**Poorly tuned channel** *Check other channels. If they are OK, retune weak one.* **Poor aerial signal** *Check all aerial plug connections, cable and aerial alignment.* **Weak signal reception area** *Consult qualified aerial installer.*
Screen blank, but sound OK	**Internal fault** *Switch TV off. Do not use. Consult qualified repairer.*
No sound	**Volume down or on mute** *Check remote control settings.* **Incorrect connection** *Make all audio connections (see Audio-visual connection leads, page 207).* **Station not tuned correctly** *Retune according to manufacturer's instructions.*

Demagnetising the screen

Move speakers and piles of videos away from television. If this fails, turn set on for 60 seconds and then off for half an hour. Repeat this three times. This should demagnetise (degauss) the screen. If it fails, call a service engineer to carry out the job with specialist equipment.

Checking the SCART connection

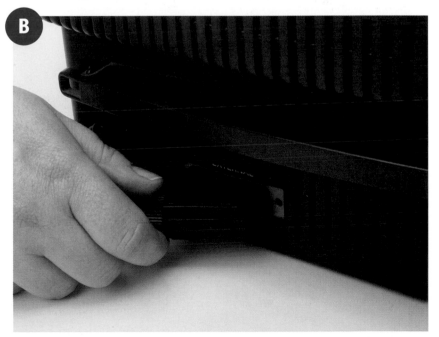

Make sure the SCART cable is firmly plugged into the back of the TV, the VCR, and any other video sources, such as a digital TV decoder or DVD player.

Video recorder

The VHS video cassette recorder (VCR) is one of the most complex devices in the home. It combines precisely aligned mechanical parts with sophisticated electronic circuits to record pictures and audio onto tape. However, despite its complexity, the VCR is a reliable and long-lived machine, and is easily kept in peak condition.

Protective cassette flap

Video cassette

Display

Control panel

> **1** As a **video cassette** is inserted a sensor detects it and the **cassette loading motor** operates to draw the cassette into the VCR.

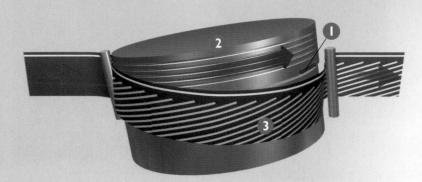

How videotape is recorded

Two video heads **1** are set on opposite sides of an angled rotating head drum **2**. The drum rotates 25 times per second. The tape moves past the drum at 24mm per second, allowing the heads to scan a helical pattern **3** on the tape at around 4.8m per second. This high speed is necessary to record the high-frequency TV signals.

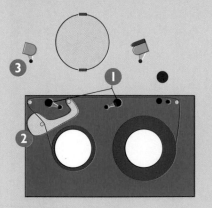

The tape path

When the cassette is lowered into the machine, two rollers **1** are positioned behind the tape. A tensioning arm **2** is also in place, ready to rotate and press the tape against the erase head **3**. When the tape loads, the rollers both move towards the rotating record/play head **4**, taking the tape and wrapping it around the head. The pinch roller **5** moves toward the capstan **6**, and the tensioning arm swings out, creating the correct tape tension.

Full erase head

Rotating video head drum

Audio and control head

Pinch roller

Cassette carriage

Capstan

Cassette loading motor

Loading mechanism

4 In playback, the magnetically recorded video information is read by the rotating heads and the audio track is read by the audio heads. Then the video and audio signals are combined and sent to a TV by S-video, SCART or RF connection (see Connecting leads, page 207).

3 During record, the **full erase head** removes any previously recorded material from the tape. The two rotating video heads in the **head drum** each record one half of the television signal. The tape then passes an audio record head, which lays down a sound track, similar to that recorded in a cassette player (see Cassette deck, page 188).

2 As the **cassette carriage** lowers into the machine, a lever opens the **protective cassette flap** and a pin disengages the spool locks. The rollers then loop the **tape around the heads** (see left). If the tape has no record tab, then the tape will start playing automatically.

Safe storage

Store video tapes vertically and in their cases, and keep them well away from magnetic sources, such as loudspeakers, which could damage the recorded magnetic signal.

Heading off trouble

Many problems with video recorders are caused by dirty heads and guides, or damaged tapes. The distance between the head and the tape is less than the depth of a fingerprint, so the slightest amount of dirt can have an effect. Regular cleaning keeps trouble at bay.

Safety first

Always unplug, disconnect or isolate any appliance when carrying out cleaning or maintenance.

Cleaning inside the recorder

A

1 Turn off and unplug the VCR. Remove the case screws and lift off the cover. Put all screws into marked containers for easy reassembly.

Maintenance

Every three months	**Clean heads** *Use a good quality head-cleaning video cassette to clean heads and rollers. Always follow the manufacturer's instructions and replace pads and liquid at indicated intervals.* **A** **Clean outside of the VCR** *Keep case free from dust by wiping down with lint free cloth. Don't spray furniture polish directly onto unit.*
Once a year	**Clean tape path** *Open case and clean route where tape runs during operation.* **A**

2 Clean the pinch roller with a slightly soaped cotton bud. Clean the capstan and any static heads (but not the video head drum) using a cotton swab dipped in pure isopropyl alcohol.

3 Use a chamois-tipped swab (available from electronics outlets) to clean the erase head. Aerosol head-cleaning fluid can be used to remove stubborn deposits.

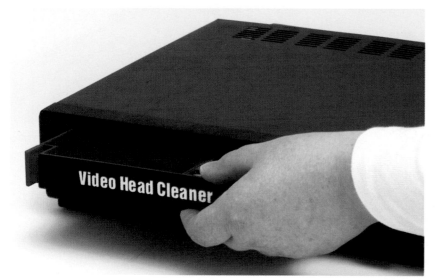

4 Use a proprietary head cleaning tape to clean the video heads. If you are in any doubt about this, consult a qualified repairer.

Removing a jammed cassette

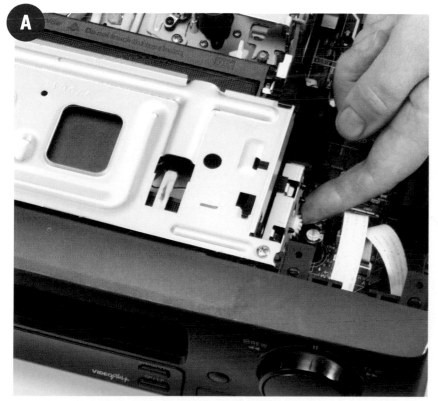

Unplug the VCR and remove the cover. Carefully try to turn the tape mechanism cog (if present) with one finger to eject the tape. If the tape is tangled in the mechanism, carefully cut it free first. Also, check the cassette carriage for obstructions in the mechanism. If in any doubt, consult a qualified repairer.

Fault diagnosis

Do not use a video cassette if the picture quality is poor. If dirty heads are to blame, then the tape may be damaged, and if the tape is worn it may deposit oxide on the heads. Eventually, permanent damage can be caused to the VCR by dirty tapes and heads.

VCR doesn't work	**No power** *Check switches, cables and fuse for faults.* **Moisture in mechanism** *Look for dew warning light. Move VCR away from condensation and allow to acclimatise for up to three hours.*
Cassette jammed	**Warped cassette** *Unplug VCR, open case and carefully try to free cassette by working it loose.* **A** **Object blocking eject system** *Open case and carefully remove blockage.* **A**
Picture quality poor	**Low quality or bad tape** *Try another tape. If it works, throw first one away and clean heads as below.* **Dirty heads** *Clean heads and rollers with a good quality head-cleaning video cassette. Always follow manufacturer's instructions.* **A** **Tracking out of alignment** *Check manufacturer's manual for instructions on how to manually adjust tracking or reset automatic tracking.* **Poor connections** *Check all connectors and cables between the VCR and TV.* **TV not tuned correctly** *Refer to manual.*
Picture bends across screen at the top	**Tape guides need adjusting** *Contact qualified repairer.* **Damaged control track on tape** *Throw away tape and clean heads as above.*
Tapes damaged by machine	**Poor quality tape** *Open case, remove tape and throw it away.* **A** **Tape guides need adjusting** *Contact qualified repairer.* **Dirty tape path** *Clean inside of the unit.* **A** **Faulty mechanism** *Contact qualified repairer.*

Recording formats

American videos are recorded in a different format from UK videos and will only play on UK machines if the unit is 'NTSC compatible'. Consult your manual to find out which formats your VCR can play.

Remote control

A wireless remote control uses pulses of infrared light to control audio-visual systems. The exact sequence of the pulses determines the task to be performed, whether it is changing a TV channel, adjusting volume, or selecting tracks on a CD player.

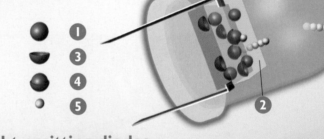

Keypad

Infrared transmitter

Printed circuit board

Batteries

1 Under the **keypad** is a **printed circuit board** made of copper conductors on an insulating non-flexible panel. As a button is pressed, a conductive contact completes a circuit.

2 The connection is detected by a processor on the circuit board, which generates a code representing the button that was pressed.

3 The processor sends the morse code-like sequence to an **infrared transmitter**. This is an LED (light emitting diode) that outputs a beam of infrared light, not visible to the human eye.

4 The infrared signal is picked up by a sensor in the device to be controlled. An electronic circuit decodes the sequence and performs the function.

Light emitting diodes

LEDs are tiny light bulbs illuminated solely by the movement of electrons in a two-layer semiconductor material. When a current flows one way through an LED, electrons **1** move from an electron-rich layer **2** to fill positively charged holes **3** in the second layer (moving right to left above). As these electrons meet holes and 'fill' them **4** spare energy is released as photons **5** of light. If the current is reversed, however, the electrons are unable to move and light is not produced. An infrared LED emits light in the non-visible infrared spectrum, as opposed to the red or green LEDs, used for digital displays.

Cleaning the buttons

A

Remove the battery compartment cover and remove any screws with a small screwdriver. Open the remote and carefully lift off the rubber keypad and clean the top surface with a damp soapy cloth. Clean the undersides of the keys with a dry, lint-free cloth and a little isopropyl alcohol. Replace keypad, screws and battery cover.

Fault diagnosis

No functions at all	**No battery power** *Test batteries in another device. Clean and retension remote battery contacts.* **Remote not functioning** *Tune a radio to medium wave and find a quiet gap between stations. Hold the remote near the radio and press a button. If the remote is working, a high-pitched sound will be heard.*
LED flashes but receiving unit doesn't respond	**Receiving unit faulty or not turned on** *If applicable, follow manufacturer's instructions for resetting unit.*
Some buttons sticking or not functioning	**Dirt inside unit** *Clean keypad. Be careful when opening case, as the keys are all separate in some remote controls. Make sure no moisture is left on the remote, and do not use abrasive cleaning products.* **A**

Video camera

Although camcorders come in various shapes and formats, they are all mechanically very similar. Light passes through a lens and an iris and falls on a charge-coupled device (CCD), which converts it into an electrical signal. The basic care and maintenance procedures are similar for all types of camcorder.

5 The electrical video and audio signals are recorded by a spinning head as magnetic patterns in angled tracks on the video tape (see Video recorder, page 198).

Zoom control

Camera control

Tape compartment

Charge-coupled device (CCD)

Viewfinder

Viewfinder display

Auto-focus device (infrared transmitter and sensor)

Battery

Lens

Iris

Focus lens

4 Sound waves are converted by the **stereo microphone** into two sets of electrical signals. The recording volume is controlled automatically by the camera.

Clock battery

1 The camera focuses automatically. Some use an **infrared transmitter and sensor**. The time it takes for the light to reach the subject and bounce back is used to calculate the distance.

Control buttons

3 Light falling on the CCD is converted to an electrical signal by red-, green- and blue-filtered light-sensitive diodes.

Foldout LCD (liquid crystal display) screen

Stereo microphone

2 The light levels are monitored and a small motor opens and closes the **iris** to change the aperture, and control the light reaching the **CCD**. Another motor moves the focus lens to produce a focused image on the CCD.

Loading the tape

Video cameras load the tape cassette and spool the tape around the tape path in much the same way as a VCR (see Video recorder, page 198). When the eject/load button is pressed, a flap ❶ opens and the cassette cartridge ❷ pops out and up, allowing the user to insert a tape cassette ❸. When the eject/load button is pressed again, the cartridge moves back into the machine and the tape is spooled around the rotating video head ❹ and pinch roller as in a VCR.

Maintenance

Before each use	**Tension tape** *Before shooting, fast-forward and then rewind tape to ensure it is tightly wound. If tape is loose, it may become tangled in mechanism or cause recording problems.* **Play 10 seconds before recording** *Don't start an important recording without playing tape for few seconds. This avoids dusty or crimped tape spoiling the beginning of the real action.* **Clean lens** *Use compressed air or a blower – never blow on it, as moisture from your breath could be harmful to lens – then wipe with a soft lint-free cloth or use professional lens-cleaning equipment.* ❹
Every month	**Clean recording heads** *These should be cleaned with a dry, non-abrasive head cleaning cassette. If you rarely use your video camera, do this only when there is noticeable deterioration in picture quality.*

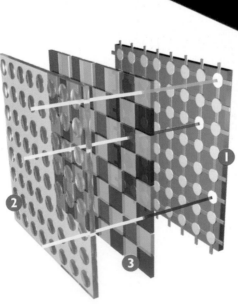

Charge coupled device (CCD)

The **CCD** is the 'retina' of a video camera. It converts light into electrons using millions of tiny light-sensitive diodes, called photosites ❶. However, each photosite can only see in black and white because it measures the intensity of light and not its colour. In order to get a full colour image from a CCD, each tiny photosite is covered with a lens ❷ and a red, green or blue filter ❸. The most common pattern of these filters is called the 'Bayer filter pattern' (shown left). There are twice as many green filters as red or blue because the human eye is more sensitive to green light. The camera then works out the various colours in the image by combining the information received from the CCD.

Cleaning the lens

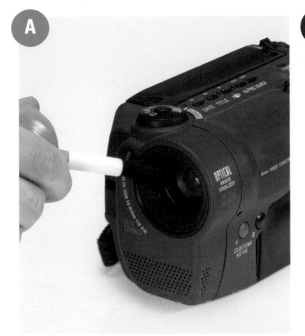

1 Use a compressed air canister or lens brush, both available from camera shops, to remove large particles of dust and dirt from the lens.

2 Apply lens-cleaning fluid to a lint-free cloth, not directly onto the lens, and then wipe gently using a circular motion. Alternatively, use a special lens-cleaning tissue.

Cleaning the contacts

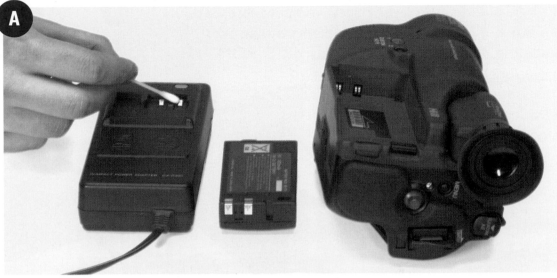

1 Carefully clean the battery contacts on the camera, battery, and charger with a cotton bud dipped in a little isopropyl alcohol. This removes greasy deposits.

2 Rub each of the contacts with a hard pencil eraser to remove corrosion. Do not use a soft eraser. Then clean the contacts and surrounding areas with an artist's brush to remove any debris.

Battery health
Nickel cadmium batteries can suffer from 'memory' problems. Always drain the battery completely before recharging, otherwise the battery's capacity will gradually be reduced.

Fault diagnosis and repair

Camera fails to operate	**Damp inside camera** *Look for 'dew' indicator. Leave camera in dry place for several hours.* **Operating temperature out of range** *Move camera to normal temperature environment.* **Battery contacts dirty** *Thoroughly clean all electrical contacts.* **A**
Tape doesn't run or is damaged	**Dirty capstan and pinch roller** *Clean with cotton bud and isopropyl alcohol.* **Foreign object in mechanism** *Use tweezers to carefully remove object.*
Battery goes flat quickly	**Charger not connected properly** *Clean and retension contacts.* **Faulty battery** *Check and replace if necessary.* **High current drain** *Avoid excessive use of zoom. Turn off LCD screen. Purchase high-capacity battery.*

DVD player

A single-sided single layer digital versatile disc (DVD) can store 4.38GB of information: more than six times the data capacity of a standard CD-ROM, and enough space for more than two hours of sound and video, plus subtitles and additional information.

3 All DVDs contain a recorded code, which is read by the **decoder** and specifies the region in which the disc will play. There are six regions covering the entire globe. A DVD from one region will not play in a player from another.

SCART socket

Tracking mechanism

2 Some DVDs have a second layer. This starts at the outside of the disc, allowing the laser to quickly focus on a different layer without the lens assembly having to move back to the centre of the disc. The DVD player adjusts for single or double-layer playing automatically.

1 A DVD player works in a similar way to a CD player (see CD player, page 182). A drive motor spins the disc as a **tracking mechanism** moves a **laser and lens assembly** over the disc's surface.

Disc

Laser and lens assembly

Decoder circuitry

LED display

6⊳ 1:38
6 7 8 9 10 11 12

DVD tracks

The laser mechanism in a DVD player has to be much more accurate than in a CD player. This is because the tracks on a DVD are closer together, the bumps are smaller, and the data may be on two layers, requiring the laser mechanism ❶ to focus through the first layer ❷ to read the second ❸. To read the layers on a double-sided disc, the disc must be turned over.

Maintenance

When required	**Keep DVD discs clean** (See Compact disc player, page 182).
Twice yearly	**Clean laser lens** Use a good quality proprietary lens cleaning CD.

Fault diagnosis

No functions	**Power supply problem** Check plug wiring, fuse and mains supply for faults.
No picture or no sound	**Poor connection to TV** Check connections are secure. If this does not work, consult qualified repairer.
No discs play	**Dirty lens** Clean lens, If this fails, consult qualified repairer.
Can't play a disc	**DVD has wrong region code for your player**

Audio-visual connecting leads

Connecting audio components together or wiring a video, DVD player or games console to a TV can involve using several different types of lead and choosing from a variety of options. Use these descriptions to help you.

Composite video

Right audio channel

Left audio channel

SCART (Syndicat des Constructeurs d'Appareils Radiorécepteurs et Téléviseurs) is a versatile lead and connector, used to link video devices to one another or to a television. Always use a fully-wired SCART lead, which can carry composite, S-video and RGB signals, and can transmit a signal that switches the TV from standby mode and changes the screen from 4:3 to 16:9 for widescreen broadcasts.

RCA audio leads (Radio Company of America) are normally used to connect audio separates such as a CD or cassette player to an amplifier. These comprise simple leads, known as coaxial leads because they have a central conductive core wrapped in an outer conducting layer. They are normally grouped as a pair – for left and right signal connections to an amplifier – or with an extra yellow RCA cable to carry a composite video signal.

Optical leads carry digital information and are normally used between CD players and MiniDisc recorders. A laser light carries audio information along a fibre-optic lead with no loss of quality, as there is no need to convert the signal from digital to analogue and back.

S-video or Super Video connectors can be found mainly on DVD players and video cameras. This is a single lead with a small multi-pin plug on either end.

Types of video signal

Composite
The red, green and blue components of a video signal are combined and transmitted down a single RCA lead. This signal does not include sound. Composite signals can also be transmitted though a SCART cable.

S-video (Super Video)
This produces a clearer picture on a television than a composite signal. The video signal is split into two channels: chrominance (colour) and luminance (brightness). S-video signals can be transmitted down a special S-video cable (with separate RCA leads for audio left and right), or through a SCART lead.

RGB (Red, Green, Blue)
This is the best way of transmitting a video signal between devices. The red, green and blue elements of a colour TV signal are separated and carried by individual leads within a fully wired SCART cable. The SCART cable carries the sound as well.

Maintenance

After installation	**Tidy leads** *Make sure all leads are away from areas where people walk, and are neatly arranged. Use lead ties and routing channels if necessary.*

Fault diagnosis

Black and white TV picture	**SCART lead partially dislodged** *Check and refit lead at both ends.*
One channel not working	**Lead disconnected** *Check all connections.*

Satellite decoder

Several delivery methods have been developed to cope with the huge data capacity required to transmit digital pictures and sound. One of the most successful of these media is satellite television, whereby digital signals are transmitted from a satellite, via microwaves, to a small parabolic reflector dish connected to the consumer's TV via a set-top box.

1 A dish picks up all available signals from the satellite and feeds them to a **tuner** and **decoder** in the **set-top box**. In a simple receiver, the user can select a single channel to be viewed. Modern receivers allow one signal to be watched while another is recorded.

Output to television

SCART socket

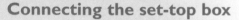

Card reader

Tuner circuits

Set-top box

SMART card

Connecting the set-top box

The satellite receiver needs to be permanently connected to a telephone line so that it can communicate with the service provider. When the viewer uses e-mail or any other interactive service (such as a game), a modem in the receiver dials the provider's computer, in a similar way to connecting to the Internet. During this time, the user's telephone line will be engaged to incoming callers. However, if the user picks up the telephone to make a call, the box will release the line.

If the viewer selects a 'pay per view' film or programme, this information is stored in the decoder and sent to the provider via the telephone connection at an off-peak time – the charge appears on the next telephone bill, unless it is a premium service, in which case information about the additional cost of these calls will be displayed prior to connection.

Parental restrictions can be applied to stop children going online without an adult's permission. This involves setting up a PIN code, which must be entered before the box will allow access to interactive services.

2 The video and audio signals are decoded and fed to the television via a **SCART socket** (see Audio-visual connecting leads, page 207). Under normal conditions, the picture and sound quality is higher than analogue TV systems. An on-screen menu allows the viewer to change preferences, quickly scan through program guides and select channels.

Looking after cables

Make sure all cables are tucked safely out of the way. Use cable ties to keep them tidy. Check that the SCART cable is plugged firmly into the receiver and the back of the VCR or TV. If necessary, remove the cable from both sockets and reinsert it carefully.

Connection to dish

Telephone connection

Secondary output to TV

Decoder circuits

3 A **SMART** card, working in conjunction with software in the receiver, determines your entitlement to view any given channel and the ability of your receiver to unscramble the signal. Some channels (like films and sport) require the purchase of additional subscription packages, controlled by the service provider via the card.

Fault diagnosis

No functions	**No power** *Check plug fuse, flex and socket outlet for faults.*
On-screen error message	**No signal received** *Check cable connections between dish and receiver, check for damaged or kinked cable (see Audio-visual connecting leads, page 207).* **Dish misaligned or receiver faulty** *Consult supplier.*
Blocky or poor quality signal	**Dish misaligned** *Consult supplier.* **Cable/receiver faulty** *Consult supplier.* **Interrupted line of sight between dish and satellite** *Adverse weather conditions may cause this condition temporarily (it may also indicate that dish is slightly off alignment – contact supplier if symptoms persist).* **Receiver overheating** *Ensure adequate ventilation.* **Processor in receiver locked up (picture freezes or can't access different channels)** *Switch off mains power to set-top receiver for a few seconds. If this does not work, reset receiver (consult supplier for precise sequence).*
Video/sound intermittent	**Faulty connections** *Check connections between receiver and VCR/TV.*

Satellite receiving and transmitting signals via microwaves

Geostationary satellites

TV satellite dishes do not move, so the satellite from which they are receiving a signal must stay in the same position in the sky in relation to the dish. This satellite is said to be in a 'geostationary' orbit. This means it always sits at a fixed height above a set point on the equator.

Since the Earth spins at a constant rate (once every 24 hours, approximately), there is only one height (around 22,000 miles) and one speed (around 7,000mph) at which any satellite can orbit, where it will stay above the same spot on the Earth's equator (and be static in relation to all dishes on the Earth's surface).

Camera

No matter how sophisticated their extras, all cameras are essentially a dark box with a hole in one end and a light-sensitive layer at the other. Most home cameras are either SLR (single lens reflex) or point-and-shoot models.

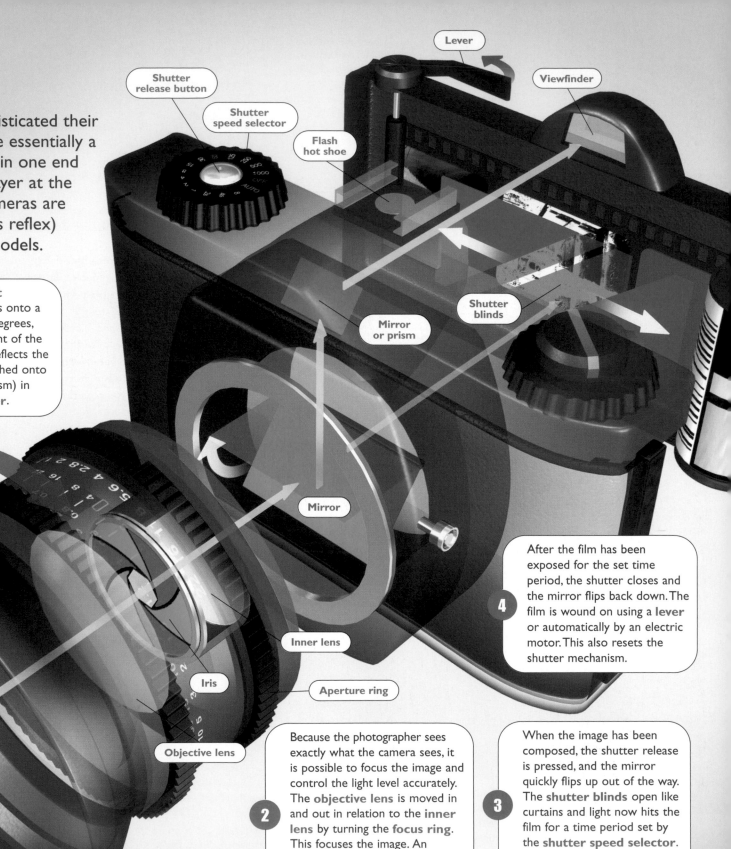

1 In an SLR camera, **light** passes through the lens onto a **mirror** angled at 45 degrees, which is directly in front of the **shutter**. The mirror reflects the image to be photographed onto another mirror (or prism) in front of the **viewfinder**.

Lever

Viewfinder

Shutter release button

Shutter speed selector

Flash hot shoe

Mirror or prism

Shutter blinds

Focus ring

Mirror

Inner lens

Iris

Aperture ring

Objective lens

Light

4 After the film has been exposed for the set time period, the shutter closes and the mirror flips back down. The film is wound on using a **lever** or automatically by an electric motor. This also resets the shutter mechanism.

2 Because the photographer sees exactly what the camera sees, it is possible to focus the image and control the light level accurately. The **objective lens** is moved in and out in relation to the **inner lens** by turning the **focus ring**. This focuses the image. An **aperture ring** opens or closes an **iris** to adjust the amount of light entering the camera.

3 When the image has been composed, the shutter release is pressed, and the mirror quickly flips up out of the way. The **shutter blinds** open like curtains and light now hits the film for a time period set by the **shutter speed selector**. The shutter speed is the length of time the blinds stay open.

Alternative design

Most **point-and-shoot** cameras take the hard work out of focusing and aperture setting, by doing it all automatically. In this model, an infrared sensor ❶ gauges distance by bouncing infrared light off the subject, and measuring the time it takes to return. A light sensor ❷ detects the average light levels and controls the amount of light that will reach the film by setting the shutter speed and aperture.

When the shutter release button is pressed slightly, small battery-powered motors move the lens ❸ to zoom in and focus the image, and also open and close the iris to control the amount of light that will reach the film. Fully pressing the shutter release causes the shutter to open for the set length of time. When the shutter has closed, the electric film advance mechanism ❹ automatically winds on the film ready for the next shot, using cogs with teeth that mesh with the holes ❺ on the film's top and bottom edges. A pressure plate ❻ keeps the film engaged with the cogs.

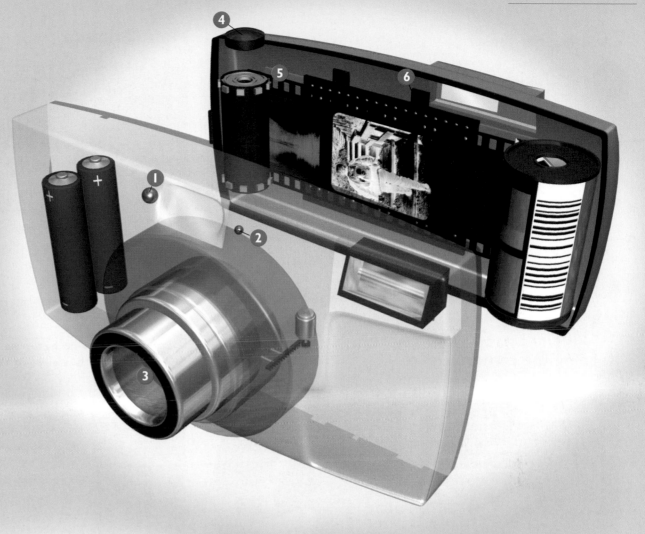

How photographic film works

Film is constructed of translucent layers, each of which is chemically changed by exposure to one of the red, green and blue components of light. When the film is developed, the blue parts of the image appear yellow ❶, the green parts, magenta ❷ and the red, cyan ❸ – these are the negatives of each colour. In order for these to be turned into a colour print, the whole process is performed in reverse by shining white light through the negative ❹ onto colour- sensitive paper. Corresponding layers in the paper react to produce a full colour image.

Advanced photo system (APS) film allows an APS-equipped camera to record details of each shot onto a transparent magnetic layer on the film. Special equipment reads the data when the pictures are developed, and can modify the shape of the final image, and improve the picture quality of each shot accordingly.

Cleaning the lens

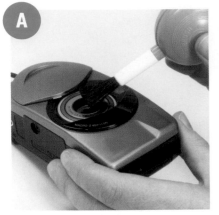

1 Wipe the lens gently with a lens brush to remove dust. Alternatively, use compressed air in cans (sold in camera shops) for blowing away dust.

2 Use a soft dry camera lens cloth or a lens tissue to clean the lens. Use a circular motion and move from the outer edge to the centre.

Keeping the camera clean

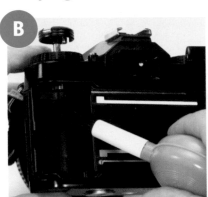

1 Open the back of the camera and use a lens blower brush to remove dust from the film compartment and pressure plate. Avoid the shutter blinds, which are fragile.

2 Brush dust off the reflex mirror in an SLR camera. Do not use compressed air here because you may blow the dust into inaccessible areas.

Keep your camera dry

When shooting in the rain, put the camera into a plastic bag and secure this around the lens with an elastic band. Make sure it is still possible to focus the image and adjust the shutter speed and aperture settings through the bag. Use a lens hood to keep water droplets off the lens.

Maintenance

Before each use	**Clean lens with a lens brush or compressed air can blower** *Then polish with a soft, dry lint-free cloth.* **A**
After each use	**Replace lens cover and store camera in its case** *If not to be used for a month or longer, remove batteries and store separately.*
When loading film	**Check interior of camera is free from dust and obstructions** *Even a small particle of dust can ruin an otherwise perfect picture. Clean inside camera regularly.* **B**

Fault diagnosis

Camera does not work at all	**Flat batteries** *Check and replace batteries if necessary.* **Batteries not making contact** *Clean battery contacts. Also check spring tension of contacts; retensioning if necessary.*
Camera does not work – display working	**Film incorrectly loaded** *Check there is film in camera and holes align with cog teeth. Reload film correctly.* **SLR lens loose** *If camera is SLR, check lens is fitted correctly and clean contacts on lens and camera body.* **Dry moving parts** *Ask qualified repairer to check camera and lubricate moving parts.*
External flash on SLR fails	**Flat batteries** *Check and replace batteries if necessary.* **Flash unit not making contact** *Clean contacts on camera shoe and flash unit.* **A**
Camera does not auto-focus	**Manual focus selected** *Check camera settings.* **SLR lens loose** *If camera is SLR, check lens is fitted correctly and clean contacts on lens and camera body.*

Cleaning SLR flash contacts

Turn the camera off. Dampen a cotton bud with a small amount of electrical contact cleaner. Rub the contacts on the top of the hot shoe, and on the base of the flash unit.

Binoculars

Developed from the telescope, binoculars use lenses and prisms to magnify objects. The lenses increase the size of, and focus, the image. The prisms increase the length of the light path to allow binoculars to be smaller than a telescope, but with the same degree of magnification.

Eyepiece

Focus wheel

4 — One of the eyepieces will have an individual focusing facility, called a **dioptre adjustment**. This is used to compensate for any focal difference in vision between the left and right eye.

Eyepiece lens

Objective lens

1 — As light, reflected from an object, enters the binoculars, the **objective lenses** magnify, mirror and invert the image.

2 — The inverted and reversed image passes through two **erecting prisms**. These turn the image the correct way up and mirror it. The light then passes through the **eyepiece lenses**.

Erecting (Porro) prisms

Dioptre adjustment

3 — A geared **focus wheel** between the eyepieces moves both objective lenses to allow the viewer to adjust the focus of the image.

Maintenance

Before use	Clean lenses Ⓐ

Fault diagnosis

Blurred image	**Lenses misaligned** Contact qualified repairer.
Sticking focus wheel	**Mechanism needs lubrication** Clean and lubricate mechanism.

Cleaning the lenses

Ⓐ

Use a soft brush or air-blower to remove dust. Then wipe lenses with a lint-free cloth dampened with proprietary lens cleaner, using a circular motion.

Alternative design

Roof prism binoculars are physically smaller than binoculars using Porro prisms (above) because they allow the objective lenses to be in line with the eyepiece. This is achieved using a more complex light path ❶ than in Porro prism binoculars.

Computer equipment

Computer

A personal computer is a combination of hardware and software, which can carry out instructions and respond to user input from a keyboard or mouse. Data flows around a computer like traffic around a city. Some streets are one-way, others allow traffic in both directions. If the processor is thought of as a factory, data, or 'goods', are being moved to and fro between ports (connecting sockets), storage facilities (memory) and consumer outlets (screen and speakers).

Graphics card

RAM

All the software data used by the computer is stored on the **hard disk**. This is a magnetic disk, much like a CD, in a case within the system unit. The disk is spun by a tiny electric motor and read by one or more drive heads that pass over it.

Information read from the hard disk flows from one place in the computer to another through 'buses', like roads. The capacity of a bus, effectively the number of lanes in the road, is known as its 'width' and determines how much data can be transmitted at one time. The clock speed of the bus, measured in MHz, indicates how fast data transfer will be, or the speed limit on that section of the road.

CD-ROM   Hard disk   Floppy disk

The computer may also include **CD-ROM** and **floppy disk** drives to read and write data to and from different types of disk. These would each be linked, by the buses, to the **processor**.

Keyboard connector

USB ports

Sound card

Processor

BIOS (ROM)

Mouse connector

The monitor and speakers are attached to the **graphics card** and **sound card** respectively. These cards convert digital signals from the processor to analogue video and sound signals, which the monitor and speakers convert to soundwaves and light.

External devices, such as **keyboard** and **mouse**, are connected to the motherboard via ports and cables. Serial (Com) and parallel ports are largely being supplanted by **USB ports** (Universal Serial Bus). The benefits of having USB are: faster data transfer; multiple use – up to 127 devices can be connected via a single port using hubs; and simplicity – hardware can be added and removed while the computer is still running.

When a program is launched from the hard disk, the processor moves the data from the disk into temporary storage in the **Random Access Memory (RAM)** while it is worked on. The processor constantly moves data back and forth between disk and memory.

System unit

The computer's brain, known as the central processing unit (CPU), is mounted on the motherboard within the system unit. The motherboard is the primary circuit board, to which all other devices are connected, either directly or via ports and cables.

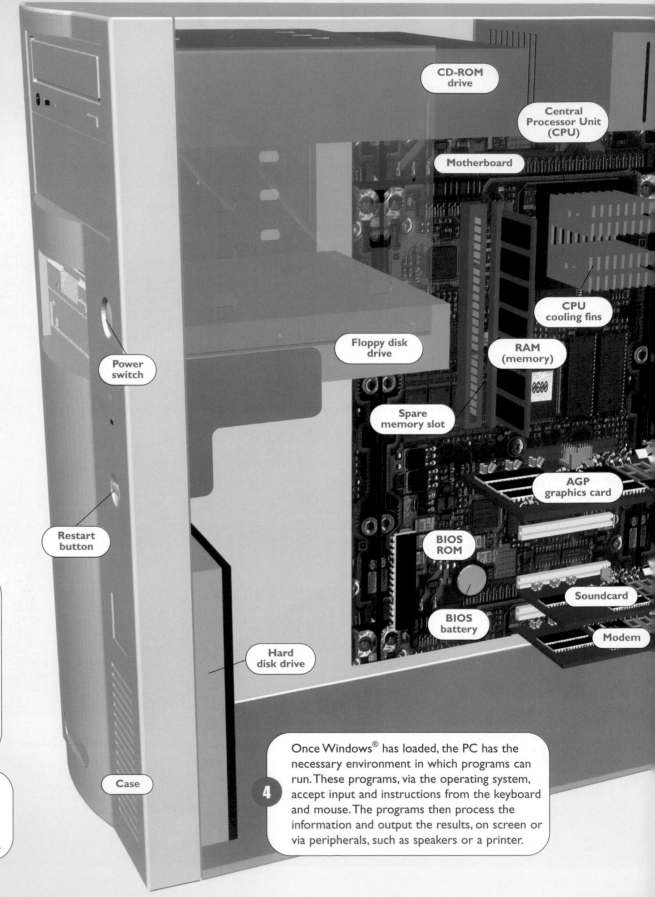

1 When the power is turned on, simple system tests and basic instructions about how to start the computer are loaded from a small section of memory called **Read Only Memory (ROM)**. These instructions are called the **BIOS** (Basic Input/Output System). Everything stored in ROM is retained when the computer is turned off and cannot inadvertently be changed or removed, which is why it is called 'read only'.

2 The operating system of a computer (Microsoft® Windows® for example) is then automatically 'loaded' from the **hard disk**, which is where all the data on a PC is stored. The operating system is loaded into the computer's main **Random Access Memory (RAM)**. This is the memory used to temporarily store files and programs that are being worked on.

3 As the operating system loads, it scans the hardware installed on the PC and loads software, called 'drivers', to control and communicate with the hardware.

4 Once Windows® has loaded, the PC has the necessary environment in which programs can run. These programs, via the operating system, accept input and instructions from the keyboard and mouse. The programs then process the information and output the results, on screen or via peripherals, such as speakers or a printer.

CD-ROM drive

Central Processor Unit (CPU)

Motherboard

CPU cooling fins

Floppy disk drive

RAM (memory)

Power switch

Spare memory slot

AGP graphics card

Restart button

BIOS ROM

Soundcard

BIOS battery

Modem

Hard disk drive

Case

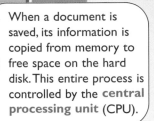

Power supply

7 When a document is saved, its information is copied from memory to free space on the hard disk. This entire process is controlled by the **central processing unit** (CPU).

6 Because all the documents currently being worked on are only temporarily stored, if the computer were turned off, this data would be lost. To avoid this, the documents must be saved to the hard disk. Data stored on the hard disk is not lost when the power is turned off.

5 While a document Is being worked on, it is stored temporarily in RAM. The processor interprets the user's instructions from the keyboard and mouse, loads required data from other parts of its memory (and the hard disk if necessary), and performs the calculations before returning the modified data to the temporary memory.

Defragmenting the hard disk

Although Windows® can usually find all the data on the hard disk quickly and easily, over time it becomes fragmented, and a single file may be split up and stored on different sections of the disk's surface. Under normal circumstances, this poses no problems since the sections of files are simply retrieved from their separate locations and put back together. However, excessive fragmentation can cause the system to slow down as it searches for bits of information all over the disk. A disk defragmenter program tracks down all the parts of the split files, and moves and recombines them on a new section of disk as complete files.

Maintenance

If using Windows Millennium Edition® (Me)	**If you have not already done so, create a startup disk** *This stores files that a computer needs to operate at the most basic level. This disk can be used to get the computer up and running so that you, or a qualified repairer, can solve underlying problem.* **A** *Windows XP®does not include the option to create a startup disk.*
Once a month	**Run Scandisk** *Scandisk checks your hard disk for data errors and physical damage and attempts to correct any problems it finds.* **(See B, page 220.)** **Run Disk Defragmenter** *Disk Defragmenter reorganises the data on hard disk to improve the efficiency of the computer.* **(See C, page 220.)** **Clean floppy drive heads** *Use proprietary floppy drive cleaning system to remove build-up on the drive heads.*
Every six months	**Uninstall unused software** *Hard disk will eventually become cluttered and slow if unused software is not removed. This is especially true if trial programs from CD-Rom or Internet are installed regularly.* **(See D, page 220.)**

Making a startup disk (in Windows Me)®

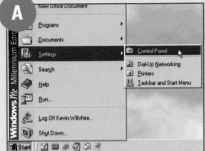

A

1 Go to the Start menu and select Control Panel. In the Control Panel window, double-click the Add/Remove programs icon.

2 Click the Startup Disk tab, then click on the Create Disk button. The computer will begin preparing the startup disk files, then prompt the user to insert a blank floppy disk into the [A:] drive on the front of the PC.

3 Insert a blank or spare floppy disk and click on the OK button. The computer will start to load the necessary startup data and diagnostic tools onto the floppy disk. The process takes a couple of minutes. When it has finished, eject the floppy, label it and store in a safe place.

Running Scandisk (in Windows XP®)

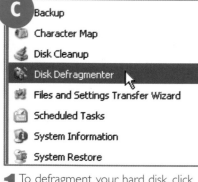

1 Scandisk is a small program supplied with Windows. Click on Start, All Programs, Accessories and choose Windows Explorer.

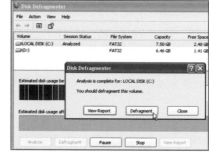

2 Click on the plus sign next to My Computer. Then, locate and right-click the drive you want to scan, shown here as LOCAL DISK (C:), and choose Properties from the pop-up menu. Click on the Tools tab and then on the Check Now button.

3 Tick both items, and click on the Start button. When windows asks you to schedule the scan for next time the PC is restarted, click Yes. After the next restart, the disk is scanned.

Defragmenting a hard disk (in Windows XP®)

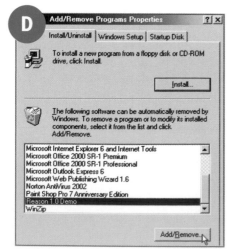

1 To defragment your hard disk, click on Start, All Programs, Accessories, System Tools and choose Disk Defragmenter.

2 Select the drive you want to defragment, and click on the Analyze button.

3 Windows quickly checks the amount of data fragmentation on the selected disk. If, after analysis, Windows indicates you need to defragment the drive, click on the Defragment button.

4 Windows reorganises the data on the disk. A coloured display indicates the progress. The process can take some time and you should leave your PC alone until it is complete.

Uninstalling programs

1 If you have a PC running Windows® 98 or Me, open the Windows control panel and double click Add/Remove Programs. Locate and select the program you want to uninstall, and click the Add/Remove button, followed by Yes.

2 If your PC is running Windows XP, click on Start and choose Control Panel. If you are in Category View (above), click on Add or Remove Programs. Otherwise, double click the Add or Remove Programs icon.

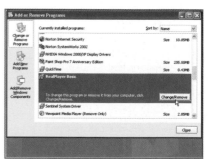

3 Select the item you want to uninstall and click on the Change/Remove button next to its name. Then click on Yes to confirm the uninstallation.

Troubleshooting Windows Me®

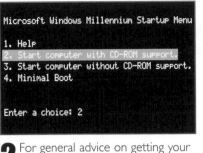

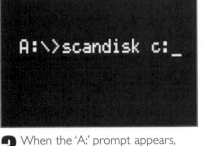

1 Insert the Startup floppy and turn on the PC. Wait while a series of diagnostic tools and a basic operating system are loaded.

2 For general advice on getting your PC going again, highlight '1. Help'. To continue, highlight '2. Start computer with CD-ROM support' and press the Return key.

3 When the 'A:' prompt appears, type 'scandisk' and a space, followed by the drive letter of your hard disk (usually C) and a colon, and press Return.

4 When asked if you want to perform a surface scan, press 'Y'. The disk is scanned for errors. If any are found, an attempt is made to repair the error.

Fault diagnosis

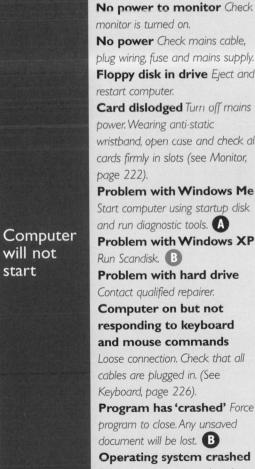

Computer will not start

No power to monitor *Check monitor is turned on.*

No power *Check mains cable, plug wiring, fuse and mains supply.*

Floppy disk in drive *Eject and restart computer.*

Card dislodged *Turn off mains power. Wearing anti-static wristband, open case and check all cards firmly in slots (see Monitor, page 222).*

Problem with Windows Me *Start computer using startup disk and run diagnostic tools.*  **A**

Problem with Windows XP *Run Scandisk.* **B**

Problem with hard drive *Contact qualified repairer.*

Computer on but not responding to keyboard and mouse commands *Loose connection. Check that all cables are plugged in. (See Keyboard, page 226).*

Program has 'crashed' *Force program to close. Any unsaved document will be lost.* **B**

Operating system crashed *Force the computer to shut down, wait a while and start it up again.*

Restarting frozen programs in Windows XP® and Me®

1 Press and hold the Ctrl key followed by the Alt and Del keys simultaneously. This brings up the Close Program dialogue box, which lists all the programs currently running on your PC, including those running invisibly.

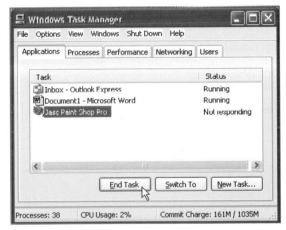

2 Scroll down the list until you see the name of the program that has crashed – it will be labelled 'Not responding' – then click the End Task button.

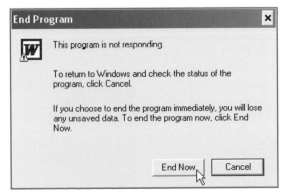

3 The crashed program should then close. If it does not, another dialogue box will open, giving you the option either to wait for the program to close by itself or to terminate the program immediately. Click on the End Now button. Restart Windows, then restart the PC. If your PC does not have a restart button on the front, hold down the on/off switch for more than four seconds to turn it off. Then start the PC again.

Monitor

The monitor is a computer's primary output device. It may be similar to a TV in size and function, or may be a flat screen composed of thousands of tiny transistors. The computer communicates with the monitor via the graphics card, which converts the ones and zeros from the processor's digital data into pictures and text.

1 In response to input from the keyboard, mouse or processor, a program tells the operating system (for example, Microsoft® Windows®) it wants to create a character or shape on the screen. The processor interprets these instructions and sends **digital data** (ones and zeros) to the **graphics card**.

Digital data (ones and zeros from processor)

2 The graphics card has memory, which stores the information required to display many common shapes and images. If the computer wants a box to be drawn, it simply tells the card to draw a box and gives it the dimensions and colour.

Different graphics cards and displays

Most graphics cards have an onboard processor specifically designed to manipulate 2D and 3D images rapidly. As much as 128MB of fast RAM may be fitted as well, in which images are 'drawn' before being sent to the monitor. If you want to play 3D accelerated games, choose a card which has 64MB of RAM or more and a built-in 3D accelerator chip. Some graphics cards also have a TV output, which can be plugged directly into a normal television. Monitors can be like CRT screens (see Television set, page 194), or may be similar to a laptop screen, which is made of thousands of transistors each of which acts as a pixel by blocking or allowing light from a fluorescent backlight. Filters provide the red, green and blue colours. These flat TFT (thin film transistor) screens are clearer than standard monitors, but may not be able to support such high resolutions.

Maintenance

Once a month	**Keep screen clean** *Use anti-static proprietary cleaning product to clean surface of screen.* **Check for updated drivers** *Most programs are constantly being improved and updated. Information and downloadable upgrades may be available on program manufacturers' Web sites.* **A**

4 The image to be displayed is split into its red, green and blue components and corresponding signals are sent from the graphics processor to the **monitor** for display. Controls on the monitor allow the user to alter brightness and contrast, and to align the image correctly onscreen.

Output to monitor

Graphics processor

Image split into red, green and blue

3 The **processor** on the **graphic card** decodes the digital ones and zeros it receives from the PC, leaving Windows® and the main computer processor free to work on other things. This maximises the PC's processing speed.

Downloading new drivers

» **Windows 95/98/Me Drivers**
» **Windows 2000 Drivers**
» **Windows XP Drivers**
» **Windows NT Drivers**
» **nForce Drivers**
» **Linux Drivers**

File Download

You are downloading the file:

WinXP_64_22.20.exe from 205.158.109.140

Would you like to open the file or save it to your computer?

Open | Save | Cancel | More Info

Always ask before opening this type of file

1 Check the manufacturer's manual for details of their Web sites. Log on to the Internet and enter their Web site address, also known as a URL (Uniform Resource Locator) in your browser's address line.

2 Locate a link marked 'support', 'help' or 'drivers' and click it. When the page loads, find your device and operating system. You may have to select from drop-down lists. Also, read the instructions on how to install.

3 Check you have the correct version of the upgrade or driver for your system, and click to download. Then click Save. When the download is complete, follow the instructions on the site to install the new software.

Keep your distance
To avoid tiredness when working at a screen for long periods, place the monitor at eye level around 50cm from your head. Always take frequent breaks.

223

Fault diagnosis

Monitor not working at all	**Poor PC connection** *Check monitor connections.* **No power to monitor** *Check mains supply cables, plugs and fuses.* **Graphics card dislodged** *Make sure graphics card is seated and screwed in properly.* **A**
Display problems when running certain games or 3D software	**Incorrect or out-of-date graphics card drivers** *Download correct drivers from Web.* **(See A, page 223.)** **Graphics card dislodged** *Make sure graphics card is seated and screwed in properly.* **A** *Check software manufacturer's Web site for compatibility issues.*
Display garbled and frozen	**Unsupported resolution selected** *Start in VGA (video graphics array) mode and select lower resolution, such as 800x600 or 640x480.* **B** **Refresh rate set incorrectly** *Start in VGA mode (as above) if screen illegible. Reset refresh rate to adapter default.* **C** **Monitor settings incorrect** *Check manual for details on how to change display geometry and monitor settings.*

Graphics card dislodged

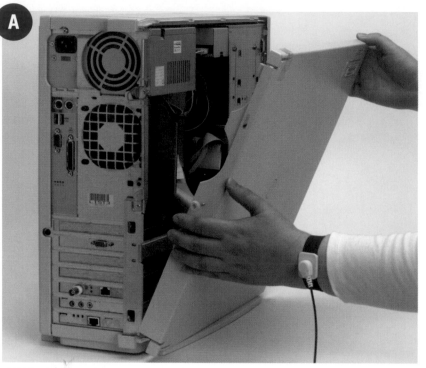

1 Wearing an anti-static wrist band throughout, turn your PC off and unplug the mains supply. Remove the cables from the back, making a note of where they go if you're unsure how to plug it back together. Place the PC on a safe work surface and unscrew the retaining screw or screws holding the case on. The whole case may lift off, or the left side may open.

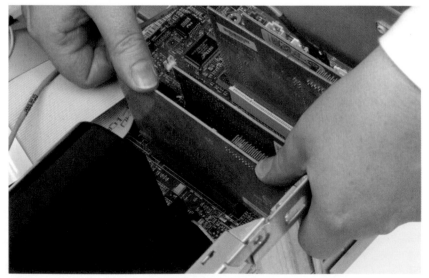

2 The graphics card is usually plugged into the brown AGP (Accelerated Graphics Port) slot (shown above). The card will always have a socket on its outer edge with 15 holes. If not in the AGP slot, it will be in a white PCI (Peripheral Component Interconnect) slot. Make sure the card is firmly seated.

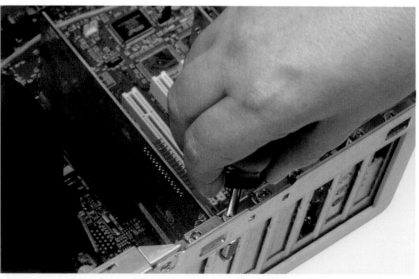

3 If necessary, unscrew the retaining screw and lift the card out of the socket. There may be a plastic lever. Then push it in firmly but gently and tighten the screw. Reassemble the PC and reconnect the cables.

Resetting the monitor resolution

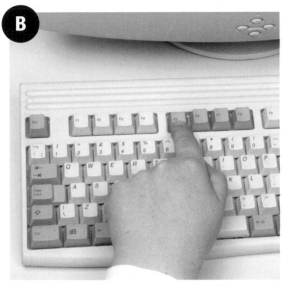

1 If the screen is legible, go to step 2. If the screen is illegible, restart your PC using the Restart button on the front of the case. When you see the words 'keyboard detected' hold down the F5 key to start in Safe Mode – this will allow you to troubleshoot the operating system to determine what is not functioning properly. When Windows® starts, click OK.

2 Click on the Start button and select Control Panel. Click on Appearance and Themes if in Category view and click Display, or double-click the Display icon in the Classic Control Panel. This opens the Display Properties dialogue box.

3 Click on the Settings tab and choose 640x480 or 800x600 from the Resolution slider. Select whichever is the lowest value available. Even the oldest monitors can work with these low resolutions. Restart your PC if necessary.

Resetting the refresh rate

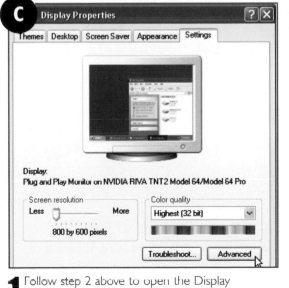

1 Follow step 2 above to open the Display Properties dialogue box. Click on the Settings tab and then the Advanced button.

2 Click on the Monitor tab and choose 60 Hertz from the drop-down menu under 'Screen refresh rate'. Or choose Adapter default if 60 Hertz is not on the list.

3 Click Apply and check that the monitor is working properly. If it is working, click on the Yes button. If not, it should revert automatically after 15 seconds.

Keyboard

The keyboard is a computer's primary input device. As well as typing characters, the user can use key combinations and special keys to control functions of a computer and its programs.

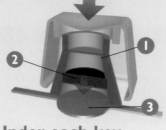

Under each key

1. Bump in flexible membrane
2. Carbon contact
3. Connector

1 Each **key** on the keyboard has a corresponding contact on the **circuit board** underneath. As the key is pressed down, it pushes on a **bump** in a **flexible membrane**, under which is a cylindrical **carbon contact**.

Keys

2 As the carbon contact touches a connector, it completes a circuit. The **processor** works out which key has been pressed, filters out bounce which might be interpreted as repeated presses, and relays the information to the PC.

3 If the key is held down, the processor recognises this as a deliberate action, and instructs the computer to repeat the character or instruction.

Shortcut keys

5 Multimedia keyboards include **shortcut keys**. There may be controls for the CD player, volume buttons and instant e-mail and Internet access keys. Pressing one of these triggers a sequence of commands to be executed quickly and easily.

LEDs

Processor

Carbon contact in each bump

4 **LEDs** on the keyboard indicate whether the number, caps or scroll lock is engaged.

Flexible membrane

Circuit board

Checking the cables

A

Turn the computer off. Check that the power supply cable is firmly plugged into the correct port. If the keyboard plug is not colour coded or clearly marked, check the manual for details.

Cleaning the keyboard

A

Turn off the PC. Spray the cleaning product onto a cloth, and wipe the keys and case gently to remove dirt. Use a lint-free or foam cotton bud to clean between the keys.

Maintenance

As required, depending on use	**Remove debris from within keyboard** Turn upside down over bin, and tap to dislodge debris from under keys. For spilt drinks, turn upside down over bucket and leave to dry. **Clean keyboard** Use proprietary computer keyboard cleaning product to remove grease and dirt from keys. **A**

Mouse

A mouse is used to control the movement of a PC's on-screen pointer. Depending on where the pointer is positioned, pressing buttons on the mouse gives the PC a variety of instructions.

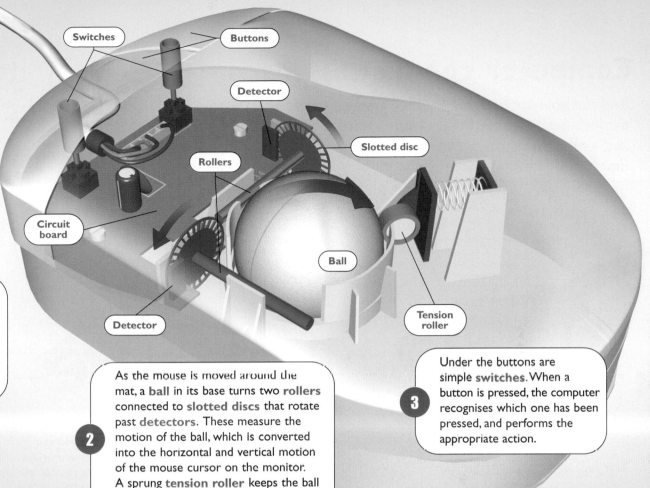

Switches

Buttons

Detector

Slotted disc

Rollers

Circuit board

Ball

Detector

Tension roller

1 A PC mouse will have at least two **buttons** – the left button selects on-screen items and the right displays drop down menus. Some mice also include a scroll wheel to allow the user to rapidly move up and down a page.

2 As the mouse is moved around the mat, a **ball** in its base turns two **rollers** connected to **slotted discs** that rotate past **detectors**. These measure the motion of the ball, which is converted into the horizontal and vertical motion of the mouse cursor on the monitor. A sprung **tension roller** keeps the ball pressed against the other rollers.

3 Under the buttons are simple **switches**. When a button is pressed, the computer recognises which one has been pressed, and performs the appropriate action.

Alternative design

Instead of a ball, an **optical mouse** detects movement using a bright light emitting diode (LED) and sensors. As the mouse is moved, changes in the way light from the LED is reflected by the surface beneath it are detected. Its circuitry interprets these changes into direction of movement. A **cordless mouse** uses a ball, but transmits radio signals in place of electrical ones down a cord.

Cleaning the mouse

A

1 Turn off the PC and remove panel on the base of the mouse. Lift out the ball and clean rollers with a cotton bud dipped in isopropyl alcohol. Use a soft plastic tool on stubborn deposits.

Maintenance

| Once a month | **Clean mouse ball and rollers** (A) *Dirt and dust can build up on rollers causing erratic pointer motion.* |

2 Wipe the ball with a soft damp cloth. Wait for the ball to dry and then reassemble the mouse and turn the PC back on.

Fault diagnosis

Mouse not working	**Cables dislodged** *Check connections (see Keyboard, page 226) and reboot PC.*
Cursor jumping	**Dirty rollers** *Clean ball and rollers.* (A) **Settings incorrect** *Change settings on your PC.* (A)
Mouse erratic	**Cordless mouse batteries flat** *Change batteries.* **Cordless mouse receiver displaced** *Move receiver.*

Changing the speed of your pointer

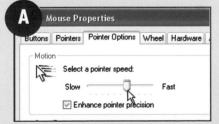

A Mouse Properties

Buttons | Pointers | Pointer Options | Wheel | Hardware

Motion

Select a pointer speed:

Slow ———————— Fast

☑ Enhance pointer precision

Click on the Start button and choose Control Panel. If the Control Panel is in Category View, click once on 'Pointers and Other Hardware'. Otherwise, double click the Mouse icon. Click on the Pointer Options tab and drag the slider to modify the tracking speed.

Computer connecting leads

It is possible to connect a wide range of peripheral devices to a computer – from printers and scanners to mobile phones and even sewing machines. However, as digital technology has developed, the ports and connection types have changed as well, requiring new styles of lead, plug and socket.

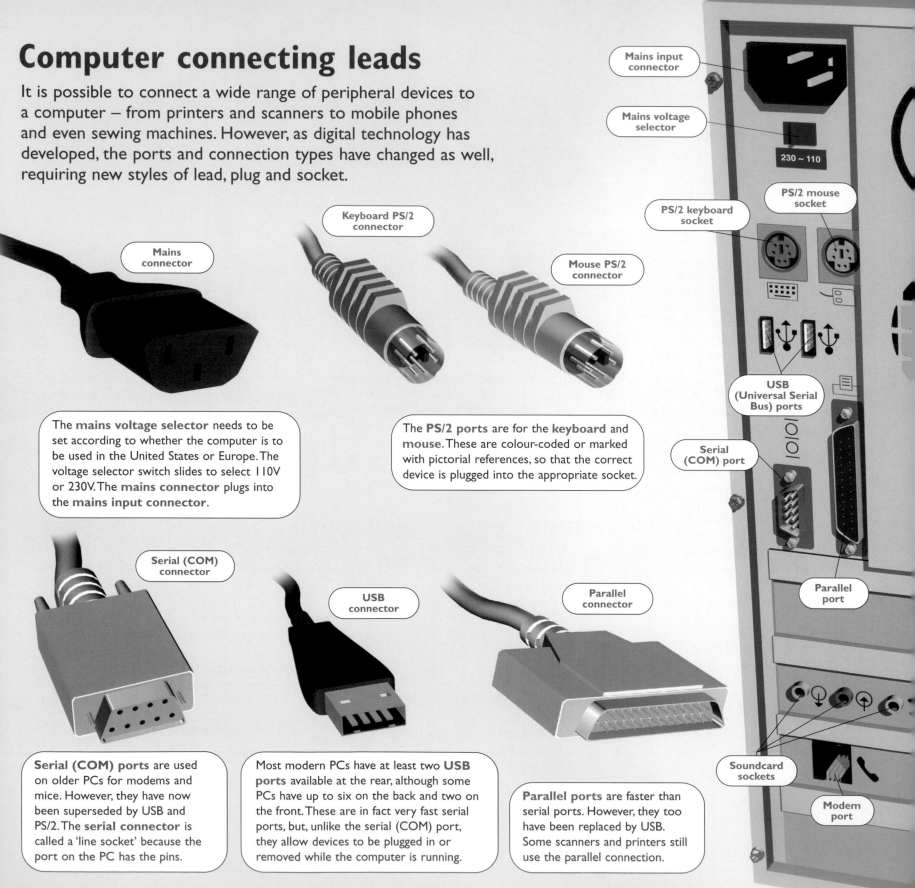

Mains input connector

Mains voltage selector

230 ~ 110

PS/2 mouse socket

PS/2 keyboard socket

USB (Universal Serial Bus) ports

Serial (COM) port

Parallel port

Soundcard sockets

Modem port

Keyboard PS/2 connector

Mouse PS/2 connector

Mains connector

The **mains voltage selector** needs to be set according to whether the computer is to be used in the United States or Europe. The voltage selector switch slides to select 110V or 230V. The **mains connector** plugs into the **mains input connector**.

The **PS/2 ports** are for the **keyboard** and **mouse**. These are colour-coded or marked with pictorial references, so that the correct device is plugged into the appropriate socket.

Serial (COM) connector

USB connector

Parallel connector

Serial (COM) ports are used on older PCs for modems and mice. However, they have now been superseded by USB and PS/2. The **serial connector** is called a 'line socket' because the port on the PC has the pins.

Most modern PCs have at least two **USB ports** available at the rear, although some PCs have up to six on the back and two on the front. These are in fact very fast serial ports, but, unlike the serial (COM) port, they allow devices to be plugged in or removed while the computer is running.

Parallel ports are faster than serial ports. However, they too have been replaced by USB. Some scanners and printers still use the parallel connection.

Monitor
connector

The computer monitor plugs into a dedicated **monitor port**, which is attached to a graphics card plugged into the motherboard. On some PCs, the monitor port is attached to the motherboard directly.

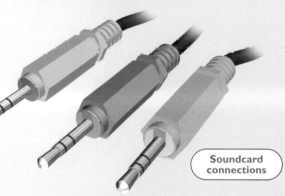

Soundcard
connections

The soundcard will usually have sockets for **speakers (line out)**, **line in** and **microphone**. These may be colour coded or will have a small image next to each socket. Check the manual if you are unsure about the connections. Here, the speaker connections are green, line-in is blue and microphone is pink.

Monitor
port

Modem
connector

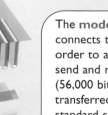

The **modem** is where your PC connects to a **telephone line** in order to access the Internet and send and receive emails. 56 kbps (56,000 bits of information transferred per second) is the standard speed for a home PC's **dial-up modem**.

Maintenance

| Before switching on | **Carefully fix cables away from feet and walking areas** Attach to desk legs with cable ties. Always keep cable layouts neat and away from walkways, pets and children. **Check plug connections** Periodically check all plugs are firmly fitted and make sure that any clips or screws are secured. |

Fault diagnosis

No functions	**No power** Check power supply for faults and connections to device, if applicable. **Data cable disconnected** Check and refit. **Cable damaged** Check and replace.
No screen display – LEDs on PC lit normally	**No power to monitor** Check power supply for faults and connections to device. Check video data cable correctly fitted to rear of the PC.
Network connection fails	**Network cable unplugged** Refit cables. **Computer problem** Restart all PCs on network. If this fails, contact qualified repairer.

Network cards

Some computers have network cards fitted. These allow you to connect two or more computers to share information and hardware, such as a printer or scanner. There are two types of connector for a home network: 'RJ45', which looks a little like a telephone plug and cable, and 'BNC', which is like a TV aerial cable. Consult your manual to find the correct cables for your network card: only one type will fit.

Ink-jet printer

Working like miniature airbrushes, ink-jet printers spray droplets of ink onto paper from hundreds of tiny nozzles. Most ink-jets print using piezoelectric technology but some use a thermal bubble process.

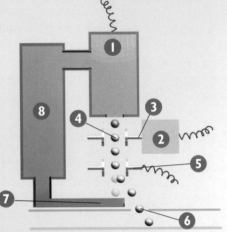

Inside a print head nozzle

How the print head works

The print head is made up of hundreds of tiny nozzles, each of which contains a piezo-electric crystal. An electric charge is supplied to the crystal causing it to vibrate **1**. This forces a constant stream of ink droplets out of the nozzle. A charging control **2** receives the electronic print data from the computer and converts it into a series of electric pulses, which turn the charge electrode **3** on and off. Any ink droplets that pass the charge electrode when it is on become charged **4**. As they continue to fall, they are diverted by the deflection plates **5**, which also carry a charge. They then pass through a hole **6** in the bottom of the nozzle assembly and on to the paper. Ink droplets that do not receive a charge are not affected by the deflection plates, so continue to drop directly into a gutter **7** and are routed back to the ink reservoir. **8**

Maintenance

Once a month	**Perform self-test and self-cleaning** *Check manual for instructions.*
Before fitting new ink cartridge	**Remove paper debris from feed path** *Fit new cartridge as described in manual.*

Bubble-jet printers

The print head of a bubble-jet printer has hundreds of nozzles operating at once. In each nozzle is a resistor, through which is passed a current that varies according to the print data of the document. This causes the resistor to heat up, which in turn causes the ink to expand in a bubble. This pushes ink out of the nozzle and directly onto the paper. As the resistor cools, the bubble contracts and more ink is drawn in from the ink reservoir.

1 When a document is sent to print, the **paper feed stepper motor** turns rubber rollers to move a sheet of paper from the **paper tray** to position it under the **print head**.

Paper tray

2 The paper feed stepper motor is synchronised with the **print head stepper motor** and **drive belt** by an internal microprocessor to position the print head accurately over the paper.

3 Microscopic ink droplets are drawn from the **ink cartridge** and then precisely targeted onto the paper by the **print head**. In some printers, the print head is integrated into the ink cartridge.

Drive belt

Stabiliser bar

4 A **stabiliser bar** ensures the print head remains the correct distance above the paper. This bar can be raised by a **lever** to prevent smudging if thicker paper is used.

Paper feed stepper motor

8 When the whole page has been printed, the print head is returned to the **park position** and the paper feed stepper motor rolls the paper out of the printer.

7 The process of stopping and starting is so quick that the print head appears to move continuously.

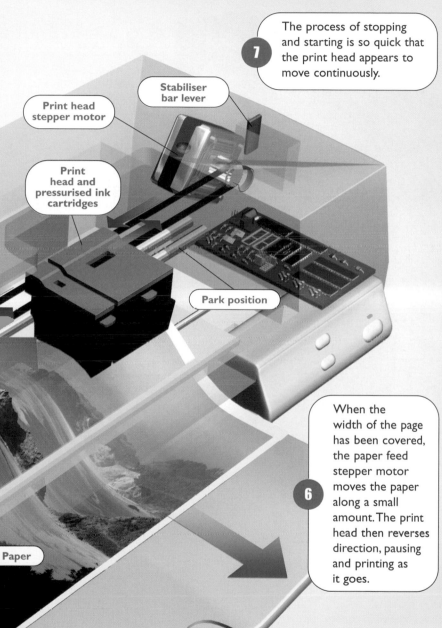

Stabiliser bar lever

Print head stepper motor

Print head and pressurised ink cartridges

Park position

6 When the width of the page has been covered, the paper feed stepper motor moves the paper along a small amount. The print head then reverses direction, pausing and printing as it goes.

Paper

5 As the print head is moved across the page, it stops every fraction of a second to spray dots of ink onto the paper. The speed and quality of the printing is determined by the dpi (dots per inch) setting. The higher the dpi, the slower the print job and the better the quality.

Fault diagnosis

Smudged ink	**Poor-quality paper** *Always use correct paper for printer.* **Paper too thick** *Raise print head using stabiliser bar lever. Return to normal position when using standard paper.* **Dirty heads** *Perform self-clean. If symptom persists, contact qualified repairer.*
Unused cartridge but no ink	**Dirty heads** *Perform self-clean. If symptom persists, contact qualified repairer.* **Heads dried out** *Replace cartridge.* **Protective tape left on print head** *Remove tape and protective covers.* **Ⓐ**
Odd characters on page	**Wrong printer selected** *If more than one printer installed in Windows® printers folder, check correct one has been selected. If there is only one printer, make it the default. Delete unused printers from folder.* **Corrupted driver** *Reinstall printer driver from manufacturer's CD-ROM or web site.* **Upgraded operating system (e.g. Microsoft® Windows® 98 to Windows® XP)** *If new operating system does not have correct driver, obtain one from printer manufacturer. Many can be downloaded via the Internet.*
Poor print quality	**Dirty heads** *Perform self-clean. If symptom persists, contact qualified repairer.*
Warning lights flashing	**Fault detected by printer** *Check documentation supplied with printer.*

Checking the print head

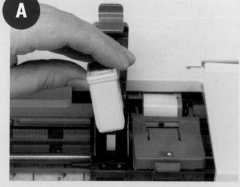

Ⓐ

Move the cartridge to its park or installation position and unclip it. Lift out the cartridge and check for protective covers or tapes. Check the manufacturer's manual for instructions if you are unsure how to do this. Remove any protective tapes or plastic covers and refit cartridge.

Laser printer

The principle at the heart of a laser printer is the same as that which causes dust to be attracted to a television screen: an electrical charge, or static. In the case of the printer, the 'dust' is particles of pigment, called toner, and the 'screen' is a photoconductive drum.

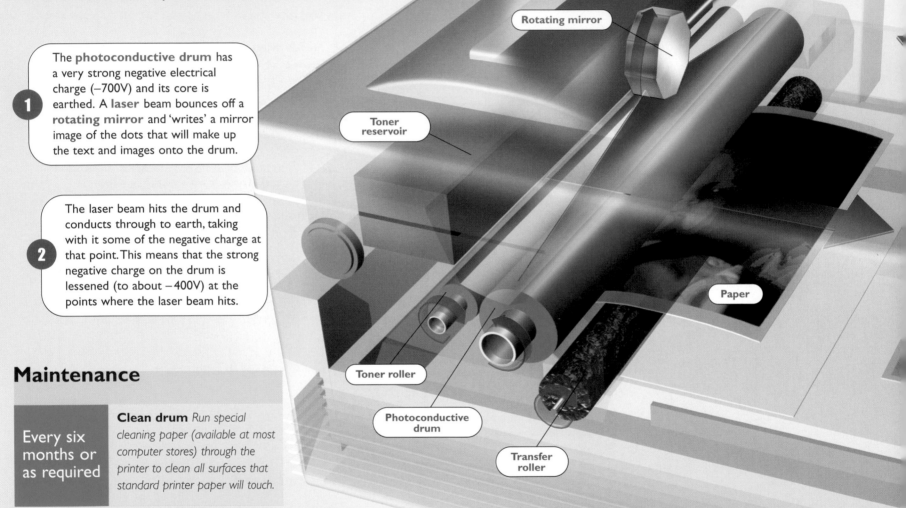

Laser

Rotating mirror

Toner reservoir

Paper

Toner roller

Photoconductive drum

Transfer roller

1 The **photoconductive drum** has a very strong negative electrical charge (−700V) and its core is earthed. A **laser** beam bounces off a **rotating mirror** and 'writes' a mirror image of the dots that will make up the text and images onto the drum.

2 The laser beam hits the drum and conducts through to earth, taking with it some of the negative charge at that point. This means that the strong negative charge on the drum is lessened (to about −400V) at the points where the laser beam hits.

Maintenance

Every six months or as required

Clean drum *Run special cleaning paper (available at most computer stores) through the printer to clean all surfaces that standard printer paper will touch.*

Colour laser printing

The entire colour spectrum can be printed using a combination of four toner colours; cyan (blue), magenta (red), yellow and black. A colour laser printer uses exactly the same technique as a monochrome printer, but repeats the process four times: once for each colour.

3 The drum then rotates past the **toner roller**, which is covered in toner from the **toner reservoir**. The toner, which also has a negative charge (−500V), consists of magnetic iron oxide, polymers and toner pigment. The toner is attracted to higher charges so only attaches to the points on the surface of the drum that correspond to the dots.

4 A piece of paper is lifted from the **paper tray** and fed past the drum at the same speed as the drum rotates. Directly under the paper is a positively charged foam roller called the **transfer roller**.

6 Finally, the paper passes through a **fuser unit**, which is made up of two rollers. The roller beneath the paper contains a heated ceramic strip. This heats through the paper and melts the polymer content in the toner, fusing it and the pigment to the paper.

Safety first

Take care when opening a laser printer, as the parts inside can be very hot.

5 The negatively charged toner particles are attracted from the drum to the positively charged transfer roller but are blocked by the paper. The mirror image of the document on the drum Is then transferred to the paper, emerging the right way round.

Paper tray

Fuser unit

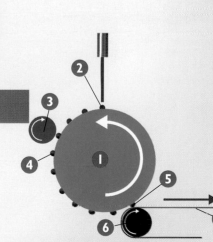

How the charges work

The drum **1** is charged at −700V except for the areas hit by the laser, which are charged at −400V **2**. The toner is charged at −500V, so that, as the drum rotates past the toner roller **3**, toner attaches itself to the areas written by the laser **4**. Then the drum comes into contact with the paper. At the point of contact **5**, there is a transfer roller **6** just beneath the paper which is charged at +200V. The toner is attracted towards the roller and hits the paper in between to create the document. **7**

Fault diagnosis

Dark streaks on print-out	**Dirt on drum** Clean drum. Consult manual for instructions. **Dirty transfer roller** Clean with lint-free cloth. **A**
Light areas on print-out	**Low toner** Remove toner cartridge, rock gently from side to side, and refit. If this fails to resolve problem, replace it. **Drum over-exposed** Put cartridge in a dark place for a few hours and then refit it. If this fails, replace it.
Odd characters coming from printer	**Computer may be using out-of-date drivers** A driver is a piece of software that allows the computer to communicate with the printer. Visit printer manufacturer's web site and download correct drivers for printer and operating system. (see Monitor, page 222).
Paper jams	**Wrong weight of paper** Check thickness setting in printer. **Dirty drum** Clean drum with a clean, dry, lint-free cloth.

Cleaning the transfer roller

Allow the printer to cool, remove the toner cartridge and place it horizontally in a safe place. Then locate the transfer roller, which is a black foam roller the width of the machine. Wipe the roller with a dry lint-free cloth to remove paper dust and debris.

233

Modem

The term modem derives from the words MODulator and DEModulator, and refers to a device that enables digital data to be transmitted over a telephone line as analogue sound waves.

5 The receiving modem 'listens' to the series of tones, and demodulates (or decodes) the digital information from the signal.

4 All data is converted, or modulated, from its digital format to an analogue signal, which can be sent down a standard telephone line as audible tones by the **DSP**.

Digital signal processor (DSP) circuits

Power switch

Power connection

Serial (COM) port

Phone socket

3 Connection speed between modems is rated in Kbps (kilobits per second).

1 When a modem call is initiated – to send or receive email, for example – the computer sends data to the modem, supplying the telephone number to be dialled.

2 The modem then checks for a dialling tone and calls the specified number. A modem at the other end responds as if picking up the telephone line. The two modems start to communicate.

Broadband connection

Asymmetric Digital Subscriber Line (ADSL) enables high-speed data communications down a standard telephone line and allows the user to make and receive phone calls while online. It is called 'asymmetric' because the upload speed **1** is much slower than the download speed **2**. ADSL uses a small portion of the telephone line's bandwidth (data capacity) for speech **3** and the rest for digital communication.

← Bandwidth →

Maintenance

Once every six months	**Update driver software** *Check the modem manufacturer's Web site for the most recent driver and instructions for installation, if necessary (see Monitor, page 222).*

Fault diagnosis

'Port already open' message	**Other software is using the modem port** *Check for fax or answering machine software running in background.*
Telephone connection interrupted or cannot connect	**Incorrect modem setup string** *Check manufacturer's Web site for help or advice.* **Too many devices plugged in socket** *Check no more than 2–3 telephone devices are plugged into the line at one time (see Telephone wiring, page 242).* **Incorrect country selection** *Check country in Modems in the Windows® Control Panel.*
Modem not detected	**No power to external modem** *Check power is on and transformer plugged in correctly.* **External modem cables disconnected** *Turn off PC and modem and check cables connected correctly.*

Scanner

A scanner converts images into digital data that can be used by a computer. The flatbed contact image sensor (CIS) scanner is one type commonly used in the home.

5 The digital data is sent to a computer, usually through a **USB port** at the back of the scanner. Software in the computer translates the data into a format that can be displayed and manipulated, effectively rebuilding the image.

1 The image to be scanned is placed face down on the **glass plate** and the **lid** is closed.

4 A **stepper motor** moves the scan head line by line under the image. As it does so, the electrical signals from the sensors are translated by an analogue to digital converter to ones and zeros.

Lid

Light emitting diodes

Scan head

USB port

Sensors

Glass plate

Drive belt

2 The light from a row of **light emitting diodes (LEDs)** mounted on the **scan head** illuminates the page directly above the head. (For more about LEDs, see Remote control, page202)

3 The head also contains a row of hundreds of light **sensors** spanning the width of the scannable area. The sensors convert the reflected light from the page into electrical signals, one line at a time.

Stepper motor

Alternative design

CCD scanners use mirrors **1** and a lens **2** to direct the reflected image of the item being scanned **3** through red, green and blue filters **4** to a **CCD (charge-coupled device) 5**. These scanners normally have a light bulb **6** on the scan head.

Maintenance

As required	**Clean glass** *Marks on glass will show on scan. Use mild detergent and lint-free cloth.*
Every six months	**Calibrate scanner** *Follow manufacturer's instructions.*

Fault diagnosis

Scans have an overall tint	**Recalibrate scanner** *Use the software provided with the scanner.*
No light	**No power** *Check mains supply, switches and fuses.* **Bulb blown (CCD scanner only)** *If scanner head moves but there is no light, replace bulb.*
Computer doesn't recognise scanner	**Get latest driver** *See Monitor, page 222.*
Hazy pattern on image	**Dots on main image** *Some images are made up of dots that distort the scanned image. Select 'Magazine print' or 'Moiré filter' from the scanner menu.*

Digital camera

Many of the components of a digital camera are similar to those in a conventional autofocus camera (see page 211). However, instead of using film, the digital camera converts light to electrical signals, which are digitised and stored on a memory card.

1 Light passes through a **lens** and is focused onto a **charge-coupled device (CCD)** (see Video camera, page 203).

2 An **infrared transceiver eye** measures the light level and works out how long the shutter will need to stay open and adjusts the **iris** to optimise the light falling on the CCD.

3 The light is converted into electrical signals, and then into a digital format.

4 The captured images are displayed on an integral **LCD screen**. They are stored on a **memory card** and can be transferred to a computer via the **connection port**.

Infrared transceiver eye

Battery

Memory card

Lens

Charge-coupled device (CCD)

Iris

Focus lens

Viewfinder focus adjuster

Viewfinder

Controls

PC connection port

Digital liquid crystal display (LCD)

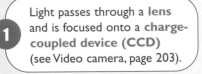

Fault diagnosis

No power	**Battery flat or faulty** Replace. *Be sparing with use of LCD and flash.*
LCD not working	**Fault in circuitry or display** *Contact qualified repairer.*
No zoom	**Motor failure** *Contact qualified repairer.*
Out of focus	**Infrared transceiver eye dirty** *Clean window.*
Pictures too dark or bright	**Incorrect mode** *Select correct mode on control pad for lighting conditions.* **Meter faulty** *Contact qualified repairer.*

Maintenance

Before each use	**Clean lens** *Use a proprietary lens cleaner and brush (see Camera, page 210). Never touch lens with fingers.* **Check battery is fully charged** *LCD and flash are power-hungry, so make sure batteries are charged.*
Once a month	**Clean lens** *Use a residual oil remover.* **Clean camera** *Clean LCD display, eyepiece and infrared transceiver eye.* **A** **Clean battery connectors** *Rub contacts with pencil eraser. Or dip a cotton bud in contact cleaner and wipe contacts (allow to dry thoroughly).*

Cleaning the camera

A

Use a soft camera lens tissue to clean the viewfinder and LCD screen. Also, clean the lens and infrared transceiver window with a lens blower brush.

Personal digital assistant

A personal digital assistant (PDA), or palmtop PC, combines many of the features of a portable computer, diary, address book and calculator in one palm-sized battery-powered unit. Some have tiny keyboards. Others accept input from a stylus and can even recognise cursive handwriting.

Processor

Touch-sensitive LCD screen

① Inside every PDA is a tiny **processor**, ROM (Read Only Memory) for built-in applications, and RAM (Random Access Memory) for data storage. The PDA is powered by **rechargeable batteries**.

Command buttons

Speaker

Rechargeable batteries

Button contact

② The user inputs information either via a tiny keyboard, or using a **stylus** directly onto a **touch-sensitive LCD screen**. The PDA recognises each character as it is completed, and converts it to text.

Stylus

Cradle connection port

③ Onscreen buttons and menus are clicked, and the cursor positioned by tapping once with the stylus. Other commands can be entered via **command buttons**. Some applications allow the user to draw diagrams or annotate text with handwritten notes.

④ Information in the PDA can be 'synchronised' with a PC. This ensures that the data is up to date on both machines and creates a back-up file. The **cradle connection port** connects the PDA to a special cradle in which it sits. The cradle is connected to the PC's serial or USB port.

Touch-sensitive screens

Just under the transparent flexible surface of the screen is a conductive sheet **①**. Beneath this is a layer of non-conductive oil **②**. The bottom layer **③** is glass coated with another conductive sheet. When the stylus **④** is pressed on the screen, it makes contact between the conductive sheets. This allows the organiser to sense the position of the stylus by registering a current flowing across the sheets from top to bottom and left to right.

Maintenance

Once a month

Back up PDA to the connected PC *Use software supplied to make a complete back-up of data and applications.*

Clean the screen *Use a lint-free cloth to remove finger marks from screen.*

Fault diagnosis

Battery goes flat quickly

Screen staying on too long *Set power saver to shorter period of inactivity. Consult manual for details.*

Not charging *Make sure cables are plugged in, or PDA seated in cradle, if it has one.*

Synchronising continuously *Make sure PDA isn't set to constantly update with PC.*

Infrared port on *Check port isn't enabled.*

TV games console

The home video game console contains similar components to a computer, but is tuned and refined specifically to play games. Some modern games consoles have hard disks and modems built in. Games are viewed through a domestic TV to which the console must be connected.

1 When the console is turned on, a simple operating system is loaded from **read-only memory (ROM)**. This allows the unit to 'talk to' the **DVD/CD-ROM disc drives** and **controller(s)**.

2 A menu loads and the player makes a selection using the **controller buttons** or joysticks and follows the on-screen instructions.

Fan

Graphics processor

Memory (RAM)

Controller port

Memory (ROM)

Input from controller

Memory card

3D graphics in 2D

To give the impression of movement through a 3D world on a two-dimensional TV screen, the console must work with a huge amount of data. The landscapes and characters are generated as wireframe shapes constructed of polygons **1**. The graphics processor then renders (covers) the image with coloured textures **2** loaded from disc. Lighting effects are also applied for extra realism. Then the whole shape is moved in response to the controller knobs and buttons.

Controller buttons

Controller

Vibration motor

238

6 If a game is stopped before it is completed, it can be stored on a **memory card** and resumed later.

Television screen

Maintenance

Once every six months	**Check ventilation slots** *Make sure that all vents are free from dirt and dust.*

Fault diagnosis

Disc fails to load or game freezes	**Dirt on disc** *Wipe from centre out in radial direction with soft lint-free cloth. Never use a circular motion as this could damage the disc.* **Dirty lens** *Use proprietary lens cleaning product.*
No display on TV	**No power** *Make sure power is on to both TV and console and check connecting cables.* **Wrong input selected** *Make sure TV is set to the correct external input.*
Cannot select items on console menu or control games	**Controller unplugged** *Check connection.* **Digital mode selected on controller** *Press button to reset to analogue. See manufacturer's manual for specific details.*

Power cable

Video output to TV

Synthesiser

5 During play, the **graphics processor** reads the movement of the controls and translates the data into movements within the game, shown on the **television screen**. Depending on the game, the player navigates through a 2D or a 3D world.

Lens

DVD/CD-ROM drive

Power switch

Positioning the console

Place the games console main unit away from dust and in a well-ventilated area. Do not place the console or power supply on carpeted floors as this may cause over-heating and a possible fire risk. Keep controller cables away from where people may trip over them.

4 Once the game has started, the music soundtrack is played back directly from disc. Sound effects are played back using the console's built-in **synthesiser**. Signals are sent to the **vibration motor**, causing it to shake the controller when a player hits an object in the game.

Eject button

3 When a game is selected, the console loads the data from the CD-ROM or DVD. Because typical consoles have only a small amount of **memory (RAM)** compared with the storage capacity of a DVD, the console loads data only when needed – this is why there may be a delay while progressing to a new level in a game.

Alternative design

Battery-powered hand-held consoles allow gamers to play on the move. Modern hand-held consoles have colour liquid crystal display (LCD) screens and built-in controllers.

Communications

Telephone wiring

Although the master telephone socket in your home must be fitted by the company that provides your telephone service, you can add extension cables and sockets yourself. The only limitation is the number of devices that can be plugged into the same phone line.

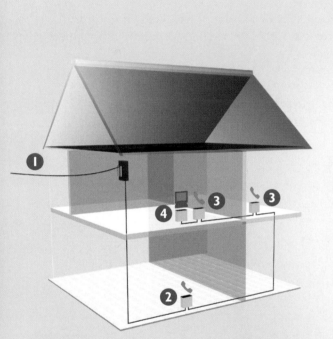

Telephone cable

When your phone number is called, a ringer signal is routed to your house from the telephone exchange. It passes through an underground or overhead cable called a drop cable ❶. The drop cable is connected to a master socket ❷, from which extensions run to other phone sockets ❸ and modem connections ❹.

Maintenance

Every six months	**Check wiring** *Make sure wiring fixed to skirting boards is not damaged. Also, check wiring run under doors is not crushed – re-route over doors if possible. Make sure connections into sockets are not loose, and that socket faceplates are secure.*

Drop cable

Terminals

Colour-coded wires

4
5
6

3
2
1

Capacitor

Resistor

ACQ 1699

Master socket

1 A **drop cable** carries the speech signal, a control signal and the ringing current into a **master socket** within the home.

2 A **capacitor** and **resistor** in the master socket separates the ring signal from the two speech signals.

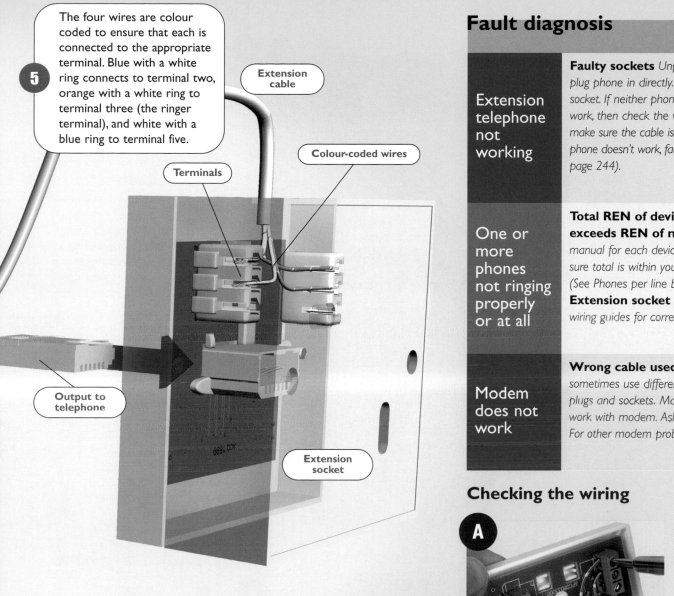

5 The four wires are colour coded to ensure that each is connected to the appropriate terminal. Blue with a white ring connects to terminal two, orange with a white ring to terminal three (the ringer terminal), and white with a blue ring to terminal five.

Extension cable

Colour-coded wires

Terminals

Output to telephone

Extension socket

4 Even though an **extension cable** normally has four wires, only three of these carry a signal to the **terminals** in the **extension socket**. See photograph (right) for the correct terminal connections.

3 The phone signals are routed from the master socket to all the extension sockets in the house in a line.

Fault diagnosis

Extension telephone not working	**Faulty sockets** *Unplug converter from master socket and plug phone in directly. Then, try extension phone in extension socket. If neither phone works, call phone company. If all phones work, then check the wiring in your extension socket **A** and make sure the cable is not kinked or crushed. If one extension phone doesn't work, fault is probably with phone (See Telephone, page 244).*
One or more phones not ringing properly or at all	**Total REN of devices attached to phone line exceeds REN of main line (usually four)** *Refer to manual for each device to check its REN number and make sure total is within your telephone supplier's recommendations (See Phones per line below).* **Extension socket not connected correctly** *Refer to wiring guides for correct connection.*
Modem does not work	**Wrong cable used** *Modems sold for use in other countries sometimes use different connections within identical looking plugs and sockets. Make sure you are using correct cable to work with modem. Ask reputable PC dealer for help if unsure. For other modem problems, see Modem, page 234.*

Checking the wiring

Make sure that the wires are properly inserted and connected properly (see above). Note that some brands of cables have their own colour-coding. In this case, follow the included instructions carefully.

Phones per line

Every telephone and modem has a rating called the Ringer Equivalence Number (REN). On most telephones this number is one (it is usually found on the underside of the phone). A single telephone circuit can handle a maximum REN of four, or four standard-rated phones. Effectively, this is the total number of ringers that the electric current in the telephone cable can supply.

Telephone

A simple telephone comprises a microphone, a speaker, and a keypad to dial the numbers.

Handset

1 When the **handset** is picked up, the **hook switch** springs up, connecting the telephone with the network. A dialling tone can be heard.

2 When a number is pressed on the **keypad** a connection is made on the circuit board and a special tone is generated corresponding to the selected number or symbol.

Speaker (earpiece)

Microphone (mouthpiece)

Hook switch

Keypad

6 At the receiving end, the phone receives the current, which is fed to the **handset earpiece**, where it is converted back to speech.

5 The signal is sent down the **phone line** to the exchange, from where it is routed to the destination.

4 Once connected, the caller's speech is converted by a **microphone** into an electrical signal.

3 The tones are transmitted down the line and detected by the local telephone exchange, which then routes the call to the desired destination.

Fault diagnosis

No dial tone	**Phone disconnected** *Reconnect.* **Mains powered phone** *Check power supply.* **Line fault** *Contact telephone provider.* **Incorrectly-wired extension jack** *Check extension jack (see Telephone wiring, page 242). Do not interfere with master wall jack, or the point at which telephone cable enters home, as this belongs to telephone service provider. Contact provider.*
Phone does not ring	**Phone disconnected** *Reconnect.* **Mains powered phone** *Check supply. Mains powered phone may still receive and make calls, but may not ring without power.* **Ringer volume at zero** *Position volume slider switch at preferred volume.* **Incorrectly-wired extension jack** *See above.* **Handset broken** *Connect different telephone to wall jack. If this doesn't work, the problem is in line or jack.*
Keys jam	**Foreign object in case** *Disconnect phone, open and clean under keys.* **A**

Mains powered phones

Telephones with advanced features or cordless devices require mains power to function. It is a good idea to keep a phone in the house which does not require power, in case of emergency.

Maintenance

Monthly	**Clean the handset** *Use cloth moistened with mild disinfectant.*
Annually	**Replace memory backup batteries** *Check manual for correct type.*

Cleaning inside the phone

A

Unplug the phone. Remove any screws and open the casing. Check for foreign objects under keys. Carefully dislodge debris with a toothpick and, if possible, clean the area under the keys with a damp cotton bud. Allow to dry before replacing the casing.

Answering machine

Modern answering machines record messages digitally on a memory chip, although some models that record onto cassette tape are still in use.

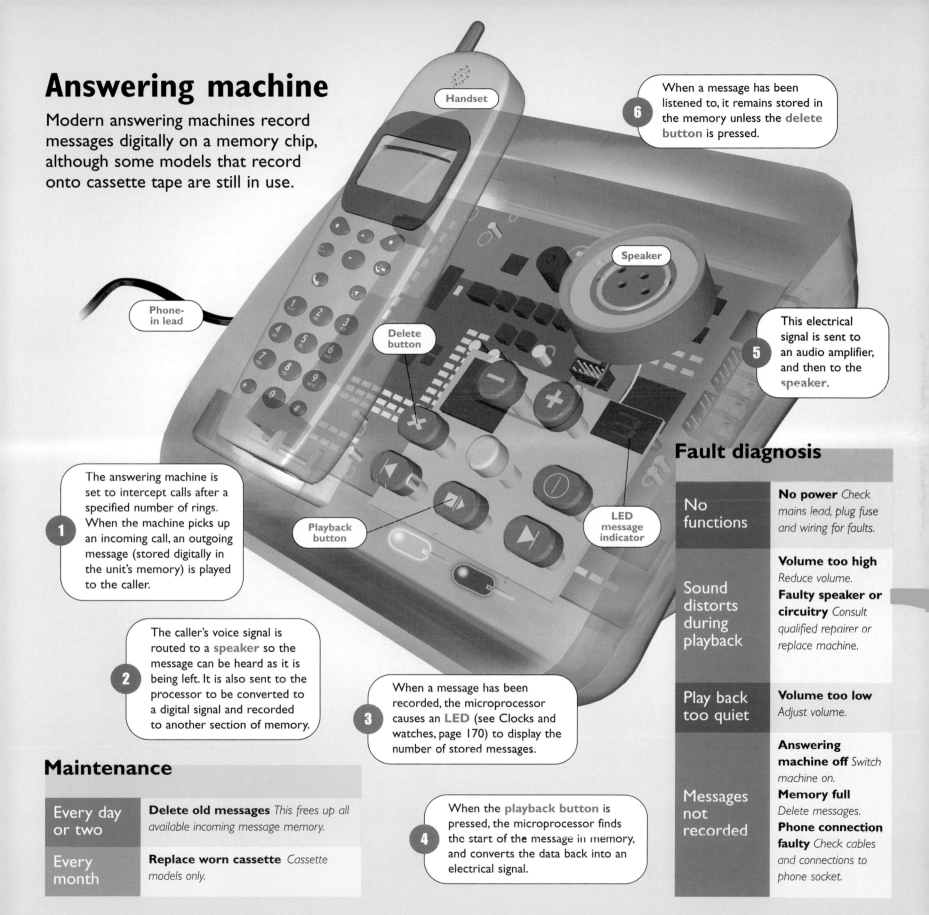

Handset

Speaker

Phone-in lead

Delete button

Playback button

LED message indicator

6 When a message has been listened to, it remains stored in the memory unless the delete button is pressed.

5 This electrical signal is sent to an audio amplifier, and then to the speaker.

1 The answering machine is set to intercept calls after a specified number of rings. When the machine picks up an incoming call, an outgoing message (stored digitally in the unit's memory) is played to the caller.

2 The caller's voice signal is routed to a speaker so the message can be heard as it is being left. It is also sent to the processor to be converted to a digital signal and recorded to another section of memory.

3 When a message has been recorded, the microprocessor causes an LED (see Clocks and watches, page 170) to display the number of stored messages.

4 When the playback button is pressed, the microprocessor finds the start of the message in memory, and converts the data back into an electrical signal.

Maintenance

Every day or two	**Delete old messages** This frees up all available incoming message memory.
Every month	**Replace worn cassette** Cassette models only.

Fault diagnosis

No functions	**No power** Check mains lead, plug fuse and wiring for faults.
Sound distorts during playback	**Volume too high** Reduce volume. **Faulty speaker or circuitry** Consult qualified repairer or replace machine.
Play back too quiet	**Volume too low** Adjust volume.
Messages not recorded	**Answering machine off** Switch machine on. **Memory full** Delete messages. **Phone connection faulty** Check cables and connections to phone socket.

Digital cordless telephone

A digital cordless phone allows you to make and receive calls up to 100m away from its base unit when indoors, and up to 300m outdoors.

Base unit

Aerial

Speaker

Answer button

Handset

Microphone

Key pad

Power connection

Battery

0123 345 6789

1 When a call is received, the **base unit** sends a radio signal to the **handset**. The signal is received through the handset's **aerial**. The microprocessor then triggers the ringer.

2 When the **answer button** is pressed, a signal is sent from the handset's transceiver, allowing the base station to connect the call.

3 The caller's speech is turned into a digital signal by the base station's analogue to digital converter. This digital signal is sent from the base unit to the handset.

4 The digital signal is processed by the handset's digital to analogue converter, then sent to the handset **speaker**.

5 When the recipient speaks into the **microphone**, the handset transmits a digital signal to the base unit, which converts it to an analogue signal and sends it to the telephone exchange.

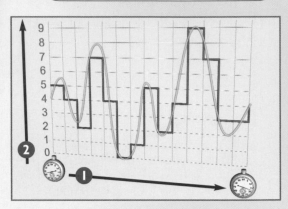

Analogue to digital (AD)

An AD converter must resolve the infinite variations of an analogue sound wave (shown in green) to manageable chunks of digital data (red) that can be transmitted from device to device or stored on a disc or in memory as ones and zeros. This process is known as sampling. At set time periods **1** the value of the sound wave is sampled on a scale of zero to nine **2**. When the sound is recreated from the digital data – for instance, in a CD player, digital phone or MiniDisc – the output sound wave is a close enough facsimile of the original to fool the ear.

Fault diagnosis

No functions	**Batteries flat** *Recharge.* **No power to base unit** *Check flex, plug fuse and wiring and mains supply for faults.*
Sound is distorted	**Interference from mobile phone** *Move mobile away.* **Out of range** *Move handset closer to base unit.*
Callers miss some speech	**Allow for delay** *Wait one second between pressing answer button when accepting an incoming call and speaking.*

Baby monitor

Essentially a tiny mains-powered radio station, a two-unit baby monitor makes it possible to hear if a child is crying in another room.

Aerial

LED visual indicators

Aerial

Transmitter unit

Microphone

Speaker

1 Both the **transmitter unit** and the **receiver unit** are connected to socket outlets, the transmitter in the room with the child, and the receiver in the room with the carer.

Volume control

2 The **microphone** in the **transmitter unit** picks up sounds in the room where it is positioned. The sound is converted to a radio signal and transmitted from the **aerial**.

4 Some units have a **channel switch**, allowing the user to choose one of two frequencies. This is useful if you are experiencing radio interference. Make sure both units are set to the same channel.

Channel switch

Receiver unit

On/off switch

Checking the channels

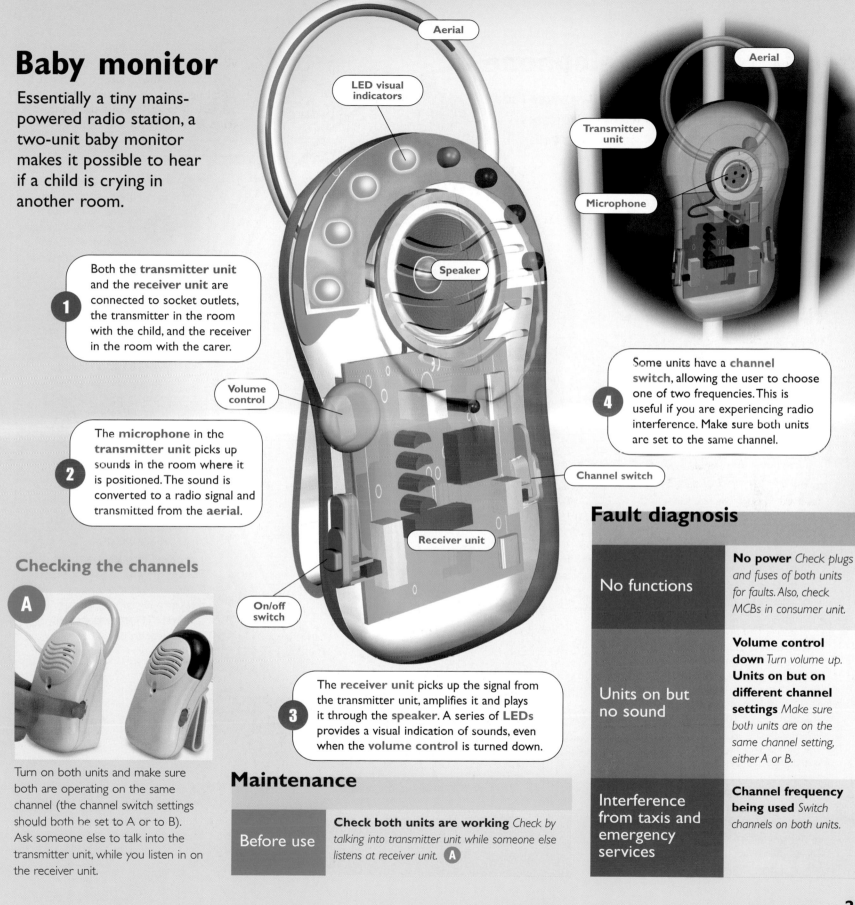

A

Turn on both units and make sure both are operating on the same channel (the channel switch settings should both be set to A or to B). Ask someone else to talk into the transmitter unit, while you listen in on the receiver unit.

3 The **receiver unit** picks up the signal from the transmitter unit, amplifies it and plays it through the **speaker**. A series of **LEDs** provides a visual indication of sounds, even when the **volume control** is turned down.

Maintenance

Before use	**Check both units are working** Check by talking into transmitter unit while someone else listens at receiver unit. **A**

Fault diagnosis

No functions	**No power** Check plugs and fuses of both units for faults. Also, check MCBs in consumer unit.
Units on but no sound	**Volume control down** Turn volume up. **Units on but on different channel settings** Make sure both units are on the same channel setting, either A or B.
Interference from taxis and emergency services	**Channel frequency being used** Switch channels on both units.

Mobile telephone

A digital mobile phone is, in effect, a two-way radio with a low power transceiver. It communicates with base stations arranged in cells. Each cell covers a specific area (of between 5km^2 and 300km^2). As you move around, the phone switches from cell to cell automatically.

Speaker

Aerial

On/off button

Headphone socket

CALL:
TERRY

LCD display

MENU

1 The phone is turned on using the **on/off button**. Control signals from the nearest base station (cell) are picked up by the **aerial**.

7 It then transmits information to your phone to connect the call. This message activates the ringer, to alert the user that a call is coming through.

Battery

2 When the network is found, the phone transmits a registration request to the base station. The network stores your cell location in a computer database. This process is constantly updated as you move from cell to cell.

6 When a call is made to your phone, the network looks up your location by cross-referencing your number – stored in your phone in the **SIM card** – with the location listed in its database.

Keypad

3 When a call is made, the number is typed into the **keypad** or selected from numbers stored on the **SIM card** or the phone memory. The phone transmits the request to make a call to the network. The call is then routed through to its destination.

5 The correspondent's speech is received through the aerial. The compressed digital signal is decompressed and routed through a digital to analogue converter. The analogue signal is then sent to the **speaker**.

SIM card (Subscriber Identification Module)

4 As the caller speaks into the **microphone**, the sound is sent to an analogue to digital converter and then compressed. The digital signal is then transmitted through the aerial.

Microphone

Keep your phone safe

Enable the PIN (Personal Identification Number) on the phone to reduce the phone's usefulness if it is stolen, and keep a note of your phone's serial number somewhere safe.

How the network works

Each network uses a portion of radio frequencies known as a spectrum. An 1800MHz mobile phone is capable of switching frequencies in the 1800MHz spectrum (1710MHz–1850MHz). This spectrum is then split into seven bands. The cells are arranged so that no adjacent cells share the same frequency band. The frequency band is then split up further to allow several mobile phones to operate at once from the same cell. In urban areas, where there are more phone users, there are more, smaller cells ❶. As you move to another cell, the network detects your new location and sends a signal telling the phone to switch frequencies. When making a call to another mobile phone, some distance away, the handset sends and receives signals from the local base station ❷. The base station sends the conversation via a satellite ❸ to the distant base station ❹. When making a call to a landline, the phone sends and receives signals from the local base station ❺ from where it is routed to the landline phone network ❻.

Frequency spectrum of cells

- ▮ 1710–1733MHz
- ▯ 1758–1781MHz
- ▮ 1806–1829MHz
- ▮ 1855–1878MHz
- ▮ 1734–1757MHz
- ▮ 1782–1805MHz
- ▮ 1830–1850MHz

Maintenance

Every six months	**Clean battery and contacts** Ⓐ **Clean SIM card** Ⓑ **Back up phone memory** *Connect phone to a computer, or use a PC SIM card reader, to back-up phone book information.*

Fault diagnosis

Display corrupted	**Phone exposed to extreme cold** *Allow phone to return to normal room temperature.* **Poor display connection** *Contact qualified repairer.*
Battery going flat quickly	**Faulty phone** *Contact qualified repairer.* **Failed charger or battery** *Contact qualified repairer.*
Cannot hear other person	**Low volume** *Turn volume up. Check manual if you're unsure how to do this.* **Defective speaker** *Contact qualified repairer.*
Phone on but buttons not working	**Phone crashed** *Remove battery, replace and retry.* **Keypad locked** *Refer to manual for unlock sequence.*
Calls disconnect	**Signal strength low** *Wait until signal level higher and try call again.* **Network busy** *Try again.*

Cleaning contacts

Ⓐ Wipe contacts on the phone and battery with an eraser. Never use anything metal on battery contacts.

Cleaning SIM card

Ⓑ ❶ Remove SIM card. Use a dry lint-free cloth to wipe down the card contacts in the phone.

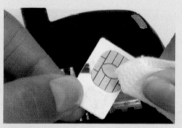

❷ Then wipe the SIM card before replacing it and reassembling the phone.

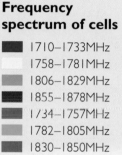

Fax machine

A fax, short for facsimile, machine is effectively a scanner, printer and modem combined in one box. The fax machine works by translating a document into a pattern of dots, which is sent down a phone line and unscrambled at the receiving end.

Maintenance

Every two months	**Use fax machine to copy a page of text** *This allows easy checking of machine's reproduction quality.* **Clean plate Ⓐ**
Every year	**Check exposure lens and mirrors are clean (if accessible)**

Cleaning the plate

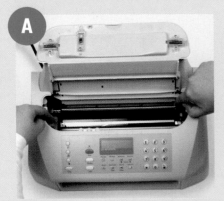

1 Disconnect fax from mains power and phone line. Lift the printing compartment cover and move the print head and cartridge to the far left side. Lift the metal plate by moving the small lever on the right.

2 Wipe the scan head with a lint-free cloth dampened with isopropyl alcohol. Let it dry thoroughly. Never spray directly into the machine – always apply fluid to the cloth first.

1 The document to be transmitted is inserted into the machine's **outgoing fax feeder tray**. The recipient's fax number is typed into the **keypad**.

2 The **start button** is pressed. A **paper feed** mechanism draws the document into the unit. An **exposure lamp** shines onto it as it passes an array of photo-sensitive diodes on the **scan head**. These 'read' the page one line at a time, translating the image into tiny dots.

3 Each dot of black or white is represented by the digit zero (0) or one (1), corresponding to the black and white of the image. Colour documents will be interpreted as black and white. This digital information is compressed ready for transmission.

4 A **modem** within the fax machine dials the recipient's number and waits for a 'handshake' – a signal from the other machine that it is ready to receive a fax.

5 The digital information is transmitted down the telephone line, using the modem. When the document has been successfully received by the other end, a signal is sent back as confirmation. Depending on the model, the fax may leave a verification stamp on the document or print a transmission report to indicate that the document has been successfully transmitted.

Paper tray for incoming faxes

Outgoing fax feeder tray

Modem

Paper feed motor

Exposure lamp

Scan head

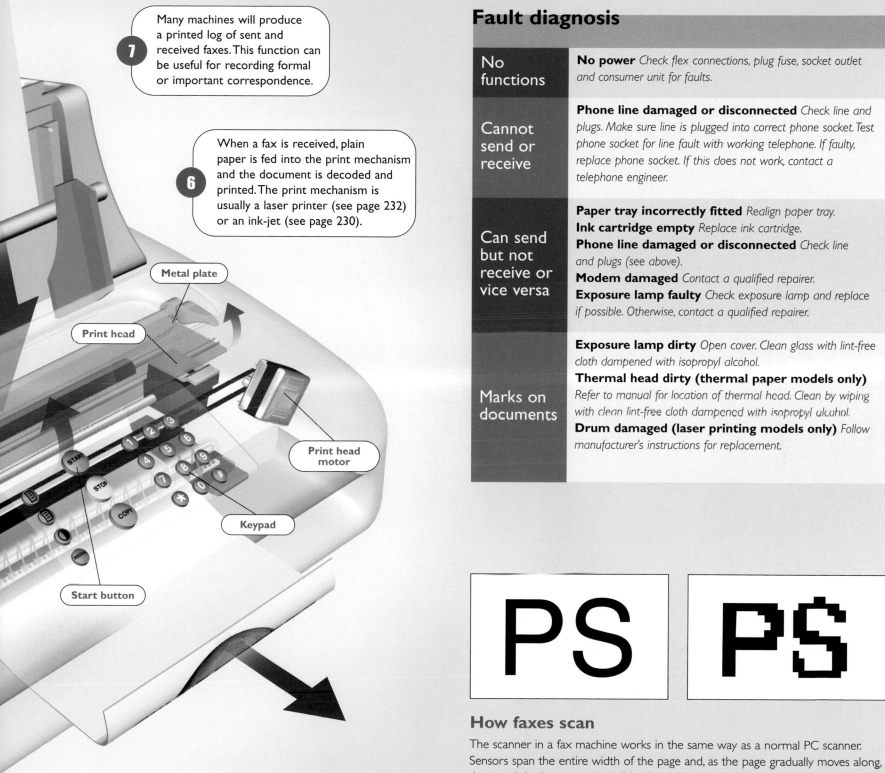

7 Many machines will produce a printed log of sent and received faxes. This function can be useful for recording formal or important correspondence.

6 When a fax is received, plain paper is fed into the print mechanism and the document is decoded and printed. The print mechanism is usually a laser printer (see page 232) or an ink-jet (see page 230).

Metal plate

Print head

Print head motor

Keypad

Start button

Fault diagnosis

No functions	**No power** *Check flex connections, plug fuse, socket outlet and consumer unit for faults.*
Cannot send or receive	**Phone line damaged or disconnected** *Check line and plugs. Make sure line is plugged into correct phone socket. Test phone socket for line fault with working telephone. If faulty, replace phone socket. If this does not work, contact a telephone engineer.*
Can send but not receive or vice versa	**Paper tray incorrectly fitted** *Realign paper tray.* **Ink cartridge empty** *Replace ink cartridge.* **Phone line damaged or disconnected** *Check line and plugs (see above).* **Modem damaged** *Contact a qualified repairer.* **Exposure lamp faulty** *Check exposure lamp and replace if possible. Otherwise, contact a qualified repairer.*
Marks on documents	**Exposure lamp dirty** *Open cover. Clean glass with lint-free cloth dampened with isopropyl alcohol.* **Thermal head dirty (thermal paper models only)** *Refer to manual for location of thermal head. Clean by wiping with clean lint-free cloth dampened with isopropyl alcohol.* **Drum damaged (laser printing models only)** *Follow manufacturer's instructions for replacement.*

How faxes scan

The scanner in a fax machine works in the same way as a normal PC scanner. Sensors span the entire width of the page and, as the page gradually moves along, they read the letters and words as individual rows of dots. These are converted to a signal that can be transmitted down a telephone line. When the information is received and printed by a fax machine at the other end, the letters, when examined closely (above right), are clearly made of up dots.

Power tools

Electric drill

A variable speed switch, reversible motor and hammer action make the modern power drill a versatile tool. Most can drive additional accessories such as sanding or polishing discs, and some may also be used as electric screwdrivers.

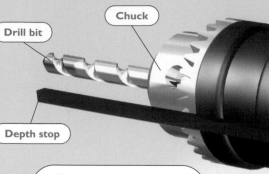

Hammer action switch

Chuck

Drill bit

Depth stop

1 The **drill bit** (or other accessory) is placed in the **chuck** and tightened by a key, or on a keyless chuck, by turning the collar.

Gears

Fixed ridged disc

Fan

2 A **variable speed switch** controls the power to, and therefore the speed of, an electric **motor** by varying the voltage.

3 The motor drives the chuck and drill bit using a series of **gears**. It is cooled by a **fan**.

Maintenance

Before use	**Check flex and plug for damage** *Make sure there are no cuts in flex, and that flex cores are connected securely to terminals in plug.*
As required	**Clean drill and unblock ventilation slots** *Keep drill casing and vents free of dust to prevent dirt getting inside casing and causing fire or deterioration of electric motor.* **A**

Dusting ventilation slots

A

Unplug the drill and wipe down its exterior to remove dust. Clear the ventilation slots of dust and debris with a clean paintbrush to prevent the motor overheating.

Lubricating the gears

A

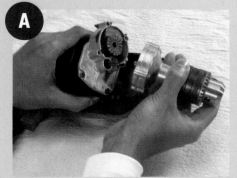

1 Unplug the drill and lay it on a workbench that has been covered with a cloth to stop small parts rolling off. Remove the screws, carefully open the drill case, then unscrew and open the gearbox.

2 Lubricate the gears and hammer action gear using spare grease from the gear case. If this has dried, use white lithium grease. Carefully refit the case screws.

Drill it straight

Before using a twist drill bit, make sure it is straight by rolling it across a flat surface. If it wobbles, the bit is bent and must be discarded. A bent bit may break, causing accidents or damage.

4 The turning direction of the drill bit can be reversed by sliding the **direction switch**, located on top of the drill.

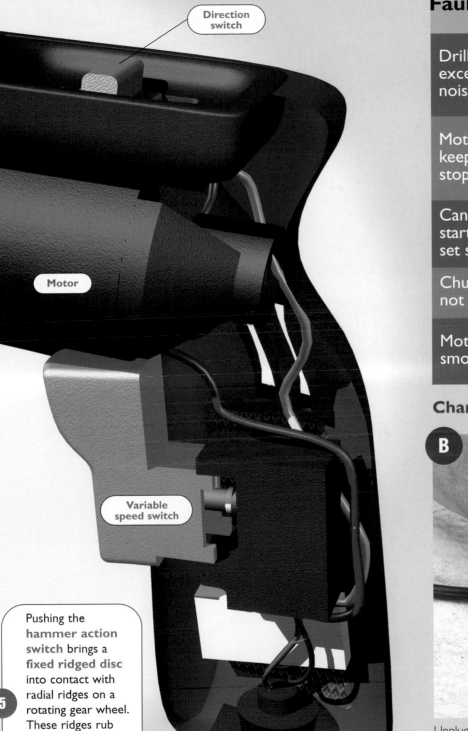

Direction switch

Motor

Variable speed switch

5 Pushing the **hammer action switch** brings a **fixed ridged disc** into contact with radial ridges on a rotating gear wheel. These ridges rub against each other creating the juddering motion of the hammer action.

Fault diagnosis

Drill excessively noisy	**Gears dried** *Open drill case and gearbox, and lubricate gears. This should only be necessary on older drills. All modern models have lifetime lubrication.* **A** **Bearings worn** *Contact qualified repairer.*
Motor keeps stopping	**Brushes worn** *Contact qualified repairer to replace worn or broken motor brushes.* **Loose connections within drill, plug or flex** *Reconnect or replace as necessary.*
Cannot start drill or set speed	**Variable speed switch not working properly** *Obtain correct replacement part and change switch.* **B**
Chuck will not turn	**Chuck jammed** *Use penetrating oil to free chuck. If badly jammed, contact qualified repairer and have chuck replaced.*
Motor smoking	**Motor overloaded** *Switch off immediately.* **Ventilation slots blocked** *Clean vents.* **Damaged motor windings** *Contact qualified repairer.*

Changing the variable speed switch

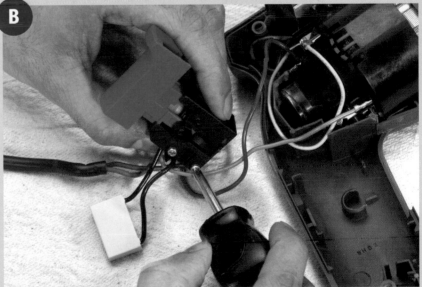

B

Unplug and carefully dismantle the drill. Label the switch wires with tags or make a diagram to aid reassembly. Unscrew the switch, unplug the wires and remove the switch unit. Connect the wires to the new switch as marked in your diagram. Screw it firmly in place. Replace casing, making sure all the parts are in their original places. If the drill has a metal casing, check the earth connection with a continuity tester (see Basic toolkit, page 12) before use.

Electric jigsaw

A simple gearing system translates the rotary power of an electric motor to the vertical motion of a jigsaw blade. The thin blade can cut straight lines if guided carefully, but it excels at cutting curves.

Most blades cut on the upstroke, which provides stability. However, blades that cut on the downstroke can be used for finer work as they cause less chipping.

Variable-speed switch

Lock-on button

Motor

Gears

Safety first
Always wear a mask and goggles when using a jigsaw: it creates a lot of dust.

1 The speed of the **motor** is controlled by a **variable-speed switch**. The harder it is squeezed, the faster the motor turns, allowing for accurate cutting.

2 A series of **gears** translates the power of the motor to the **blade**, which moves up and down at up to 3,500 strokes per minute.

Blade clamp

Blade guide

Soleplate

Blade

A few saws have scrolling knobs to rotate the blade holder and blade, which helps with cutting tight curves.

3 As the jigsaw is pushed along, the **soleplate** keeps the blade perpendicular to the surface of the material being cut.

Some saws have a pendulum action, moving the blade slightly to and fro, as well as up and down, for a more aggressive cut action.

Maintenance

Before each use	**Inspect mains flex** *Make sure that plug is fitted properly and there are no cuts or nicks in flex. Wrap any areas of nicked flex with insulating tape. Badly damaged flex must be replaced and the tool removed from use until the repair has been made.* **Make sure the soleplate screw and blade are secure**
After each use	**Clean appliance thoroughly** *Remove resin deposits with white spirit.* **Empty dust bag** *Dispose of dust carefully: fine particles constitute a fire hazard.*
As necessary	**Change a damaged or worn blade**

Fault diagnosis

No function	**No power** *Check plug fuse, flex and socket outlet for faults.* **Switch or motor faulty** *Consult qualified repairer.*
Unit overheats	**Inappropriate force being used** *Cut small amounts at a time and never force the blade.* **Ventilation holes blocked** *Clear blockage.* Ⓐ **Wrong blade for material** *Use correct blade: 32 teeth per inch (tpi) for metals and thin plastic sheet; 14tpi for general use on metals, plastics, plywood, hardboard and coated chipboard; 10tpi for plywood, uncoated chipboard, blockboard and solid wood, with or across the grain; and 8tpi for cutting solid wood with the grain.*
Vibration and noise	**Worn bearings** *Contact qualified repairer.* **Worn blade** *Replace blade.* Ⓐ **Motor fault** *Contact qualified repairer.*
Blade overheats cutting metal	**Use a suitable metal lubricant** *Light machine oil is ideal.*

How a jigsaw cuts

The motor turns a drive shaft which turns a large cog ❶. This has a pin ❷ attached that sticks through a horizontal slot in the blade mounting. As the cog turns, the pin moves first to the right and down ❸ and then to the left and up ❹. As it moves, it pushes the blade mounting and blade up and down rapidly.

Changing the blade

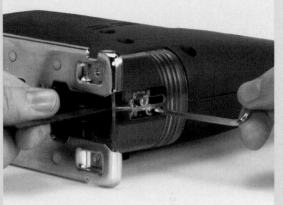

Turn the jigsaw off, unplug it and allow it to cool. Undo the clamp holding the old blade in place. This is usually a clip with a screw fixing, but some models have a tool-free system. Remove the old blade and then insert the new one with the serrated edge facing the front of the jigsaw. Refasten the clip to fix the new blade in place. Check that it is securely held.

Cleaning the jigsaw

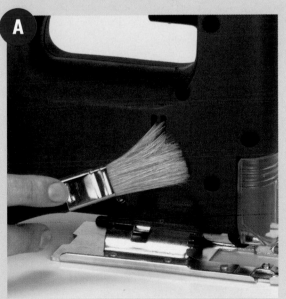

Turn the jigsaw off, unplug it and allow it to cool. Then use a clean, dry paintbrush to clear out the ventilation slots, making sure that dust does not fall inside the casing through the slots.

Angle grinder

At the heart of an angle grinder is a durable rough disc which is spun at high speed. This disc can be held against hard surfaces, such as stone or metal, to grind away rust, protruding nails and irregularities, and can cut through metal or paving stones. A wire brush can be used in place of the disc to get into tight corners and to scour away rust or loose paint.

Safety warning ⚠️
Always wear eye protection when using an angle grinder. Flying debris can cause serious injury.

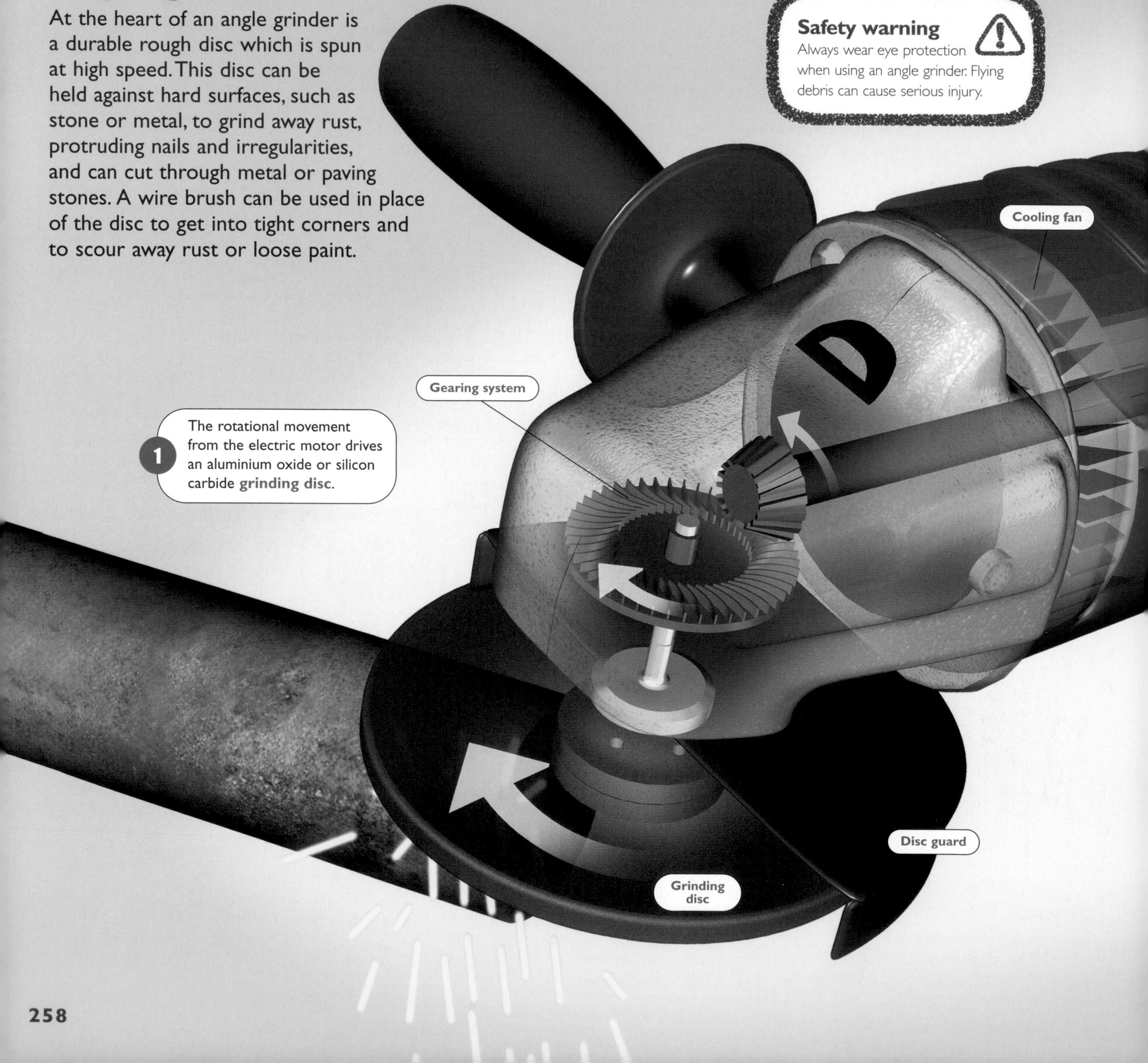

Cooling fan

Gearing system

1 The rotational movement from the electric motor drives an aluminium oxide or silicon carbide **grinding disc**.

Disc guard

Grinding disc

2 The **gearing system** increases the torque (rotational force) so that the electric motor will not stall when force is applied to the grinding disc.

Electric motor

On/off switch

Maintenance

Before each use	**Check grinding disc** *Make sure disc is right size for model, correct type for material to be cut, and is not worn or damaged. Check it is properly attached.*
After each use	**Clean vents** *Dust can cause damage to electric motor and gearbox.* **A**
Once a year	**Check gearbox lubricant** *Consult manufacturer's instructions on how to do this.* **A**

Fault diagnosis

No functions	**No power** *If mains powered, check flex, plug fuse and consumer unit fuse for faults. Also check MCB has not tripped. If cordless, check battery condition with battery tester.*
Extreme vibration	**Worn or cracked disc** *Replace disc.* **A** **Gearbox needs lubricating** *Consult manufacturer's instructions on how to lubricate.* **A**

Cleaning and lubricating

A

1 Unplug the grinder or remove the battery, as appropriate. Using a clean dry paint brush, clear away dust from the vents around the motor and gearbox. Remove the grinding disc and the disc guard and brush around the drive shaft.

2 Brush away all dirt from the gearbox housing before removing the securing screws. Open the case and apply lithium grease to the cogs. Replace all the parts once finished. Check manual for specific instructions on cleaning and lubricating gearbox.

Changing the disc

A

Switch off and unplug the unit. Use the supplied tool to unscrew the securing cap from the grinding disc. There may be one on each side of the grinder, depending on its design. Take out the disc, noting its orientation. Fit the new disc, making sure the securing cap(s) are tightly fitted.

Electric circular saw

For long straight cuts in wood or man-made boards, a hand-held circular saw, with a blade that rotates at around 4000rpm, is the ideal tool. The exact depth of cut can be varied and a vacuum cleaner hose can be attached to remove most of the sawdust. The soleplate can be adjusted to any angle between 0° and 45°.

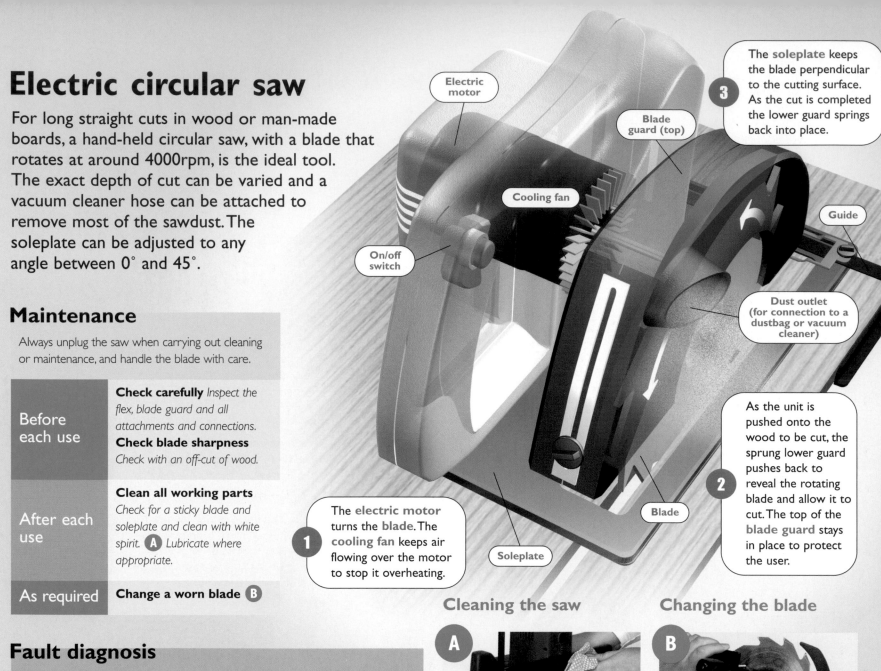

Electric motor

Blade guard (top)

The **soleplate** keeps the blade perpendicular to the cutting surface. As the cut is completed the lower guard springs back into place. **3**

Cooling fan

Guide

On/off switch

Dust outlet (for connection to a dustbag or vacuum cleaner)

The **electric motor** turns the **blade**. The **cooling fan** keeps air flowing over the motor to stop it overheating. **1**

Soleplate

Blade

As the unit is pushed onto the wood to be cut, the sprung lower guard pushes back to reveal the rotating blade and allow it to cut. The top of the **blade guard** stays in place to protect the user. **2**

Maintenance

Always unplug the saw when carrying out cleaning or maintenance, and handle the blade with care.

Before each use	**Check carefully** *Inspect the flex, blade guard and all attachments and connections.* **Check blade sharpness** *Check with an off-cut of wood.*
After each use	**Clean all working parts** *Check for a sticky blade and soleplate and clean with white spirit.* **A** *Lubricate where appropriate.*
As required	**Change a worn blade** **B**

Fault diagnosis

No function	**No power** *Check flex, plug fuse, wiring and mains outlet.*
Saw ceases to cut properly	**Blade is blunt** *Replace blade.* **Motor bearing clogged or needs lubrication** *Consult qualified repairer.*
Saw guard fails to lift	**Guard jammed** *Stop the saw, unplug it from the mains and consult the manual on how to release it.*
Sawdust does not clear from cutting area	**Blocked outlet or full dustbag** *Stop saw and unplug it from the mains. Then clear the outlet or empty the bag.*

Cleaning the saw

A

Unplug from the mains and allow to cool. Clean the bottom of the soleplate with white spirit and a cloth. Use an emery cloth to remove any scratches. Then polish the base with car wax. Clean wood resin from the blade guards with white spirit.

Changing the blade

B

Switch off the saw. unplug it from the mains and allow to cool. 'Jam' the blade with a screwdriver to stop the spindle from turning. Use the tool(s) supplied with the saw or a spanner to loosen the nut (see instruction manual). Remove the old blade, insert the new one and retighten the nut.

Electric planer

Planers cut a thin layer from the top of wood and fibreboards to reduce thickness and produce a flat surface ready for sanding.

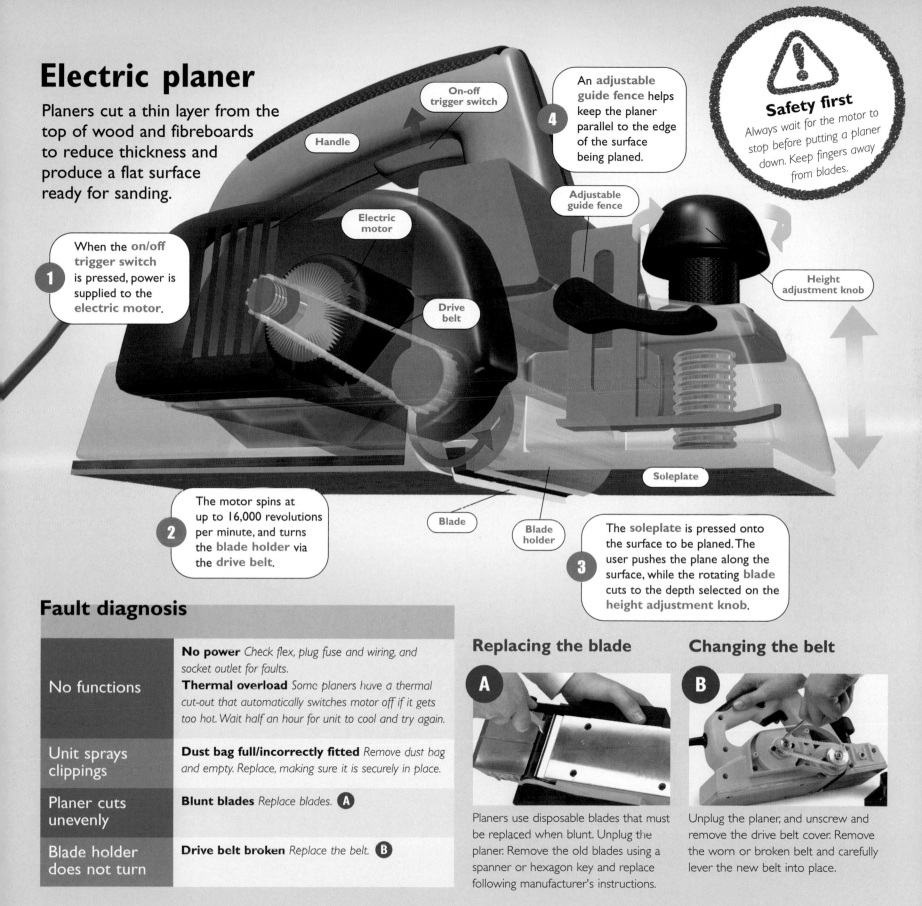

Handle

On-off trigger switch

4 An **adjustable guide fence** helps keep the planer parallel to the edge of the surface being planed.

Safety first
Always wait for the motor to stop before putting a planer down. Keep fingers away from blades.

1 When the **on/off trigger switch** is pressed, power is supplied to the **electric motor**.

Electric motor

Adjustable guide fence

Height adjustment knob

Drive belt

2 The motor spins at up to 16,000 revolutions per minute, and turns the **blade holder** via the **drive belt**.

Blade

Blade holder

Soleplate

3 The **soleplate** is pressed onto the surface to be planed. The user pushes the plane along the surface, while the rotating **blade** cuts to the depth selected on the **height adjustment knob**.

Fault diagnosis

No functions	**No power** Check flex, plug fuse and wiring, and socket outlet for faults. **Thermal overload** Some planers have a thermal cut-out that automatically switches motor off if it gets too hot. Wait half an hour for unit to cool and try again.
Unit sprays clippings	**Dust bag full/incorrectly fitted** Remove dust bag and empty. Replace, making sure it is securely in place.
Planer cuts unevenly	**Blunt blades** Replace blades. **A**
Blade holder does not turn	**Drive belt broken** Replace the belt. **B**

Replacing the blade

A

Planers use disposable blades that must be replaced when blunt. Unplug the planer. Remove the old blades using a spanner or hexagon key and replace following manufacturer's instructions.

Changing the belt

B

Unplug the planer, and unscrew and remove the drive belt cover. Remove the worn or broken belt and carefully lever the new belt into place.

Electric sander

Through moving or vibrating abrasive paper, electric sanders can smooth wood, plaster and other surfaces. There are three types: the orbital sander (shown here), rotary sander and belt sander.

1 When the **on/off switch** is pressed or slid, power is supplied to the **electric motor**. Some sanders also have a lock-on switch for lengthy usage. The motor turns around 10,000 times a minute.

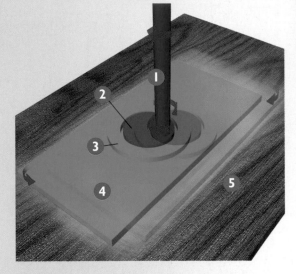

Orbital sanding

The motor shaft **1** is connected off-centre to a cam **2**, which rotates within a circular guide **3**. This is attached to the sanding plate **4** under which is the abrasive paper. As the shaft is turned by the motor, the cam forces the plate to move rapidly in a circular direction, sanding the surface **5**.

Maintenance

After each use	**Clean sander** *Using clean brush, remove sanding dust from casing and vent holes.*

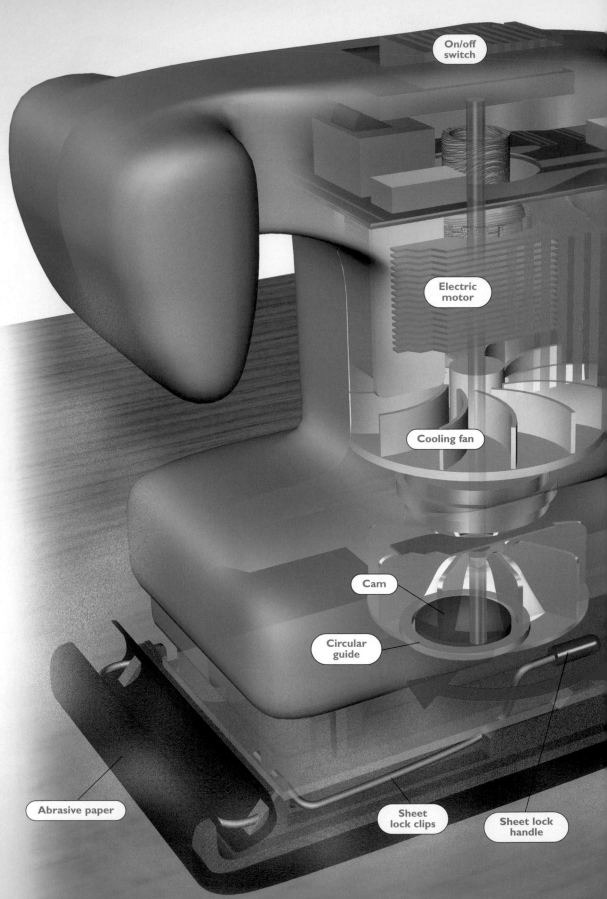

On/off switch

Electric motor

Cooling fan

Cam

Circular guide

Abrasive paper

Sheet lock clips

Sheet lock handle

Sanders use removable sheets of **abrasive paper**, which may be perforated with holes that align with openings in the sanding plate, allowing dust **3** to be extracted to a dustbag, or to a vacuum cleaner by attaching its hose to the **vacuum cleaner connection**. Sanding sheets are connected to the sanding plate with **clips**.

Vacuum cleaner connection

The rotation from the electric motor is translated into an off-centre (eccentric) **2** movement through a shaft and cam (see far left) that are attached to the **sanding plate**.

Sanding plate

Rotary sanders

These use circular sanding discs that sand as they spin. Rubber attachments for holding sanding sheets are available that fit into the chuck of a drill, and you can also obtain sanding attachments for an electric hobby tool, such as a Dremel.

Belt sanders

There are three types of belt sander: handheld, bench-mounted and floor. All use an electric motor to drive a replaceable sanding belt. A handheld belt sander is used for heavy-duty sanding, particularly in carpentry. Bench mounted sanders are useful for smoothing rough cut edges.

Floor sanders, which look a little like an upright vacuum cleaner, are used exclusively for removing dirt, varnish and stain from natural wood floors.

Fault diagnosis

No functions	**No power** Check mains lead, plug fuse and wiring, and socket outlet for faults.
Sheet wears on one side	**Uneven pressure** Make sure not to apply pressure to sander: let it do the work.
Sanding sheet keeps tearing	**Sheet is loose** Applies to orbital, belt or floor sanders. Refit sheet. **A** **Sheet misaligned** Applies to orbital sanders, with or without a dust extract facility.
Sparks from vents	**Dust on motor** Turn unit off and shake out dust.
Sparks from plate	**Contact with metal** Nails and other metal objects may produce sparks when sanded. Check surface before sanding.

Refitting a sanding sheet

Unclip the abrasive sheet from the plate. Replace it if it is worn. Otherwise, refit, making sure it is stretched tightly across the plate and attached firmly.

Bench grinder

An electric bench grinder rotates two abrasive wheels at high speed. The machine is attached to a work bench, leaving the user's hands free to sharpen tools against the wheels or to shape pieces of metal.

3 **Adjustable guides** can be used to keep tools perpendicular to the grinding wheels while they are being sharpened.

2 Plastic **eye protectors** are hinged over the grinding wheels to prevent sparks or metal fragments from hitting the face of the operator.

Safety first
Never use without the eye protectors down and always wear goggles for extra protection.

Eye protector

Grinding wheel

Electric motor

Wheel guard

On/off switch

Adjustable guide

1 An **electric motor** drives two abrasive **grinding wheels**. One wheel has a medium grit surface for initial grinding work. The other wheel has a finer grit for detailed and finishing work.

Replacing grinding wheel

A

Switch the unit off and unplug from the socket outlet. Before changing a wheel, refer to the manufacturer's instructions. Remove the wheel guard. Use an adjustable spanner to remove the old wheel and fit the new one.

Maintenance

After use	**Gently scrub grinding wheels** *Use wire brush to prevent particles embedding in grit. Clean other surfaces with dry cloth to remove dust.*
Every six months	**Grease axle at either side of motor** *Refer to manufacturer's instructions for recommended lubricant.*

Fault diagnosis

No functions	**No power to unit** *Check plug, plug wiring, fuse and mains supply for faults.* **Burnt out motor** *Contact qualified repairer.*
Unit does not grind efficiently	**Grinding wheel worn** *Replace wheel.* **A**

Hot air stripper

When removing old paint and varnish, a heat gun is a useful tool to melt and loosen the finish. Great care must be taken when using one, however. There is a risk of burns as the air produced is between 300°C and 500°C: hot enough to set fire to paint, wood and fabrics.

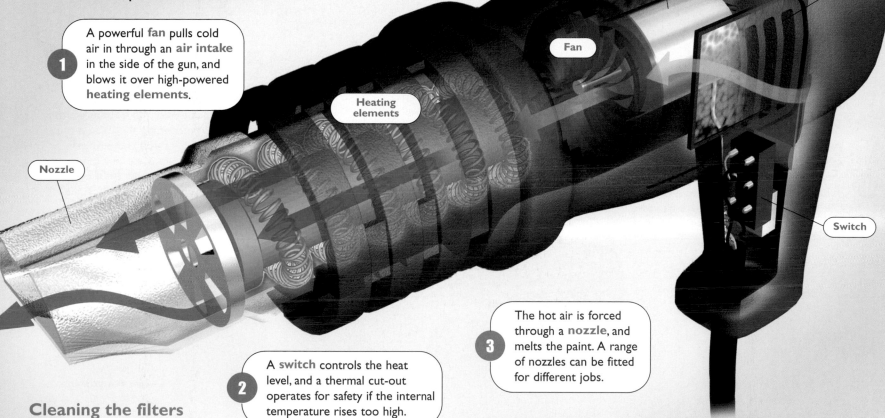

Motor

Air intake vents and filter

Fan

Heating elements

Nozzle

Switch

1 A powerful **fan** pulls cold air in through an **air intake** in the side of the gun, and blows it over high-powered **heating elements**.

2 A **switch** controls the heat level, and a thermal cut-out operates for safety if the internal temperature rises too high.

3 The hot air is forced through a **nozzle**, and melts the paint. A range of nozzles can be fitted for different jobs.

Cleaning the filters

A

If the hot air stripper has been in use, turn it off, unplug it and allow it to cool for at least 30 minutes. Then use a clean, dry paintbrush to work out any debris and dust from the air intake vents and filter.

Maintenance

Before each use	**Check the air intake vents** *Use an old paint brush to clear inlet vents of debris and dust. Also, make sure filter, if any, is not clogged.* **A**

Fault diagnosis

No functions	**No power** *Check flex, plug fuse and wiring, and mains outlet for faults.* **Thermal cut-out tripped** *Wait for stripper to cool, clean clogged filters* **A** *and try again when cut-out has reset.*
Motor works but no heat	**Broken element** *Contact qualified repairer.* **Faulty switch** *Contact qualified repairer.*
Motor heats but cuts out	**Faulty motor** *Contact qualified repairer.*

Spray paint gun

To achieve even paint coverage of large surfaces, such as car bodywork, spray paint guns use compressed air to atomise paint and spray it as a fine mist.

3 Turning the **air cap** adjusts the width of the spray pattern, from a fine line through to a 'full fan' pattern that covers a large area.

Safety warning ⚠️
Never use a finger to clear paint from the nozzle. It can result in serious injury from sharp parts inside. When spraying, always use a face mask, goggles and safety clothing.

Air control knob

Air cap

Nozzle

Needle

Fluid control knob

Air valve

Trigger

1 When the **trigger** is pulled, it opens an **air valve** allowing compressed air to flow over the top of the tube from the **paint container**. This draws paint up the tube and blows it out through a narrow aperture, creating a fine spray.

2 The trigger controls the position of the **needle**, which in turn controls the amount of paint flowing through the **nozzle**. Maximum paint flow can be regulated by the **fluid control knob** at the rear of the gun.

Cleaning the spray gun

A

1 Repeatedly flush the gun and paint container with solvent until it is free of paint and the solvent runs clear. Clean the exterior of the gun and paint container with solvent.

2 Remove the needle, nozzle and air cap and clean them carefully with solvent. Make sure all parts are clean and dry before reassembling the gun.

Paint container

Compressed air supply hose

Maintenance

Before use	**Mix paint** *Thin paint with water or solvents if required.*
After each use	**Make gun safe** Disconnect all air and fluid hoses. **Lubricate gun** *Use non-silicone lubricant and keep it away from possible contact with paint.* **Clean the gun** Ⓐ

Fault diagnosis

Paint will not flow	**Nozzle blocked** *Clean or replace.* **Tube loose** *Tighten.* **No air to paint container** *Look for air leaks.*
Leakage at the front of the gun	**Damaged needle** *Replace.* **Nozzle dirty** *Clean the gun.* Ⓐ **Fluid adjustment screwed out** *Rotate fluid control knob clockwise.* **Impurities in paint** *Strain paint.*

Air pump

Electrically powered compressed air pumps are useful for inflating car or bicycle tyres. An air pump should inflate an average car tyre from flat in around three minutes.

Gauge

Outlet valve

Electric motor

Inlet valve

Pumping chamber

Piston

Cam

1 The **shroud** at the end of the **hose** is pushed and locked onto the valve of the object to be inflated.

2 Electricity is supplied to the **motor** from the mains supply or a car battery through the 12V input plug. This is connected to the cigarette lighter or dedicated 12V socket.

Shroud

5 The air pressure inside the object being inflated is measured by the **gauge**.

Maintenance

Regularly	**Check for leaks** *Turn pump on and lock shroud lever. Put hose under water. Check for bubbles.*

Fault diagnosis

Unit does not start	**No mains power** *Check power lead and cigarette lighter socket or 12V socket is 'live' using a multimeter (see Basic toolkit, page 12).* **Poor plug connection** *Check, clean and retension plug and socket contacts.* **Car lighter fuse blown** *Confirm by plugging in lighter. Replace fuse if necessary.* **Plug dislodged** *Make sure plug is securely in socket.*
Inflation slow	**Hose constricted or leaky** *Make sure nothing is constricting hose and check hose for leaks.* **Shroud not correctly fitted to valve** *Make sure shroud is secure.*

3 The motor turns a **cam**, which pushes the **piston** up and down inside the **pumping chamber**.

4 As the piston moves down, the **outlet valve** closes and air is drawn into the pumping chamber through an **inlet valve** in the top of the chamber. As the piston moves up, the inlet valve closes, the outlet valve opens and air is forced down the hose and into the item being inflated.

Hose

Nail gun

A nail gun automates the process of nailing or stapling wood and other materials together. Most household models feature springs and a simple solenoid (electromagnet), and use special nails.

Spring

1 When the **safety catch bar** is pressed against a solid surface a safety catch is released, allowing the **trigger** to operate.

Solenoid

Trigger

Piston

2 When the trigger is pulled it activates a **solenoid** (see right), which pushes the **piston** and **hammer** forward at high speed.

Hammer

Magazine springs

Magazine

Nails

Safety warning ⚠

Nail guns can be useful tools, but must always be handled with care. Never point the gun at any surface other than the one to be fixed, and never attempt to fire the gun at a person or animal.

Safety catch bar

3 The **hammer** hits a **nail**, supplied from a strip of nails glued together and held in the **magazine**. This strip is pushed upwards by **magazine springs**.

Cleaning a nail gun

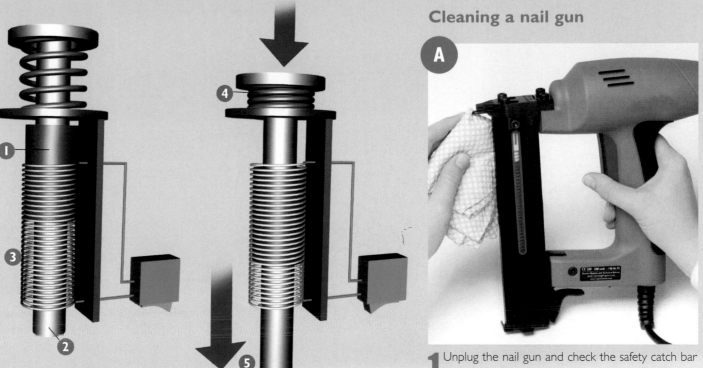

When one nail has left the chamber, the next nail is loaded into position by the magazine springs. A second **spring** in the body of the gun pulls the hammer back, ready for the next firing.

5

The nail is driven into the surface, creating friction. This melts the glue coating, helping the nail to adhere more strongly to the material.

4

How a solenoid works

The nail gun's power comes from a solenoid. This is a simple combination of an iron or steel collar **1** mounted on a non-magnetic bar **2**, positioned within a coil of wire **3**. When a current passes through the wire, it generates a magnetic field. This pulls the iron collar and bar into the coil, compressing the spring **4** and pushing the bar assembly out of the coil at high speed **5**. When the power is turned off, the bar is pulled back by the spring to its resting position. This simple device is used in doorbells, electric door catches, valves and switches.

Maintenance

| Before each use | **Check safety catch bar** *Keep clean of debris that may cause jams.* **A** |
| | **Check for bent nails** *These can cause unit to jam.* |

Fault diagnosis

| No function | **No power** *Check mains flex, plug fuse and socket outlet for faults.* |
| Nails fire when gun not in contact with a surface | **Safety catch bar jammed** *Stop using unit immediately. Clean safety catch bar.* **A** |

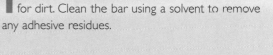

1 Unplug the nail gun and check the safety catch bar for dirt. Clean the bar using a solvent to remove any adhesive residues.

2 Making sure the nail gun is unplugged, and that there are no nails in the magazine, apply a few drops of oil where the safety catch bar meets the main body of the gun. Press the safety catch bar to test for smooth sliding movement.

Garden equipment

Electric hover mower

The most common form of lawnmower uses rotating blades to scythe the grass. Other mowers, often favoured by professional gardeners and groundsmen, use a cylindrical blade. Some lawnmowers have a roller, usually driven by a petrol motor (see page 276), to help to propel the mower forward, but most models need to be pushed back and forth by the user. The electric hover mower makes it easy for the user to push, by creating a cushion of air beneath the mower.

1 A spring-loaded grip-style **safety switch** controls the power supply to an **electric motor**, which is mounted vertically above the blades. The motor operates only when the switch is gripped.

2 The motor is covered by a housing, which contains vents with a **foam filter** to prevent grass and dirt getting inside. The motor drives the **fan** and **blades** directly.

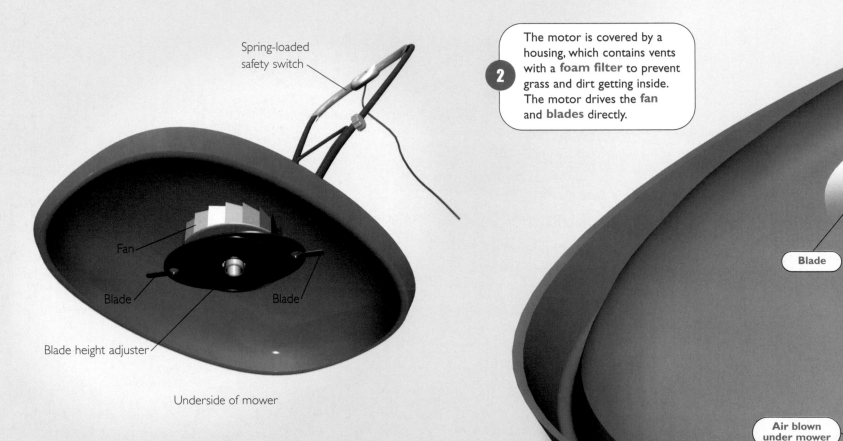

Spring-loaded safety switch

Fan

Blade

Blade

Blade height adjuster

Underside of mower

Blade

Air blown under mower

Alternative design

Some electric rotary mowers and all electric cylinder mowers use **metal blades** instead of plastic ones. The blades need to be kept sharp if a mower is to maintain its cutting efficiency (see Petrol lawnmower, page 276). Always refer to the manufacturer's instructions before starting repairs.

3 The fan draws air in through the housing and blows it out beneath the mower to create a cushion of air upon which the mower hovers. The blades, which can be metal or plastic, rotate at high speed and the sharp edges cut the grass.

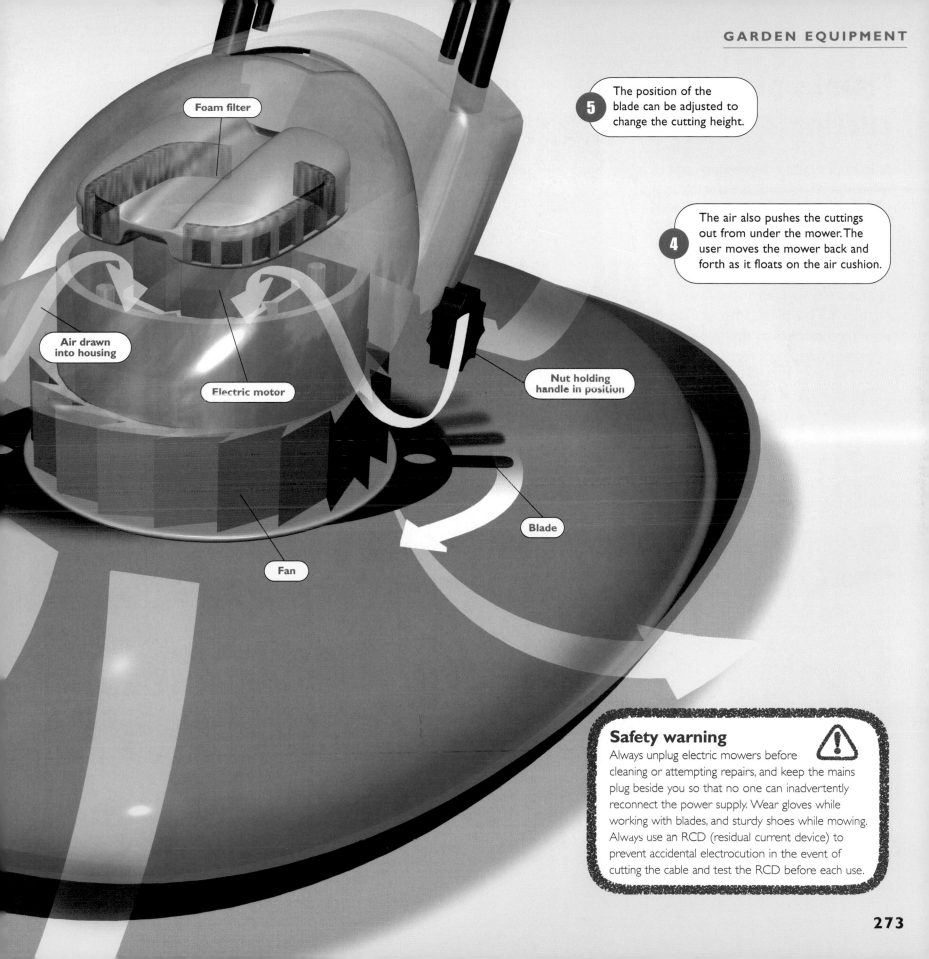

Foam filter

Air drawn
into housing

Electric motor

Fan

Nut holding
handle in position

Blade

5 The position of the blade can be adjusted to change the cutting height.

4 The air also pushes the cuttings out from under the mower. The user moves the mower back and forth as it floats on the air cushion.

Safety warning ⚠️

Always unplug electric mowers before cleaning or attempting repairs, and keep the mains plug beside you so that no one can inadvertently reconnect the power supply. Wear gloves while working with blades, and sturdy shoes while mowing. Always use an RCD (residual current device) to prevent accidental electrocution in the event of cutting the cable and test the RCD before each use.

Maintaining a cutting edge

It is important to keep any electric motor well ventilated during use to prevent it overheating. The air vents and internal workings of a lawnmower can quickly become clogged with grass cuttings, so it is essential to clean the mower regularly. The blades must also be well maintained to ensure that the mower keeps cutting cleanly.

Maintenance

Before each use	**Check area to be mowed for objects such as stones and twigs** *These could damage blades or be ejected at high speed and cause injury.* **Check mains flex for wear and cuts** *Do not use mower if flex is damaged. Replace damaged flex with correct flex type and size (1mm² 2-core flex up to 30m in length; 1.5mm² 2-core flex up to 50m).*
After each use	**Unplug the mower and thoroughly clean motor vents, underside and blades** *Also remove mud and grass from any wheels and rollers once it has dried hard.* **A**
Once every three months	**Check and tighten all nuts and bolts** *Remove motor housing and check for dirt and damage in area around motor.* **Lubricate moving parts** *Check manual and apply a small amount of light oil to indicated lubrication points. Wipe off excess oil immediately.* **Sharpen metal blades** *Dull blades will tear grass, cause excessive noise, and impose extra strain on motor. (See Petrol lawnmower, page 276, for details).*
Before storing for winter	**Clean all parts of mower** *Coil up mains flex carefully. Spray all bare metal parts with aerosol lubricant and apply light oil to indicated lubrication points.*

Cleaning the mower

1 Unplug the flex and use a stiff brush to dislodge dirt and grass from the motor housing and outside of the mower.

2 Make sure the power is disconnected. Use a wooden kitchen spatula or plastic utensil to scrape the underside of the mower, blades and surrounding area to remove caked-on grass cuttings. Wipe down the whole mower with a damp cloth, avoiding the switches and motor area.

Changing the blade height

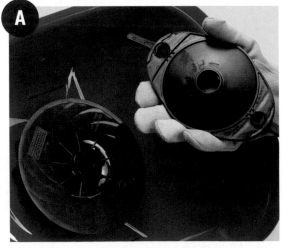

The blades on most hover mowers have a high and low cutting position. To change the cutting height, wear heavy duty work gloves and grip the blade mounting firmly. Twist the mounting to free the blade. Turn the blade over and reinsert it into the attachment. Check the manual for specific details.

Changing the blade

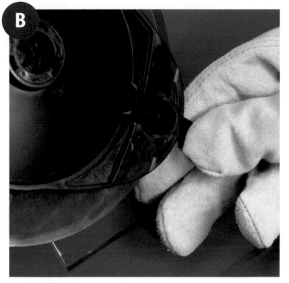

On mowers with interchangeable plastic blades, push the blade upwards and inwards to remove it. Simply slot in a replacement blade. Always wear work gloves. Consult the manual for details.

Cleaning the motor and vents

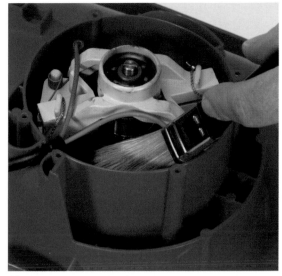

1 Unplug the mower and clean the motor housing and vents with a stiff brush. Then undo the retaining screws and lift off the housing. Remove the foam filters from the housing and gently clear away dried grass cuttings with your fingers or a soft brush.

2 Dust around inside the motor with an old paintbrush and inspect it for visible faults or bad connections. Tighten any loose connections, apply lubricant (if indicated in your manual) and refit the filters and housing.

Fault diagnosis

Mower not working	**Thermal cut-out activated (if fitted)** *Reset or wait a few minutes for automatic reset to occur.* **No power** *Check plug fuse, wiring and mains supply for faults.* **Blades jammed** *Free blades and clean area.* (A) **Motor assembly faulty** *Contact qualified repairer.* **Faulty on-off switch** *Contact qualified repairer.*
Grass not being cut	**Height adjustment too high** *Adjust cutting height.* (A) **Blades blunt** *Sharpen blades or replace if plastic.* (B) **Grass too wet** *Wait until grass is dry.* **Grass too long** *Use a strimmer.* **Underside clogged up with cut grass** *Clean underside.*
Motor cutting out after short time	**Thermal cut-out activated (if fitted)** *Reset or wait a few minutes for automatic reset to occur.* **Motor overheating** *Clear blocked vents and clean motor.* (C) **Cooling fan broken** *Check and replace fan.* (D) **Blades clogged up with grass** *Clean blade area.* (A)

Changing the fan

Unplug the mower and turn it over. Remove the blade height adjuster complete with the blades, see (A), and then lift off the fan assembly. Refer to the manual for specific instructions. Replace the fan with the correct part for the model.

Petrol lawnmower

Most modern petrol lawnmowers have compact four-stroke engines, which take unleaded petrol. Depending upon the model, the motor powers either rotary or cylindrical blades.

Handlebar

Cable

Starter cord

1 Most small engines require the operator to pull a **starter cord** to 'kick' start the motor. Some larger self-propelled models may have a battery and starter motor.

Four-stroke petrol engine

Air filter

Spark plug

Grassbox channel

Carburettor

2 The **petrol engine** turns the **blades** directly. On some models there may be a separate brake to stop the blades.

Petrol tank

Cooling fins

Exhaust

Blade

3 The speed of the blades is adjusted by the throttle on the **handlebar**. This pulls a **cable** that opens and closes a valve in the **carburettor**, to control the amount of fuel delivered to the engine and, therefore, its speed.

Front wheel adjustment lever

Mower deck

4 The rotating **blade** under the **mower deck** lifts and cuts the grass as it spins. Grass cuttings are blown through the **grassbox channel** and deposited on the lawn or in a box, if fitted.

The four-stroke cycle

Inside the cylinder of a petrol engine, the cycle begins with the piston ❶ moving down and drawing a mixture of air and fuel into the combustion chamber ❷ through the intake valve ❸.

The piston then begins to move upwards, the intake valve closes and the air/fuel mixture is compressed. This stage is called the compression stroke.

When the piston is nearly at the top of its travel, the combustion stroke starts. The spark plug ❹ fires and ignites the air/fuel mixture, which expands and forces the piston down at high speed.

The last stage is the exhaust stroke. Here the momentum of the engine forces the piston back up and the exhaust valve ❺ opens allowing the spent fuel gases to escape.

Rear wheel adjustment lever

5 The cutting height is determined by adjusting the height of the front and rear wheels. This is done by moving **levers**.

Grass collection

Because the blades ❶ have twisted ends they act like propellers, drawing air under the outer edge of the mower. This lifts the grass, making it easier to cut, and also blows the grass cuttings out of a channel ❷ on the rear of the mower into a grassbox ❸. A grille ❹ in the rear of the box allows the air to escape while the grass stays inside. If the box is not fitted, a flap covers the channel and the cuttings drop onto the lawn.

Working on a petrol mower

Before doing any maintenance or cleaning work on a petrol lawnmower, switch off the engine, allow it to cool and always detach the spark-plug cable. Unless the engine is cool before you start work, any turn of the blades while cleaning or sharpening could start the engine.

Maintenance

Before each use

Keep engine and blades clean *Small engines are air-cooled and dirt prevents heat dissipation and slows blades. Brush away grass and debris from air intake, fins and blade area.* **A**

Check oil *Four-stroke engines require oil of type 10W-30 or 10W-40 depending on model (check manufacturer's instructions). Low oil results in overheating and wear on engine. When changing oil, be careful not to overfill reservoir.*

Add fresh fuel, if required *Open fuel cap and make sure no foreign objects get into tank while filling.*

After about 25 hours of use

Clean air filter *If air filter is blocked, fuel/air mixture will be too rich, causing carbon build-up inside engine.* **B**

Lubricate moving parts *All cables and pivot points should be lubricated using light oil or grease. Brush away dirt and clean before applying lubricant. Perform this task before storing the lawnmower for winter.*

After about 50 hours of use

Remove and check spark plug *Electrodes in a four-stroke engine should be light brown. Clean with solvent and wire brush or replace if there is excessive damage to porcelain insulator or electrodes.*

Drain fuel from carburettor *Check manufacturer's instructions on location of spring-loaded drain plug under carburettor.*

Cleaning the mower

1 Stop the engine. Unplug the spark plug and allow the mower to cool. Use a stiff brush to dislodge dried grass from the air intake, cooling fins, exhaust, oil and fuel filler caps and all cables and links.

2 Protect working area against possible petrol leakage, then use a wide blade screwdriver wrapped in cloth to scrape off caked-on grass and dirt from under the mower. Spray bare metal areas with an aerosol lubricant to protect from corrosion.

Cleaning foam filters

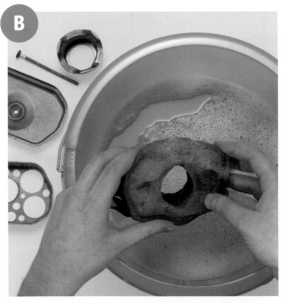

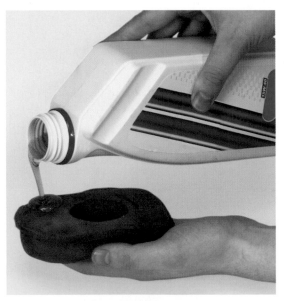

1 Unscrew air-filter casing, remove foam filters and wash in detergent and warm water. Rinse with clean water, gently squeeze to remove excess water, then allow to dry in the air.

2 Apply a teaspoon of engine oil to filter and squeeze to distribute before refitting.

Fault diagnosis

Engine will not start	**No fuel** *Check fuel level. Also open fuel tank and look for dirt in fuel. Drain the tank if fuel is dirty – consult manufacturer's manual.* **Fuel valve turned off** *Make sure valve is in correct position.* **Blocked carburettor** *Consult qualified repairer.* **No spark** *Consult qualified repairer.*
Black smoke from exhaust	**Air filter blocked** *Check and clean if necessary.* **B** **Fuel mixture screw needs adjustment** *Check mixture setting (refer to manufacturer's instruction manual).* **A** **Oil overflow** *Check oil levels.* **Worn piston rings** *Consult qualified repairer.*
Idles badly	**Mixture incorrectly set** *Adjust idle mixture screw.* **A** **Blocked air filter** *Clean air filter.* **B**
Uneven cutting	**Blunt, twisted or unbalanced blade** *Check, sharpen and rebalance the blade.* **B** **Dried clippings and dirt under mower** *Clean area and blade.*

Adjusting the mixture

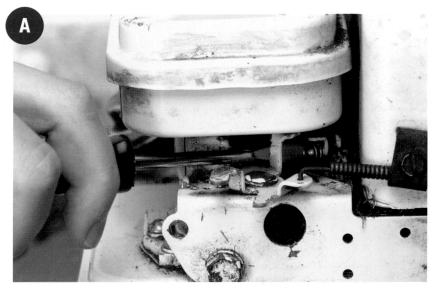

Allow the engine to reach running temperature and set the throttle to idle. Turn the idle mixture screw – located on the carburettor – clockwise slowly until the engine speed begins to decrease. Turn the idle mixture screw anti-clockwise slowly until the engine speed, after increasing, begins to decrease again. Count the turns and position the screw mid-way between the two points.

Sharpening and balancing the blades

1 Disconnect the spark plug cable to prevent accidental starting of the motor. Put on heavy-duty work gloves and firmly wedge the blade with a piece of wood. Hold the blade with one hand and remove the retaining bolt, or bolts. Check the blade and any other parts for damage. Always replace damaged parts. Then clamp the blade to a worktop at its centre, and sharpen using a medium-rough flat file.

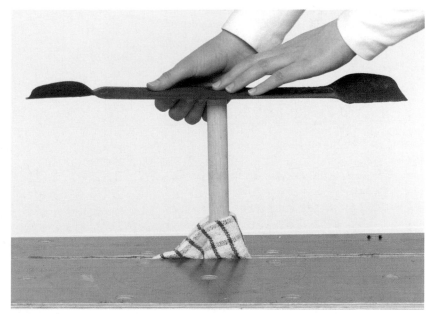

2 Carefully check that the blade balances using a screwdriver or broom handle as a pivot. If the blade is unbalanced, file away metal from the heavy end, avoiding the cutting edge. When the blade is sharpened and balanced, refit it, making sure the lift wing on each end points towards the mower deck, not the ground.

Electric grass trimmer

Trimming lawn edges and cutting back weeds near stone edges would blunt or break metal mower blades. Instead of a blade, a grass trimmer cuts grass and weeds with a short nylon line that spins at speeds of up to 10,000rpm.

Handle

Electric motor

1 When the trigger switch on the **handle** is squeezed, the **electric motor** spins the **rotating head**.

Nylon line

2 A length of **nylon line** wrapped on a **bobbin** scythes grass and weeds as it spins and as the trimmer is swept from side to side.

Rotating head

Nylon line on bobbin

Guard plate

Safety warning

Always use a residual current device (RCD) when operating a mains-powered trimmer.

4 As the worn line snaps through use, a fresh length must be fed from the bobbin. Some models have an automatic feed system.

3 Only the section of nylon line protruding from the rotating head is used for cutting. A **guard plate** protects the user from injury.

Cleaning the grass trimmer

Unplug trimmer from the mains. Wipe the casing down with a slightly damp cloth, avoiding the switch and motor areas. Use a soft brush or vacuum to clear blockages around the ventilation slots. Use a stiff brush to remove debris from around the line feed area and under the guard plate.

Replacing the nylon line

Unplug from the mains. Remove the bobbin and the old line. Secure one end of the new line to the tie clip in the bobbin, then wind the rest uniformly in a clockwise direction around the bobbin. Feed 10cm of line through the small hole in the rotating head, then push the bobbin back into its surround.

Maintenance

After each use	**Check condition of mains flex** *Because flex is constantly being moved, and is vulnerable to damage from nylon line, it should be checked regularly for cuts.* **Clean/inspect cutting area** *The cutting area must be kept clear of dried grass and dirt.*
Once a month	**Clean body of grass trimmer** *Also, brush out or vacuum dirt and dry grass/leaves from vents and underneath.* **A**
Once a year	**Check guard fixing and condition** *Make sure spool, cover and guard are mounted properly and are not damaged.* **Lubricate where necessary** *Consult manufacturer's manual to see whether trimmer needs lubrication. If so, check where lubrication points are.*

Fault diagnosis

Cutting head won't turn	**Head blocked with grass or debris** *Unplug trimmer and clean cutting area.* **A** **Line tangled on reel** *Unplug trimmer, carefully unravel line and refit.* **A** **Motor fault** *Contact qualified repairer.*
No functions	**No power** *Check mains flex, plug fuse and wiring, and mains outlet for faults.* **Faulty switch** *Disconnect from mains and contact qualified repairer.* **RCD tripped** *Check flex and plug for damage. If all is in order, reset RCD. If it trips again, unplug trimmer and consult qualified repairer.*

Electric chainsaw

Light to medium-duty chainsaws are mains powered. An electric motor drives a hinged toothed chain, which cuts through small branches. Heavy-duty chainsaws have small petrol engines and have the power to tackle bigger jobs.

1 When the unit is switched on, and both **triggers** are pressed, current flows to the **electric motor**.

2 Linking the motor and the **chain** is a **sprocket-wheel** that engages with the chain.

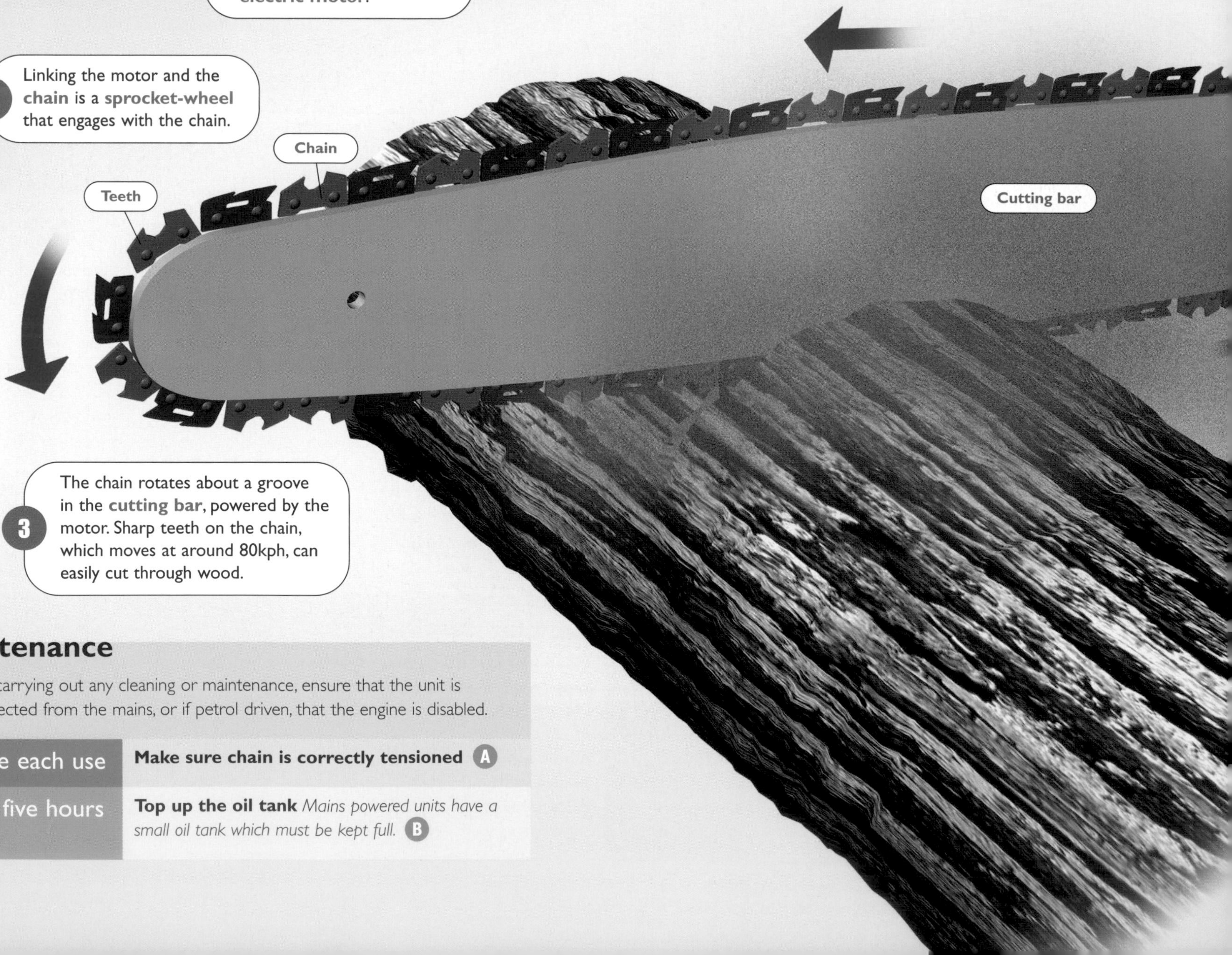

Teeth

Chain

Cutting bar

3 The chain rotates about a groove in the **cutting bar**, powered by the motor. Sharp teeth on the chain, which moves at around 80kph, can easily cut through wood.

Maintenance

Before carrying out any cleaning or maintenance, ensure that the unit is disconnected from the mains, or if petrol driven, that the engine is disabled.

Before each use	**Make sure chain is correctly tensioned** Ⓐ
After five hours use	**Top up the oil tank** *Mains powered units have a small oil tank which must be kept full.* Ⓑ

Guard plate

Triggers

Oil tank filler cap

Handle

Sprocket-wheel

Electric motor

4 The electric motor automatically stops when either trigger is released, cutting the power should the user get into any difficulty.

Topping up the oil tank

B

Check manufacturer's instructions, then remove the oil tank filler tap and fill the tank with light machine oil.

Replacing the chain

A

Undo the bolts and pull the cutting bar backwards to release the chain. Fit new chain, retension and retighten bolts. Wear gloves to protect your hands.

Tightening the chain

A

1 Undo the cutting bar retaining bolts using a spanner or a large flat-head screwdriver, depending on model.

2 Move the adjusting screw until the chain is taut when pulled from underneath. Retighten the bolts.

Fault diagnosis

Motor does not run	**No power** *Check mains lead, plug fuse and wiring, and mains outlet for faults.*
Chain wears out quickly	**Chain incorrectly tensioned** *Check chain tension and tighten if necessary.* **A**
Chain pulling to one side	**Uneven teeth in chain** *File teeth so they are all same length.* **Blunt chain teeth** *Chains damaged by rocks can pull unevenly. Replace chain.* **A**
Cutting badly	**Chain teeth worn** *Replace chain.* **A**

Hedge trimmer

The back-and-forth movement of the serrated blades of a hedge trimmer cuts through twigs and shoots easily. A residual current device (RCD – see Outdoor electricity, page 36) is vital when using any mains-powered appliance outdoors.

Safety first
Never use a mains-powered hedge trimmer on a wet or damp hedge, or when it's raining.

5 If the unit overheats, it trips a thermal overload cut-out (TOC), which switches the unit off.

Front switch

Back switch

Electric motor

Rack-and-pinion gearbox

1 Both front and back **switches** must be pressed at the same time so that the user's hands are clear of the blades before a circuit is completed, supplying power from the mains to the **electric motor**.

Fixed serrated blade

Moving serrated blade

4 When shoots and leaves enter the gaps between fixed and moving blades they are trapped and sheared.

2 The rotational movement of the electric motor is translated into a linear movement of a movable blade using **rack-and-pinion gearing**.

3 The **moving serrated blade** moves backwards and forwards over a **fixed serrated blade**.

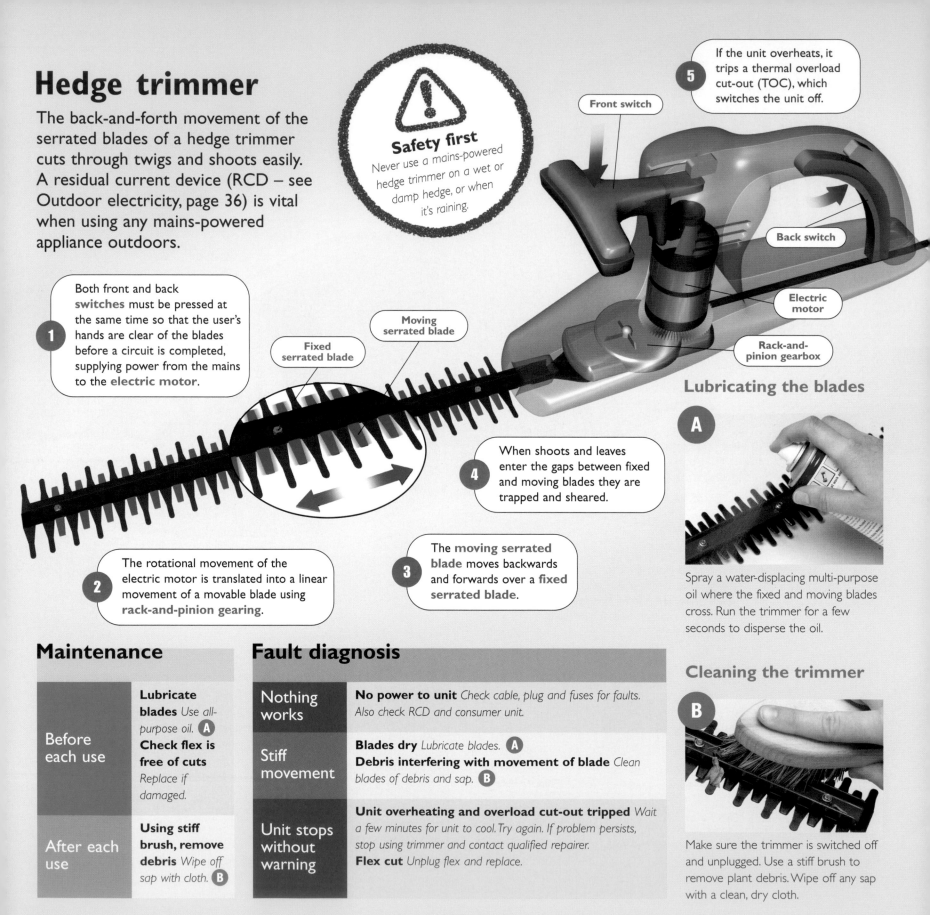

Lubricating the blades

A

Spray a water-displacing multi-purpose oil where the fixed and moving blades cross. Run the trimmer for a few seconds to disperse the oil.

Cleaning the trimmer

B

Make sure the trimmer is switched off and unplugged. Use a stiff brush to remove plant debris. Wipe off any sap with a clean, dry cloth.

Maintenance

Before each use	**Lubricate blades** Use all-purpose oil. **A** **Check flex is free of cuts** Replace if damaged.
After each use	**Using stiff brush, remove debris** Wipe off sap with cloth. **B**

Fault diagnosis

Nothing works	**No power to unit** Check cable, plug and fuses for faults. Also check RCD and consumer unit.
Stiff movement	**Blades dry** Lubricate blades. **A** **Debris interfering with movement of blade** Clean blades of debris and sap. **B**
Unit stops without warning	**Unit overheating and overload cut-out tripped** Wait a few minutes for unit to cool. Try again. If problem persists, stop using trimmer and contact qualified repairer. **Flex cut** Unplug flex and replace.

Garden shredder

Acting as a heavy-duty waste disposal unit, an electric garden shredder reduces leaves, twigs, grass and other prunings to small manageable chunks for recycling or easy disposal. Most small shredders are mains-powered. However, a petrol-driven model will be required for heavy-duty work.

Intake funnel

Feeding chute

Circular blade plate

Electric motor

Discharge area

Wheels

Blade

Flap

3 As waste material hits the blades, it is shredded. Two **flaps** on the underside of the disc act as a fan, blowing the shredded material out of the **discharge area**.

1 Garden waste is fed by hand into the **intake funnel** in small amounts. A plunger can be used to feed larger twigs and branches.

Safety warning

Always use an RCD adaptor when working with mains-powered devices in the garden. Wear ear and eye-protection and heavy-duty protective gloves while shredding. Avoid wearing loose-fitting clothes.

2 An **electric motor** turns a **circular blade plate** directly under the **feeding chute**. Two **blades** are bolted onto the plate, near the outer edge.

Maintenance

Before each use	**Check cables and plugs** *Look for cuts or breaks in mains flex, check plug for damage and test RCD.*
Once a month	**Clean blades** *Consult manufacturer's manual for details.*
Once a year	**Lubricate mechanisms** *Consult manufacturer's manual for lubrication points. Spray metal areas with water-repellent lubricant.*

Fault diagnosis

Always unplug (or detach the spark plug cable on a petrol version) before attempting cleaning or repair.

Shredder jams	**Wet material clogging blades** *Open case and remove material.* **Blades blunt** *Reverse (if reversible) or replace.* **A** **Motor failing or overheating** *Unplug and check for clogs. Make sure motor is clear of debris. If motor failed, consult qualified repairer.*
No power	**Thermal switch tripped** *Wait 15 minutes and try again. If this fails, unplug and check for clogs. Consult qualified repairer.* **Cables and connections** *Check cables, plugs and RCD for faults.*
Unusual vibration	**Blades broken** *Stop using shredder immediately. Unplug and replace blades.* **A** **Motor bearing worn or failed** *Consult qualified repairer.*

Changing the blades

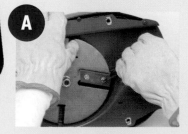

A Unplug the shredder. Clip open the case and replace the blades using a hexagon key (some models may require a different tool).

Pressure washer

The principle of an electric pressure washer is simple: water is forced at high speed through a fine nozzle, which produces a strong jet to dislodge dirt. Most models also allow you to add detergent to the water, which increases the cleaning power of the jet.

1 The **cold-water feed hose** is attached to the domestic water supply and the unit is turned on.

Detergent intake

High-pressure pump

2 The **electric motor** drives the **pump** which pressurises the water. When the water reaches operational pressure (usually around 110–120bar), a pressure switch inside the pump is activated, turning off the electric motor. The water remains under pressure in the pump.

On/off switch

Electric motor

Power flex

Maintenance

After each use	Wipe machine casing
Every month	**Check connections for wear or water damage** *Make sure that hoses, pipes and connectors are in good condition.* **Clean nozzles (A)** **Check flex and plug** **Clean filters (B)**

Spray lance

Valve

3 When the **trigger** is pressed it opens a **valve**, causing the water to flow along the **pressure hose** into the **spray lance**.

Pressure hose

Trigger

4 The lance is fitted with an **adjustable nozzle**, which widens or narrows the hole from which the water exits. This reduces or increases the pressure of the water jet.

Safety warning

An extension lead should be no longer than 8m, rated at up to 3kW and suitable for outdoor use. Uncoil the lead completely and keep the adaptor well away from the area you are cleaning. When using electrical appliances outside always use a residual current device (RCD).

Pressure hose

Cold-water feed hose

Fault diagnosis

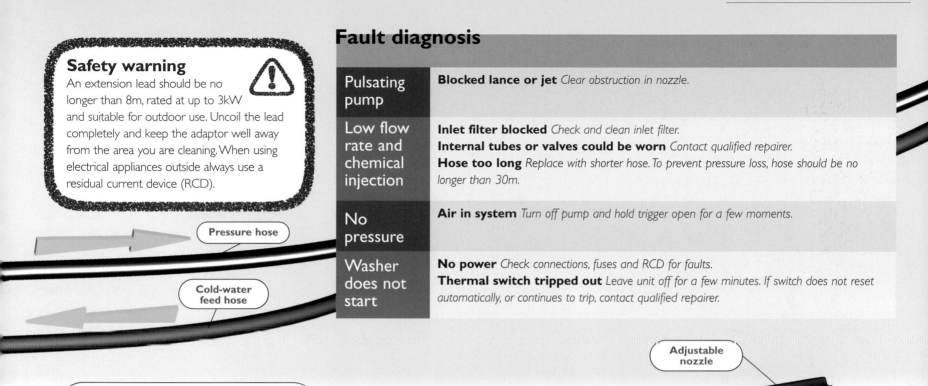

Pulsating pump	**Blocked lance or jet** *Clear obstruction in nozzle.*
Low flow rate and chemical injection	**Inlet filter blocked** *Check and clean inlet filter.* **Internal tubes or valves could be worn** *Contact qualified repairer.* **Hose too long** *Replace with shorter hose. To prevent pressure loss, hose should be no longer than 30m.*
No pressure	**Air in system** *Turn off pump and hold trigger open for a few moments.*
Washer does not start	**No power** *Check connections, fuses and RCD for faults.* **Thermal switch tripped out** *Leave unit off for a few minutes. If switch does not reset automatically, or continues to trip, contact qualified repairer.*

Adjustable nozzle

5 When the trigger is pressed, the motor is turned back on. The pump then continues to pressurise the water entering from the mains until the trigger is released.

Alternative design

In some pressure washers the electric motor runs constantly, recirculating the water in the pump even when the trigger is closed. A **thermal switch** prevents this type of washer from overheating. If the temperature exceeds safe levels, the switch turns the machine off.

Cleaning the nozzle

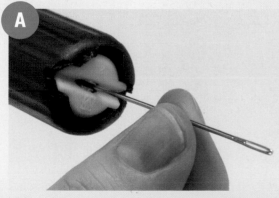

Unplug the washer from the mains supply. Flush the jet through with clean water and clear the nozzle with a fine needle. Be careful not to widen the hole.

Cleaning the filter

1 Detach the cold-water hose, unscrew the inlet nozzle and carefully remove the inlet filter with a pair of long-nosed pliers.

2 Wash the inlet filter under running water. Make sure all dirt is removed. If necessary, use an old toothbrush to remove stubborn debris.

On wheels

Bicycle

The bicycle is essentially a simple machine. The cyclist turns a pair of pedals, which rotate a chainset with a number of chainrings. A chain and sprocket-wheel assembly transfers the motion to the rear wheel and propels the bicycle forwards.

1 The cyclist turns the **pedals**, which are connected directly to the **chainset**. The chainset has three different sized **chainrings**, which have drive teeth (sprockets) around their outer edge.

2 The teeth engage with a **chain** made up of steel rollers, linked by side plates and joined together with rivets.

3 As the chain is turned, the rollers engage with one of the **sprocket-wheels** connected to the **rear wheel**. This turns the rear wheel and drives the bicycle forwards.

Seat or saddle

Saddle height adjust lever

Seat tube

Rear vee brake

Rear wheel

Sprocket-wheels

Rear derailleur

Chain

Front derailleur

Chainset

Chainrings

Pedal

Frame size and safety

It is important, for both safety and comfort, to choose a bike of the right frame size, and to adjust the saddle and handlebars correctly. When buying a bike, stand astride the frame flat-footed on the ground. If the bike is a mountain bike (right) there should be a minimum 7.5cm clearance between the top tube and your body. With a conventional racing design (not shown here), the distance should be around 2.5cm. Never buy an oversized bike for a child to grow into.

Using the **saddle height adjust lever** and **handlebar adjust lever**, alter the seat and handlebar height so that the leg is not quite straight at the lowest point of pedal travel, with the foot flat against the pedal – consult an expert if you are in doubt about making any adjustments. If you do make adjustments, check that all quick-release levers, nuts and bolts are securely tightened before riding.

4 The cyclist steers the bicycle by turning the **handlebars**, which are connected to the **front wheel** by the steerer tube, inside the **head tube**, and the **forks**. The bicycle moves in the direction that the wheel is pointed.

5 A series of **chainrings** works in conjunction with the rear sprocket-wheels to increase or decrease the number of revolutions of the back wheel compared with the number of revolutions of the pedals (see Bicycle gears, page 294).

Thumb gear-shifters

Stem

Expander bolt

Handlebar adjust lever

Top tube

Down tube

Brake lever

Handlebars

Head tube

Front vee brake

Front wheel

Brake pad

Forks

Spokes

Hub

Tyre

Wheel rim

Choosing a bicycle

Choose a mountain bike for use off-road only. The gears are very low and the tyres are best-suited for riding on mud. For most commuters and leisure cyclists, a hybrid bike is a better selection. These have pot-hole-resistant wheels and heavy-duty tyres adapted for efficient riding on the road, and more suitable gearing. Select a sports or racing bike for speed and long-distance comfort. The best mountain bikes are fitted with both front and rear suspension, but the cheapest option is a solid frame without suspension. A good compromise for comfort is to choose a 'hard tail' (with front suspension only), but look for forks with either air or liquid damping, not just 'elastomer' damping.

1 The **handlebars** are clamped in the **stem**, which fits inside the steerer tube. The steerer tube is part of the forks. This is mounted on upper and lower adjustable bearings, called the headset, which are carried by the **head tube**.

6 The cyclist can stop the bike by pulling the **brake levers**. These are connected via a series of cables and levers to a set of **brake pads** on the front and back wheels. When the brake handles are pulled the pads are pressed against the wheel rims to slow the bike down (see Bicycle brakes, page 296).

Fault diagnosis

Bike difficult to steer	**Bearing races damaged** *Replace the headset. This requires special tools, so contact a qualified repairer.* **Steering misaligned** *Do not continue to ride bike. Loosen the expander bolt and re-align the handlebars at 90° to the wheel. Make sure the bolt is tightened.*

Bicycle wheels and tyres

The spokes and rim of a bicycle wheel are designed to be strong enough to support the weight of the rider and transmit the rider's pedal power efficiently to the road. Around the edge of the rim is an inflated tube within a tough rubber tyre, which is held in shape by rigid hoops.

Choosing replacement tyres

Replace badly worn tyres as soon as you notice they are worn. When buying tyres, look for that ones made of silica rubber with a kevlar anti-puncture strip. These seldom puncture and last longer, although they cost about 50 per cent more than standard tyres. Replace the tyre and tube if the wheel has suffered more than one puncture.

Maintenance

Before each ride	**Check pump and puncture kit** **Squeeze tyres to check they are pumped up hard** *If tyres are too soft, it will increase rolling resistance, making cycling hard work (for off-road cycling, tyres should be slightly less inflated to create a greater area of traction).* **Make sure quick-release levers are securely fixed in place and have not loosened**
Regularly	**Tweak spokes with fingers to check they are tight** *If not, get spokes retensioned by trained cycle mechanic.* **Spin wheels in frame** *Using brake pads as a fixed point, it should be possible to see if the rim wanders off true. If it does, get wheel adjusted by cycle mechanic.*

Fault diagnosis

Wheel rim rubs	**Rim is warped or not true** *Get the wheel adjusted by a trained cycle mechanic.*
Tyre goes flat	**Faulty or damaged valve** *Check for escaping air and, if found, replace inner tube.* **Tyre has a puncture** *Repair or replace inner tube.* Ⓐ

Nipple

Spokes

1 On most modern bikes, the wheels are fitted with a **quick-release lever** to make it easy to remove and refit them. The quick-release consists of a cam device operated by a short lever on one side of the **hub**.

2 Steel or carbon fibre **spokes** join the hub to the **rim**. Each spoke crosses over two or three other spokes, building in resilience and making the ride more comfortable for the rider. The end of each spoke is threaded and is held in a hole in the rim with a **nipple**, which can be tightened or loosened with a nipple key.

Hub

Quick-release lever

5 Mountain bike tyres have a deep **tread** for cutting through or gripping loose surfaces. Sports and racing bikes have much narrower tyres inflated to a higher pressure. These have even less rolling resistance for greater speed, at the cost of a more uncomfortable ride.

Inner tube

4 The beads fit under ledges on the inner face of the rim. As the tyre is pumped up to between 60 and 120 pounds per square inch (psi), depending on the type of bike, the beads are pushed under the ledges and so the tyre stays on the wheel.

Valve

Beads

Tread

Rim

Tyre

3 A bicycle wheel has a **tyre** and **inner tube**. The tube is made of a type of rubber that does does not allow air to escape through it, and is protected from punctures by the tyre. Tyres usually have a thick tread section, thinner side walls and strong **beads** made of steel or kevlar, around the edges.

Repairing a puncture

A

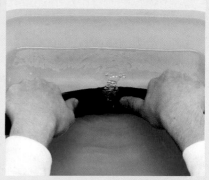

1 Turn the bike upside-down, loosen the brakes and remove the wheel. Squeeze any remaining air out of the tyre, then lever it from the rim on one side by inserting tyre levers and working around the wheel. When the tyre is free from the rim, unscrew the valve nut, free the valve and remove the inner tube.

2 To find the puncture, partly inflate the inner tube and immerse it in water. Bubbles will indicate where the hole is. If no water is available, inflate the tyre and rotate it past your face to feel for escaping air. Check the whole tube in case there is more than one puncture. Dry the tube and mark the location of the puncture with the crayon provided in the repair kit.

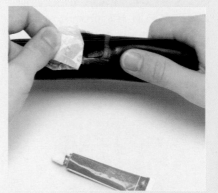

3 If the tube is badly torn, or the bubbles indicate multiple holes, replace it with a new one. If there is just one hole, roughen the surface of the inner tube with abrasive paper and then glue a rubber patch over the puncture hole. Sprinkle chalk over the patch to stop it sticking to the inside of the tyre. Remove anything sharp lodged in the tyre that may have caused the puncture.

4 To refit the inner tube, or to fit a new one, insert the valve and tighten the valve nut, then partly inflate the tube and tuck it inside the tyre. Press one side of the tyre onto the rim, then use the levers to secure the other side, being careful not to snag the inner tube. Loosen the valve nut and adjust the valve, then tighten it and inflate the tyre. Replace the wheel, ensuring that it is properly aligned and that the quick-release wheel nut is securely fastened. Reconnect the brakes.

Bicycle gears

Most modern bicycles use the Derailleur, or derailer, gear system, which works by literally derailing the chain and moving it to another sprocket-wheel (cog). An alternative gear system, popular on basic bicycles, is the three-speed internal hub gear.

1 The front cogs are called **chain wheels**, and the rear the **sprocket-wheels**. The set of sprocket-wheels is known as the freewheel. Because the number of sprockets (teeth) is greater on the chain wheel than on the sprocket-wheel the rear wheel turns faster than the pedals. For instance, if the chain wheel has 48 teeth and the sprocket-wheel has 12 teeth, the back wheel turns four times for every one turn of the pedals.

Maintenance

When required	**Keep bicycle clean and lubricate gears and chain** *Lubricate once a week if bike is ridden every day.*  *Keep oil well away from brake pads and rims.*

Lubricating the gears

Use white spirit to remove any caked-on oil and dirt. Lubricate chain on inside edge and spray bicycle oil or put a drop of light machine oil onto sprocket-wheels, chain wheels and derailleur.

Tensioning the cable

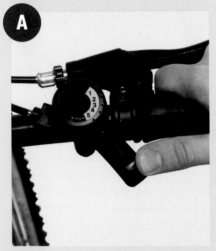

1 Before you start, shift to the highest gear (smallest freewheel cog). Push the shifter to the end of its travel so that the cable is as loose as it can get.

2 Turn the index adjuster wheel a half turn counter-clockwise and test the gears again on a short ride. Repeat this process until the gears can be selected smoothly.

Freewheel

Sprocket-wheels

Top jockey wheel

2 The freewheel has between five and ten differently sized sprocket-wheels. The gears are controlled by a shifter that pulls a cable connected to the **rear derailleur mechanism**. Moving the shifter changes the position of the **top jockey wheel**, dragging the chain from one sprocket-wheel to the next. The mechanism is sprung so that the **bottom jockey wheel** keeps the chain taut.

Rear derailleur mechanism

Bottom jockey wheel

4 For speed, the rider should select the large chain wheel and one of the smaller sprocket-wheels. This rotates the wheel many times for each turn of the chain wheel. If the pedals become hard to turn, select a larger sprocket-wheel. To climb a steep hill, the rider should use the smallest chain wheel and one of the largest sprocket-wheels.

Front derailleur mechanism

Chain wheels

Gear cable

3 Most modern bikes have two or three chain wheels. The **front derailleur mechanism** moves the chain between them in the same way as at the rear. With this system it is possible to have as many gears as there are combinations of chain position. For example, a bike with three chain wheels and eight sprocket-wheels would have 24 gears.

Alternative design

The **epicyclic internal hub gearing system** (or three-speed internal hub gear) is popular on basic utility and children's bikes. At the centre of the rear hub is a fixed axle connected to a fixed cog called the sun pinion, shown in green **1**. This is surrounded by four rotating cogs called the planet pinions, in grey **2**. These are mounted in a rotating planet cage (gold) **3** and contact the teeth on the inside of the gear ring (blue) **4**. As the planet cage rotates 90°, the gear ring rotates 120°, thus creating a gear ratio of 3:4. To pedal at speed, the rider selects third gear, where the sprocket-wheel turns the planet cage. This turns the gear ring, which is attached to the rear wheel. The sprocket-wheel turns three times to produce four rotations of the rear wheel. In first gear, the sprocket-wheel drives the gear ring and the planet cage drives the wheel. This time, the sprocket-wheel turns four times to turn the wheels three times, making it easier to climb hills. Second gear is simply a direct connection between the sprocket and wheel, with a 1:1 ratio.

Fault diagnosis

Most bicycle gear problems are the result of cable problems. Indexed gears (where the gear shifter clicks when you select a gear) won't change properly if the inner cable is loose or unable to move smoothly. Modern cables require little lubrication, but some light oil on unprotected and tightly curved sections helps avoid problems.

Gears not matching click stops on shifter	**Cable too loose** *Tension cable by turning knurled wheel at shifter or cable stop.* **A**
	Inner cable sticking *Lubricate or replace cable.*
	Bent derailleur *Take to qualified repairer.*

Bicycle brakes

There are several different types of braking system for modern bicycles. Most brakes work by pressing a rubber or similar pad against the rim of the wheel – the pressure is transmitted from hand-operated levers on the handlebars by means of steel cables. However, top-of-the-range models now use disc brakes.

Cable to rear brakes

Safety first
Always go over your work several times to check brakes are safe.

Brake lever

Outer cable tube

Rubber gaiter

Cable clamp

Inner cable

Brake arm

1 On nearly all bikes, the brake levers fitted to the handlebars are connected to the brakes by **outer cables**. These are made of spiral-wound metal wire covered with plastic. Inside the outer cable is an **inner cable**, made of many strands of twisted wire.

2 The inner cable has a drum or pear-shaped stud that fits into the **brake lever**. When the brake lever is pulled, the outer cable stays still while the inner pulls against the spring-loaded **brake arms**.

Brake pad

Pivots fixed to the fork stanchion

Pivot bolt

Maintenance

Before each ride	**Check brakes.** *Pull brake lever as hard as you can. If lever reaches or almost reaches handlebar, do not go out on bike until you have fixed brakes (see Fault diagnosis).*
Every six months	**Put a couple of drops of oil on inner cable and pivots** *If oil gets on tyres or wheels, make sure it is wiped off carefully. Then operate brake several times. As oil works in, brakes should work more smoothly and require less effort.*

Brake arm pivot

4 The wheel must always revolve a little as the brakes are applied. If a wheel locks, the tyre will lose its adhesion to the road and the bike will skid. The brake arms also act as levers, so their length is carefully chosen to balance the design of the brake lever to prevent skidding.

3 With vee brakes (shown here) the **brake arms** pivot at the bottom. The inner cable is connected to the **cable clamp** and pulls the brake arms together, causing the **brake pads** to press against the wheel rim. This generates friction. The harder the brake pad presses, the more friction is created and the quicker the bike stops.

Alternative design

Dual pivot brakes are now standard on sports and racing bikes. The brake levers, cables and pads work in a similar way to vee brakes (left) but the pivots of the brake arms are on a separate back plate **①**, not welded to the frame. The whole design is very compact, so the brake arms **②** have less leverage than the long brake arms of vee brakes. As the rider pulls on the brake lever, the cable pulls the lower arm upwards. The cable passes through a tube fixed to the upper arm, allowing the two arms to scissor together, pressing the brake pads onto the rims.

Fault diagnosis

Excessive travel on brake lever	**Worn brake pads** Replace pads. **A** **Inner cable loose** Adjust cable. **B**
Brake lever stiff or jerky	**Brake lever dirty** Clean lever pivot and lubricate. **Faulty cable** Replace cable.
Brakes snatching or locking	**Worn brake pads** Replace pads. **A** **Inner cable loose** Adjust cable. **B**
Brakes squealing or juddering	**Pads misaligned** Adjust toe-in of pads. Consult manufacturer's instructions.

Replacing worn brake pads

A

1 Check the brake pads to see whether they are down to the marked wear line, are worn to near the bottom of the slots, or are ridged. Identify the type of pad arrangement.

2 Obtain correct replacement pads and fit them, using a spanner to align the brakes either side of the wheel. Consult instructions for toe-in alignment to avoid squealing or judder.

Tightening inner cable

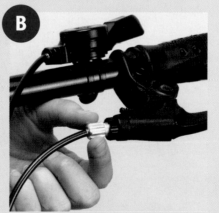

B

1 Undo the locking nut and turn the knurled adjuster anti-clockwise one turn, then check brakes. Do not forget to tighten the lock nut on the adjuster when adjustment is finished.

2 If you can still pull the brake lever up to the handlebar, use a spanner to loosen the cable clamp. Grip the end of the cable with pliers and pull it through. Re-tighten the clamp.

Micro-scooter

Riding a micro-scooter is like skateboarding but with steering and a rudimentary brake. Many scooters fold up for carrying and storage.

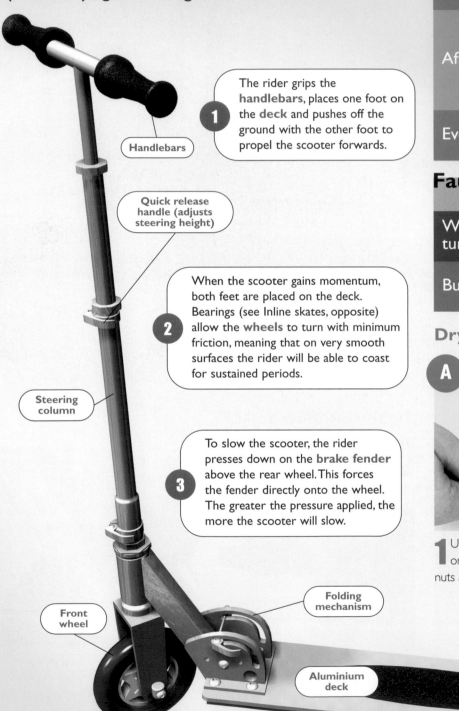

Handlebars

1 The rider grips the **handlebars**, places one foot on the **deck** and pushes off the ground with the other foot to propel the scooter forwards.

Quick release handle (adjusts steering height)

2 When the scooter gains momentum, both feet are placed on the deck. Bearings (see Inline skates, opposite) allow the **wheels** to turn with minimum friction, meaning that on very smooth surfaces the rider will be able to coast for sustained periods.

Steering column

3 To slow the scooter, the rider presses down on the **brake fender** above the rear wheel. This forces the fender directly onto the wheel. The greater the pressure applied, the more the scooter will slow.

Front wheel

Folding mechanism

Aluminium deck

Brake fender

Rear wheel

Maintenance

Before each use	**Check quick release mechanisms** *Make sure catches, bolts, levers and screws are tightened, and that steering column is securely locked in correct position.*
After each use	**Clean scooter** *Using emery cloth, remove any sharp burrs and ridges that can appear on aluminium body and which may cause cuts in an accident.* **Dry the bearings** *If wheels get wet, dry the bearings with a hair dryer to prevent rust.* **A**
Every month	**Clean bearings** *(see Inline skates, opposite).* **Swap wheels round** *This helps keep wear even.*

Fault diagnosis

Wheels won't turn freely	**Dirt in bearings** *(see Inline skates, opposite).* **Bearings rusted** *Replace bearings.*
Bumpy ride	**Debris on wheels** *Remove dirt and debris.* **Wheels worn** *If badly worn they should be replaced.*

Drying the bearings

A

1 Unscrew wheels using a hexagon key or supplied tool. Make sure all the nuts are stored somewhere safe.

2 Use a hair drier on the bearings for a few minutes to evaporate any moisture. Replace the wheels.

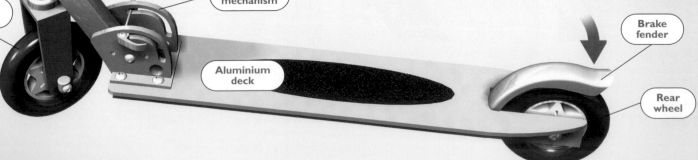

Inline skates

Until the 1990s the most popular type of roller skate had four wheels mounted as on a car. This design has been superseded by inline skates (rollerblades) where the four wheels are arranged in a row.

Swapping the wheels

Lay both skates flat and remove the wheels. Turn the wheels over, so that the inside of each faces you. Swap the wheels from one boot to the other, and then on each boot, swap the front and back wheels with the middle two. Finally, replace the wheels.

Cleaning the bearings

Remove the bearing from the wheel if possible. Using a soft moist cloth and citrus-based cleaner, wipe away dirt and debris. Do not add oil or grease: they will attract more dirt. If it is not possible to remove the bearing, clean its exposed surfaces.

Maintenance

After each use	**Remove dirt** *Use a vacuum cleaner with a brush attachment on dry debris.* **Dry the bearings** *(see Scooter opposite).*
Once a month	**Swap wheels round** *This keeps wear even.* **A** **Clean bearings** **B**

Fault diagnosis

Skates veer to one side	**Uneven wear** *Swap wheels* **A** *. If this does not cure problem, replace wheels.*
Skates run roughly	**Debris on wheels** *Remove dirt and debris.*
Wheels won't turn	**Dirt in bearings** *Remove the bearing and clean.* **B** **Bearings rusted** *Replace bearings.*

1 Inline skates rely on lubricated ball bearings to keep the **wheels** running freely.

2 As the skater pushes along, the bearings transfer the force and rotate within two cylinders, called races.

Liner

Cuff

Strap and clip buckle

Shell

Frame

Axle

Heel brake

Wheels

3 To slow down, the skater moves one skate forward and tilts it back so that the **heel brake** drags against the ground.

How bearings work

A simple ball bearing has an inner **1** and outer race **2**. Between these are steel ball bearings **3** and grease. Since the points at which the bearings touch the races are very small, friction is kept to a minimum. This means that the wheel **4** (which grips the outer race) can easily rotate around the axle **5** (which is gripped by the inner race), reducing wear.

Pushchair

Because they fold on two axes, pushchairs can collapse to occupy a small space. The idea was developed from the retractable landing gear of a Boeing aircraft.

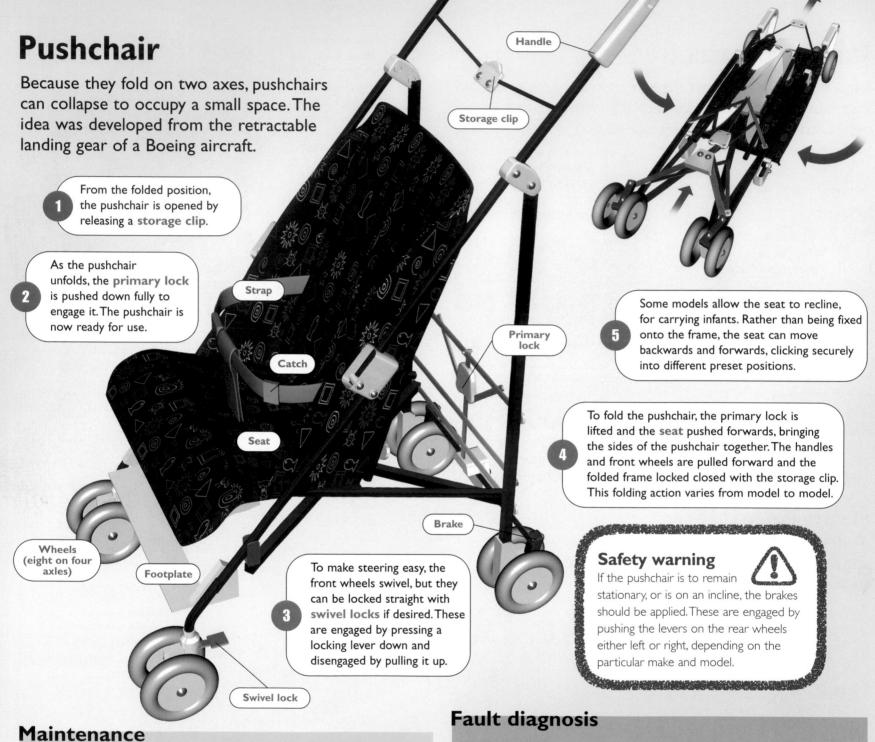

Handle

Storage clip

1 From the folded position, the pushchair is opened by releasing a **storage clip**.

2 As the pushchair unfolds, the **primary lock** is pushed down fully to engage it. The pushchair is now ready for use.

Strap

Catch

Seat

Primary lock

5 Some models allow the seat to recline, for carrying infants. Rather than being fixed onto the frame, the seat can move backwards and forwards, clicking securely into different preset positions.

4 To fold the pushchair, the primary lock is lifted and the **seat** pushed forwards, bringing the sides of the pushchair together. The handles and front wheels are pulled forward and the folded frame locked closed with the storage clip. This folding action varies from model to model.

Wheels (eight on four axles)

Footplate

Brake

3 To make steering easy, the front wheels swivel, but they can be locked straight with **swivel locks** if desired. These are engaged by pressing a locking lever down and disengaged by pulling it up.

Swivel lock

Safety warning ⚠

If the pushchair is to remain stationary, or is on an incline, the brakes should be applied. These are engaged by pushing the levers on the rear wheels either left or right, depending on the particular make and model.

Maintenance

| Every month | **Check seat for damage** If seat fabric has been torn by mechanism, replace pushchair. |
| Every six months | **Lubricate axles and joints** Use light multipurpose oil. |

Fault diagnosis

| Mechanism sticking | **Joints dry** Lubricate with small amount of multipurpose oil. **Metal scuffed** Remove burrs on frame with metal file and abrasive paper. |
| Wheels do not turn | **Brakes applied** Push brake levers to opposite side to release. |

Radio controlled car

A simple radio controlled car has four main parts: a handset, which controls the toy using radio waves; a receiver within the toy, which receives and decodes the signals; a motor; and a power source.

Aerial

Microprocessor

Electric motor

Cogs

1 The **handset** allows the user to control the speed, direction and steering of the car. This works in a similar way to a games console controller, (see Games console, page 238).

Steering mechanism

Solenoid

2 When the **joystick controls** are moved, the transmitter in the handset sends out a coded radio frequency (see Portable radio, page 178). This signal is picked up by the **aerial** in the model car.

Batteries

Magnets

Rear wheels (driven)

Front wheels

Joystick controls

3 The signals are then sent to a **microprocessor**, which decodes the signal and switches on circuits to control the **electric motor** and **steering mechanism**.

4 The **rear wheels** are driven by a motor via two **cogs**. The **front wheels** are steered by a **solenoid**, (see Nail gun, page 268) that pulls on magnets to turn the wheels to the left or right.

Handset

Adjusting the tracking

A

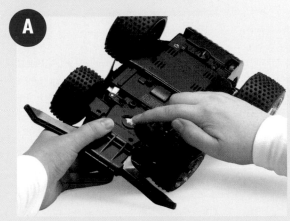

Turn the car upside down. On the base there should be a tracking adjustment. If the car is veering slightly to the left, adjust the tracking to the right. If it is veering to the right, adjust the tracking to the left. Try operating the car again and repeat as necessary until the car keeps a straight course.

Maintenance

| After each use | **Take out batteries** *Remove from both car and handset.* |
| | **Clean car** *Check axles for fluff, string or thread. Clean any dirt from the car, and dry completely before storage.* |

Fault diagnosis

No power	**Batteries dead** *Check batteries in both handset and car. Clean and retension battery contacts.*
Faulty steering	**Tracking misaligned** *Adjust.* **A**
Car stops responding	**Car out of radio range** *Move closer to car until signal is restored.* **Radio waves blocked** *Move away from large concrete or metal structures.* **Batteries low** *Replace.*

Glossary

Words defined elsewhere in the Glossary are shown in italics.

A

Activated charcoal Carbon that has been treated with oxygen so that it traps (adsorbs) odours and certain impurities in air and water. Used in cooker hood filters.

▼

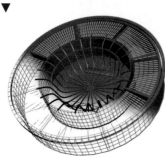

ADC Analogue to digital converter. An electronic device that converts analogue information into digital ones and zeros. Used in digital cameras, MiniDisc recording and computers.

AGP Accelerated graphics port. A slot on a computer *motherboard* that accepts AGP-compatible graphics cards, designed to process 3D image information rapidly and to output images at high resolution.

Alpha radiation The most easily absorbed type of radiation. It consists of a stream of alpha particles that produce ionisation in matter, making it suitable for use in smoke detectors.

AM Amplitude modulation. A method of transmitting audio waves by varying the amplitude (volume) of a sine wave, the carrier.

Anode A positively charged electrode.

Anti-skate control On a record deck, a small weight that can be adjusted manually, via a knob, to centre the stylus in a record groove and prevent it slipping across the record's surface.

Aperture The lens opening formed as the *iris* on a camera opens and closes.

ADSL Asymmetric digital subscriber line. A form of high-speed Internet access technology which uses a standard copper wire telephone line.

Auger Any of a variety of hand tools, typically having a threaded shank and cross handle, used for boring holes or unblocking pipes.

Auto-focus A system in a camera or camcorder, which uses an electronic system coupled with tiny motors to focus the image.

Axle The pin or spindle around which a wheel revolves, or which revolves with a wheel.

B

Baking soda Sodium bicarbonate; a compound used in effervescent drinks, baking and as an antacid. Useful for cleaning surfaces, such as the inside of a fridge.

Ball valve A device controlling the supply of water in a tank, cistern, or toilet by means of a float. The latter is connected to a valve that opens or closes with changes in water level.

Bayer filter pattern The most common pattern of red, green and blue filters in a CCD (charge-coupled device) in a television set. Behind each red, green or blue filter is a *photosensitive diode*.

Bayonet fitting Lamp holder in which a light bulb slots into place and is held by two pins on either side of its metal base. The alternative is a screw fitting, also known as an Edison screw, where the bulb has a screw-in metal base.

Bearing A device, usually spherical, which supports, guides, and reduces the friction of motion between fixed and moving machine parts.

Bearing race A track or channel in which a ball bearing rolls or slides; specifically a groove (as for the balls) in a *bearing*.

Bevel gear A type of gear in which two cogs mesh at an angle. Used where a motor is at right angles to the object being turned, such as an angle grinder.

Bimetallic strip A device that bends in response to a change in temperature. Normally used to switch the power on or off in a circuit when the temperature reaches a set value. Used as a thermostat in irons and kettles.

▼

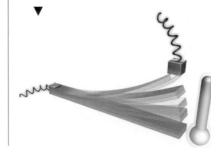

BIOS Basic Input Output System. A set of instructions stored in a computer's *ROM* (read-only memory) that enables it to start the operating system and to communicate with the various devices in the system.

Bleed valve A small tap in the top of a central heating radiator used to release trapped air.

Bus (computing) A parallel circuit that joins the major components of a computer, allowing the transfer of data or power from one connected component to another.

C

Cam An elliptic or multiply curved wheel mounted on a rotating axle, used to produce variable or reciprocating motion in another engaged or contacted part, known as the follower.

Cantilever Small strip at the end of a record deck arm under the headshell, into which the stylus is inserted.

Capstan shaft Operates in conjunction with the pinch roller to move the tape in a cassette or video from spool to spool during recording or playback.

Casement window A type of window that opens outward by means of hinges positioned at the side or top.

Catchpot A small container in a washing machine with no lint filter, designed to trap debris.

Cathode A negatively charged electrode.

CCD Charged-coupled device. Light-sensitive electronic device used in camcorders and digital cameras. Each CCD chip consists of an array of *photosensitive diodes*.

Centrifugal force The outward force on any object that is moving in a circular path.

Ceramic discs A pair of ceramic cylinders within a tap which, by rotating in relation to each other, permit or prevent water flow.

▼

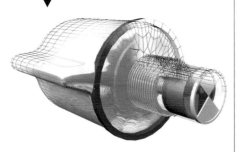

Chuck A cylindrical grip that connects drill bits and accessories, such as sanding discs, to the body of a power drill. Can be tightened using a chuck key or, in some models, by hand.

Circuit breaker A safety device specially designed to cut the power instantly in an electrical wiring circuit if it detects current leaking to earth. Also known as a trip switch.

CO Carbon monoxide. Colourless, odourless, highly poisonous gas formed during incomplete combustion of carbon or carbon-based fuels, such as natural gas.

Coaxial lead A connecting cable that consists of a tube of electrically-conductive material surrounding a central conductor. It is normally used to transmit television signals between aerial and set. A different form is used in some computer networks.

Combination boiler Central heating unit that heats tap water and central heating water directly as it passes through the boiler, rather than storing the hot water in a tank as in a conventional system.

Condenser boiler Energy-efficient type of central heating boiler that uses heat from escaping flue gases to pre-warm the water before it passes through a heat-exchanger.

Composite In this type of connection, the combined red, green and blue components of a video signal are transmitted down a single *RCA* or *SCART* lead.

Counterweight A weight on a record deck at the opposite end of the tone arm to the stylus. It allows the user to set the stylus pressure for optimal sound quality.

▼

CPU Central processing unit. The 'brains' of a computer, comprising the processor and main memory. The term is often used to refer to the processor alone.

Crosshead (tap) The top part of a rising spindle tap that is turned to control the flow of water.

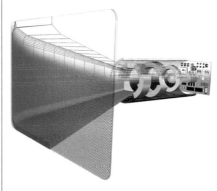

▲

CRT Cathode ray tube. In its most basic form, a glass flask containing a cathode and an anode within a vacuum. Colour versions are used to generate the picture on television screens and computer monitors.

Cursor A flashing indicator on a computer text display, marking the position at which a character can be entered, corrected or deleted. Sometimes used to refer to the mouse pointer.

D

DAC digital to analogue converter. Opposite of an *ADC*. Converts the ones and zeros of digital information into an analogue form.

Demodulator Used in a tuner in a radio to extract the audio content of radio signals so it may be amplified.

Distortion An undesired change in the waveform of a signal due to interference, overdriven speakers or amplifying transistors. Causes a reduction in or loss of quality in reception or sound reproduction.

Drainage system The system which links a house with the mains sewer to carry away waste water.

Driver (computer) A piece of software that enables a computer operating system to communicate with a *peripheral* device, such as a printer.

Drop cable Overhead or underground cable connecting the master telephone socket in a building to the local telephone exchange. It carries the speech signal, a control signal and the ringing current.

E

Earthing bond A safety cable linking the consumer unit or fuse box in a house to an earthed conductor so that, if a fault occurs, current may be conducted away through the earth safely.

Electrolyte Any solution that conducts electricity.

Electromagnet A magnet comprising a coil of wire wrapped around an iron core, which only becomes magnetised if a current flows through the wire.

F

Faceplate The front of a socket outlet or light switch.

FCU Fused connection unit. A mains outlet with a fuse, which has an appliance flex wired directly into its terminals, rather than plugged into a socket.

Filament A fine wire heated electrically in an electric light bulb until it emits light in the visible wavelength.

▼

FM Frequency modulation. Radio signals in which audio information is transmitted by varying the frequency of a sine wave.

FMV Full motion video. Sequences of film in a console game, typically at important points in the game-play. FMV does not use the 3D power of the graphics processor; instead it is simply a video played directly from disc (CD-ROM or DVD).

Fuse A safety device that protects a conductor from excessive current. It consists of a metal element that melts when the current flowing through it exceeds a specific value (described as the fuse rating).

G

Gasket Any of a wide variety of seals or packings used between parts or around joints to prevent the leakage of a gas or fluid.

Gear A toothed machine part, in the shape of a wheel or cylinder, which meshes with another toothed part to transmit rotary motion.

Geostationary Located at a fixed point in orbit, relative to the earth's surface.

Graphics processor A microchip or series of microchips, designed to create images on a monitor screen from digital information supplied by a *central processor* in a computer or games console.

H

Halogen bulb A light bulb containing halogen gas instead of nitrogen or argon, as in a standard light bulb. It produces whiter light of a higher intensity than a standard bulb. It also lasts longer.

▲

Hard disk A magnetic disk that spins within a computer's drive unit, which is used for storing digital data. The heads write magnetic information in the same way as a tape head writes on audio tape.

I

Hardware (computing) The physical devices that make up a computer.

HEPA filter High efficiency particle arresting filter. A type of air filter that blocks 99.97 percent of particles averaging 0.3 micron in diameter.

I

Impedance rating Indicates the maximum resistance and reactance level of the audio speakers that can be connected to a particular amplifier. Both the amplifier and speaker's impedance ratings must match.

Infrared transmitter An *LED* that transmits infrared instead of visible light waves.

Internet Global network of millions of computers, where a wide range of operating systems and types of computer can communicate using a common language (protocol).

Iris Overlapping plates that move over each other to shrink or expand the aperture in a camera, therefore controlling the amount of light reaching the film or *CCD* (in a digital camera).

J

Joystick A manual control consisting of a vertical handle that can move freely forwards and backwards and from left to right; used as an input device for computers or computer-controlled devices.

K

Kite mark The British Standards Institution Kite Mark is a recognised symbol of quality, indicating the product to which it relates has undergone rigorous testing and conforms to a published specification.

▼

L

LCD Liquid crystal display. Used to present data and information on watches, *PDAs* and laptops.

LED Light emitting diode. Used in digital clocks and other devices to make indicators on a display glow. Also used in a remote control, where infrared light is emitted.

LPG Liquid petroleum gas (also known as propane). A fuel used in portable gas heaters and LPG cars.

M

Magneto-optical disc A small disc (MiniDisc), which is primarily used for digitally recording and playing back music.

▼

Magnetron The component of a microwave oven that generates the microwaves.

MCB Miniature circuit breaker. A small switch in a consumer unit, which trips if the current flowing through it exceeds its rated amount, thus acting like a fuse.

Microchip Semiconductor which can be programmed to carry out specified control functions in electronic equipment and appliances.

Motherboard The primary circuit board within a computer, to which all other devices are connected.

N

National grid UK network of power stations, overhead and underground cables and substations, which provide the mains electricity to domestic and industrial premises.

NTSC National Transmission Standards Committee. The US standard for video recording. Most modern video cassette recorders are compatible with NTSC and PAL (Phase Alternation Line), which is the European TV standard.

O

Objective lens The first lens or lens system in a microscope, binoculars or other optical instrument to receive light rays from the object.

Output power A rating indicating the power, in watts, that an audio amplifier can deliver.

P

Parabolic dish Reflector used in communication systems and telescopes to focus radio waves or light for transmission or reception.

PDA Personal digital assistant. A hand-held battery-powered computer, used as a diary, address book, calculator and, in some models, to access the *Internet* and e-mail.

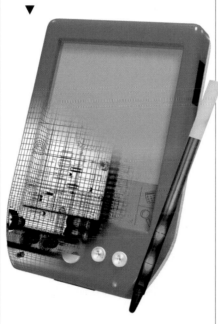

PDP Plasma display panel. Alternative type of TV and computer monitor screen which uses tiny electrically-stimulated sealed cells containing low-pressure neon and xenon gas instead of a cathode ray tube to make the dots of an image.

Peripheral (computer) An external auxiliary device, such as a printer or scanner, that is attached to and works in conjunction with a computer.

Phono lead A simple *coaxial cable* used to attach hifi and video devices to amplifiers and televisions.

Phosphor dots Tiny spots, which glow when struck by electrons. Used to form the image on a TV screen or computer monitor.

Photosensitive diode An electronic device that produces an electric current when exposed to light. Also known as a light-sensitive diode.

Piezoelectricity The electricity generated when a *piezoelectric crystal* is struck or compressed.

Piezoelectric crystal A crystal which produces a charge when compressed. It also vibrates in the presence of an electric charge.

PIN Personal identification number. A security code, typically comprising four numbers, used with mobile phones and credit or debit cards.

Pinch roller A rubber cylinder within a video or cassette tape recorder. It works with the *capstan shaft* to move the tape from spool to spool.

Pointer An onscreen indicator, usually an arrow, which allows a computer user to select items, click buttons and menus and drag and drop objects.

Porro prism A type of prism found in binoculars which, when combined with an identical prism at right angles, corrects the inverted mirrored image created by the objective lenses.

Ports Connection sockets, usually found at the rear of a computer case, to which *peripherals*, such as a printer, can be attached for data transmission.

Preamplifier The part of an amplifier that receives and augments weak signals, then feeds them to the main amplifier for further amplification.

Prism A transparent geometric shape (usually glass), which internally refracts or reflects light. Used in binoculars.

Processor (computing) The central 'brains' microchip in a computer, usually rated by speed in MHz (megaHertz). It controls all the *peripherals*, the memory and processes data.

PS/2 port IBM's personal system/2 port. Used to connect a mouse and a keyboard to a modern PC.

PUK Personal unlocking key. A unique security code for mobile phones. If the wrong PIN number is keyed in more than three times, the phone is blocked until a PUK code is entered.

Q

Quartz crystal A crystal which oscillates 32,768 times a second when a current is applied across its faces. Used as the basis of the timing device in clocks and watches.

R

RAM Random access memory. A computer's main working memory, measured in MB (megabytes). It is so called because it can be written and read non-sequentially.

RCA Radio Corporation of America. RCA connectors are used to connect audio and video devices. Two leads are required for the left and right channels in a stereo audio signal; three are required when a video signal is transmitted as well

▼

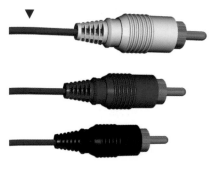

RCD Residual current device. Component that cuts the power to a wiring circuit immediately if an imbalance is detected. It is fitted to modern consumer units, and is used as a stand-alone plug-in device to protect outdoor users of electricity.

Reflective plate/reflector A sheet of shiny metal, fitted behind the heating elements of an electric or gas fire to reflect heat out into the room.

Region code (DVD) Every DVD player or drive has a region code stored in ROM. If a DVD is put in a drive which does not have the matching code stored on it, the disc will not play. The code is also printed on the back of a DVD package. It is used to prevent the unauthorised duplication of copyrighted material and to control worldwide release dates of new films.

Regulator Device on the top of a liquid petroleum gas cylinder, which controls the release of gas.

▼

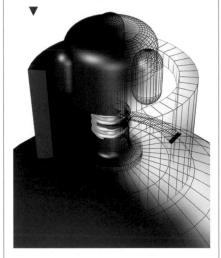

REN Ringer equivalency number. The total number of ringers – usually four – that the electric current in the telephone cable can activate.

RGB Red green blue. The standard way of indicating colours is by the proportions of red, green and blue in their make-up. Televisions use three *cathodes* (guns), one for each of the three colours, to create a final full-colour image.

Ring main The electrical circuit running to and from the consumer unit, on which there may be a number of socket outlets and *FCUs*. A house will usually have separate ring circuits for upstairs and downstairs.

Rising main The main water pipe in the house, fed from the service pipe in the drive or garden.

RJ45 A type of computer network connector, which looks similar to a telephone plug.

ROM Read-only memory. Used to store information that does not need to be updated or changed regularly or rapidly. Unlike *RAM*, it is only possible to rewrite the information in ROM using a process known as flashing.

Roof prism The popular alternative to Porro prisms in binoculars, allowing the design to be more compact.

S

Scandisk A program that checks for faults on a computer's hard or floppy disk. Scandisk works in tandem with Windows' disk defragmenter.

SCART Syndicat des Constructeurs d'Appareils Radiorécepteurs et Téléviseurs. A connection standard that defines how video signals are transmitted. SCART cables are used to connect audiovisual equipment.

Sealed service cut-out A safety cut-out positioned between the electricity meter and the consumer unit or fuse box. Repairs are the responsibility of the local electricity supply company.

Semi-permeable membrane A 'skin' that allows some molecules to pass through but not others. Used in a carbon-monoxide detector.

Service cable Cable along which mains power is delivered to the home from the local substation.

Service pipe (water system) The pipe that connects the property to the outdoor stoptap.

Service provider An organisation that provides a service, such as Internet access or digital television.

Shadow mask An extremely thin metal screen with tiny slots in it, lying just behind a *CRT* television screen. It focuses the electron beams (red, green and blue) that create the image.

SIM Subscriber identification module. A card that identifies a mobile phone user to their network. It contains a microchip that stores information about the user's account, including some phone numbers and security numbers (*PIN* and *PUK*).

SLR Single lens reflex. A type of camera where light entering the lens is reflected through the eyepiece.

▼

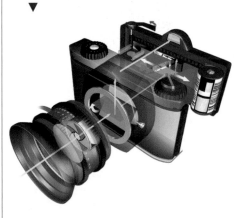

SMART card Credit-card sized piece of plastic, which is inserted into a set-top satellite TV decoder box. It contains the viewer's account information and allows the service provider to control access to channels.

Socket outlet A wall-mounted point for connecting electrical appliances to the mains power supply using plugs.

Software (computing) A written program or procedure which can be run on *hardware*. Examples are the Microsoft® Windows® operating system and applications such as Word® or Excel®.

Solenoid Similar to an *electromagnet*, a solenoid uses the magnetic field around a coil of wire to open a valve or door lock, or in a nail gun.

▼

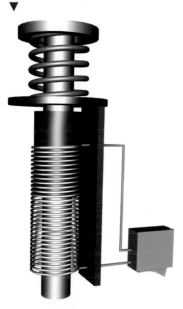

Sole plate A metal plate at the base of an iron or power tool, designed to keep it perpendicular to the surface on which the user is working.

Soundcard A removable circuit board attached to a computer *motherboard*, which reproduces sounds, such as game effects, CD music and program warning sounds.

Split pin A nail-like small pin which has one end split so that it may be spread open to secure it in its place.

Spring A coiled or bent piece of metal, used to provide support, the power for a clockwork device or to apply force to hold an object in place.

Sprocket Any of various tooth-like projections arranged on a cog (the sprocket-wheel). These engage with the links of a chain.

Stepper motor A small electric motor used in a printer or fax machine to move an ink cartridge or scan head across a page, or to move the paper.

Stylus A tool used to input information into a *PDA* (personal digital assistant) by writing on the touch-sensitive *LCD* screen. Also, the playing needle of a record deck.

S-VIDEO Separated video. A method of transmitting video signals, split into colour (chrominance) and brightness (luminance) information, down a connecting cable.

T

Thermal cut-out An electronic safety switch that temporarily cuts off power to a system if the temperature rises above a set point.

Thermal fuse A safety device, which cuts off electrical power by burning out when overheated. It must be replaced once it has blown.

Thermometer A device for measuring temperature.

Thermoresistor An electrical component that changes its resistance to electrical current with changes in ambient temperature. Used in some digital thermometers.

Transceiver A transmitter and receiver together in a single unit and having some circuits in common, often for portable use such as a mobile phone.

Transducer A device that transforms one type of energy into another – for instance, sound, temperature, pressure and electricity.

Transistor An electrical component comprising layers of impure (doped) silicon, which is used by an amplifier to increase the volume of electrical signals, or by a *processor* as a switching device.

Trap A U-shaped pipe or a bottle, which retains a small amount of waste water in order to prevent foul gases entering the house from the waste system pipes.

▼

Trip switch See *circuit breaker*.

Tuner A radio component that filters out all the received radio signals from the aerial, except for the frequency selected by the tuning control, which it then outputs to a *demodulator* and an amplifier.

Tweeter A small speaker, which reproduces the high audio frequency component of sounds. Sometimes referred to as the treble speaker.

▼

U

URL Uniform resource locator. An address referring to a document located on a computer anywhere in the world wide web (for example, http://www.readersdigest.co.uk/shopping/index.htm). This usually consists of the access protocol 'http', the domain name 'wwwreadersdigest.co.uk', and optionally the path to a file residing on that server, in this case 'shopping'.

USB Universal serial bus. A way of connecting external *peripheral* devices, such as a scanner, to a computer using inexpensive cable.

V

VCR Video cassette recorder. A device used to record and play television pictures and sound onto and from VHS (video home system) video tape cassettes.

VGA Video graphics array. The minimum video display standard for colour computer monitors, of 16 colours at a resolution of 640 x 480 pixels.

W

WAP Wireless application protocol. One of the standards that regulates access to *Internet* sites. Specifically designed for WAP mobile phones.

Woofer A large speaker, which reproduces the low frequency component of sounds. Usually coupled with a tweeter within a speaker cabinet.

Useful Contacts

Around the house

Builders
Federation of Master Builders
020 7242 7583
www.fmb.org.uk

Electrical contractors
Electrical Contractors' Association
020 7413 4800
www.eca.co.uk

Institution of Electrical Engineers
www.iee/org/publish/wireregs

Electricity and gas supply
Energywatch
0845 906 0708
www.energywatch.org.uk

Energy efficiency
Energy Savings Trust
0845 727 7200
www.saveenergy.co.uk

Gas central heating
CORGI (The Council for Registered Gas Installers)
01256 372200
www.corgi-gas.com

Plumbing
The Institute of Plumbing
01708 472791
www.plumbers.org.uk

Security
The Association of Chief Police Officers (ACPO) Crime Prevention Initiatives
020 7227 3423
www.securedbydesign.com

Appliances

Trade associations
Association of Manufacturers of Domestic Appliances (AMDEA)
020 7405 0666

Domestic Appliance Service Association (DASA)
01920 872464
www.dasa.org.uk

Manufacturers
Aeg
08705 350350
www.aeg.co.uk

Aga-Rayburn
0845 712 5207
www.aga-rayburn.co.uk

Alba
020 8787 3000

Ariston
01494 755600
www.ariston.co.uk

Belling
01709 579902
www.belling.co.uk

Bosch
08702 400060
www.boschappliances.co.uk

Braun
0800 783 7010
www.braun.co.uk

Bush (see Alba)

Candy
08705 400600
www.gias.co.uk

Cannon
08701 546474
www.cannongas.co.uk

Creda
08701 546474
www.creda.co.uk

Daewoo
0118 925 2577
www.daewoo-electronics.co.uk

DeLonghi
0845 600 6845
www.delonghi.co.uk

Dirt Devil
020 8787 3000
www.dirtdevil.com

Dyson
01666 827200
www.dyson.co.uk

Electrolux
08705 950950
www.electrolux.co.uk

Goodmans (see Alba)

Hinari (see Alba)

Hoover
08705 400600
www.gias.co.uk

Hotpoint
08701 506070
www.hotpoint.co.uk

Indesit
01895 858200
www.merloni.com/Indesit

Lec
01243 863161
www.lec.co.uk

Morphy Richards
08450 777700
www.morphyrichards.com

Neff
01908 328300
www.neff.co.uk

Panasonic
08705 357357
www.panasonic.co.uk

Philips
0870 900 9070
www.philips.co.uk

Rowenta
0845 602 1454
www.rowenta.co.uk

Russell Hobbs
0161 947 3000
www.russell-hobbs.co.uk

Samsung
020 8391 0168
www.samsungelectronics.co.uk

Sanyo
01923 246363
www.sanyo.co.uk

Siemens
01908 328400
www.siemensappliances.co.uk

Smeg
0870 990 9907
www.smeguk.com

Tefal
0845 602 1454
www.tefal.co.uk

Vax
0870 606 1248
www.vax.co.uk

Whirlpool
0870 600 8989
www.whirlpool.co.uk

Zanussi
08705 727727
www.zanussi.co.uk

Audio-visual

Trade associations
British Radio and Electronic Equipment Manufacturers' Association (BREMA)
020 7331 2000
www.brema.org.uk

Radio Electrical and Television Retailers' Association (RETRA)
01234 269110
www.retra.co.uk

Manufacturers
Aiwa
020 8897 7000
www.aiwa.co.uk

Alba
020 8787 3000

Bang & Olufsen
0118 969 2288
www.bang-olufsen.com

Bose
0870 741 4500
www.bose.com
Bush (see Alba)

Canon
0870 241 2161
www.canon.co.uk

Daewoo
0118 925 2577
www.daewoo-electronics.co.uk

Denon
01753 888447
www.denon.co.uk

Goodmans (see Alba)

Hitachi
01628 643000
www.hitachi.co.uk

JVC
0870 330 5000
www.jvc.co.uk

Kodak
01442 845710
www.kodak.co.uk

Kenwood
01923 816444
www.kenwood-electronics.co.uk

Konica
020 8751 6121
www.konicaphoto.co.uk

LG
0870 607 5544
www.lgelectronics.co.uk

Minolta
02908 200400
www.minolta.co.uk

Nikon
020 8481 6875
www.nikon.co.uk

Panasonic
08705 357357
www.panasonic.co.uk

Philips
0870 900 9070
www.philips.co.uk

Pioneer
01753 789789
www.pioneer.co.uk

Samsung
020 8391 0168
www.samsungelectronics.co.uk

Sanyo
01923 246363
www.sanyo.co.uk

Sharp
08705 274277
www.sharp.co.uk

Sony
08705 111999
www.sony.co.uk/support/support.asp

Toshiba
0115 976 6958
www.home-entertainment.toshiba.co.uk

Computer equipment

Manufacturers
Acer
020 7365 2486
www.acer.co.uk

Compaq
0870 559 2000
www.compaq.co.uk

Dell
0870 152 4699
www.dell.co.uk

Fujitsu Siemens
08705 353325
www.fujitsu.com

Handspring
020 7294 0157
www.handspring.co.uk

Hewlett Packard
08705 474747
www.hewlett-packard.com

IBM
01475 892000
www.ibm.com/uk

Logitech
020 7309 0127
www.logitech.com

Microsoft
0870 601 0100
www.microsoft.com/uk

NEC
0870 333 6322
www.nec-online.co.uk

Packard Bell
01628 512400
www.packardbell.co.uk

Palm
0118 9278 700
www.palm.com/uk

Sony
08705 111999
www.sony.co.uk

Time
0870 830 3116
www.timecomputers.com

Tiny
0870 830 3116
www.tiny.com

Toshiba
0870 444 8944
www.computers.toshiba.co.uk

Communications

Industry Regulator
Office of Telecommunications (Oftel)
020 7634 8700
www.oftel.gov.uk

Manufacturers
Ericsson
See Sony Ericsson

Handspring
020 7294 0157
www.handspring.co.uk

Motorola
0500 555555
www.motorola.co.uk

Nokia
08700 555777
www.nokia.co.uk

Panasonic
08705 357357
www.panasonic.co.uk

Philips
0870 900 9070
www.philips.co.uk

Pogo
020 7961 4100
www.pogo-tech.com

Samsung
020 8391 0168
www.samsungelectronics.co.uk

Siemens
08705 334411
www.my-siemens.com

Sony Ericsson
01444 234567
www.sonyericsson.com/uk

Trium
0800 912 0020
www.mitsubishi-telecom.com

Power tools

Manufacturers
Black & Decker
01753 574277
www.europe-blackanddecker.com

Bosch
08702 400060
www.boschappliances.co.uk

Dremel
08459 395 395
www.dremel.co.uk

Hitachi
01908 354700
www.hitachi-powertools.co.uk

JCB
0500 144444
www.jcbworks.com

Panasonic
08705 357357
www.panasonic.co.uk

Power Devil
01788 547547

Garden equipment

Manufacturers
Black & Decker
01753 574277
www.europe-blackanddecker.com

Flymo
01325 300303
www.flymo.co.uk

JCB
0500 144444
www.jcbworks.com

Qualcast
01449 742130
www.qualcast.co.uk

On wheels

Trade associations
Association of Cycle Traders
01892 526081
www.cyclesource.co.uk

Bicycle Association
02476 553838
www.bicycle-association.org.uk

Manufacturers
K2
01527 510570 (UK distributor)
www.k2sports.com

Micro Mobility
0118 973 6222
www.micro-mobility.com

Raleigh
0115 942 0202
www.raleighbikes.com

Rollerblade
1306 501668
www.rollerblade.com

Tamiya
01525 385798 (UK distributor)
www.tamiya.com

Trek
01908 282626
www.trekbike.co.uk

Index

PLANET THREE PUBLISHING NETWORK

Edited, designed and produced by
Planet Three Publishing Network
Northburgh House, 10 Northburgh Street, London EC1V 0AT

PROJECT EDITOR Kevin Wiltshire • **ART EDITOR** Susan Gooding
DEVELOPMENT EDITOR Jon Asbury • **ART DIRECTOR** Paul Southcombe
SUB EDITORS Jonas Crabtree   Barbara Gledhill   James Snodgrass
DESIGNERS Sam Fishburn   Yuen Ching Lam   Terry Sambridge
ILLUSTRATORS Peter Cerpnjak   Paul Jackson   Paul Southcombe

FOR READER'S DIGEST
Editor Alison Candlin • **Art Editor** Julie Bennett
Editorial Assistant Rachel Weaver
Proofreaders Barry Gage   Ken Vickery
Pre-press Accounts Manager Penny Grose

READER'S DIGEST GENERAL BOOKS
Editor Cortina Butler • **Art Director** Nick Clark
Executive Editor Julian Browne • **Development Editor** Ruth Binney
Managing Editor Alastair Holmes • **Picture Resource Manager** Martin Smith
Style Editor Ron Pankhurst
Book Production Manager Fiona McIntosh • **Pre-press Manager** Howard Reynolds

CONTRIBUTORS
We would like to thank the following individuals and
organisations for their assistance in producing this book

Consultants Barry Aylett-Warner   James Bird   Roger Bisby   Pat Clarke
Graham Dixon   John Durrant   Steve Farrow   Simon Gilham   David Holloway
Mike Lawrence   Paul Marchant   John McGowan   Fred Milson
Mirashade/Matt Gould   Jack Whitehead

Indexer Laura Hicks

Photography Steven Bartholomew   Martin Cameron   Jeff Carroll
John Freeman   Howard Jones
Set construction Tim Tizzard

Assistance and resources Dan Collins, Association of British Locksmiths (AOBL);
Matt Conway, DEFRA; Thomas Holland, Kate's Skates; David Olive, The Original Sash
Window Company; Darren Poole, AV Studios; Argos; Centre Hobbies; Delonghi;
Energy Development Co-operative Ltd; Hewlett Packard; Kärcher; Potterton; Triton;
Recreation Group plc

How Everything in the Home Works

Origination: Colour Systems Ltd
Printing and binding:
Mateu Cromo, Madrid, Spain

⚠ Repairs and Safety

The Reader's Digest Association Ltd cannot be held
responsible for any accidents or expenses incurred as a
result of following the information held within this book.
Always check the details of any warranty before starting work on an
appliance, as attempting repairs yourself may render the original or
extended warranty void. Always consult the manufacturer's maintenance
or operating manual for instructions specific to your particular model
and take heed of any safety warnings given in the manual or on the
device itself, as well as following the safety procedures recommended
at the beginning of and throughout this book. Take care to follow
manufacturers' operating instructions when using tools and machinery.
Although the editors have made every effort to ensure accuracy, the
reader remains responsible for the selection and use of tools, materials
and methods. Contact a qualified repairer if you are, at any point, unsure
of your ability to carry out a repair or maintenance task safely yourself.

CONCEPT CODE IE 0067/G
BOOK CODE 400 047 01
ISBN 0 276 42720 3